MW01133004

THE FEDERALIZATION OF CORPORATE GOVERNANCE

The Federalization of Corporate Governance

Marc I. Steinberg

The Federalization of Corporate Governance. Marc I. Steinberg.

Oxford University Press is a department of the University of Oxford. It furthers the University's objective of excellence in research, scholarship, and education by publishing worldwide. Oxford is a registered trademark of Oxford University Press in the UK and certain other countries.

Published in the United States of America by Oxford University Press
198 Madison Avenue, New York, NY 10016, United States of America.

Library of Congress Cataloging-in-Publication Data
Names: Steinberg, Marc I., author.
Title: The federalization of corporate governance / Marc I. Steinberg.
Description: New York : Oxford University Press, 2018. | Includes bibliographical references and index.
Identifiers: LCCN 2017039724 | ISBN 9780199934546 ((hardback) : alk. paper)
Subjects: LCSH: Corporate governance—Law and legislation—United States. | Federal government—United States. | United States. Securities and Exchange Commission.
Classification: LCC KF1422 .S74 2018 | DDC 346.73/0664—dc23
LC record available at https://lccn.loc.gov/2017039724

9 8 7 6 5 4 3 2 1

Printed by Edwards Brothers Malloy, United States of America

Note to Readers
This publication is designed to provide accurate and authoritative information in regard to the subject matter covered. It is based upon sources believed to be accurate and reliable and is intended to be current as of the time it was written. It is sold with the understanding that the publisher is not engaged in rendering legal, accounting, or other professional services. If legal advice or other expert assistance is required, the services of a competent professional person should be sought. Also, to confirm that the information has not been affected or changed by recent developments, traditional legal research techniques should be used, including checking primary sources where appropriate.

(Based on the Declaration of Principles jointly adopted by a Committee of the American Bar Association and a Committee of Publishers and Associations.)

This book is dedicated to my wonderful sister Nancy Burman with all of my love. My sister, who is four years older than me, is a remarkable person. As a single mother for many years, she raised three daughters who today are happily married, have beautiful children, and wonderful careers. During that time, she was an elementary school teacher in the Columbus, Ohio public schools. Nancy is also the best sister that a brother could have. Through the years, she always has been supportive, loving, and empathetic. She indeed is perhaps the kindest person I know. Dedicating this book to my sister Nancy is a small way for me to convey to her how much she has meant to me throughout my life.

Summary Contents

Detailed Contents

About the Author

MARC I. STEINBERG is the Rupert and Lillian Radford Professor of Law at the Southern Methodist University (SMU) Dedman School of Law. He is the Director of SMU's Corporate Directors' Institute, the Director of the SMU Corporate Counsel Externship Program, the former Senior Associate Dean for Academics, and the former Senior Associate Dean for Research at the Law School. Prior to becoming the Radford Professor, Professor Steinberg taught at the University of Maryland School of Law, the Wharton School of the University of Pennsylvania, the National Law Center of the George Washington University, and the Georgetown University Law Center. His experience includes appointments as a Visiting Professor, Scholar and Fellow at law schools outside of the United States, including at universities in Argentina, Australia, China, England, Finland, Germany, Israel, Italy, Japan, New Zealand, Scotland, South Africa, and Sweden. In addition, he has been retained as an expert witness in several significant matters, including Enron, Martha Stewart, Belnick (Tyco), and Mark Cuban.

In addition to his university appointments, Professor Steinberg has lectured extensively both in the United States and abroad, including at the Lauterpacht Centre of International Law at the University of Cambridge, the Aresty Institute of Executive Education at the University of Pennsylvania, The American Bar Association's Annual Meeting, the PLI Annual Institute on Securities Regulation, the University of Texas Annual Securities Law Conference, the International Development Law

Institute in Rome, the Hong Kong Securities and Futures Commission, the Taiwan "SEC" in Taipei, the New Zealand Securities Commission, the Australian Law Council Section on International Law in Melbourne, the David Hume Institute in Edinburgh, the German-American Lawyers' Association in Munich, the International Law Society of South Africa, the Buenos Aires Stock Exchange, the Finnish Banking Lawyers Association in Helsinki, the Swedish Banking Lawyers Association in Stockholm, and the Ministry of Internal Affairs, Economic Crimes Department of the Russian Federation in Moscow. He also has served as a member of the FINRA National Adjudicatory Council (NAC).

Professor Steinberg received his undergraduate degree at the University of Michigan and his law degrees at the University of California, Los Angeles (JD) and Yale University (LLM). He clerked for Judge Stanley N. Barnes of the U.S. Court of Appeals for the Ninth Circuit, extern clerked for Judge Anthony J. Celebrezze of the Sixth Circuit, was legislative counsel to U.S. Senator Robert P. Griffin, and served as the adviser to former U.S. Supreme Court Justice Arthur J. Goldberg for the Federal Advisory Committee Report on Tender Offers.

Professor Steinberg was an enforcement attorney at the U.S. Securities and Exchange Commission, and thereafter became special projects counsel. In that position, he directly assisted the SEC's General Counsel in a wide variety of projects and cases and served as the General Counsel's confidential legal adviser.

Professor Steinberg has authored more than 150 law review articles as well as 36 books, is editor-in-chief of *The International Lawyer*, editor-in-chief of *The Securities Regulation Law Journal*, and is an adviser to *The Journal of Corporation Law*. Professor Steinberg is a member of the American Law Institute.

Acknowledgments

I AM DELIGHTED that this project has come to fruition. It certainly was challenging and interesting. As the contents of the book indicate, a wide array of subjects are explored. The analysis herein hopefully will prove useful to academics, practitioners, students, judges, and legislators.

My research assistants provided tremendous support and I thank them. Three former students merit special mention. Mr. Dean Galaro, Ms. Theresa Melia, and Mr. Colby Roberts. Their efforts indeed were exceptional. I also appreciate the assistance of a number of other research assistants and practitioners: Mr. Matt Hortenstine, Ms. Ekaterina Long, and Mr. Abel Ramirez. I also thank my current research assistants, Mr. Hayden Baker and Mr. Logan Weissler, for their diligent proofreading of the manuscript.

From the faculty, I thank Dean Jennifer Collins for her strong support of this project and Mr. Greg Ivy, Associate Dean for Library and Technology, for his invaluable research guidance. In addition, Ms. Carolyn Yates, law school administrative assistant, merits kudos for her diligent and superb contribution.

During this project, I was fortunate to receive two summer research grants. These grants were funded in part by the David D. & Virginia Jackson Law Fund and the Barbara and Michael Lynn Faculty Research Fund. I very much thank the donors for their generous support of my scholarship.

I also express my appreciation for the strong support I have received for nearly three decades as a faculty member of this superb law school.

1

AN EVOLUTIONARY PROCESS—THE FEDERALIZATION OF CORPORATE GOVERNANCE

I. Introduction

This book focuses on a very timely subject: the federalization of corporate governance. Today, federal law impacts the governance of publicly-traded companies to a greater degree than ever before in U.S. history. Nonetheless, traditionally, the states have regulated the sphere of corporate governance—encompassing the relations among and between the subject corporation, its directors, its officers, its stockholders, and other stakeholders (including its creditors, employees, and communities where the subject corporation principally conducts its business).[1] Through

[1] Corporate governance has been described as "a system of overlapping legal, regulatory, organizational, and contractual mechanisms designed to protect the interests of a company's owners (the shareholders) and limit opportunistic behavior by corporate managers who control the company's operations." International Organization of Securities Commissions (IOSCO), June 2009 Final Report of the Task Force, *Protection of Minority Shareholders in Listed Issuers*, and February 2005 Final Report of the Task Force, *Strengthening Capital Markets Against Financial Fraud*, available at www.iosco.org/library/pubdocs/pdf/IOSCOPD295.pdf and www.iosco.org/library/pubdocs/pdf/IOSCOPD192.pdf. Stated in different terms, corporate governance may be deemed "a reaction to agency problems, associated with the separation between owners and managers" in a publicly-traded company. Andrea Beltratti, *The Complementarity Between Corporate Governance and Corporate Social Responsibility*, The Geneva Papers 373, 375 (2005).

Literally dozens of books and treatises have been written on state corporation law. *See, e.g.*, American Bar Association, Section of Business Law, Committee on Corporate Laws, *Corporate Director's Guidebook* (6th ed.

The Federalization of Corporate Governance. Marc I. Steinberg.

the enactment of enabling corporation statutes, commencing in the last decade of the nineteenth century, the states emerged as the primary regulator of corporate governance.[2] Much of this phenomenon may be explained by the widespread recognition of the "internal affairs" doctrine whereby the law that governs the relations among and between the corporation, its fiduciaries, and its stockholders is the law of the subject corporation's state of incorporation.[3]

The respective states had a clear objective in this endeavor—namely, the substantial revenues to be derived from state chartering.[4] Focused on this goal, in 1896, New Jersey enacted the initial modern liberal corporation law.[5] The Act was a success, attracting the incorporation of the New Jersey trusts, such as the old Standard Oil Company.[6] However, in 1913, at then Governor Woodrow Wilson's urging, New Jersey tightened its corporation statute.[7]

2011); American Bar Association, Committee on Corporate Laws, *Model Business Corporation Act Annotated* (4th ed. 2013); American Law Institute, *Principles of Corporate Governance: Analysis and* Recommendations (1994); Stephen Bainbridge, *Corporate Governance After the Financial Crisis* (2012); Henry Winthrop Ballantine, *Ballantine on Corporations* (1946); R. Franklin Balotti and Jesse A. Finkelstein, *The Delaware Law of Corporations and Business Organizations* (2003); Douglas M. Branson, *Corporate Governance* (1993); Robert Charles Clark, *Corporate Law* (1986); James D. Cox and Thomas Lee Hazen, *Business Organizations Law* (3d ed. 2011); William Mead Fletcher, *Fletcher Cyclopedia of the Law of Private Corporations* (1972) (revised 1993); Franklin A. Gevurtz, *Corporation Law* (2d ed. 2010); Henry G. Henn and John R. Alexander, *Laws of Corporations and Other Business Enterprises* (3d ed. 1983); Norman D. Lattin, *The Law of Corporations* (1971); Marc I. Steinberg, *Developments in Business Law and Policy* (2012); Rodman Ward, Jr., Edward P. Welch, and Andrew J. Turezyn, *Folk on the Delaware General Corporation Law* (2005). *See also*, Marco Ventoruzzo, et al., *Comparative Corporate Law* (2015).

Increasingly, corporate governance has become politicized. *See, e.g.*, Dan Stewart, *Britain's Theresa May Takes Power with Brexit in Her Sights*, Time, July 25, 2016, at 14, 15 (stating that Prime Minister Theresa May "has signaled a shift toward economic popularism with plans to overhaul corporate governance and narrow the gap between the rich and the poor").

[2] *See* William L. Cary, *Federalism and Corporate Law: Reflections Upon Delaware*, 83 Yale L.J. 663 (1974).

[3] *See CTS Corp. v. Dynamics Corp. of Am.*, 481 U.S. 69 (1987); Richard Buxbaum, *The Threatened Constitutionalization of the Internal Affairs Doctrine in Corporate Law*, 75 Cal. L. Rev. 29 (1987).

[4] *See* Cary, *supra* note 2, at 664–68.

[5] *See* Christopher Grandy, *New Jersey and the Fiscal Origins of Modern American Corporation Law* 43 (1993). *See also*, Comment, Theodore H. Davis, Jr., *Corporate Privileges for the Public Benefit: The Progressive Federal Incorporation Movement and the Modern Regulatory State*, 77 Va. L. Rev. 603, 617 (1991):

> The New Jersey Act was by far the most liberal ever passed. Its provisions allowed corporate promoters to determine their own capitalization values, place stockholders into preferred or common classifications, receive perpetual charters for "any lawful business or purpose whatever," issue stock in exchange for either money or property, and, perhaps most importantly, exercise some control over information transmitted to stockholders.

[6] *See* E. Merrick Baker and Ralph J. Dodd, *Cases and Materials on Corporations* 38 (2d ed. 1951); Cary, *supra* note 2, at 664.

[7] *See* sources cited *supra* note 6.

This void was effectively filled by Delaware, which is today the preeminent state where publicly-held corporations elect to incorporate.[8] As SEC Chairman William L. Cary stated:

> Delaware understandably does not wish to surrender its lead.... It likes to be number one. With some justification Delaware corporate counsel take pride in their role and enjoy the fees that flow from it.... Most important, the raison d'etre behind the whole system has been achieved—revenue for the state of Delaware.[9]

Due to its alleged pro-management bias, critics claim that Delaware has won "the race for the bottom."[10] From a broader perspective, as the distinguished scholar, Professor Ernest Folk, reflected:

> Almost without exception, the key movement in corporation law revisions is toward ever greater permissiveness.... Indeed, the new statutes seem to be exclusively concerned with only one constituent of the corporate community—management—and have disregarded the interests of shareholders and creditors....[11]

Arguably, during the past few decades, state corporation law, particularly that of Delaware, has become more attentive to shareholder interests.[12] Nonetheless, permissive state substantive standards regulating the normative conduct of corporate fiduciaries continue to draw criticism.[13] Indeed, these lax standards were a factor in

---

[8] *See* Douglas M. Branson et al., *Business Enterprises: Legal Structures, Governance, and Policy* 7 (3d ed. 2016); Jill E. Fisch, *Leave It to Delaware: Why Congress Should Stay Out of Corporate Governance*, 37 Del. J. Corp. L. 731 (2013); Joel Seligman, *A Brief History of Delaware's General Corporation Law of 1899*, 1 Del. J. Corp. L. 249 (1976).

[9] Cary, *supra* note 2, at 668. For a harsh review, *see* Comment, *Law for Sale: A Study on the Delaware Corporation Law of 1967*, 117 U. Pa. L. Rev. 861 (1969) (asserting that "[t]he sovereign state of Delaware is in the business of selling its corporation law").

[10] *See* sources cited *supra* note 9. *See generally* Seligman, *supra* note 8, at 287 ("What is most troubling about Delaware's General Corporation Law is that this statute which affects 215 million Americans is written by a handful of Wilmington attorneys unaccountable to anyone but their corporate clients....").

[11] Ernest L. Folk III, *Some Reflections of a Corporation Law Draftsman*, 42 Conn. B.J. 409, 410 (1968). *See* Bayless Manning, *The Shareholder's Appraisal Remedy: An Essay for Frank Coker*, 72 Yale L.J. 223, 245 n.37 (1962) (characterizing state corporation statutes as "towering skyscrapers of rusted girders, internally welded together and containing nothing but wind").

[12] *See* Lucran Ayre Bebchuk and Assaf Hamdani, *Vigorous Race or Leisurely Walk: Reconsidering the Competition over Corporate Charters*, 112 Yale L.J. 553, 562 (2002) (stating that "supporters of state competition ... view it as a powerful mechanism working to benefit shareholders").

[13] *See id.* at 562–63; Guhan Subramanian, *The Influence of Antitakeover Statutes on Incorporation Choice: Evidence on the "Race" Debate and Antitakeover Overreaching*, 150 U. Pa. L. Rev. 1795 (2002).

inducing Congress to legislate specified corporate governance enhancements pursuant to the Sarbanes-Oxley Act of 2002 and the Dodd-Frank Act of 2010.[14]

Interestingly, the view that federal legislation as well as vigorous judicial scrutiny and SEC activism were necessary to protect shareholder interests is not recent. For example, the SEC shareholder proposal rule was implemented during World War II.[15] Moreover, through the years, the SEC has sought to impact normative fiduciary conduct through the strategy of disclosure. Under this rationale, mandating disclosure of directors' and officers' improper conduct and self-dealing transactions may have the effect of deterring such behavior, thereby enhancing shareholder protection.[16] In addition, some proponents urged that Section 10(b) of the Securities Exchange Act and SEC Rule 10b-5 promulgated thereunder[17] be adapted to encompass substantive fiduciary wrongdoing.[18] Indeed, nearly 50 years ago, Professor Donald E. Schwartz perceived that Rule 10b-5 was being employed at that time to serve as a type of federal corporation law.[19] Professor Schwartz opined that the federal securities laws:

> have been expanded from merely requiring disclosure to investors and prohibiting fraud to providing substantive protection for the rights of shareholders by imposing, in fact if not in form, a federal fiduciary standard. To a large extent this has been necessitated by the plain fact that state corporation law has, in the main, abandoned all efforts to regulate corporations in the interests of

---

[14] *See* Marc I. Steinberg, *Securities Regulation* 320–21 (7th ed. 2017); Daniel J. Morrissey, *Catching the Culprits: Is Sarbanes-Oxley Enough?*, 2003 Colum. Bus. L. Rev. 801 (2003); discussion of these Acts in Chapters 5, 6 herein.

[15] The SEC shareholder proposal rule was adopted in 1942. *See* Securities Exchange Act Release No. 3347 (1942); discussion in Chapter 4 herein. As another example, in 1940, the SEC recommended the implementation of certain board committees comprised of independent directors. Three decades later, the Commission issued a formal release expressing its support for this development. Subsequently, in 1977, the New York Stock Exchange adopted rules mandating that a listed company must have an audit committee composed solely of independent directors. *See* discussion in Chapter 6 herein; Douglas Branson et al., *supra* note 8, at 383; *Report of the Task Force of the ABA Section of Business Law Corporate Governance Committee on Delineation of Governance Roles and Responsibilities*, 65 Bus. Law. 107 (2009); Roberta S. Karmel, *American Law Institute's Corporate Governance Project: Independent Directors: The Independent Corporate Board: A Means to What End?*, 52 Geo. Wash. L. Rev. 534 (1984).

[16] *See* Marc I. Steinberg, *Securities Regulation: Liabilities and Remedies* §§ 1.01–1.10 (2017); Ralph C. Ferrara, Richard M. Starr, and Marc I. Steinberg, *Disclosure of Information Bearing on Management Integrity and Competency*, 76 Nw. U.L. Rev. 555 (1981).

[17] Rule 10b-5, 17 C.F.R. § 240.10b-5, was promulgated by the SEC under its authority pursuant to Section 10(b) of the Securities Exchange Act, 15 U.S.C. § 78j(b) (2012).

[18] *See, e.g.*, Richard W. Jennings, *Federalization of Corporate Law: Part Way or All the Way*, 31 Bus. Law. 991 (1976). *See also*, Roberta S. Karmel, *Is It Time for a Federal Corporation Law?*, 57 Brook. L. Rev. 55 (1991).

[19] Donald E. Schwartz, *Federal Chartering of Corporations: An Introduction*, 61 Geo. L.J. 71 (1972).

> shareholders. Mainly as an interpretation of the SEC's rule 10b-5, courts have created a federal common law of corporations to advance shareholder rights.[20]

It may well be that Professor Schwartz's characterization was overstated, particularly as evidenced by the U.S. Supreme Court's subsequent decision in *Santa Fe Industries* (decided in 1977) that thoroughly rejected invocation of Rule 10b-5 as a federal corporation mandate.[21] Focusing on the primacy of disclosure under the federal securities laws, the Court reasoned that fairness and other such substantive aspects of a transaction are within the purview of state corporation law.[22] Thus, the *Santa Fe* Court definitively resolved the parameters of Rule 10b-5, holding that the Rule, consistent with the objectives of the federal securities laws, is premised on principles of disclosure. Substantive fairness, the Court opined, is a matter of state corporate law and not within the province of Rule 10b-5.[23]

Consistent with its decision in *Santa Fe*, the Supreme Court has been reluctant to invoke federal law to govern normative corporate fiduciary conduct. As stated by the Supreme Court:

> Corporations are creatures of state law, and investors commit their funds to corporate directors on the understanding that, except where federal law expressly requires certain responsibilities of directors with respect to stockholders, state law will govern the internal affairs of the corporation.[24]

---

[20] *Id.* at 81. Interestingly, the Report of the Corporation Law Revision Commission of New Jersey, issued in 1968, stated: "It is clear that the major protections to investors, creditors, employees, customers, and the general public have come, and must continue to come, from Federal legislation and not from state corporation acts. . . ." N.J. Stat. Ann, § 14A, at x (1969), as quoted in Cary, *supra* note 2, at 666.

[21] *Santa Fe Industries, Inc. v. Green*, 430 U.S. 462 (1977).

[22] *Id.* at 477–80.

[23] The Supreme Court stated:

> Federal courts applying a "federal fiduciary principle" under Rule 10b-5 could be expected to depart from state fiduciary standards. . . . Absent a clear indication of congressional intent, we are reluctant to federalize the substantial portion of the law of corporations that deals with transactions in securities, particularly where established state policies of corporate regulation would be overridden. . . .
>
> . . . There may well be a need for uniform federal fiduciary standards to govern mergers such as those challenged in this complaint. But those standards should not be supplied by judicial extension of § 10(b) and Rule 10b-5 to "cover the corporate universe."

Id. at 479–80. *See* Ralph C. Ferrara and Marc I. Steinberg, *A Reappraisal of Santa Fe: Rule 10b-5 and the New Federalism*, 129 U. Pa. L. Rev. 263 (1980); Mark J. Loewenstein, *Delaware as Demon: Twenty-Five Years After Professor Cary's Polemic*, 71 U. Colo. L. Rev. 497 (2000).

[24] *Cort v. Ash*, 422 U.S. 66, 84 (1975).

This theme has been repeated in numerous Supreme Court and lower federal court decisions.[25] Stated succinctly by Judge Frank Easterbrook, "[f]ederal securities laws frequently regulate process while state corporate law regulates substance."[26]

For over 100 years, this deference to state substantive corporate governance standards has been criticized. As discussed in this book, legislative as well as judicial attempts were undertaken to elevate federal regulation as the primary source for establishing minimum standards of corporate fiduciary accountability and governance. For the most part, until recently, these efforts did not meet with significant success. During the past two decades, the landscape has fundamentally changed. With the enactment of the Sarbanes-Oxley Act of 2002, the Dodd-Frank Act of 2010, SEC rules adopted under the authority of these statutes, and the emergence of stricter substantive listing requirements mandated by the stock exchanges, federal fiduciary principles and enhanced shareholder activism are now firmly established.[27]

This book addresses, from both historical and contemporary perspectives, the federalization of corporate governance in the United States. Nonetheless, it is clear that state corporate law remains vital with respect to the propriety of substantive fiduciary conduct as well as setting forth the relations among and between the corporation, its fiduciaries, its shareholders, and its other stakeholders. Accordingly, the ensuing discussion focuses on key aspects of state corporate law to illustrate the continued importance of state company law impacting corporate governance.

II. State Corporate Law Impacting Corporate Governance

The following discussion highlights several state law principles that impact substantive corporate conduct in a fundamental manner. A comprehensive analysis of state corporate governance is not the objective of this discussion. After all, dozens of treatises (many of which are comprised of several volumes) have been published on this subject.[28] The purpose of the following discussion is more limited—to illustrate, in a succinct manner, several of the wide-ranging matters that remain firmly entrenched within the confines of state corporate governance.

---

[25] *See, e.g., Burks v. Lasker*, 441 U.S. 471, 478 (1979) ("Congress has never indicated that the entire corpus of state corporate law is to be replaced simply because a plaintiff's cause of action is based upon a federal statute."). *Accord, Kamen v. Kemper Fin. Servs., Inc.*, 500 U.S. 90 (1991); *Amanda Acquisition Corp. v. Universal Foods Corp.*, 877 F.2d 496 (7th Cir. 1989).

[26] *Amanda Acquisition Corp. v. Universal Foods Corp.*, 877 F.2d 496, 503 (7th Cir. 1989).

[27] *See* discussion in Chapters 2–7 herein.

[28] *See* books and treatises cited in *supra* note 1.

A. GOVERNANCE OF THE CORPORATE ENTERPRISE

Under state corporate law, the board of directors is charged with managing or overseeing the business and affairs of the corporation.[29] Directors are elected (or removed) by the subject corporation's shareholders as authorized by corporate statutes as well as pursuant to provisions in such corporation's articles of incorporation and bylaws that do not contravene constitutional or statutory mandates.[30] These sources control such governance matters as the requisite notice, quorum, nomination, election, and board committee regimen. For example, pursuant to state corporate law and a subject company's articles of incorporation and bylaws, such company may opt for: straight (or cumulative) voting for directors,[31] election of directors by a plurality of shareholder votes,[32] shareholder access to

---

[29] *See* Model Business Corporation Act § 8.01(b) (2016) (With certain exceptions, "[a]ll corporate powers shall be exercised by or under the authority of and the business and affairs of the corporation managed by or under the authority of its board of directors. . . ."). For removal of directors, *see id.* at § 8.08.

[30] *See id.* at § 7.28. With respect to the allocation of power between a company's board of directors and its shareholders, the Delaware Supreme Court reasoned in *MM Companies, Inc. v. Liquid Audio, Inc.*, 813 A.2d 1118, 1126 (Del. 2003) (citations omitted):

> The most fundamental principles of corporate governance are a function of the allocation of power within a corporation between its stockholders and its board of directors. The stockholders' power is the right to vote on specific matters, in particular, in an election of directors. The power of managing the corporate enterprise is vested in the shareholders' duly elected board of representatives. Accordingly, while these fundamental tenets of Delaware corporate law provide for a separation of control and ownership, the stockholder franchise has been characterized as the ideological underpinning upon which the legitimacy of the directors' managerial power rests.

[31] Model Business Corporation Act § 7.28(b) (2016). Under straight voting, shareholders are entitled to "one vote for each share of stock they own for each director." Branson, et al., *supra* note 8, at 349. With respect to cumulative voting, "shareholders may 'cumulate' their votes," thereby providing a stockholder "with the possibility of electing one or more directors even if that shareholder does not own a majority of the outstanding shares. Under cumulative voting, a shareholder has a number of *votes* equal to the number of shares that the shareholder owns multiplied by the number of directors to be elected." *Id.* (emphasis in original).

[32] *Id.* at § 7.28(a). The traditional rule opts for plurality as the shares needed for a director to be elected. *Id.* Pursuant to their articles of incorporation, many corporations today call for a director-nominee to resign (or offer to resign) if he or she receives a majority of votes against or that are withheld. For example, two alternative model guidelines are:

> (1) Any nominee for Director who receives a number of votes "withheld" from or "against" his or her election greater than a majority of the outstanding shares entitled to vote in such election shall tender his or her resignation for consideration by the Corporate Governance and Nominating Committee. The Corporate Governance and Nominating Committee shall recommend to the Board the action to be taken with respect to such resignation.
>
> (2) Any nominee for Director in an uncontested election as to whom a majority of the shares of the Company that are outstanding and entitled to vote in such election are designated to be "withheld" from or are voted "against" his or her election shall tender his or her resignation for consideration by the Corporate Governance and Nominating Committee. The Corporate Governance and

nominate director-candidates on the company's ballot,[33] and a staggered board of directors.[34]

Traditionally, shareholders in a corporation have relatively little power. They may elect or remove directors, seek the inclusion of eligible shareholder proposals in the subject company's proxy materials, vote on matters presented at shareholder meetings, amend the bylaws, and vote on fundamental changes (such as an amendment to the articles of incorporation, the sale of substantially all assets, and most merger transactions).[35] If displeased, they can seek to replace incumbent directors or exercise

---

> Nominating Committee shall evaluate the best interests of the Company and its shareholders and shall recommend to the Board the action to be taken with respect to such tendered resignation.

Martin Lipton and David A. Katz, Wachtell, Lipton, Rosen & Katz, *Majority Vote to Elect Directors* (June 28, 2005), www.wlrk.com/docs/mved.pdf. *See generally* William K. Sjostrom, Jr. and Young Sang Kim, *Majority Voting for the Election of Directors*, 40 Conn. L. Rev. 459 (2007).

Moreover, consistent with state law and stock exchange listing rules, some publicly-held corporations opt for dual classes of stock with one class having super-voting rights, hence being able to elect the majority or all of the directors. *See, e.g.*, § 212 of the Delaware General Corporation Law; § 6.01 of the Model Business Corporation Act; *Williams v. Geier*, 671 A.2d 1368 (Del. 1996); Spencer G. Feldman, *IPOs in 2016 Increasingly Include Dual-Class Shareholder Voting Rights*, 48 Sec. Reg. & L. Rep. (BNA) 1342 (2016).

[33] An increasing number of corporations have amended their bylaws to authorize shareholders who meet specified eligibility criteria to nominate director-candidates on the corporation's ballot. Former SEC Chair Mary Jo White estimated that 35 percent of the 500 largest publicly-held U.S. corporations have adopted such director-nominee access bylaws. *See H & R Block Denied SEC No-Action Relief on Proposal to Amend Proxy Access Bylaws*, 48 Sec. Reg. & L. Rep. (BNA) 1549 (2016). Note that pursuant to the Dodd-Frank Act of 2010, the SEC adopted the proxy access rule entitling a company's largest shareholder (or group of shareholders) who did not seek control and owned at least 3 percent of the company's shares to nominate the greater of one director-nominee or up to 25 percent of the total number of directors on the company's board. *See* Securities Exchange Act Release No. 62764 (2010). Subsequently, the U.S. Court of Appeals invalidated these rules. *See Business Roundtable v. SEC*, 647 F.3d 1144 (D.C. Cir. 2011); discussion Chapters 4, 5, 6 herein. *See generally* Justice Henry DuPont Ridgely, *The Emerging Role of Bylaws in Corporate Governance*, 68 SMU L. Rev. 315 (2015).

[34] *See* Model Business Corporation Act § 8.06 (2016). With respect to a staggered board, directors generally are divided into two groups (if there are, for example, eight directors) or three groups (if there are, for example, nine directors). One group stands for election each year, signifying that a two- or three-year period must elapse before an entire incumbent board of directors can be replaced. Staggered boards, coupled with removal of directors only for cause, serve as an anti-takeover defense. *See* George S. Geis, *Ex-ante Corporate Governance*, 41 J. Corp. L. 609, 615 (2016) (stating that due to institutional shareholder pressure and the making of shareholder proposals, "the prevalence of staggered boards has plummeted").

[35] *See, e.g.*, Model Business Corporation Act §§ 7.28, 8.08, 10.01, 11.04, 12.02 (2016). *See generally* J. Robert Brown and Lisa L. Casey, *Corporate Governance: Cases and Materials* 349–84 (2011). With respect to the shareholder franchise, Chancellor Allen reasoned in *Blasius Industries, Inc. v. Atlas Corp.*, 564 A.2d 651, 659 (Del. Ch. 1988):

> It has, for a long time, been conventional to dismiss the stockholder vote as a vestige or ritual of little practical importance. It may be that we are now witnessing the emergence of new institutional voices and arrangements that will make the stockholder vote a less predictable affair than it has been. Be that as it may, however, whether the vote is seen functionally as an unimportant formalism, or as an important tool of discipline, it is clear that it is critical to the theory that legitimates the exercise of power by some (directors and officers) over vast aggregations of property that they do not own. Thus, when viewed from a broad, institutional

the "Wall Street" rule—namely, sell their stockholdings.[36] Notably, during the last two decades, the influence of institutional shareholders has increased dramatically, enabling shareholders to have meaningful input in corporate governance practices.[37] This shareholder activism has evolved to play an instrumental role in the governance of publicly-held companies.[38]

If an election for directors is contested, such as in a proxy fight,[39] state law standards apply to ascertain the fairness of the challenged conduct.[40] For example, with respect to the legitimacy of an incumbent board of directors engaging in conduct that interferes with shareholder voting, a strict duty of loyalty applies—requiring that the defendant directors establish a compelling justification for the action(s) taken.[41] Moreover, when an incumbent board of directors and management act with the objective of perpetuating themselves in office, inequitable conduct will not be

---

> perspective, it can be seen that matters involving the integrity of the shareholder voting process involve considerations not present in any other context in which directors exercise delegated power.

36 *See, e.g., Schnell v. Chris-Craft Indus., Inc.*, 285 A.2d 437 (Del. 1971). The Wall Street Rule posits that dissatisfied shareholders in a publicly-traded company that has an active trading market may opt to sell their shares. If a sufficient number of shares are sold, this "signal" likely will adversely impact the subject company's stock price, thereby raising the specter of a third-party takeover bid (for example, by means of a proxy contest or hostile tender offer).

37 *See* Corporate Governance Committee, American Bar Association Section of Business Law, *Report of the Task Force of the ABA Section of Business Law Corporate Governance Committee on the Delineation of Governance Roles and Responsibilities*, 65 Bus. Law 107, 139 (2008):

> Active shareholder engagement in governance issues by institutional investors—initially led by pension funds such as CalPERS, CalSTRS, TIAA-CREF, and the AFSCME and AFL-CIO pension funds—has played a significant role in urging boards to become more active, engaged, and objective . . . While the data is not definitive, there is evidence that focus by large, long-term shareholders and greater activation by independent boards is associated with better corporate performance. . . .

38 *See generally id.*; Imar Anabtawi and Lynn Stout, *Fiduciary Duties for Activist Shareholders*, 60 Stan. L. Rev. 1255 (2008); John C. Coffee, Jr. and Darius Palia, *The Wolf at the Door: The Impact of Hedge Fund Activism on Corporate Governance* 41 J. Corp. L. 545 (2016); K.A.D. Camara, *Classifying Institutional Investors*, 30 J. Corp. L. 219 (2005); Ronald J. Gilson and Jeffrey N. Gordon, *The Agency Costs of Agency Capitalism: Activist Investors and the Revaluation of Governance Rights*, 113 Colum. L. Rev. 863 (2013); Virginia Harper Ho, *Risk-Related Activism: The Business Case for Monitoring Nonfinancial Risk*, 41 J. Corp. L. 647 (2016).

39 *See* Randall S. Thomas and Catherine T. Dixon on *Aranow & Einhorn on Proxy Contests for Corporate Control* (1992).

40 *See, e.g., Schnell v. Chris-Craft Indus., Inc.*, 285 A.2d 437 (Del. 1971). Nonetheless, the federal securities laws and SEC rules and regulations thereunder govern the disclosure process and certain procedural matters in proxy contests, thereby having a significant impact. *See, e.g., GAF Corporation v. Heyman*, 724 F.2d 727 (2d Cir. 1983).

41 *See, e.g., Blasius Indus., Inc. v. Atlas Corp.*, 565 A.2d 651 (Del. Ch. 1988). Vote buying also is vigilantly scrutinized. As the court stated in *Schreiber v. Carney*, 447 A.2d 17 (Del. Ch. 1982):

> Vote-buying, despite its negative connotation, is simply a voting agreement supported by consideration personal to the stockholder, whereby the stockholder divorces his discretionary voting power and votes as directed by the offerer. . . .

deemed enforceable solely because it is authorized by statute and the company's articles and bylaws.[42] In a case involving management's adoption of a bylaw amendment that advanced the date of the corporation's annual shareholders' meeting, thereby preventing the insurgents from launching a proxy contest, the Delaware Supreme Court opined:

> [M]anagement has attempted to utilize the corporate machinery and the Delaware Law for the purpose of perpetuating itself in office; and, to that end, for the purpose of obstructing the legitimate efforts of dissident stockholders in the exercise of their rights to undertake a proxy contest against management. These are inequitable purposes, contrary to established principles of corporate democracy. The advancement by directors of the by-law date of a stockholders' meeting, for such purposes, may not be permitted to stand. . . .[43]

Likewise, state law standards apply to determine the legitimacy of such governance mechanisms as voting agreements,[44] irrevocable proxies,[45] stock transfer restrictions,[46] and agreements among shareholders that impinge upon the authority of the board of directors.[47]

> [T]he agreement [at bar] . . . was not void per se because the object and purpose of the agreement was not to defraud or disenfranchise the other stockholders but rather was for the purpose of furthering the interest of all [subject company] stockholders. The agreement, however, was a voidable act. Because the loan agreement was voidable, it was susceptible to cure by shareholder approval. Consequently, the subsequent ratification of the transaction by a majority of the independent stockholders, after a full disclosure of all germane facts with complete candor, precludes any further judicial inquiry of it.

Id. at 23, 26 (citations omitted).

[42] *See, e.g., Schnell v. Chris-Craft Indus., Inc.*, 285 A.2d 437 (Del. 1971).

[43] *Id.* at 439. With respect to a shareholder's inspection rights to corporate books and records, *see* § 220 of the Delaware General Corporation Law (2011) ("proper purpose" required); *Seinfeld v. Verizon Commc'ns, Inc.*, 909 A.2d 117, 118 (Del. 2006) (requiring shareholder under § 220 "to show some evidence to suggest a credible basis for wrongdoing. . . .").

[44] *See, e.g.*, Model Business Corporation Act §§ 7.31, 7.32 (2016); *Ringling Bros. Combined Shows v. Ringling*, 53 A.2d 441 (Del. 1947); *Triggs v. Triggs*, 413 N.Y.S. 2d 325 (N.Y. Ct. App. 1978).

[45] *See, e.g.*, Model Business Corporation Act § 7.22(d) (2016). Generally, a proxy is revocable unless it is coupled with an interest. "Appointments coupled with an interest include the appointment of: (1) a pledgee; (2) a person who purchased or agreed to purchase the shares; (3) a creditor of the corporation who extended credit under terms requiring the appointment; (4) an employee of the corporation whose employment contract requires the appointment; or (5) a party to a voting agreement under section 7.31." *Id.*

[46] *See, e.g.*, Model Business Corporation Act § 6.27 (2016); *Lash v. Lash Furniture Co.*, 296 A.2d 207 (Vt. 1972); *Jones v. Harris*, 388 P.2d 539 (Wash. 1964).

[47] *See, e.g.*, Model Business Corporation Act § 7.32(2016). Such unanimous shareholder agreements are frequently found in closely-held enterprises. *See, e.g., Lehrman v. Cohen*, 222 A.2d 800 (Del. 1966); *Galler v. Galler*, 203 N.E. 2d 577 (Ill. 1964); *Clark v. Dodge*, 199 N.E. 641 (N.Y. 1936).

B. FIDUCIARY DUTIES OF CORPORATE DIRECTORS AND OFFICERS

Corporate directors and officers owe the corporation and such corporation's shareholders collectively the duties of care and loyalty.[48] Generally, the duty of care calls for the subject fiduciary to exercise that degree of care that a person in a like position reasonably would use in like circumstances.[49] In practice, corporate officers and directors are rarely held liable for breach of the duty of care.[50] This largely is due to the application of the business judgment rule and the implementation by corporations of exculpation provisions. The business judgment rule provides insulation from liability if the subject fiduciary made a deliberative decision, in good faith without a disabling conflict of interest, being adequately informed, and with such decision having a rational basis.[51] As the Delaware Supreme Court has held, to rebut the presumption of the business judgment rule, a plaintiff must show that no deliberative decision was made, that a conflict of interest existed, or that the fiduciaries acted with gross negligence (due to either being inadequately informed or with respect to the rationality of the determination made).[52] Directors (but not officers) are further protected by exculpation or "raincoat" provisions that are included in the subject company's articles of incorporation. Generally, under these provisions, unless a director breaches the duty of loyalty, is responsible for the declaration of an illegal distribution, or violates another statute (such as the securities laws), such

---

[48] *See, e.g., Stone v. Ritter*, 911 A.2d 362 (Del. 2006*); Brane v. Roth*, 590 N.E.2d 587 (Ind. 1993); *State ex rel. Hays Oyster Co. v. Keypoint Oyster Co.*, 391 P.2d 979 (Wash. 1994). Note that when a corporation is insolvent, these duties are owed collectively to the creditors of the corporation. *See North American Catholic Educational Programming Found., Inc. v. Gheewalla*, 930 A.2d 92 (Del. 2007).

[49] *See, e.g., Francis v. United Jersey Bank*, 432 A.2d 814, 822 (N.J. 1981) (stating that "directors are bound to exercise ordinary care," "are under a continuing obligation to keep informed about the activities of the corporation," and "should maintain familiarity with the financial status of the corporation by a regular review of [such corporation's] financial statements").

[50] *See* Joseph W. Bishop, Jr., *Sitting Ducks and Decoy Ducks: New Trends in the Indemnification of Corporate Directors and Officers*, 77 Yale L.J. 1078 (1967); David A. Hoffman, *Self-Handicapping and Managers' Duty of Care*, 42 Wake Forest L. Rev. 803 (2007); Lynn A. Stout, *On the Proper Motives of Corporate Directors*, 28 Del. J. Corp. L. 1 (2003).

[51] *See, e.g.*, American Law Institute, *Principles of Corporate Governance: Analysis and Recommendations* § 4.01(c) (1992) (providing protection from liability if the subject officer or director made a business decision in good faith, "is not interested in the subject matter of his business judgment; is informed with respect to the subject of the business judgment to the extent the director or officer reasonably believes to be appropriate under the circumstances; and rationally believes that the business judgment is in the best interests of the corporation").

[52] *See Smith v. Van Gorkom*, 488 A.2d 858, 873 (Del. 1985) ("While the Delaware cases use a variety of terms to describe the applicable standard of care, our analysis satisfies us that under the business judgment rule director liability is predicated upon concepts of gross negligence.") (citation omitted). *See Gimbal v. Signal Cos.*, 316 A.2d 599 (Del. Ch.), *aff'd*, 316 A.2d 619 (Del. 1974). Note that many courts applying the business judgment rule hold that the rationality of the decision made is outside the ambit of the rule. *See, e.g., WLR Foods, Inc. v. Tyson Foods, Inc.*, 65 F.3d 1172 (4th Cir. 1995) (interpreting Virginia law).

director can be held monetary liable only for engaging in "knowing misconduct."[53] Thus, under an applicable raincoat provision, a director who acts with gross negligence in a duty-of-care scenario cannot be held monetarily liable.[54]

The duty of loyalty encompasses situations where, for example, a subject fiduciary engages in self-dealing, usurps a corporate opportunity, fails to act in good faith, or otherwise has a disabling conflict of interest. In addition, fiduciaries owe shareholders a duty of candor, which, depending on the circumstances, may implicate the duty of care and/or the duty of loyalty.[55] These duties are placed not only on directors and officers. In parent-subsidiary self-dealing situations (such as cash-out mergers where adequate protective safeguards are not provided to the subsidiary's minority shareholders), the parent corporation, as the controlling shareholder, must act with entire fairness in undertaking and consummating the transaction.[56]

Self-dealing often arises in the context of related party transactions, such as interested director transactions.[57] With a corporate fiduciary being on both sides of the transaction (often a controller such as a majority shareholder or the chief executive

---

[53] *See, e.g.*, Delaware General Corporation Law § 102(b)(7) (2011). The raincoat provision thus authorizes inclusion of a provision in a Delaware corporation's articles of incorporation that eliminates or limits the liability of a director, except such a provision cannot provide such exculpation: "(i) For any breach of the director's duty of loyalty to the corporation or its shareholders; (ii) for acts or omissions not in good faith or which involve intentional misconduct or a knowing violation of law; (iii) under § 174 of this title [relating to the knowing authorization of illegal distributions]; or (iv) for any transaction from which the director derived an improper personal benefit." The Delaware statute has been widely adopted by other states. *See generally* Elizabeth A. Nowicki, *Director Inattention and Director Protection under Delaware General Corporation Law Section 102(b)(7): A Proposal for Legislative Reform*, 33 Del. J. Corp. L. 695 (2008).

[54] *See, e.g., Malpiede v. Townson*, 780 A.2d 1075 (Del. 2001).

[55] *See, e.g., Malone v. Brincat*, 722 A.2d 5 (Del. 1998), discussion *infra* notes 57–69 and accompanying text. Note that other obligations also apply in the duty-of-loyalty context, such as to refrain from unfairly competing with the subject corporation. *See, e.g.*, American Law Institute, *Principles of Corporate Governance: Analysis and Recommendations* § 5.06 (1994).

[56] *See, e.g., Weinberger v. UOP, Inc.*, 457 A.2d 701 (Del. 1983) Self-dealing in this context "occurs when the parent [corporation], by virtue of its domination of the subsidiary, causes the subsidiary to act in such a way that the parent receives something from the subsidiary to the exclusion of, and detriment to, the minority stockholders of the subsidiary." *Sinclair Oil Corp. v. Levien*, 280 A.2d 717, 720 (Del. 1971). Nonetheless, in a short-form merger (where the parent corporation owns at least 90 percent of the subsidiary prior to such merger), the entire fairness test does not apply. Absent fraud or illegality, appraisal is the minority shareholder's exclusive remedy. *Glassman v. Unocal Exploration Corp.*, 777 A.2d 242 (Del. 2001). *See* Marc I. Steinberg, *Short-Form Mergers in Delaware*, 27 Del. J. Corp. L. 489 (2002). However, even in long-form mergers, if the merger is conditioned on a special committee comprised of independent directors who are granted authority to meaningfully bargain with the parent corporation and if the merger is conditioned upon the informed approval of a majority of the minority shares, the business judgment rule is the applicable standard. *See Kahn v. M & F Worldwide Corp.*, 88 A.3d 635 (Del. 2014). Nonetheless, contrary to Delaware, a number of states mandate that, absent fraud or illegality, appraisal is the sole remedy for a minority shareholder complaining of a cash-out merger. *See, e.g., Yanow v. Teal Indus., Inc.*, 422 A.2d 311 (Conn. 1979).

[57] *See, e.g.*, Delaware General Corporation Law § 144 (2011).

officer), the test of entire fairness must be met—namely, that the transaction is both procedurally and substantively fair to the corporation.[58] On the other hand, when the transaction is approved by disinterested directors after being sufficiently informed of the requisite facts and circumstances underlying the transaction, the business judgment rule is the prevailing standard that is applied by the courts.[59] With the specter of structural bias, the actuality of detached disinterested director scrutiny of these related party transactions has been questioned.[60]

The corporate opportunity doctrine arises when a corporate fiduciary allegedly takes for her benefit an opportunity that properly belongs to the corporation. A number of tests have been employed by the courts to assess the propriety of fiduciary conduct in this setting, including the expectancy test,[61] the line of business test,[62] and the fairness test.[63] In addition, the American Law Institute has promulgated a test that has been adopted in a number of jurisdictions.[64] From a general perspective, depending on the circumstances presented, key factors in ascertaining whether a

---

[58] *See, e.g., Benihana of Tokyo, Inc. v. Benihana Inc.*, 906 A.2d 114 (Del. 2006); *Fliegler v. Lawrence*, 361 A.2d 218 (Del. 1976); *Remillard Brick Co. v. Remillard-Dandini Co.*, 241 P.2d 66 (Cal. App. 1952).

[59] *See, e.g., Marciano v. Nakash*, 535 A.2d 400, 405 n.3 (Del. 1987) (stating that "approval by fully-informed disinterested directors under section 144(a)(1), or disinterested shareholders under section 144(a)(2), permits invocation of the business judgment rule").

[60] "Structural bias" may be defined as "inherent prejudice . . . resulting from the composition and character of the board of directors [and management]." Note, *The Business Judgment Rule in Derivative Suits Against Directors*, 65 Cornell L. Rev. 600, 601 n.14 (1980). *See generally* Harold M. Marsh, Jr., *Are Directors Trustees? Conflict of Interest and Corporate Morality*, 22 Bus. Law. 35 (1966–1967).

[61] As applied today, the "interest or expectancy" test generally examines whether the subject company had expressed an interest in the particular opportunity that the fiduciary seeks to take for his or her own benefit. *See, e.g., Farber v. Servan Land Co.*, 662 F.2d 371 (5th Cir. 1981) (applying Florida law).

[62] The "line of business" test generally provides that any opportunity that is in the identical or closely-related line of the corporation's business is a corporate opportunity. This inquiry ordinarily focuses on the company's existing as well as prospective plans so long as such contemplated plans are deemed sufficiently concrete. *See, e.g., Broz v. Cellular Info. Sys.*, 673 A.2d 148 (Del. 1996); *PJ Acquisition Corp. v. Skoglund*, 453 2d 1 (Minn. 1990).

[63] The fairness test first focuses on whether the transaction constituted a corporate opportunity, either pursuant to the expectancy test or the line-of-business test. If so, the court then applies a fairness inquiry, assessing such factors as "whether the fiduciary learned of the opportunity in her personal or official capacity, whether the fiduciary is an inside or outside director, whether the corporation had the financial ability to exploit and profit from the opportunity, and whether the fiduciary used any corporate resources to gain the opportunity." Marc I. Steinberg, *Developments in Business Law and Policy* 191 (2012). *See Miller v. Miller*, 222 N.W. 2d 71 (Minn. 1974).

[64] *See* American Law Institute, *Principles of Corporate Governance: Analysis and Recommendations* § 5.05(b) (1994). Under the ALI test, a corporate opportunity is:

> (1) Any opportunity to engage in a business activity of which a director or senior executive becomes aware, either:
>
> > (A) In connection with the performance of functions as a director or senior executive, or under circumstances that should reasonably lead the director or senior executive to believe that the person offering the opportunity expects it to be offered to the corporation; or

director or officer usurped a corporate opportunity may include whether: the corporation focused on the opportunity, the opportunity was within the current or prospective line of the corporation's business endeavors, the fiduciary used corporate resources to exploit the opportunity, the fiduciary learned of the opportunity in her corporate or personal capacity, and the corporation had the financial wherewithal to pursue the opportunity. The usurpation of a corporate opportunity by the offending fiduciary may well carry with it a harsh sanction—the levying of a constructive trust for the corporation's benefit on the property improperly taken.[65] To protect oneself from such claims, prudent fiduciaries disclose the opportunity and the material facts to the subject company's board of directors or other appropriate decision-maker. Ordinarily, a decision by a majority of the disinterested directors declining to pursue the opportunity will entitle the subject fiduciary to procure the opportunity for her personal benefit without undue risk of liability exposure.[66]

A fiduciary's failure to act in good faith implicates another area of concern. Viewed as part of the duty of loyalty by the Delaware Supreme Court,[67] this obligation may be breached even when the subject fiduciary does not financially benefit from the transaction.[68] This situation may arise when a subject fiduciary is under the control of a majority shareholder or chief executive officer and fails to adhere to his responsibilities to act in the corporation's best interests. As the Delaware Supreme Court has opined, the failure to act in good faith may arise in the following contexts:

> A failure to act in good faith may be shown, for instance, where the fiduciary intentionally acts with a purpose other than that of advancing the best interests

---

(B) Through the use of corporate information or property, if the resulting opportunity is one that the director or senior executive should reasonably be expected to believe would be of interest to the corporation; or

(2) Any opportunity to engage in a business activity of which a senior executive [thereby excluding an outside director] becomes aware and knows is closely related to a business in which the corporation is engaged or expects to engage.

See Northeast Harbor Club, Inc. v. Harris 725 A.2d 1018 (Maine 1999) (adopting ALI test).

[65] *See, e.g., Broz v. Cellular Info. Sys.*, 673 A.2d 148 (Del. 1996); *Miller v. Miller*, 222 N.W. 2d 71 (Minn. 1974); *Northeast Harbor Club, Inc. v. Harris*, 725 A.2d 1018 (Maine 1999); *Today Homes, Inc. v. Williams*, 634 S.E. 2d 737 (Va. 2006); Steinberg, *supra* note 63, at 191. The levying of a constructive trust may be ordered, thereby requiring the fiduciary to transfer the ill-gotten opportunity to the corporation. *See Brandt v. Somerville*, 692 N.W. 2d 144 (N.D. 2005).

[66] *See, e.g.*, American Law Institute, *Principles of Corporate Governance: Analysis and Recommendations* § 5.05(a) (1992) & comment thereto (stating that "under § 5.05(a)(1) disclosure of all material facts known to the director or senior executive concerning the conflict of interest and the corporate opportunity should be made to the corporate decisionmaker [e.g., the independent directors] reviewing the matter").

[67] *Stone v. Ritter*, 911 A.2d 362 (Del. 2006).

[68] *Id.* at 370.

> of the corporation, where the fiduciary acts with the intent to violate applicable positive law, or where the fiduciary intentionally fails to act in the face of a known duty to act, demonstrating a conscious disregard for his duties.[69]

With great frequency, alleged breaches of the duty of care or loyalty give rise to derivative litigation—actions that are brought by a shareholder on behalf of the corporation.[70] Before these suits may be brought by a shareholder, a demand ordinarily must be made on the subject company's board of directors to review the allegations at issue and make a determination whether the case should be pursued.[71] An increasing number of states require universal demand, signifying that, except where the corporation would suffer irreparable injury, a shareholder demand on the board of directors is mandated.[72] Other states, including Delaware, excuse the making of a demand on the board of directors if deemed futile to do so.[73] For example, under Delaware law, an interested director transaction, whereby a majority of the current directors financially benefitted from the transaction, would be an instance where demand would be excused.[74]

In situations where demand on the board of directors is required, the prevailing standard applies the business judgment rule to a determination by the disinterested directors that the litigation should be dismissed as not being in the corporation's best interests.[75] Often, these decisions are delegated to a special litigation committee (SLC) comprised of independent directors, who, with the assistance of legal

---

[69] *In re Walt Disney Company Derivative Litig.*, 906 A.2d 27, 67 (Del. 2006). *See In re Abbott Labs. Derivative Shareholders Litig.*, 325 F.3d 795 (7th Cir. 2003) (applying Delaware law); *McCall v. Scott*, 239 F.3d 808, *amended*, 250 F.3d 997 (6th Cir. 2001) (applying Delaware law). *See generally* Marc I. Steinberg and Matthew D. Bivona, *Disney Goes Goofy: Agency, Delegation, and Corporate Governance*, 60 Hastings L.J. 201 (2008).

[70] *See, e.g., Tooley v. Donaldson, Lufkin & Jenrette, Inc.*, 845 A.2d 1031 (Del. 2004).

[71] *See, e.g.*, § 7.42 of the Model Business Corporation Act; *Aronson v. Lewis*, 473 A.2d 805 (Del. 1984). One source sets forth three reasons supporting the demand requirement:

> [F]irst, to relieve the courts of the necessity of interfering in the management of routine, internal corporate business affairs; second, to afford a measure of protection to corporate directors against harassment by dissident minority shareholders who may disagree with such directors on matters involving business judgment; and third, to discourage so-called "strike" suits in which stockholders make charges, without regard to their truth, for the purpose of coercing corporate management into settling worthless claims in order to get rid of them.

Edward Brodsky, *Law of Corporate Officers and Directors: Rights, Duties and Liabilities* § 9.6 (2003).

[72] *See, e.g.*, § 7.42 of the Model Business Corporation Act (2016); *In re Guidant Shareholders Derivative Litig.*, 841 N.E. 2d 571 (Ind. 2006).

[73] *See, e.g., Aronson v. Lewis*, 473 A.2d 805 (Del. 1984).

[74] *See, e.g., Zapata Corp. v. Maldonado*, 430 A.2d 779 (Del. 1981).

[75] *See, e.g., Aronson v. Lewis*, 473 A.2d 805, 817 (Del. 1984).

counsel and other advisers, assesses the merits of the claims alleged and recommends whether the litigation is in the corporation's best interests.[76]

Where demand is excused, a SLC likewise is ordinarily appointed. As studies have indicated, the SLC usually recommends that the subject lawsuit be dismissed.[77] While some courts apply the business judgment rule to the SLC's recommendation,[78] other courts apply more rigorous standards. For example, in a number of jurisdictions, the SLC must show that it was independent, acted in good faith, conducted a reasonable investigation, and had reasonable grounds for its recommendation.[79] Thus, while some shareholder derivative suits are pursued with vigor, many others are dismissed at an early stage without judicial scrutiny of the alleged fiduciary misconduct.

The foregoing discussion succinctly illustrates the application of state corporate law to determine the propriety of fiduciary conduct. Both historically and today, assessment of the substantive characteristics of a subject decision made by corporate fiduciaries has been and remains a matter of state law.

C. THE USE OF DEFENSIVE TACTICS IN TAKEOVER BIDS

This discussion briefly focuses on the use by incumbent management of defensive tactics to fend off hostile prospective acquirers. Although certain takeover matters are a matter of federal law,[80] the legitimacy of defensive actions undertaken by target management remains a function of state corporate law. For example, the target

---

[76] *See Harhen v. Brown*, 730 N.E. 2d 859 (Mass. 2000).

[77] *See, e.g.*, Minor Myers, *The Decisions of Corporate Special Litigation Committees: An Empirical Investigation*, 84 Ind. L.J. 1309 (2009). *See also*, *Thompson v. Sci. Atlanta, Inc.*, 621 S.E. 2d 796, 798–99 (Ga. Ct. App. 2005) (applying business judgment rule to SLC's determination that the derivative suit was not in the corporation's best interests and referring to the SLC's "over 900-page report").

[78] *See, e.g., Boland v. Boland,* 31 A.3d 529 (Md. 2011); *Auerbach v. Bennett*, 419 N.Y.S. 2d 920, 393 N.E. 2d 994 (1979); *Desigoudar v. Meyercord*, 108 Cal. App. 4th 173 (2003).

[79] *See. e. g., Zapata Corp. v. Maldonado*, 430 A.2d 779 (Del 1981). Some courts apply this level of scrutiny irrespective of whether demand is required or excused. *See, e.g., Alford v. Shaw*, 358 S.E. 2d 323 (N.C. 1987). In Iowa, the members of a special litigation committee are to be appointed by the court. *See Miller v. Register & Tribune Syndicate, Inc.*, 336 N.W. 2d 709 (Iowa 1983). *See generally* James Cox and Harry L. Munsinger, *Bias in the Boardroom: Psychological Foundations and Legal Implications of Corporate Cohesion*, 48 Law & Contemp. Prob. 83 (Summer 1985); George Dent, *The Power of Directors to Terminate Shareholder Litigation: The Death of the Derivative Suit?*, 75 Nw. U.L. Rev. 96 (1980); Marc I. Steinberg, *The Use of Special Litigation Committees to Terminate Shareholder Derivative Litigation*, 35 U. Miami L. Rev. 1 (1980).

[80] *See, e.g.,* Sections 14(d), (e) of the Securities Exchange Act, 15 U.S.C. §§ 78n(d), (e) (2012) and SEC rules promulgated thereunder. Several of these provisions have meaningful impact on the tender offer process. Their mandates include those relating to a shareholder's right to proration, to withdraw shares previously tendered, and to receive the best price offered by the subject bidder, and that the offer be open to all shareholders. For further discussion, *see* Chapter 3 herein.

board's adoption and deployment of poison pills, rendering the corporation more difficult to acquire, is a matter within the purview of state law.[81] Another example is the target board's execution of a long-term business plan that has the effect of fending off a prospective acquirer.[82] The same holds true with respect to lockups extended to favored bidders. Such lockups, including the issuance of shares and options to purchase specified assets of the target corporation, are measured by principles of state corporate law.[83] A number of these lock-ups have been invalidated by state courts, including the grant of an option to a favored bidder to purchase attractive assets of the target when the target corporation had elected to put itself up "for sale."[84]

The impact of state law as the key determiner in assessing the substantive propriety of fiduciary conduct in corporate control transactions is huge. In such mergers and tender offers, billions of dollars in a global marketplace are at issue. One would reasonably conclude that, given the public policy issues at stake from both United States and global perspectives, these issues would be evaluated under federal law. But that is not the situation. Instead, the internal affairs doctrine prevails, signifying that the Delaware courts often will determine the outcome of major takeover bids that have domestic and international ramifications.[85]

D. ANTI-TAKEOVER, STAKEHOLDER, AND RELATED STATUTES

A last example for illustrative purposes is the adoption by several states of anti-takeover, stakeholder, and benefit corporation statutes. Seeking to protect

---

[81] *See, e.g., Versata Enters., Inc. v. Selectica, Inc.*, 5 A.3d 586 (Del. 2010); *Unitrin, Inc. v. Am. Gen. Corp.*, 651 A.2d 1361 (Del. 1995); *Unocal Corp. v. Mesa Petroleum Co.*, 493 A.2d 946 (Del 1985). Generally, a poison pill is "an antitakeover provision (also called a 'shareholder rights plan') whereby certain securities (such as rights or warrants) of the target company, upon consummation of an enumerated transaction or event, are convertible into the common stock or other security of the target (or of the acquirer) or into cash." Marc I. Steinberg, *Understanding Securities Law* 494 (6th ed. 2014).

[82] *See, e.g., Paramount Commc'ns, Inc. v. Time, Inc.*, 571 A.2d 1140 (Del. 1990). This decision was criticized by the author. *See* Marc I. Steinberg, *Nightmare on Main Street: The Paramount Picture Horror Show*, 16 Del. J. Corp. L. 1 (1991).

[83] *See, e.g., Omnicare, Inc. v. NCS Healthcare, Inc.*, 818 A.2d 914 (Del. 2000); *Smith v. Van Gorkom*, 488 A.2d 858 (Del. 1985).

[84] *See, e.g., Paramount Commc'ns, Inc. v. QVC Network, Inc.*, 637 A.2d 34 (Del. 1994); *MacAndrews & Forbes Holdings v. Revlon, Inc.*, 506 A.2d 173 (Del. 1986).

[85] *See Federal Preemption of State Anti-Takeover Legislation*, Remarks of David S. Ruder, Chairman, Securities and Exchange Commission, before the 28th Annual Corporate Counsel Institute, at 8–9 (Chicago Oct. 7, 1987), reported in, Fed. Sec. L. Rep. (CCH) No. 1256, at 8–9 (1987) (asserting that "it is imprudent for states to use their authority over matters of internal governance as a means of regulating the interstate market for corporate control"). Of course, such acquisitions may be precluded by the federal antitrust laws. *See, e.g., Marathon Oil Co. v. Mobil Corp.*, 669 F.2d 378 (6th Cir. 1981) (preliminarily enjoining prospective acquisition of Marathon by Mobil, finding that such acquisition would violate the federal antitrust laws).

locally-situated companies and their various stakeholders (such as employees and communities) within their respective jurisdictions, states have enacted anti-takeover statutes that supplement takeover defenses implemented by target corporations.[86] These statutes raise constitutional and public policy issues.[87] Although a number of the earlier state statutes were declared unconstitutional,[88] more recent state statutes have passed constitutional scrutiny, thus surviving challenges to their validity.[89] As succinctly described by Professor (and former SEC Commissioner) Roberta Karmel:

> [M]anagement and labor groups were able to persuade state legislatures to pass anti-takeover statutes. Early statutes either unduly delayed the takeover process or permitted state blue-sky commissioners to conclude that takeovers were unfair. Such a statute was struck down by the U.S. Supreme Court as unconstitutional. Later state statutes, which imposed delays in the tender offer process, prohibited control share merger transactions for a period of years, or endorsed the consideration by corporate managers of nonshareholder constituencies in control contests, were upheld by the federal courts.[90]

With respect to stakeholder statutes, these statutes generally provide that, in exercising their fiduciary duties in the corporation's best interests, directors may consider the interests of stakeholders in addition to stockholders. These stakeholders may include employees, customers, suppliers, and the communities in which the corporation conducts business. Whereas many states apply this standard to the conduct of

---

[86] *See generally* Symposium, *Delaware Antitakeover Statute*, 65 Bus. Law. No. 3 (2010); Richard A. Booth, *The Promise of State Takeover Statutes*, 86 Mich. L. Rev. 1635 (1988); C. Steven Bradford, *Protecting Shareholders from Themselves? A Policy and Constitutional Review of a State Takeover Statute*, 67 Neb. L. Rev. 459 (1988); Harry N. Butler and Larry E. Ribstein, *State Anti-Takeover Statutes and the Contract Clause*, 57 U. Cin. L. Rev. 611 (1988); Thomas L. Hazen, *State Anti-Takeover Legislation: The Second and Third Generations*, 23 Wake Forest L. Rev. 77 (1988); Alan R. Palmiter, *The CTS Gambit: Stanching the Federalization of Corporate Law*, 69 Wash. U. L.Q. 445 (1991); Arthur R. Pinto, *The Constitution and the Market for Corporate Control: State Takeover Statutes After CTS Corp.*, 29 Wm. & Mary L. Rev. 699 (1988); Roberta Romano, *The Political Economy of Takeover Statutes*, 73 Va. L. Rev. 111 (1987); Manning Gilbert Warren, III, *Developments in State Takeover Regulation: MITE and Its Aftermath*, 40 Bus. Law 671 (1985).

[87] *See* sources cited *supra* note 86.

[88] *See, e.g., Edgar v. MITE Corp.*, 457 U.S. 624 (1982) (holding Illinois anti-takeover statute unconstitutional on interstate commerce grounds).

[89] *See, e.g., CTS Corp. v. Dynamics Corp. of Am.*, 481 U.S. 69 (1987) (holding that Indiana's control share acquisitions statute not violative of the Constitution on either preemption or interstate commerce grounds); *Amanda Acquisition Corp. v. Universal Foods Corp.*, 877 F.2d 496 (7th Cir. 1989) (upholding Wisconsin anti-takeover statute); *BNS Inc. v. Koppers Co.*, 683 F. Supp. 458 (D. Del. 1988) (upholding Delaware anti-takeover statute).

[90] Roberta S. Karmel, *Appropriateness of Regulation at the Federal or State Level: Reconciling Federal and State Interests in Securities Regulation in the United States and Europe*, 28 Brook J. Int'l L. 495, 534 (2003).

directors in general, a number of other states limit the scope of the subject statute to the takeover situation.[91]

More recently, a majority of states have enacted public benefit statutes. These statutes authorize companies to opt into a governance framework that requires directors to balance all stakeholder interests when making decisions—including those of stockholders, customers, suppliers, employees, and the public.[92] Thus, unlike the traditional and still firmly established principle of the corporate objective being profit maximization for its shareholders in a law-compliant manner,[93] the "benefit corporation" embraces a broader mandate. Today, a majority of U.S. jurisdictions, including Delaware, have enacted public benefit corporation statutes.[94] As stated by one source, these public benefit corporation statutes

> follow the same three-part formula: the corporate charter must contain a clearly articulated corporate purpose, the directors must balance or consider interests beyond shareholder profit, and the company must report regularly on [its] efforts to promote or maintain [its] chosen social purpose.[95]

Whether the benefit corporation will remain a niche option or emerge as a vehicle regularly utilized by for-profit corporations remains to be determined.[96] The widespread enactment of these statutes serves as further evidence of the states' fundamental role in being an essential player in the regulation of corporate governance.

E. SUMMATION

The foregoing examples illustrate that state law continues as a principal regulator of corporate governance. By no means exhaustive, the myriad of examples set forth above refute the assertion that federal law has displaced the states in regulating the corporate governance of publicly-held companies. Nonetheless, to a significant

---

[91] *See* Stephen M. Bainbridge, *Interpreting Nonshareholder Constituency Statutes*, 19 Pepp. L. Rev. 971 (1992); Marleen O'Conner, *Malaise—Stakeholder Statutes: Cause or Cure?*, 21 Stetson L. Rev. 3 (1991); Richard B. Tyler, *Other Constituency Statutes*, 59 Mo. L. Rev. 373 (1994).

[92] *See* Frederick H. Alexander, *Public Benefit Corporations*, 49 Rev. Sec. & Comm. Reg. 155 (2016).

[93] *See Dodge v. Ford Motor Co.*, 170 N.W. 668 (Mich. 1919).

[94] *See* Alexander, *supra* note 92, at 156 (stating that 31 jurisdictions, including Delaware, have enacted public benefit corporation statutes).

[95] Michael Vargas, *The Next Stage of Social Entrepreneurship: Benefit Corporations and the Companies Using This Innovative Corporate Form*, Bus. Law Today, at 1 (July 2016).

[96] *Id.* at 4. Moreover, note that a number of states have adopted merit regulation with respect to their state securities laws. These statutes focus not only on the adequacy of disclosure in the registered securities offering context but also whether such offering is "fair, just, and equitable." Thus, the concept of fairness also applies under

extent, federal law either has replaced or supplemented several areas of state corporate law. The following discussion provides a succinct analysis with respect to this transformation.

III. Federal Law Impacting Corporate Governance

This book focuses on the federalization of corporate governance in the United States. The ensuing chapters analyze federal law developments that have replaced or supplemented areas traditionally within the purview of the states. For purposes of this chapter, the discussion that follows provides a number of examples to illustrate this principle.

Certainly, the starting point is the enactment of the Securities Act of 1933 and the Securities Exchange Act of 1934. Among other objectives, these Acts focus on disclosure of material information to the securities markets and to the investing public.[97] Although fiduciaries under state law have a duty of candor when communicating to shareholders,[98] the federal securities laws are predominant with respect to the primacy of disclosure. As a condition of offering securities for sale and being a publicly-held company,[99] subject corporations must comply with rigorous disclosure mandates.[100] Moreover, by means of disclosure directives—namely, federal statutes, SEC rules and regulations, and self-regulatory organization rules—federal regulators (and SROs that are subject to SEC oversight) initiate enforcement actions with

---

the securities laws of several states. *See generally*, Joseph C. Long, Michael Kaufman, and John Wunderlich, *Blue Sky Law* § 1.04 (2016); Symposium, *Blue Sky Anniversary Edition*, 50 Washburn L.J. No. 3 (2011) (commemorating the 100th anniversary of the Kansas securities law).

[97] 15 U.S.C. § 77a et seq. (2012) 15 U.S.C. § 78a et seq. (2012). *See generally Santa Fe Indus., Inc. v. Green*, 430 U.S. 462 (1977); Louis Loss, Joel Seligman, and Troy Parades, *Securities Regulation* (5th ed. 2015).

[98] *See, e.g., Malone v. Brincat*, 722 A.2d 5 (Del. 1998); *Stroud v. Grace*, 606 A.2d 75 (Del. 1992); *Lynch v. Vickers Energy Corp.*, 383 A.2d 278 (Del. 1978).

[99] The term "publicly-held company" encompasses enterprises that are reporting companies under the Securities Exchange Act (see §§ 12, 13(a), 15(d) of the Securities Exchange Act). Generally, the common stock of such companies is listed on a national securities exchange, such as the New York Stock Exchange and the Nasdaq Stock Market.

[100] *See, e.g.*, SEC Regulations S-K (sets forth the disclosure requirements for the non-financial statement parts of SEC filings), S-X (sets forth the accounting rules and procedures with respect to financial statements filed with the SEC). Items required to be disclosed within Regulation S-K, by way of example, include: description of the registrant's (and its subsidiaries') business, property, legal proceedings, and securities; furnishing of selected financial data; management's discussion and analysis of financial condition and results of operations (MD&A); disclosure focusing on directors, executive officers, promoters, and control persons; disclosure of executive compensation; and furnishing of risk factors.

frequency based on allegedly deficient disclosure.[101] The constant presence of private litigation based on alleged disclosure violations also is a mainstay of the federal securities law regimen.[102]

Through the decades, the SEC has sought to improve standards of conduct through the guise of disclosure. For example, although the substantive terms of an interested director transaction are a matter of state corporate law,[103] disclosure of these transactions is mandated by SEC rule.[104] The same holds true with respect to management compensation.[105] Indeed, the SEC rules requiring details of management remuneration are exhaustive, resulting in disclosures in corporate filings that are dozens of pages in length.[106] As a last example, if a director fails to attend 75 percent of the subject company's board of director meetings, that fact must be disclosed to shareholders pursuant to SEC rule.[107]

At times, displeased with judicial outcomes, the SEC has sought to modify fiduciary substantive conduct through the guise of disclosure. A poignant example is the Commission's adoption of Rule 13e-3[108] after the Supreme Court's decision in *Santa Fe Industries*.[109] In *Santa Fe*, the Supreme Court held that Section 10(b) and Rule 10b-5 adopted thereunder are focused on disclosure, not on substantive fairness. Accordingly, the plaintiff's claim that he was treated unfairly in the context of a going-private merger transaction was held to be outside the scope of these

---

[101] *See* Marc I. Steinberg and Ralph C. Ferrara, *Securities Practice: Federal and State Enforcement* (2d ed. 2001 and 2017–2018 supp.) (addressing, inter alia, actions initiated by the SEC, the U.S. Department of Justice, state regulators, and the self-regulatory organization authorities).

[102] For the seminal treatise on this subject, *see* Alan R. Bromberg, Louis D. Lowenfels, and Michael J. Sullivan, *Securities Fraud & Commodities Fraud* (2016).

[103] *See supra* notes 57–60 and accompanying text.

[104] *See* Item 404 of Regulation S-K (requiring disclosure of related party transaction(s) between the registrant and the subject related person wherein such related person had or will have a direct or indirect material interest during any 12-month period involving an amount exceeding $120,000).

[105] *See* Item 402 of Regulation S-K (mandating disclosure of executive compensation). *See generally* Jennifer S. Martin, *The House of Mouse and Beyond: Assessing the SEC's Efforts to Regulate Executive Compensation*, 32 Del. J. Corp. L. 481 (2007).

[106] For example, discussion of executive compensation pursuant to SEC regulations typically runs at least 25 published pages in proxy statements filed by subject companies. *See, e.g.,* the 2016 proxy statements of American Express, Exxon Mobil, General Motors, IBM, Southwest Airlines, and Walmart.

[107] *See* Item 407(b)(1) of Regulation S-K (requiring the registrant to "[n]ame each incumbent director who during the last fiscal year attended fewer than 75 percent of the aggregate of: (i) The total number of meetings of the board of directors. . . . ; and (ii) The total number of meetings held by all committees of the board on which he served. . . .").

[108] 17 C.F.R. § 240.13e-3 (2017); Securities Exchange Act Release No. 16075 (1979). Interestingly, as proposed by the SEC, going-private transactions were required to be both procedurally and substantively fair to minority stockholders. *See* Securities Exchange Act Release No. 14185 (1977).

[109] *Santa Fe Indus., Inc. v. Green*, 430 U.S. 462 (1977).

provisions, thereby not constituting a violation of federal law.[110] In response, the SEC adopted Rule 13e-3,[111] which is directed at going-private transactions (namely, those transactions whereby a merger or other transaction is consummated with the effect that a publicly-held company goes private and its minority shareholders are cashed-out).[112] Among its many requirements, the Rule obligates the subject company (or affiliate that makes the filing) to disclose whether it "reasonably believes" that the going-private transaction is fair or unfair to minority shareholders and the "material factors" upon which such belief is based.[113] As a consequence, failure to disclose that a going-private transaction is unfair to minority shareholders or the providing of materially false representations in connection therewith will give rise to an SEC enforcement action as well as a private damages lawsuit.[114]

On certain occasions, the SEC will act in a manner that, in practical impact, largely displaces state law. The SEC shareholder proposal rule, first adopted in 1942, provides such an example.[115] A chapter in this book focuses on the impact of this Rule.[116] Another example is the law of insider trading. Cognizant that the states declined to hold corporate fiduciaries sufficiently accountable for trading on the basis of (and tipping) material nonpublic information,[117] the SEC filled this void, resulting in determinations as to the legality of insider trading conduct today principally being a matter within the federal securities laws.[118] A last example is an actual

---

[110] *Id.* at 479–80. *See supra* notes 21–26 and accompanying text. *See generally* Mark J. Loewenstein, *The Supreme Court, Rule 10b-5 and the Federalization of Corporate Law*, 39 Ind. L. Rev. 17 (2005).

[111] 17 C.F.R. § 240.13e-3 (2017); Securities Exchange Act Release No. 16075 (1979); *supra* note 108.

[112] *See, e.g., Weinberger v. UOP, Inc.*, 457 A.2d 701 (Del. 1983). Going-private transactions also may arise in the form of a first-step tender offer whereby the acquirer purchases over 90 percent of the target's stock, followed by a second-step short-form merger. Absent fraud or illegality, a minority shareholder's sole remedy in the short-form merger context is the right to an appraisal. *See, e.g., Glassman v. Unocal Exploration Corp.*, 777 A.2d 242 (Del. 2001). Although not frequent, a going-private transaction may take the form of a sale of substantially all assets transaction. *See, e.g.*, § 271 of the Delaware General Corporation Law; § 12.02 of the Model Business Corporation Act.

[113] *See* SEC Schedule 13E-3, Item 8; Item 1014 of Regulation M-A; Marc I. Steinberg, *Securities Regulation: Liabilities and Remedies* § 11.03 (2017) (stating that Rule 13e-3 requires the subject company or affiliate to "giv[e] its opinion whether it reasonably believes that the going private transaction is fair or unfair to unaffiliated security holders and the material factors upon which the belief is based").

[114] *See, e.g., Howing Co. v. Nationwide Corp.*, 826 F.2d 1470 (6th Cir. 1987); *In the Matter of FSC Corp.*, 22 SEC Docket 1374 (SEC 1981). *See generally* Ndiva Kofele-Kale, *Some Unfinished Business, Some Unresolved Issues: Section 13(e) and the Going-Private Rules After* Howing, 20 Toledo L. Rev. 625 (1989); discussion in Chapter 3 herein.

[115] Rule 14a-8, 17 C.F.R. § 240.14a-8 (2017). *See* Securities Exchange Act Release No. 3347 (1942).

[116] *See* discussion in Chapter 4 herein.

[117] *See, e.g., SEC v. Texas Gulf Sulphur Co.*, 401 F.2d 833 (2d Cir. 1968) (en banc); *In re Cady Roberts & Co.*, 40 S.E.C. 907 (1961). *See generally* Marc I. Steinberg and William K.S. Wang, *Insider Trading* (3d ed. Oxford University Press 2010).

[118] *See United States v. O'Hagan*, 521 U.S. 642 (1997); *Dirks v. SEC*, 463 U.S. 646 (1983); *Chiarella v. United States*, 445 U.S. 222 (1980). Additional provisions impacting insider trading under federal law include Section

reversal of state law by the SEC. In *Unocal*, the Delaware Supreme Court upheld the validity of an exclusionary issuer tender offer that precluded a hostile bidder from participating in the target company's self-tender offer.[119] In response thereto, the SEC amended Rule 13e-4, thereby prohibiting exclusionary issuer tender offers from being made as a matter of federal law, thereby signifying that such tender offers must be open to all shareholders.[120]

The culmination in this process is the enactment of the Sarbanes-Oxley Act of 2002[121] and the Dodd-Frank Act of 2010.[122] Aspects of these Acts, by affirmative mandate, displace state law. Chapters of this book address these Acts. For purposes here, three examples are provided. First, the propriety of loans to directors and executive officers traditionally was viewed within the ambit of state corporate law.[123] Today, under federal law, with certain exceptions, publicly-held companies are prohibited from making such loans.[124] Second, the qualification of individuals to serve as directors and officers is viewed as within state law.[125] However, today, individuals who have engaged in a securities fraud violation and are deemed unfit may be barred

---

16 of the Securities Exchange Act (focusing on short-swing trading by directors, officers, and 10 percent shareholders within a six-month period), Rule 14e-3 (regulating insider trading in the tender offer context), and Regulation FD (prohibiting selective disclosure of material nonpublic information as set forth in the Regulation). For further discussion, *see* Chapter 3 herein.

Some states deem trading by corporate fiduciaries based on material nonpublic information to constitute a breach of the duty of loyalty. *See, e.g., Kahn v. Kolberg Kravis Roberts & Co., L.P.*, 23 A.3d 831 (Del. 2011); *Diamond v. Oreamuno*, 24 N.Y. 2d 494, 301 N.Y.S. 2d 78, 248 N.E. 2d 910 (1969). Other states, however, decline to provide a remedy for allegedly improper trading by insiders. *See, e.g., Freeman v. Decio*, 584 F.2d 186 (7th Cir. 1978) (applying Indiana law); *Schein v. Chasen*, 313 So. 2d 739 (Fla. 1975). *See* discussion in Chapter 3 herein.

119 *Unocal Corp. v. Mesa Petroleum Co.* 493 A.2d 946, 958 (Del. 1985) (holding that the board of directors had the authority "to undertake a selective stock exchange made in good faith and upon a reasonable investigation pursuant to a clear duty to protect the corporate enterprise").

120 *See* SEC Rules 13e-4(f)(8), 14d-10(a)(1), 17 C.F.R. §§ 240.13e-4(f)(8), 14d-10(a)(1) (2017) (requiring that issuer and third-party tender offers be open to all shareholders); Securities Exchange Act Release No. 23421 (1986); discussion in Chapter 3 herein.

121 Sarbanes-Oxley Act of 2002, Pub. L. No. 107-204, 116 Stat. 745 (2002).

122 Dodd-Frank Wall Street Reform and Consumer Protection Act of 2010, Pub. L. No. 111-203, 124 Stat. 1376 (2010).

123 *See, e.g.*, § 143 of the Delaware General Corporation Law; *Aronson v. Lewis*, 473 A.2d 805, 817 (Del. 1984) (With respect to the company's $250,000 interest-free loan to a corporate fiduciary, the court stated that "the complaint does not allege facts indicating the wastefulness of such arrangements [and] the mere existence of such loans, given the broad corporate powers conferred by Delaware law, does not even state a claim.").

124 *See* § 402 of the Sarbanes-Oxley Act, *amending*, § 13(k) of the Securities Exchange Act. Certain limited types of loans are allowed if such loans are extended in the ordinary course of the company's business and are granted to the recipient on the same terms as loans are made to the general public.

125 *See, e.g.*, §§ 141 ("Board of Directors; Powers; Number, Qualifications, Terms and Quorum. . . .") and 142 ("Officers; Titles, Duties, Selection, Term. . . .") of the Delaware General Corporation Law.

from serving as a director or officer of *any* publicly-held company.[126] Third, state corporate law (along with a subject company's internal governance documents, such as its articles and bylaws), prescribes the establishment of board committees and their functions in a myriad of contexts.[127] Focusing on perhaps the most important board committee for a publicly-held corporation—the audit committee—federal legislation precludes a national stock exchange from listing a subject company's securities on such exchange unless that company has an audit committee comprised solely of independent directors.[128] In this regard, federal law sets forth: circumstances that preclude a director from being deemed independent for audit committee service, functions of the audit committee, specified requirements pertaining to adequate audit committee funding, and such committee's authority to retain outside experts.[129]

The foregoing discussion illustrates the emergence and now acknowledgment of the federalization of corporate governance. Federal law today is a vibrant player with respect to standards of conduct to which U.S. publicly-held companies and their fiduciaries must adhere. Hence, during the past two decades, the regulatory landscape has fundamentally changed. Federal standards of corporate governance today are firmly entrenched and are likely to remain vital for the foreseeable future.

IV. Focus of This Book

This book focuses on the very timely and important subject of the federalization of corporate governance in the United States. The evolution and development of corporate governance from a federal law perspective from the commencement of the twentieth century to the present will be explored. Much has changed in corporate governance practices and expectations during this period. Nonetheless, a constant theme emerges: the tension between state and federal regulation of corporations, their fiduciaries, their stockholders, and other stakeholders. This book examines this tension, analyzes the historical developments, explains the ramifications of the federal legislation enacted during the past two decades, and recommends corrective measures that should be undertaken. Thus, the book seeks to provide an original, historical, and contemporary analysis of this important subject that impacts this country's economic well-being in a very fundamental way.

---

[126] *See* § 305 of the Sarbanes-Oxley Act, *amending*, § 20(e) of the Securities Act and § 21(d)(2) of the Securities Exchange Act. Previously, pursuant to legislation enacted in 1990 (The Securities Law Enforcement Remedies Act), the standard was "substantially unfit." *See generally* Jayne W. Barnard, *Rule 10b-5 and the "Unfitness" Question*, 47 Ariz. L. Rev. 9 (2005); discussion in Chapter 5 herein.

[127] *See, e.g.*, § 8.25 of the Model Business Corporation Act.

[128] *See* § 301 of the Sarbanes-Oxley Act, *codified at*, 15 U.S.C. § 78j-1(m) (2012).

[129] *Id. See* discussion in Chapters 5, 6 herein.

2

TWENTIETH CENTURY LEGISLATIVE PROPOSALS—FEDERAL INCORPORATION AND RELATED EFFORTS

I. Introduction

Attempts at federal incorporation arose in order to combat increasing liberalization of corporate laws at the state level.[1] In the latter part of the nineteenth century, New Jersey enacted what has been viewed as the first modern liberal corporation statute.[2] Until this time, corporations were created by special acts of the state legislatures; however, these corporations came to be viewed as "monopolistic" and "anti-egalitarian."[3] Thus, relatively little corporate law existed in the country for much of the nineteenth century.[4]

This situation changed dramatically in 1896 with the passage of the first "modern liberal corporation statute" being adopted in New Jersey.[5] The New Jersey statute allowed corporations to "merge or consolidate at will, set their own capitalization

---

[1] Melvin I. Urofsky, *Proposed Federal Incorporation in the Progressive Era*, 26 Am. J. Legal Hist. 160, 164 (1982).

[2] William L. Cary, *Federalism and Corporate Law: Reflections on Delaware*, 83 Yale L.J. 663, 664 (1974). *See Liggett Co. v. Lee*, 288 U.S. 517 (1933).

[3] Cary, *supra* note 2, at 663–64.

[4] *See id.* (For example, New York revised its Constitution in 1846 to prohibit corporations being created by special act "except . . . in cases where, in the judgment of the legislature, the objects of the corporation cannot be attained under general laws.").

[5] *Id.* at 664.

values, and secure the stock of other firms through outright purchase or exchange of their own stock," while also giving broad discretion to directors in determining what information was to be transmitted to shareholders and when to utilize proxy votes.[6] Other states, most notably Delaware,[7] were quick to follow suit, and by 1901 overcapitalization[8] and mergers[9] had risen to an all-time high.[10]

In reaction to this perceived "race to the bottom,"[11] reformers and politicians began to call for federal regulation of corporate entities.[12] As early as 1898, concerns over trusts and monopoly power led Congress to establish the Industrial Commission.[13] The Commission conducted hearings on "all aspects of the new industrial order" over a period of 18 months.[14] In its final report, the Commission recommended a system of chartering all corporations engaged in interstate commerce.[15] In the Industrial Commission hearings, the subject of overcapitalization was addressed (namely, the perception that businesses were being bought on the market for inflated prices).[16] Many of the bills discussed in this chapter include provisions that sought to ensure that subject corporations were not overcapitalized.

In responding to these developments, Congress in 1903 established the Department of Labor and Commerce, and within it, the Bureau of Corporations.[17] The Bureau of Corporations was established essentially as an investigatory agency, with little enforcement power; it "played a secondary role to the judiciary and the

[6] Urofsky, *supra* note 1, at 164.

[7] Cary, *supra* note 2, at 164; Mark J. Roe, *Delaware's Competition*, 117 Harv. L. Rev. 588 (2003); Charles M. Yablon, *The Historical Race-Competition for Corporate Charters and the Rise and Decline of New Jersey: 1880–1910*, 32 J. Corp. L. 323 (2007).

[8] Overcapitalization may be viewed as occurring when a corporation has issued more debt and equity than its assets are worth (*see* Marjorie E. Kornhauser, *Corporate Regulation and the Origins of the Corporate Income Tax*, 66 Ind. L.J. 53, 78 (1990)).

[9] *See Merger, Black's Law Dictionary* (10th ed. 2014) ("The absorption of one organization (esp. a corporation) that ceases to exist into another that retains its own name and identity and acquires the assets and liabilities of the former.").

[10] *See* Gabriel Kolko, *The Triumph of Conservatism: A Reinterpretation of American History, 1900–1916*, at 19 (4th printing, 1963) (In 1895, 43 firms disappeared because of mergers while merger capitalizations were equal to $41 million; by 1901, 423 firms disappeared as a result of mergers with capitalizations topping out at over $2 billion.).

[11] *See* Cary, *supra* note 2, at 664–65 (commenting that Delaware "took the lead [in 1913 when New Jersey drastically tightened its corporation law] and has never lost it").

[12] Urofsky, *supra* note 1, at 164–66.

[13] *Id.* at 166–67.

[14] *Id.* at 167.

[15] *Id.*

[16] United States Industrial Commission, *Preliminary Report on Trusts and Industrial Combinations, Together with Testimony, Review of Evidence, Charts Showing Effects on Prices, and Topical Digest* (Washington Govt. Printing Office 1900) 1, 6.

[17] Urofsky, *supra* note 1, at 169.

Department of Justice, which together determined how illegal restraints of trade as established by the 1890 Sherman Antitrust Act[18] were interpreted and enforced."[19] The Bureau of Corporations did not have power to compel testimony or to require the production of records; instead, its main role was "gathering, compiling, publishing, and supplying useful information about interstate corporations and those engaged in foreign trade."[20] The Bureau of Corporations was eventually replaced by the Federal Trade Commission (FTC) with the passage of the Federal Trade Commission Act in 1914.[21]

Many of the bills discussed below sought to give the Bureau and its chairman, the Commissioner of Corporations, more power.[22] As set forth above, the Bureau of Corporations was eliminated pursuant to the enactment of the Federal Trade Commission Act, with the Bureau's Commissioner of Corporations, Joseph Davies, becoming the first chairman of the FTC.[23]

Overall, more than two dozen bills aimed at federal incorporation were introduced between 1900 and the 1930s.[24] At times, these bills enjoyed a broad spectrum of support; however not one made it into law.[25] Although the bills themselves did not survive, several of their provisions or concepts have found their way into modern corporate governance law at both the state and federal level.[26]

Although much has been written regarding the concepts of federal chartering and federal minimum standards,[27] this chapter meaningfully adds to this dialogue

---

[18] 15 U.S.C. §§ 1 et seq. (2012) (The Sherman Act was passed in order to give the government power to limit anticompetitive practices among business, and to break up powerful trusts that were leading to monopolies).

[19] Elizabeth Kimball McLean, *Joseph E. Davies, The Wisconsin Idea and the Origins of the Federal Trade Commission*, 6 J. Gilded Age and Progressive Era 249, 256 (2007).

[20] Arthur M. Johnson, *Theodore Roosevelt and the Bureau of Corporations*, 45 Miss. Valley Hist. Rev. 571, 575 (1959).

[21] *Id.* at 589. Coincidently, 1914 was the year that my terrific father, Gerald S. Steinberg, was born (March 3, 1914).

[22] *See, e.g.*, H.R. 10704, 59th Cong. (1906), *infra* notes 74–94; and the Taft-Wickersham Bills, *infra* notes 224–261 & accompanying text.

[23] McLean, *supra* note 19, at 280.

[24] *See* Urofsky, *supra* note 1, at 176.

[25] *See id.* (noting that not a single federal incorporation bill introduced between 1901 and 1914 made it out of committee).

[26] *See* discussion on modern day relevance, *infra* notes 554–585 & accompanying text.

[27] Thus, many articles have been authored over the last century with respect to federal chartering of corporations as well as the enactment of federal minimum standards. One particularly poignant article was authored by former SEC Chairman William L. Cary. *See* William L. Cary, *Federalism and Corporate Law: Reflections Upon Delaware*, 83 Yale L.J. 663 (1974). At the time he authored this article, the author was a law professor at Columbia University. Viewing the concept of federal incorporation as "unrealistic," Professor Cary called for federal standards of corporate responsibility—namely, "prescribing minimum corporation law provisions which shall be applicable to companies doing business in interstate commerce and construed by federal judicial standards." *Id.* at 700–01. The provisions of such a federal law, according to Professor Cary, might include: "(1) federal fiduciary standards with respect to directors and officers and controlling shareholders;

by examining the dozens of bills that have been introduced in Congress on this subject since 1903. By providing this historical presentation in conjunction with analysis of the modern-day relevance of these legislative proposals, the chapter significantly contributes to the development of the law with respect to the federalization of corporate governance.

II. The Height of Interest in Federal Incorporation (1903–1914)

At no point in American history was the idea of federal incorporation more debated in Congress than the 1903–1914 period.[28] In his address to Congress in 1905, President Theodore Roosevelt condemned government oversight of corporate power as it then existed, stating:

> The fortunes amassed through corporate organizations are now so large, and vest such power in those that wield them, that it makes it a matter of necessity to give the sovereign... some effective power of supervision over their corporate use... [S]uch regulation and supervision can only be effectively exercised by a sovereign whose jurisdiction is co-extensive with the field of work of corporations—that is, by the National Government.[29]

---

(2) an 'interested directors' provision prescribing fairness as a prerequisite to any transaction; [and] (3) a requirement of certain uniform provisions to be incorporated in the certificate of incorporation, [such as] authority to amend by-laws, initiate corporate action, or draw up the agenda of shareholders' meetings shall not be vested exclusively in management...." *Id.* at 702. For other works focusing on this subject, *see, e.g.*, Ralph Nader, et al., *Taming the Giant Corporation* (1976); Symposium, *Federal Chartering of Corporations*, 61 Geo. L.J. No. 1 (1972); Robert B. Ahdieh, *Trapped in a Metaphor: The Limited Implications of Federalism for Corporate Governance*, 77 Geo. Wash. L. Rev. 255 (2009); Lucian Arye Bebchuk and Assaf Hamdani, *Vigorous Race or Leisurely Walk: Reconsidering the Competition over Corporate Charters*, 112 Yale L.J. 553 (2003); Roberta S. Karmel, *Is It Time for a Federal Corporation Law?*, 57 Brook. L. Rev. 55 (1991); Peter V. Letsou, *The Changing Face of Corporate Governance Regulation in the United States: The Evolving Roles of the Federal and State Governments*, 46 Willamette L. Rev. 149 (2009); Henry G. Manne, *Our Two Corporation Systems: Law and Economics*, 53 Va. L. Rev. 259 (1967); Mark J. Roe, *Delaware's Competition*, 117 Harv. L. Rev. 588 (2003); Donald E. Schwartz, *A Case for Federal Chartering of Corporations*, 31 Bus. Law. 1125 (1976); Melvin I. Urofsky, *Proposed Federal Incorporation in the Progressive Era*, 26 Am. J. Leg. Hist. 160 (1982); Ralph K. Winter, Jr., *State Law, Shareholder Protection, and the Theory of the Corporation*, 6 J. Legal Stud. 251 (1977); Note, Harris Berlack, *Federal Incorporation and Securities Regulation*, 49 Harv. L. Rev. 396 (1936); Note, H.L. Wilgus, *Need of a National Incorporation Law*, 2 Mich. L. Rev. 358 (1903–1904); Note, Theodore H. Davis, Jr., *Corporate Privileges for the Public Benefit: The Progressive Federal Incorporation Movement and the Modern Regulatory State*, 77 Va. L. Rev. 603 (1991).

[28] *See* Urofsky, *supra* note 1, at 176.

[29] Federal Trade Commission, Report on Utility Corporations, No. 69A, at 18 (Sept. 15, 1934) (hereinafter FTC Report).

Likewise, promoting his own bill, President William Howard Taft stated that it was necessary for the federal government to take control over corporations so as to prevent the "abuses which have arisen under state control."[30] With this as a backdrop, the bills introduced during this time period offered the most comprehensive attempts to provide for federal incorporation.

A. 1903 BILL—HOUSE OF REPRESENTATIVES—H.R. 66

The first bill aimed at curbing corporate excess, introduced in 1903, was titled "A bill to provide for the organization of corporations to engage in commerce with foreign nations and among the several states."[31] The bill was introduced by Representative Henry Palmer of Pennsylvania who believed that it was in the best interest of the American people that corporations be "directly accountable to the sovereign power of the Federal Government rather than to any one State."[32] The bill proposed to accomplish this accountability by requiring corporations to file a certificate of incorporation with the secretary of the Department of Commerce and Labor; if the secretary approved the certificate, the corporation was allowed to engage in interstate commerce.[33]

The bill required that every corporation set out: its name; location; names of shareholders, officers, and directors; amount of capital stock; the value of the corporation's real and personal property; and the highest amount of liability that could be incurred by the corporation or its shareholders.[34] In this regard, the bill was somewhat similar to then existing Delaware law.[35] However, unlike Delaware law, this bill required that the authorized capital stock be at least $2,000 and that the par value of each share be at least $25.[36] Additionally, the bill required that notice of intention to incorporate be published in newspapers in both Washington, DC, and the location of the corporation's principal place of business.[37]

Unlike later, stricter, attempts, H.R. 66 only required that 50 percent of the authorized capital stock of the subject corporation be subscribed for before business

---

30 *Id.*

31 H.R. 66, 58th Cong. (1903).

32 *Id.*

33 *Id.* at § 7.

34 *Id.* at § 3.

35 *Cf.* Delaware General Incorporation Act, 21 Del. Laws 273, §7 (1899) (requiring: name of corporation, principal office location, nature of business, name of shareholders, amount of capital stock, value of property and liability of shareholders and corporation); *see also* Joel Seligman, *A Brief History of Delaware's General Corporation Law of 1899*, 1 Del. J. Corp. L. 249, 280 (1976).

36 H.R. 66, 58th Cong., § 3 (1903).

37 *Id.*

could commence; furthermore, only 10 percent of such stock had to actually have been paid in full.[38] Sections eleven and twelve of H.R. 66 set out the requirements for directors and officers.[39] The bill required that the president of the corporation "shall be chosen from among the directors."[40] Additionally, the bill required the board of directors to make an annual report of the company's financial condition.[41] This report had to be filed with the company's treasurer and made available to shareholders at all reasonable times.[42]

One important aspect of this bill was that it expressly sought to protect against corporate fraud.[43] Section 17 provided that stock could be purchased through a transfer of real property, and it was the duty of the directors to determine the fair value of the property.[44] If the directors, through fraud or gross negligence, overestimated the value of the property accepted for payment of stock, they were jointly and severally liable to the corporation for the difference between the amount received and the actual value of the property.[45] Whereas Section 17 thus created liability for a specific act, Section 22 provided for broad liability for the making of knowingly material false statements by officers and directors.[46] In relevant part this section states:

> That if the directors or officers of any corporation organized under the provisions of this Act shall *knowingly* cause to be published or given out any written statement or report of the condition or business of the corporation that is false

---

[38] *Id.* at § 10. *Compare* S. 4874, 60th Cong. (1908) (requiring 75 percent subscription and 50 percent paid in full before commencing business).

[39] *Id.* at § 11 (Every corporation "shall be managed by a board of not less than three directors, each of whom shall hold in his own right not less than ten shares of capital stock; they shall hold office until their successors are respectively elected and qualified; a majority of directors shall constitute a quorum for the transaction of business; they shall be chosen annually by stockholders at the time fixed by the by-laws and may fill any vacancy, however arising, in their board or in the offices of the company for the unexpired portion of the term. . . ."); *Id.* at § 12 ("[E]very corporation organized under this Act shall have a president, secretary, and treasurer, who shall be chosen either by the directors or the stockholders, as the by-laws may direct, and shall hold their offices until their successors are chosen and qualified; the president shall be chosen from among the directors; the secretary shall be sworn to the faithful discharge of his duties, and shall record all the votes of the corporation and the minutes of its transactions in a book to be kept for that purpose, and perform such other duties as shall be assigned to him; the treasurer may be required to give bond in such sum and with such sureties as shall be provided by the by-laws for the faithful discharge of his duties; the secretary and treasurer may or may not be the same person.").

[40] *Id.* at § 12.

[41] *Id.* at § 11.

[42] *Id.*

[43] *See id.* at §§ 17, 22.

[44] *Id.* at § 17.

[45] *Id.*

[46] *See id.* at § 22.

> in any *material respect*, the officers and directors *causing* such report or statement to be published or given out, or assenting thereto, shall be, *jointly and severally, individually liable for any loss or damage resulting therefrom*.[47]

On its face, this language suggests that officers and directors who knowingly gave out false information would be liable not only to the corporation or its shareholders, but also to any complainant who suffered loss due to those misstatements.

This bill was flexible in allowing companies to hold, purchase, sell, and transfer stocks, bonds, and securities of other corporations.[48] The bill also allowed for the merger of two companies engaged in the same business after a two-thirds shareholder approval and approval by the Secretary of Commerce and Labor.[49]

B. 1904 BILL—HOUSE OF REPRESENTATIVES—H.R. 8883

The next piece of legislation on this topic was a two-page bill brought by Representative Nehemiah Sperry of Connecticut in 1904 entitled "A bill to regulate the powers and privileges of corporations."[50] The bill's author believed that state incorporation led to interstate trusts, which in turn led to monopolies.[51] Congressman Sperry believed that the solution was to confine the rights, powers, and privileges of a corporation to the state in which it was created.[52] Furthermore, directors and officers were required to be "bona fide citizens" of the state in which the business was incorporated.[53]

Additionally, no corporation organized under the general laws of any state was allowed to purchase or control any corporation created by another state.[54] If such a purchase did occur, it was legally void and had no effect.[55] Under the bill, when it became necessary to promote interstate commerce or to further the best interests of the states, Congress had the authority to create an interstate corporation, which would be subject to congressional rules and regulations.[56]

Congressman Sperry reasoned that a corporation has no right to contract outside of its state of incorporation because "a corporation is neither a citizen nor a person

---

47 *Id.* (emphasis added).

48 *Id.* at § 26.

49 *Id.* at § 31.

50 H.R. 8883, 58th Cong. (1904).

51 *Id.*

52 *Id.* at § 1.

53 *Id.* at § 2.

54 *Id.* at § 3

55 *Id.*

56 *Id.* at § 4

and is, therefore, not entitled to the privileges conferred by the constitutional doctrine of the comity of States."[57] If passed, this bill would have directly overturned Supreme Court precedent and upended the traditional legal fiction of corporate personhood.[58] Not surprisingly, the constitutionality of this bill was questioned.[59]

C. 1905 BILL—SENATE—S. 6238

The next bill was offered in 1905, and was the first one to provide for the creation of a corporate oversight body.[60] The bill called for the President, with the advice and consent of the Senate, to appoint four persons to be members of the National Board of Corporations ("National Board").[61] The Secretary of the Department of Commerce and Labor would serve as the Board's fifth member and be ex officio chairman.[62]

According to the bill, a corporation could not engage in the transaction of any business in any state other than its state of incorporation without first filing a sworn statement with the National Board.[63] The statement verified by oath of the company's president or vice president had a total of 19 required items and was required to be filed every year that the corporation was in existence.[64] The filing required such items as: the name of the corporation, the location of its principal place of business, the cash value of its assets, the amount of the corporation's indebtedness and in what manner such indebtedness is secured, and the number of shares of capital stock issued and amount received for that stock.[65] Additionally, a corporation would be required to list the amount of shares in other corporations held by it, along with the

---

[57] *Id.* at § 1.

[58] *See Santa Clara Cty. v. S. Pac. R.R. Co.*, 118 U.S. 394 (1886) (setting forth that a corporation is treated as a person within the confines of the Fourteenth Amendment's equal protection clause); *Christian Union v. Yount*, 101 U.S. 352, 356 (1879) ("In harmony with the general law of comity obtaining among the States composing the Union, the presumption should be indulged that a corporation of one state, not forbidden by the law of its being, may exercise within any other state the general powers conferred by its own charter unless it is prohibited from so doing either in the direct enactments of the latter state, or by its public policy to be deduced from the general course of legislation or from the settled adjudications of its highest court."). *See generally* Gregory A. Mark, *The Personification of the Business Corporation in American Law*, 54 U. Chi. L. Rev. 1441 (1987).

[59] FTC Report, *supra* note 29, at 34.

[60] *See, e.g.*, "A bill to create the National Board of Corporations and to provide for the regulation thereby of corporations engaged in interstate, Territorial, District, or insular possession business. . . ." S. 6238, 58th Cong. (1905).

[61] *Id.* at § 1 (Although it is not explicit in the bill, the National Board presumably would have replaced the Bureau of Corporations, also within the Department of Labor and Commerce.).

[62] *Id.*

[63] *Id.* at § 7.

[64] *Id* at §10.

[65] *Id.*

percentage of capital stock that those shares represent.[66] The filing also called for a certification to be filed stating that: no other stock had been issued, the business engaged only in the type of business listed in the articles, no voting pool existed which would prevent shareholders from exercising their voting rights, and no part of the capital stock is owned, controlled, or voted on by another corporation or the officers of another corporation.[67] Furthermore, the bill also set forth special requirements for corporations that were common carriers, engaged in the coal business, or provided life insurance.[68]

In addition to the filings that were required annually, the bill also mandated sworn statements of the company's officers certifying, inter alia, that: "the corporation is solvent; it is incorporated for a legitimate business purpose; it is not a party to a contract or agreement in restraint of trade or which results in unfair advantage; and it is not in contract with any other corporation that would create a monopoly or destroy competition."[69]

This bill gave the National Board of Corporations the power to compel books, records, and documents that would be "necessary to the investigation of any question affecting the right of any corporation to engage in business under the provisions of this Act."[70] The Board had the power to compel the attendance of witnesses to testify in connection with an enforcement proceeding under the Act.[71] If a corporation disagreed with a Board decision, it could appeal to the appellate court in the jurisdiction where the corporation was formed.[72] While the court had the authority to adjudicate the appeal, "the decision of the Board on all questions of fact or the sufficiency of proof" was not subject to review.[73]

D. 1906 BILL—HOUSE OF REPRESENTATIVES—H.R. 10704

Similar to the Senate bill above, H.R. 10704 required interstate corporations to register with a public agency, mandating that companies register with the newly created

---

[66] *Id.*

[67] *Id.*

[68] *Id.* For example these special requirements included that: a company engaged in coal production make a certification that it did not receive any rebate, deduction, or advantage on its shipping rates; and life insurance companies were forbidden from having directors who were members of or held an interest in any other life insurance company or banking entity.

[69] *Id.* at § 7.

[70] *Id.* at § 5.

[71] *Id.*

[72] *Id.* at § 10.

[73] *Id.*

"Bureau of Corporations."[74] This was the first attempt to give the Bureau, a purely investigative agency, the power to issue corporate licenses. This bill would apply to any company, partnership, corporation, joint stock company, or association that engaged in commerce with foreign nations or with the several states whose total sales for the previous year exceeded $1 million.[75] The bill required any corporation fitting this description to apply and procure a license from the Commissioner of Corporations (the head of the Bureau).[76] The bill did not set out a specific licensure procedure—only that the license will be in "such form as the Secretary of Commerce and Labor may direct."[77] The bill did, however, explicitly require that the president, secretary, or chairman of the company's board of directors make a sworn statement in writing that included specified information regarding the company,[78] such as: the state of the company's incorporation, amount of capital stock, list of stockholders, total value of gross sales, and a listing of dividends paid for the previous year along with the amount of surplus on hand.[79]

The bill also required each subject corporation to submit annual reports to the Commissioner of Corporations.[80] These reports must set forth "the receipts and disbursements as shown by the auditing department, a list of officers and the salary received by each, and such other information as the Commissioner of Corporations may require."[81] Additionally, the bill gave the Commissioner the power to appoint a person to examine the company's books, records, and affairs, including the ability to examine any of the company's officers and agents under oath.[82] On its face, the bill evidently granted the Commissioner unilateral power to initiate such an investigation "whenever [he or she] may deem it necessary."[83]

If, under H.R. 10704, a corporation wanted to increase its capital stock, it could do so only with approval from the Commissioner of Corporations.[84] A company wishing to increase capital had to set forth the reasons why the increase was "necessary

[74] "A Bill to require all corporations engaged in commerce with the several States, with the Territories, and with foreign nations to secure a license from the General Government, and to impose a license fee for the same. . . ." H.R. 10704, 59th Cong. § 2 (1906); *see supra* notes 17–23 & accompanying text for discussion of the Bureau of Corporations.

[75] *Id.* at § 1.

[76] *Id.* at § 2.

[77] *Id.*

[78] *Id.* at § 3.

[79] *Id.*

[80] *Id.* at § 6 (This section gave the Commissioner power to request reports more often if he so desired, but set the statutory minimum at one year.).

[81] *Id.*

[82] *Id.*

[83] *Id.*

[84] *Id.* at § 11.

for the continued development and for the proper transaction of its business. . . ."[85] The bill also gave the Commissioner the power to require that a corporation increase either its total capital stock or the amount of its stock actually paid.[86]

This bill listed several civil and criminal penalties for different violations of the bill. For instance, one provision granted the Commissioner power to impose penalties in an instance of false statements.[87] It provided:

> That a false statement of facts . . . shall be adjudged a misdemeanor, and the officers and directors of said offending interstate corporation shall each be subject to a fine of not less than five thousand dollars nor more than twenty thousand dollars, or imprisonment for not less than six months nor more than five years, or both.[88]

It is worth noting that the bill did not explicitly require that a false statement be knowingly made—only that one exist in the statement of facts.[89] The bill also directed that any officer or director who violated the Act, the Interstate Commerce Act, the Sherman Act, or the Department of Commerce and Labor Act shall be subject to the same penalties as listed above.[90]

Additional penalties included a fine of $1,000 for every day after the deadline that a corporation failed to file for a license under the Act.[91] Furthermore, failure to file could result in an injunction against continuing business until the license is applied for pursuant to the bill's provisions.[92] Two or more violations of the Act could result in a corporation forfeiting its license to engage in interstate commerce.[93] In addition to the statutory penalties, the bill gave the U.S. attorneys the power to bring suit or

---

[85] *Id.*

[86] *Id.* at § 9.

[87] *Id.* at § 5.

[88] *Id.*

[89] *Compare* Section 17(a)(2) of the Securities Act of 1933 (compiled at 15 U.S.C. § 77q (2012) (imposing liability on anyone who seeks "to obtain money or property by means of any untrue statement of a material fact or any omission to state a material fact necessary in order to make the statements made, in light of the circumstances under which they were made, not misleading"); *see Aaron v. SEC*, 446 U.S. 680 (1980) (finding that § 17(a)(2) & (3) require only that the SEC establish a defendant's negligence in order to prove a violation); *see also* Marc I. Steinberg, *Understanding Securities Law* 314 (6th ed. 2014) (The SEC need only prove a defendant's negligence to establish a violation of § 17(a)(2); thus, this section is "an attractive enforcement weapon to the SEC."). *See generally* Marc I. Steinberg, *Section 17(a) of the Securities Act of 1933 after* Naftalin *and* Redington, 68 Geo. L.J. 179 (1979).

[90] H.R. 10704, 59th Cong. § 17 (1906).

[91] *Id.* at § 7.

[92] *Id.*

[93] *Id.* at § 17.

institute proceedings "before any circuit court of the United States whenever the Commissioner of Corporations directs."[94]

E. 1905 BILL—HOUSE OF REPRESENTATIVES—H.R. 473

H.R. 473 was introduced in 1905 and was entitled "a bill to regulate corporations, joint stock companies, and other associations engaging in interstate and foreign commerce in food and fuel supplies."[95] The bill applied only to associations whose business was in "cattle, sheep, swine, dressed meats, meat products, poultry, poultry products, dairy products, grain, cereals, breadstuffs, coal, oil, or other food or fuel supplies."[96] Specifically, the bill required that any association engaging in interstate commerce in one of these businesses had to obtain a license from the Secretary of the Department of Commerce and Labor before engaging in such trade or commerce.[97]

Unlike previous bills, the licensing procedure did not require a filing with a federal regulator setting out such information as capital stock, shareholders, assets, and liabilities. Rather, a corporation applying for a license had to show that it was not overcapitalized and that its capitalization represented a fair valuation of the rights and property actually owned by the corporation.[98] Furthermore, the business had to show that it was not engaging in any activity that operated as a restraint on trade in violation of U.S. laws.[99]

The license was perpetual and would last for the legal life of the corporation.[100] Once a company obtained a license, it was required to file annual reports with the Secretary of Commerce and Labor.[101] These reports (which were required to be signed by the president, treasurer, general manager, and a majority of the board of directors[102]) were to include information on the company's "organization, capitalization, properties, earnings, profits, dividends, and business methods."[103] A failure to file a report would result in suspension of the license.[104]

---

[94] *Id.* at § 16.

[95] H.R. 473, 59th Cong. (1905).

[96] *Id.* at § 1.

[97] *Id.*

[98] *Id.* at § 2.

[99] *Id.* (such as conspiring with another person, corporation, or company to monopolize "any part of the trade or commerce" mentioned in the bill).

[100] *Id.* at § 3.

[101] *Id.* at § 4.

[102] *Id.* Interestingly, today a majority of a company's board of directors must sign a Securities Act registration statement (*see* § 6(a) of the Securities Act, 15 U.S.C. § 77f(a) (2012)) and the company's annual Form 10-K report (*see* Securities Act Release No. 6231 (1980)).

[103] H.R. 473, 59th Cong. § 4 (1905). (The term "business methods" is not defined in the bill.).

[104] *Id.* at § 4; Similarly, the Securities Exchange Act of 1934 gives the SEC the power to revoke a company's registration or suspend the trading of its securities when it has failed to timely file an annual report. *See* U.S.

The bill provided that the U.S. Attorney General was to bring an action against any corporation that violated the U.S. Acts outlawing restraints against trade and monopolies.[105] A successful action would result in forfeiture of a corporation's license.[106] After an adverse determination, a corporation could appeal to the Secretary of Commerce and Labor, and upon a showing that it had removed the unlawful features from its business, the Secretary had the discretion to grant the subject corporation a second license.[107] However, if such a corporation was found guilty of a second violation, its license would be forfeited and it was barred from engaging in interstate commerce.[108]

Penalties for violation of the bill itself were relatively less harsh. A corporation that violated any provision would be deemed guilty of a misdemeanor and punished by a fine of not more than $5,000.[109] Officers, directors, and agents who violated the Act would be subject to the same fine and/or imprisonment not to exceed one year.[110] Any corporation that operated in interstate commerce in the listed business without a license would be subject to seizure of its property by the United States.[111]

F. 1906 BILL—SENATE—S. 6287

Following the introduction of the food and fuel supplies bill,[112] another specialized bill was introduced—this time dealing with railroads and common carriers.[113] This bill applied to corporations formed for the purpose of constructing, equipping, maintaining, improving, extending, or operating a line (or lines) of railroad or navigation between points in different states.[114] It also applied to those corporations formed for the purpose of acquiring by purchase or lease any such line.[115]

The bill set out the powers given to subject corporations.[116] The powers listed were standard corporate necessities such as power to: assume a name, sue or be sued,

---

Securities and Exchange Commission, Investor Bulletin: Delinquent Filings (2013), *available at* http://www.sec.gov/investor/alerts/ib_delinquent_filers.htm.

105 H.R. 473, 59th Cong. § 5 (1905).

106 *Id.*

107 *Id.*

108 *Id.*

109 *Id.* at § 6.

110 *Id.*

111 *Id.* at § 7.

112 H.R. 473, 59th Cong. (1905).

113 *See* "A bill for the formation of national corporations for railroad and navigation lines engaged in interstate and foreign commerce. . . ." S. 6287, 59th Cong. (1906).

114 *Id.* at § 1.

115 *Id.*

116 *See id.* at § 2.

issue capital stock and bonds, adopt bylaws, make contracts, incur liabilities, manage its business, and elect officers and directors.[117] The bill also gave subject railroad companies the right to hold stock in other railroad corporations whose operations were incidental to the management of that subject railway's operation.[118]

The creator of the bill, Senator Francis Newlands of Nevada, was concerned about the capitalization of railroad companies; thus, the bill provided that a corporation could only issue amounts of stock and bonds that were necessary to improve or construct railroad equipment and lines.[119] Any issuance of stock or bonds required approval by the Interstate Commerce Commission (ICC) after a public hearing on the matter.[120] Apparently this approval was required every time a subject corporation issued stock, as the bill stated that the issuance of stock and bonds "shall in every case" be subject to approval by the ICC.[121] Furthermore, the bill instructed that stock may only be issued in consideration for money paid or for property acquired at such property's actual cash value.[122]

The bill set forth the requirements of the certificate of incorporation.[123] In addition to the customary provisions, a corporation was required to set out the routes of the railways that were built or proposed to be built.[124] Additionally, ICC approval was required for any railway proposed in a certificate of incorporation.[125] Before the ICC approved a certificate containing such a proposal, it was obligated to hold a public hearing to determine whether public convenience or necessity required the construction. If after the hearing the Commission believed the construction was warranted, the plan became part of the certificate of incorporation.[126] This provision applied to extensions to current railways as well.[127] The bill also required that an engineer's report be filed along with the certificate of incorporation when a corporation proposed to build or acquire a new line.[128] Such report was directed to show

---

[117] *Id.*

[118] *Id.*

[119] *Id.* at § 3. Although this bill did not make it out of Committee, the Senator's interest in regulating railroads seems to have survived as he was Chairman of the Committee on Interstate Commerce from the Sixty-Third to the Sixty-Fifth Congress. Biographical Directory of the United States Congress, Francis Griffith Newlands (1846–1917), *available at* http://bioguide.congress.gov/scripts/biodisplay.pl?index=N000069 (last visited Nov. 23, 2015).

[120] S. 6287, 59th Cong. § 3 (1906).

[121] *Id.*

[122] *Id.*

[123] *Id.* at § 4.

[124] *Id.*

[125] *Id.* at § 5.

[126] *Id.*

[127] *Id.*

[128] *Id.* at § 6.

the "character, structure, grades, cost of duplication, cost of construction, and the manner of construction" of the lines being proposed.[129]

The ICC was charged with establishing rules to govern meetings of stockholders, notices thereof and quorums required, election of directors, appointment of officers, and adoption of bylaws.[130] The rules were to provide that every corporation subject to the bill has between five and fifteen directors, along with an executive committee that would have managing powers.[131] Additionally, a corporation's bylaws were not effective until approved by the Commission.[132] The bill specifically provided that a director may be removed by a two-thirds shareholder vote.[133]

The ICC was given approval power over specified issuances of stocks and bonds. For instance, the bill required that, before a subject company issued bonds, the Commission first had to approve "the amount and time and term thereof and the rate of interest."[134] Furthermore, before being offered to the general public, all bonds were required to be offered to current shareholders "at not less than par."[135] If bonds were issued, the amount of the total obligation would be determined by the ICC, not the corporation.[136] Different classes of stock were permitted, provided that such classes were approved by a two-thirds shareholder vote and also approved by the ICC.[137]

The bill required the treasurer of a corporation to maintain books and records that accounted for "all transactions."[138] The secretary was required to keep a record of all meetings of the shareholders, board of directors, and executive committee.[139] These records were open to inspection by the ICC at any time, and to shareholders at "any reasonable time."[140] The bill also provided that the Commission had the authority to require reports from time to time, although the bill did not explicitly require annual reports.[141]

---

129 *Id.*

130 *Id.* at § 7.

131 *Id.*

132 *Id.* Today, under state corporate law, corporations have executive committees that, with certain exceptions (such as with respect to the declaration of dividends or the adoption of bylaws), have managing powers. *See, e.g.*, § 8.25 of the Model Business Corporation Act (2016).

133 S. 6287, 59th Cong. § 7 (1906).

134 *Id.* at § 8.

135 *Id.*

136 *Id.* at § 11.

137 *Id.* at § 10.

138 *Id.* at § 14 ("[T]he treasurer shall keep proper books of account of all transactions of the corporation. . . .").

139 *Id.*

140 *Id.*

141 *Id.* at § 15.

Some of the more interesting provisions of the bill dealt with the relationship of the corporation to its employees. For example, one provision stated that a pension fund be established,[142] which was to be paid to former employees of the corporation due to injury on the job or age.[143] The bill required that any fines imposed due to violation of the Act were to be paid to the pension fund, not the government.[144] Additionally, the bill provided that the ICC would act as a "board of conciliation" for any dispute arising between the corporation and its employees with respect to such matters as compensation, hours, conditions of labor, and protection of life and limb.[145]

The bill set forth penalties for violation of its provisions.[146] For example, a fraud provision stated:

> Any officer, director, or agent of such corporation who shall willfully make, assist in making, cause or direct to be made any false statement, material misrepresentation, or false entry in any book, report, return, account, or certificate required by or under this Act to be kept, shall be, upon conviction, subject to a fine . . . or imprisonment for not more than one year, or both, . . . and *shall furthermore be liable in a civil action for damages caused to any creditor or stockholder thereby.*[147]

Note that this may well be the first bill of its kind to expressly create a civil private right of action.[148] Furthermore, the right of action belonged not only to shareholders,

---

[142] *Id.* at § 21.

[143] Although S. 6287 was never enacted, Senator Newland's concern over railroad workers being compensated for injury was addressed in the Federal Employer's Liability Act of 1908 (FELA), 45 U.S.C. § 51 (2012). *See* Richard J. Butler and John D. Worrall, *Wage and Injury Response to Shifts in Workplace Liability*, 61 Indus. and Labor Relations Rev. 181, 181–82 (2008) (discussing the reasons for establishment of FELA); Marc I. Steinberg, *The Federal Employers' Liability Act and Judicial Activism: Policymaking by the Courts*, 12 Willamette L.J. 79 (1975) (asserting that the U.S. Supreme Court has engaged in judicial activism in its interpretation of the Act); *see also Wilkerson v. McCarthy*, 336 U.S. 53 (1949) (Douglas, J., concurring) (stating that FELA "was designed to put on the railroad industry some of the cost for the legs, eyes, arms, and lives which it consumed in its operations").

[144] S. 6287, 59th Cong. § 23 (1906).

[145] *Id.* at § 22.

[146] *See id.* at § 23.

[147] *Id.* (emphasis added). Note that the monetary amount of the fine was left blank in the provision.

[148] *Compare* Section 18 of the Securities Exchange Act, 15 U.S.C. § 78r (2012). This provision creates an express cause of action for aggrieved purchasers and sellers of securities against any person who made, or caused to be made, a materially false statement in a filing with the SEC under the Securities Exchange Act of 1934. Note that the provision in S. 6287 was broader in that it provided a remedy to creditors and holders of stock. *See generally* Marc I. Steinberg, *The Propriety and Scope of Cumulative Remedies under the Federal Securities Laws*, 67 Cornell L. Rev. 557 (1982).

but to creditors as well. Additionally, any officer, director, or agent who willfully or negligently refused to perform a duty required by the bill was subject to a fine of not more than $5,000, imprisonment of not more than one year, or both.[149] There were also penalties for a corporation that failed to comply with the bill, which included an undetermined fine. [150] In addition, every day that a subject corporation failed to comply constituted a separate violation.[151] As an additional provision, the bill provided a monetary fine for any corporation that funded or aided a political candidate or party.[152]

The bill provided that a subject corporation was a citizen in any state where its lines were located for purposes of private suits and government suits.[153] Additionally, the Interstate Commerce Commission could apply to any federal appellate court through which the corporation's lines ran for the appointment of a receiver.[154] Appointment of a receiver was a suitable penalty for any violation of the Act or for violation of the Interstate Commerce Act.[155] If deemed appropriate, the appellate court had the power to revoke the charter of a corporation organized under the Act, due to its continued violation of the Act's terms.[156]

G. 1907 BILL—SENATE—S. 383

S. 383, introduced by Senator Porter McCumber of North Dakota, was aimed at regulating all corporations that were or would become a part of interstate commerce.[157] Each corporation subject to the bill was required to file a copy of its articles of incorporation with the Secretary of Commerce and Labor.[158] The articles were to be signed by "all persons uniting to form the association."[159] The articles of incorporation were to contain the corporation's name, location, number of directors or trustees, amount of capital stock, and number of shares.[160] Also required was a

---

[149] S. 6287, 59th Cong. § 23 (1906).

[150] *Id.*

[151] *Id.*

[152] *Id.* This issue is still debated today; recently, the Supreme Court found that these types of limits violate the corporation's First Amendment rights. *See Citizens United v. Federal Election Commission*, 558 U.S. 310 (2010).

[153] S. 6287, 59th Cong. § 24 (1906) (in case of suits by the government for fines or penalties, jurisdiction may be had in the circuit court where the corporation has its principal place of business).

[154] *Id.* at § 25.

[155] *Id.*

[156] *Id.*

[157] "A bill to provide for the incorporation, control, and government of associations organized to carry on business entering into, or becoming a part of, interstate commerce. . . ." S. 383, 60th Cong., § 1 (1907).

[158] *Id.* at § 3.

[159] *Id.*

[160] *Id.* at § 2.

statement that the company consent to "submit its books and records for inspection and examination by any person designated for that purpose, by [the Secretary of Commerce and Labor]."[161] Furthermore, a subject corporation was prohibited from issuing stock in excess of the value of its assets and that such issuance would only occur after Secretary approval.[162] Once the articles were transmitted to the Secretary, he was required to make an investigation into the facts therein.[163] After a satisfactory investigation, the Secretary would issue to the company a "certificate of incorporation," which authorized the corporation to conduct business in interstate commerce.[164]

The bill provided that it was a subject corporation's obligation to provide annual reports to the Secretary.[165] These reports were to include a "full statement of its business" for the specific year, the corporation's gross and net earnings, improvements or additions made and the cost thereof, value of its assets, expenditures made, and other information as the Secretary may require.[166] In addition to his duty to require annual reports, the Secretary had the power to require reports at any interval that he deemed "advisable."[167] These reports were to address the corporation's financial condition and its "manner of conducting business."[168]

The bill also gave the Secretary of Commerce and Labor the duty to appoint "a sufficient number of competent accountants and appraisers, whose duty it shall be to investigate . . . all associations organized under the provisions of this Act."[169] These accountants and appraisers were required to file reports with the Secretary regarding the financial condition of each such corporation.[170] On its face, the bill would seem to have required government accountants and appraisers to periodically investigate each subject corporation and present a report of their findings to the Secretary.[171]

---

[161] *Id.*

[162] *Id.* at § 7.

[163] *Id.* at § 4.

[164] *Id.*

[165] *Id.* at § 8.

[166] *Id.*

[167] *Id.* at § 7.

[168] *Id.*

[169] *Id.* at § 12.

[170] *Id.* at § 13.

[171] Although such widespread mandatory audit provisions have not been implemented in regards to private companies, a similar mandate exists pertaining to government corporations. In 1945 Congress established the Division of Corporate Audits in the General Accounting Office (now the Government Accountability Office). It is the job of this division to perform mandatory audits of all government corporations. *See* Gary J. Previts and Barbara D. Merino, *A History of Accountancy in the United States: The Cultural Significance of Accounting* 330–31 (1998); Lawrence A. Cunningham, *A New Product for the State Corporation Law Market: Audit Committee Certifications*, 1 Berkeley Bus. L.J. 327, 350 n.60 (2004).

In contrast to S. 6287, which provided for numerous penalties and a civil action, S. 383 had only one penalty—dissolution. The bill provided that "upon the failure of any corporation organized under this [A]ct to conform to all the requirements thereof, the Secretary of Commerce and Labor shall by order annul and cancel [the] certificate of corporation, [and such] cancellation shall effect a dissolution of such corporation."[172]

H. 1908 BILL—SENATE—S. 4874

Two months after Senator McCumber's bill was introduced, Senator Knute Nelson of Minnesota introduced a similar bill entitled "a bill for the incorporation and regulation of corporations engaged in interstate commerce."[173] The bill applied to any "interstate commerce corporation," which is defined as any corporation engaging in interstate commerce.[174] In turn, interstate commerce was defined as business between two or more states or territories, or between a state and territory, and all commerce within any territory or within the District of Columbia.[175]

Similar to H.R. 10704, Senator Nelson's bill required that a corporation subject to the bill's provisions file its articles of incorporation with the Commissioner of Corporations of the newly created Bureau of Corporations.[176] Once the articles were approved by the Commissioner and a fee of $100 paid, a certificate of incorporation would be issued.[177] A copy of that certificate then had to be filed in every state in which the company intended to carry on business.[178] The directors of the corporation were to be jointly and severally liable for the accuracy of the information contained in the articles' statement of facts.[179] Hence, the directors were personally responsible for "any loss or damage which *may occur to any person* by reason of the falsity of any part of such statement of the facts."[180]

The bill set forth the powers of each corporation.[181] Included was the right to acquire, "hold, enjoy, improve, lease, encumber, and convey such real and personal property as may be necessary for the purposes of its operation, *except stock or bonds*

---

[172] S. 383, 60th Cong. § 9 (1907).

[173] S. 4874, 60th Cong. (1908) (S. 383 was introduced in December of 1907, and this bill in February of 1908.).

[174] *Id.* at § 3.

[175] *Id.* at § 2.

[176] *Id.* at § 5. For discussion of H.R. 10704, *see supra* notes 74–94 & accompanying text. For discussion of the Commissioner of Corporations, *see supra* notes 17–23 & accompanying text.

[177] S. 4874, 60th Cong. § 5 (1908).

[178] *Id.*

[179] *Id.* at § 7.

[180] *Id.* (emphasis added).

[181] *Id.* at § 6.

in any other corporation."[182] Thus, this provision seemingly precluded investments in other corporations as well as the effectuation of merger transactions.[183] The bill also provided that a subject corporation could not commence business until at least 75 percent of its capital stock had been subscribed for and 50 percent of such capital stock had been paid in full.[184]

The bill prohibited stock to be traded for property or labor unless the person trading that property or labor was an original subscriber of the stock.[185] In that case, the board of directors was to assign a fair value to the property or labor at issue.[186] In an attempt to curb self-dealing by directors, the bill provided that:

> In case such appraisal [of the property or labor] is actually or constructively fraudulent, or palpably and clearly excessive or materially beyond the fair value, the board of directors, and each of them, shall be jointly and severally personally liable and accountable to the company, its stockholders, and creditors for any loss or damage which any of them may sustain in consequence thereof.[187]

In this respect, this provision essentially codified a director's duty of loyalty to act in the best interest of the corporation. The bill also required that: "No dividend stock, or stock in whole or in part for dividends, shall ever be issued by the company or its officers."[188]

This bill required that companies maintain specified books and records, which could be inspected at any time by the Department of Justice and the Department of Commerce and Labor.[189] For example, the bill called for the board of directors to keep "Stock Books" which were to include: the name and address of every subscriber of original stock, along with the number of shares subscribed for and price paid for those shares; the total number of shares of stock issued and outstanding; and the total amount paid for the subject shares (divided into the amount paid in cash, property, and labor).[190] These "Stock Books" were to be open for inspection to

---

[182] *Id.* (emphasis added).

[183] Mergers had become an especially attractive means of acquiring monopoly power in the early 1900s; this is due in part to late nineteenth century Supreme Court decisions outlawing cartels. *See* William H. Page, *Standard Oil and U.S. Steel: Predation and Collusion in the Law of Monopolization and Mergers*, 85 S. Cal. L. Rev. 657, 662–68 (2012).

[184] S. 4874, 60th Cong. § 8 (1908).

[185] *Id.* at § 11.

[186] *Id.*

[187] *Id.*

[188] *Id.*

[189] *See id.* at §§ 13, 17, 18, 21, 29.

[190] *Id.* at § 13. (If stock was transferred from an original purchaser, the books were required to have the name and address of the person to whom they were transferred.)

shareholders and creditors, and "to all persons whom the company has served in its interstate business."[191]

The board of directors also was required to keep a "directors' book," which would contain "a full, true, and correct record of all acts and transactions of the board pertaining to the business and property of the company occurring and taking place at its meeting or elsewhere, and a record of the vote on every resolution, motion, or proposition presented to or acted upon by the board [as well as] the names of the directors voting in the affirmative on any proposition and the names of those voting in the negative on the same."[192] The directors' book was to be open for inspection by all shareholders during reasonable business hours.[193] Failure to keep or negligent destruction of the book would result in a fine of not more than $5,000, imprisonment of not more than two years, or both.[194] Additionally, the directors were to be "jointly and severally liable in a civil action for all damages which any person may sustain," because of such failure or destruction.[195]

Likewise, the secretary of the corporation was required to keep a "Stockholders' Book," which recorded the business transacted at shareholder meetings, and provided a tally of votes taken at such meetings.[196] This book was to be available for inspection by the officers and shareholders of the company at all reasonable business hours.[197] Failure to keep such a book, or negligent destruction of that book, would result in the same penalties as listed above.[198]

The bill required that subject corporations issue annual reports to the Commissioner of Corporations.[199] Additionally, a corporation was required to file a notice with the Commissioner any time additional stock or bonds were to be issued.[200] In order for the corporation to issue more stock, its action would have to be approved by a two-thirds vote of the issued and outstanding stock.[201] Immediately following such approval, a copy of the resolution authorizing the issuance was required to be filed with the Commissioner.[202] A written report also was

---

[191] *Id.*

[192] *Id.* at § 17.

[193] *Id.*

[194] *Id.*

[195] *Id.*

[196] *Id.* at § 18.

[197] *Id.*

[198] *Id.*

[199] *Id.* at § 22.

[200] *Id.* at § 21.

[201] *Id.*

[202] *Id.*

mandated that was to include the number of shares issued and disposed of, their price, and to whom they were transferred.[203]

The bill included an extensive list of penalties for fraudulent or negligent acts, thereby providing:

> [E]very officer, agent, or employee of the company *who shall knowingly and willfully subscribe or make any false statement, false report, or false entry in or upon any of the books, papers, or other documents* . . . or shall knowingly and willfully subscribe or exhibit any false paper, book, or document *with intent to deceive any person or officer* authorized to examine the financial condition of any such corporation, or shall knowingly and willfully subscribe or make any false report whatsoever shall be guilty of a crime, and on conviction thereof shall be punished by a fine of not more than five thousand dollars or by imprisonment for a term not exceeding two years. . . .[204]

Furthermore, the bill stated that "[e]very officer, director, or agent of the company charged with or undertaking the execution or performance of any trust, duty, or work in its behalf who shall fail to execute or perform the same *improperly, negligently, or carelessly*, shall be deemed guilty of a misdemeanor. . . ."[205] Not only was a neglectful director guilty of a misdemeanor, he was also liable in a civil action for "all loss or damage sustained by the company or any person whomsoever in consequence" of such misconduct.[206] Likewise, the bill provided additional penalties for publishing false or misleading statements of the condition, business, or income of the company, or for "any scheme or device to unduly depress or unduly enhance the market price of the stock or bonds of the company," or for purchasing or selling property at an unreasonably excessive price.[207]

i. 1908 BILL—HOUSE OF REPRESENTATIVES—H.R. 19745

The next bill that was intended to tighten the reins on corporations did so by attempting to amend the Sherman Antitrust Act of 1890.[208] In March 1908, Representative

---

[203] *Id.*

[204] *Id.* at § 25 (emphasis added).

[205] *Id.*

[206] *Id.*

[207] *Id.* at § 27. Hence, this provision in part was directed at proscribing stock manipulation. Sections 9, 10(b), and 15(c) of the Securities Exchange Act, 15 U.S.C. §§ 78i, j(b), o(c) (2012) prohibit this misconduct.

[208] The bill was brought on the urging of President Theodore Roosevelt who believed that in order to effectively regulate those corporations that were causing harm to the public, the federal government should be

William Hepburn of Iowa introduced a bill entitled "a bill to regulate commerce among the several States or with foreign nations, and to amend the Act . . . entitled 'An Act to protect trade and commerce against unlawful restraints and monopolies.' "[209] The bill sought to amend Section 8 of the Sherman Act to require that any subject corporation file a written application with the Commissioner of Corporations.[210] The application was to include information about the corporation's organization, financial condition, contracts, and corporate proceedings.[211] Additionally, the bill would have vested power in the executive branch to prescribe further regulations regarding the necessary information to be provided in the application.[212]

Once the application had been filed with a written statement setting forth the company's charter and bylaws, place of its principal office, and its directors or managing officers and standing committees, the Commissioner of Corporations[213] would register the corporation under the Act.[214] If the Commissioner found the application was deficient or contained false statements of fact, he could, after providing 30 days notice to the subject corporation, cancel such corporation's registration.[215] All appeals of Commissioner decisions went to the Supreme Court for the District of Columbia.[216]

Representative Hepburn's bill included a novel provision that allowed corporations to file their contracts with the Commissioner of Corporations.[217] The Commissioner, with the concurrence from the Secretary of Commerce and Labor, would then review the contract or combination to determine whether it represented an unreasonable restraint of trade or commerce.[218] If so, the Commissioner was authorized to enter an order declaring that, in his opinion, the contract constituted an unreasonable restraint of trade or commerce.[219] If no such order was made within

---

granted supervisory power over interstate corporations. 43 Cong. Rec. 2320, 2321 (Statement of Hon. Charles G. Washburn).

209 H.R. 19745, 60th Cong. (1908).

210 *Id.* at § 8.

211 *Id.*

212 *Id.*

213 For discussion of the Commissioner of Corporations, *see supra* notes 17–23 & accompanying text.

214 H.R. 19745, 60th Cong. § 8 (1908).

215 *Id.*

216 *Id.* During the Reconstruction period following the Civil War, Congress replaced the district and circuit courts in the District of Columbia with the Supreme Court of the District of Columbia. This court was given the same powers as the circuit court. In 1936 Congress changed the name of the Supreme Court to the District Court for the District of Columbia. *See Federal Courts of the District of Columbia*, Federal Judicial Center, http://www.fjc.gov/history/home.nsf/page/courts_special_dc.html (last visited Oct. 1, 2015).

217 H.R. 19745, 60th Cong. § 10 (1908).

218 *Id.*

219 *Id.*

30 days, with certain exceptions, the corporation would be immune from prosecution based on that contract.[220] The bill would also have amended Section 11 of the Sherman Act to provide the same protection to common carriers.[221]

The bill provided a private right of action for any person injured in his business or property as a result of conduct forbidden by the Act.[222] It also allowed for the recovery of litigation costs and reasonable attorney's fees.[223]

J. TAFT-WICKERSHAM BILL OF 1910—HOUSE OF REPRESENTATIVES AND SENATE—H.R. 20142 AND S. 6186

February 1910 saw the introduction of S. 6186 and H.R. 20142.[224] These identical bills, known collectively as the "Taft-Wickersham Bill" (hereinafter referenced to as "the bill"), were designed to offer voluntary federal incorporation.[225] The bill provided that "[a]ny five or more persons, citizens of the United States, . . . may, upon complying with the requirements of this Act, form a corporation to engage in trade or commerce with foreign nations, or among the several States. . . ."[226] Corporations that wished to avail themselves of the bill's protections were required to file Articles of Association with the Commissioner of Corporations.[227] These articles were to contain the usual requirements such as corporate name, location of principal business office, object for which the corporation is to be established, dollar amount of capital stock, and the number of shares and par value of such shares.[228] Additionally, the corporation's existence was limited to 50 years.[229] Once the articles were approved by the Commissioner, the corporation would be registered as a "national corporation," subject to the requirements and advantages of the Act.[230]

---

[220] *Id.* (providing no defense existed on this basis if the contract or combination was "in unreasonable restraint of trade or commerce among the several States or with foreign nations").

[221] *Id.* at § 11.

[222] *Id.* at § 7.

[223] *See id.* at § 3 (stating that "no suit for damages under said section seven of the said Act, based upon a right of action accruing prior to the passage of this Act, shall be maintained unless the same shall be commenced within one year after the passage of this Act").

[224] "A Bill to provide for the formation of corporations to engage in interstate and international trade and commerce. . . ." S. 6186, 61st Cong. (1910); "A Bill to provide for the formation of corporations to engage in interstate and international trade and commerce. . . ." H.R. 20142, 61st Cong. § 1 (1910). FTC Report, *supra* note 29, at 39.

[225] FTC Report, *supra* note 29, at 39.

[226] S. 6186, 61st Cong., § 1 (1910); H.R. 20142, 61st Cong. § 1 (1910) [hereinafter S. 6186].

[227] S. 6186 at § 2.

[228] *Id.*

[229] *Id.* (The corporation was required to list "the period limited for the duration of the company, not exceeding fifty years.").

[230] *Id.* at §§ 2, 3.

The bill set forth the general powers of the corporation.[231] These included the power to adopt a corporate name and seal, to have succession, to conduct interstate commerce and foreign trade, and to produce or manufacture goods in any state.[232] The bill kept the legal fiction of corporate personhood, and allowed the corporation to sue or be sued as if it were a natural person.[233] Under this bill, a corporation was required to file its bylaws with the Bureau of Corporations.[234]

The bill contained strict provisions regarding mergers, effectively outlawing them.[235] Section 8 provided that:

> *No corporation formed pursuant to this Act shall purchase, acquire, or hold stock in any other corporation*, nor shall any corporation organized under this Act *or under the law of any state or foreign country* for the purpose of or engaged in carrying on the like business to that of a corporation formed pursuant to this Act acquire or hold the stock of such last-mentioned corporation, and any attempted transfer of such stock contrary to this provision shall be *null and void.*[236]

Thus even if a corporation chose not to incorporate under the Act, it would not be able to purchase stock in a corporation formed pursuant to the Act, if the two were engaged in a "like" business. The bill did allow for a subject company to sell all of its assets to another corporation organized under the Act, if the company obtained an 80 percent shareholder vote approving such.[237] It required that the company file the terms of the sale with the Bureau of Corporations (that was created in 1903) prior to the shareholder vote.[238] Once requisite shareholder approval was obtained, the corporation had to file a copy of the minutes of the shareholder meeting with the Bureau.[239] No sale was final until approved, in writing, by the Commissioner of Corporations.[240]

The bill required that a corporation have at least five board members who were to be elected every year.[241] The board could delegate much of its power to an executive

---

[231] *See id.* at § 5.

[232] *Id.*

[233] *Id.*

[234] *Id.* For discussion of the Bureau of Corporations, *see supra* notes 17–23 & accompanying text.

[235] S. 6186, 61st Cong. § 8 (1910).

[236] *Id.* (emphasis added).

[237] *Id.* at § 30.

[238] *Id.* For discussion of the Commissioner of Corporations, *see supra* notes 17–23 & accompanying text.

[239] S. 6186, 61st Cong. § 30 (1910).

[240] *Id.*

[241] *Id.* at § 9.

committee comprised of a majority of its board members.[242] This committee generally was authorized to exercise the power of the entire board, except that it could not declare dividends.[243] This section also allowed a corporation to indemnify its directors who did not serve on the executive committee against liability, requiring only that such directors exercise good faith and due diligence in matters considered in board of director meetings which were attended by them.[244]

The bill gave every corporation the power to create "two or more kinds of stock" so long as these different classes were contained in the original articles of association or an amendment thereto.[245] The creation of these classes required approval by the Commissioner of Corporations.[246] Additionally, a subject corporation was not authorized to issue preferred stock unless it specified such in the original articles of association or a resolution was passed authorizing such by two-thirds shareholder vote.[247] The bill required the filing of a certificate with the Bureau of Corporations with respect to payment of every installment of capital stock, along with a sworn statement from two officers, stating "the amount of the capital paid, and whether paid in cash or property; and the total amount of capital stock if any previously paid and reported. . . ."[248]

This bill required that notice be given to the Bureau of Corporations if the company wished to purchase property through an issuance of stock.[249] The notice was a rather detailed filing that was to contain: a full description of the property; the number of shares issued as payment for the property and the par value of such shares; the names and addresses of the sellers of said property along with a statement stating whether they own shares in the corporation; the terms of the agreement; and, in the event that the stock to be issued for payment of the subject property has a par value, an evaluation made by two independent appraisers, who must be approved in writing by the Commissioner of Corporations.[250] This section provided that, should the statement or appraisal be false in a material respect, the directors participating in that statement were to be jointly and severally liable to all subscribers and holders of stock and "to all persons to whom the corporation may thereafter become indebted, for any damage sustained by them by reason of the issue" of that stock.[251]

---

[242] *Id.*

[243] *Id.* This restriction is similar to current state law. *See, e.g.*, Model Business Corporation Act § 8.25(e)(1) (2016).

[244] S. 6186, 61st Cong. § 9 (1910). For current Delaware treatment of director indemnity, *see* Del. Gen. Corp. Law § 145.

[245] S. 6186, 61st Cong. § 11 (1910).

[246] *Id.*

[247] *Id.*

[248] *Id.* at § 19.

[249] *Id.* at § 17.

[250] *Id.*

[251] *Id.*

The bill mandated yearly reports to be made containing information as the Commissioner required.[252] These reports were to be filed along with an oath or affirmation signed by the president or treasurer of the corporation along with the signatures of at least three directors.[253] Furthermore, the bill gave the Commissioner the power to call for special reports whenever necessary to "secure a full and complete knowledge" of a corporation's condition.[254]

The bill required that dividends come only from the corporation's surplus or net profits.[255] If the directors approved a distribution in violation of the statute, acting with negligence or willful intent, those directors were liable to the company's creditors for six years after the issuance of such distribution.[256] A director could avoid liability by entering a dissent in the minutes of the meeting authorizing the distribution, or entering a dissent after the fact if the director was not present at said meeting.[257]

Notably, the bill gave the Commissioner power to appoint a "special agent" to ascertain a corporation's financial condition whenever it "failed to pay off any of its written obligations."[258] The agent was to examine the corporation to determine whether it was unable to pay its debts.[259] If, upon reviewing the agent's report, the Commissioner determined that the corporation was insolvent or in such a financial condition so that continuance of its business would damage public welfare, the Commissioner was authorized to appoint a receiver.[260] The receiver, under the direction of the Commissioner, was empowered pursuant to court order to sell the company's property in order to pay the remaining debts.[261]

K. 1911 BILL—SENATE—S. 1377

The next bill, offered in the Senate, took a different approach to regulating corporations. Instead of obliging a corporation to register with a national agency or

---

[252] *Id.* at § 18.

[253] *Id. Cf.* Sarbanes-Oxley Act of 2002, Pub. L. No. 107-204, §§ 302(a), 906 (requiring CEO & CFO certifications); for a more detailed discussion of these provisions, *see* modern day relevance *infra* notes 576–578 & accompanying text.

[254] S. 6186, 61st Cong. § 18 (1910).

[255] *Id.* at § 23.

[256] *Id.*

[257] *Id.* This use of a director entering a dissent in this manner is consistent with current statutory law. *See, e.g.*, Model Bus. Corp. Act § 8.24(d) (2016).

[258] S. 6186, 61st Cong. § 31 (1910).

[259] *Id.*

[260] *Id.*

[261] *Id.*

bureau, S. 1377 required that a corporation "be organized under the law of a State or Territory in which its chief place of business . . . is located and its directors' meetings regularly held."[262] Under this bill, a corporation would not be allowed to hold stock of any other corporation or to do anything outside of its state of incorporation that it was not allowed to do therein.[263]

The bill prohibited directors and officers from being shareholders, officers, directors, or employees of any company engaged in the same business.[264] The bill contained a general rule that capital stock could not exceed $5 million.[265] However, a corporation could apply to a competent court to authorize a greater capital stock upon a finding that such stock was not being held to operate as a restraint on trade.[266] This provision did not apply to common carriers, or to any business engaged in banking, insurance, or public utility, or to any business "the substantial bulk of which is carried on in foreign countries or in any one State or Territory or district, and which does not involve the customary transmission of goods from one State or Territory or District to another. . . ."[267]

Any corporation or association that was found to have violated the Act would be subject to a fine not exceeding 10 percent of the corporation's capital stock, and also subject to a "perpetual injunction against engaging in interstate commerce."[268] In addition, any person who violated the Act was subject to a fine not greater than $10,000.[269] If the violation was willful and committed with the intent to defraud or "to create a monopoly," imprisonment of up to five years was authorized.[270] Moreover, any contract that was made in violation of the Act would be void.[271]

L. 1911 BILL—HOUSE OF REPRESENTATIVES—H.R. 12809

The same year—1911—a bill was filed in the House entitled "A bill relating to the regulation and transactions of corporations engaging in interstate commerce."[272]

---

[262] "A bill to prescribe the conditions under which corporations may engage in interstate commerce, and to provide for penalties for otherwise engaging in the same. . . ." S. 1377, 62d Cong. § 1 (1911).

[263] *Id.*

[264] *Id.*

[265] *Id.*

[266] *Id.*

[267] *Id.* at § 2 (The bill did not specify what constitutes a "substantial bulk" of business carried on in foreign nations.).

[268] *Id.* at § 5.

[269] *Id.*

[270] *Id.*

[271] *Id.* at § 3.

[272] H.R. 12809, 62d Cong. (1911).

The bill was brought by Representative William C. Adamson who, at the time, was the chairman of the Committee on Interstate and Foreign Commerce.[273] This bill provided that any corporation that engaged in interstate commerce in any transaction whatsoever was required to file a certificate with the Secretary of Commerce and Labor.[274] The certificate was required to be from the state in which the corporation was incorporated, stating that such corporation was properly and lawfully organized, that its capital stock was fully paid, and that the funds had "been applied faithfully to the equipment and organization of the business. . . ."[275]

Additionally, the certificate was to set forth that the corporation was not engaged in anticompetitive behavior.[276] Corporations were barred from holding stock in any other corporation, and directors and officers were not allowed to be directors or officers in competing companies.[277] If the filing contained a materially false statement, the person responsible would be guilty of a misdemeanor and subject to a fine not exceeding $10,000, imprisonment of not more than 10 years, or both.[278] In addition, if any director or stockholder held a director position in a competing company, a fine not exceeding $1,000, imprisonment for a period not to exceed one year, or both, could be imposed in the court's discretion.[279]

The bill required an annual sworn statement of the "chief officer of such corporation" attesting that the facts contained in the original filing were still true.[280] Additionally, the officer had to include an itemized list of the assets of the corporation, and a statement that the market value of those assets exceeded the company's liabilities.[281] The bill included a per diem fine of $1,000 for every day after the deadline that the corporation failed to file its statement.[282] Furthermore, if the report contained a falsity, the officer responsible for making that report "shall be deemed guilty of perjury" and punished as such.[283]

---

[273] Biographical Directory of the United States Congress, William Charles Adamson (1854–1929), *available at* http://bioguide.congress.gov/scripts/biodisplay.pl?index=A000051 (last visited Oct. 1, 2015).

[274] H.R. 12809, 62d Cong. § 1 (1911).

[275] *Id.*

[276] *Id.*

[277] *Id.*

[278] *Id.*

[279] *Id.* at § 3.

[280] *Id.* at § 4.

[281] *Id. Cf.* certifications required of a publicly-held company's chief executive officer and chief financial officer pursuant to Sections 302 and 906 of the Sarbanes-Oxley Act. *See infra* notes 576–578 & accompanying text; discussion Chapter 5 herein.

[282] H.R. 12809, 62d Cong. § 4 (1911).

[283] *Id.*

The bill provided that it was illegal to merge or to combine two competing companies "for the purpose of or with the effect of suppressing or destroying, preventing, or lessening competition between them to any extent. . . ."[284] Under its language, violation of this provision could have imposed strict liability—meaning that, if such a merger resulted in unduly lax competition, it was a violation regardless of intent.[285] An agent or officer responsible for this violation would have been criminally liable, and "on conviction would have been subject to a fine in a sum not exceeding ten thousand dollars or imprisonment for a period not exceeding ten years, either one or both in the discretion of the court."[286]

M. 1912 BILL—HOUSE OF REPRESENTATIVES—H.R. 17932

A year later, Representative Ernest Roberts of Massachusetts introduced a lengthy bill designed to increase the power of the Commissioner of Corporations.[287] Although the bill's title suggests that it applies to all interstate corporations, the bill did not extend to national banks, insurance providers, corporations created by special acts of Congress, or any corporation whose aggregate capital stock and earnings did not exceed $5 million.[288] The bill sought to amend the Act that created the Department of Commerce and Labor.[289]

The bill required that those seeking to form a corporation submit an "agreement of association" with the Commissioner.[290] This agreement of association was to include the corporate name and purpose, the state in which the corporation was to be located, the total amount of its capital stock, the par value and number of

---

[284] *Id.* at § 6.

[285] *Id.* ("It shall be unlawful for any two or more corporations of any character engaged in any line of business which compete with one another, reasonably or unreasonably, any one of which is to any extent engaged in interstate commerce or the operation or products of one of which enter into or affect interstate commerce, reasonably or unreasonably, to merge or combine for the purpose of *or with the effect of* suppressing or destroying, preventing, or lessening competition between them to any extent, reasonably or unreasonable, *if the purpose or result* of said combination is to engage in interstate commerce *regardless of* the extent of the competition destroyed or prevented or lessened, or the power or extent of the new combination") (emphasis added). *See also, Strict-Liability Crime, Black's Law Dictionary* (10th ed. 2014) ("An offense for which the action alone is enough to warrant a conviction, with no need to prove a mental state; specif., a crime that does not require a mens rea element, such as traffic offenses and illegal sales of intoxicating liquor.").

[286] *Id.*

[287] "A bill to provide for the formation and regulation of corporations engaged in any form of interstate commerce. . . ." H.R. 17932, 62d Cong. (1912). For discussion of the Commissioner of Corporations, *see supra* notes 17–23 & accompanying text.

[288] H.R. 17932, 62d Cong. § 1 (1912).

[289] *Id.* at § 2.

[290] *Id.* at § 9.

shares, and the amount of shares taken by each subscriber.[291] The agreement (or in lieu thereof, a sworn statement setting forth generally the contents of the agreement) would then be submitted to the Commissioner of Corporations. Upon the Commissioner's approval, the subject corporation's officers would transmit the statement and the Commissioner's endorsement to the Secretary of Commerce and Labor, who in turn would "cause a certificate in the form of a charter to be issued to said corporation. . . ."[292] Notably, a corporation would not be allowed to commence business until it filed a sworn statement with the Commissioner of Corporations stating that all of its capital stock had been paid in full.[293]

This bill did not require pre-approval from the Commissioner before increasing capital stock.[294] Instead, a corporation that increased capital would be required to file a certificate with the Commissioner setting forth the amount of the increase along with the details of payment.[295] This certificate had to be filed within 30 days of payment of the last installment.[296] The bill explicitly provided that no subject corporation could hold stock in any other corporation.[297] Failure to dispose of the stock of another corporation would be ground for dissolution.[298] This outright ban did not apply to directors and officers; instead, the bill allowed directors and officers to serve as directors and officers in up to four other corporations at the same time.[299]

The bill did require that each corporation subject to the Act file annual reports.[300] The reports were to contain the date of the annual meeting, the amount of capital stock, the identity of each shareholder and the number of shares held by each such stockholder, and the assets and liabilities of the corporation.[301] Additionally, an independent auditor's report was to be included with the filing. The auditor's report was to verify that such report represented the "true condition of the affairs of

---

[291] *Id.* at § 4.

[292] *Id.* at § 10.

[293] *Id.* at § 14.

[294] *Id.* at § 55.

[295] *Id.*

[296] *Id.*

[297] *Id.* at § 65.

[298] *Id.*

[299] *Id.* at § 64. The rationale of allowing directors and officers to serve the same positions in multiple companies came under fire in the late twentieth century as well. *See* Judith H. Dobrzynski, *When Directors Play Musical Chairs: Seats on Too Many Boards Spell Problems for Investors*, N.Y. Times, Nov. 17, 1996, *available at* http://www.nytimes.com/1996/11/17/business/seats-on-too-many-boards-spell-problems-for-investors.html?pagewanted=all. For a further discussion of interlocking directorates, *see* modern day relevance *infra* note 547 & accompanying text.

[300] H.R. 17932, 62d Cong. § 53 (1912).

[301] *Id.*

such corporation as disclosed by its books at the time of making the audit."[302] If the corporation failed to file reports for two consecutive years, the district court, upon application by the Commissioner and after notice and hearing, was authorized to decree such corporation's dissolution.[303]

The president of the corporation and its directors could be held personally liable for consenting to a dividend that rendered the corporation insolvent, and could also be liable for making loans to shareholders.[304] Additionally, the president, directors, and treasurer were liable for signing any statement that misrepresented the value of real or personal property accepted in exchange for stock.[305] Furthermore, the directors and all officers were liable for signing any certificate that they knew to be false and for debts contracted before the original capital stock was paid (and the certificate of such payment had been duly filed).[306] Directors and officers who knowingly violated the Act were subject to a "fine of not less than one thousand dollars and imprisonment for one year."[307]

N. 1912 BILL—HOUSE OF REPRESENTATIVES—H.R. 18662

The next bill to be brought was titled "a bill to control and regulate corporations engaged in commerce among the several States or foreign nations."[308] This bill called for the President, with the advice and consent of the Senate, to appoint a deputy commissioner of corporations in each of the several states.[309] The deputy commissioners would be part of the Bureau of Corporations, within the Department of Commerce and Labor, and would be supervised by the Commissioner of Corporations.[310] This bill would apply to all corporations engaged in interstate commerce except banks.[311]

---

[302] *Id.*

[303] *Id.* at § 54.

[304] *Id.* at § 40 ("The president and directors shall be so liable ... For making or consenting to a dividend if the corporation is or thereby is rendered insolvent, to the extent of such dividend ... [and] For debts contracted between the time of making or assenting to a loan to a stockholder and the time of its repayment to the extent of such loan.").

[305] *Id.*

[306] *Id. Cf.* Sarbanes-Oxley Act of 2002, Pub. L. No. 107-204, §§ 302(a), 906 (requiring CEO & CFO certifications). For a more detailed discussion of these sections, *see* modern day relevance *infra* notes 554–585 & accompanying text; Chapter 5 herein.

[307] H.R. 17932, 62d Cong. § 39 (1912).

[308] *See* H.R. 18662, 62d Cong. (1912).

[309] *Id.* at § 2.

[310] *Id.* For discussion of the Commissioner of Corporations, *see supra* notes 17–23 & accompanying text.

[311] H.R. 18662, 62d Cong. § 1 (1912).

The bill gave the federal circuit courts jurisdiction in any action brought by the Commissioner, the deputy commissioners, or the Attorney General.[312]

The bill required that each corporation file an agreement of association, which set forth the corporate basics such as name, location of principal office, purposes for which formed, nature of business to be transacted, and amount of capital stock.[313] After the first meeting of a majority of shareholders, a majority of directors was required to sign and "make oath" to a "true copy" of the agreement of association, along with the date of the first meeting, the amount of stock issued, the amount of stock paid for in cash, the amount paid for with property (along with a description of the property and the value thereof), and the names and addresses of all officers.[314] This would be known as the "articles of organization."[315] The articles would then be submitted to the deputy commissioner in the state where the business was located who, upon approval, would issue a "certificate of incorporation" to the company.[316]

The bill provided for steep penalties for knowingly false statements in the initial filings. Any director who signed the articles, knowing them to be false, would be liable to any stockholder for damages caused as a result of the falsity.[317] Such a director would also be guilty of a felony and subject to a fine between $1,000 and $10,000, imprisonment between one and ten years, or both.[318]

The bill permitted a corporation to purchase property with stock.[319] However, a corporation had to disclose this fact in all subsequent filings.[320] If additional stock were sought to be issued, the corporation had to file another certificate with the deputy commissioner setting out the current amount of stock, the amount of additional stock to be issued, and a description of any property for which the stock was being issued.[321] Under the bill, a director was jointly and severally liable for signing a certificate that he knew to be false, and was subject to the same penalties described above.[322]

Under this bill, a corporation, with certain exceptions, was allowed to purchase and hold the stock of other companies, including those engaged in the same

[312] *Id.* at § 3.
[313] *Id.* at § 5.
[314] *Id.* at § 8.
[315] *Id.* at § 9.
[316] *Id.* at § 10.
[317] *Id.* at § 9.
[318] *Id.*
[319] *Id.* at § 14.
[320] *Id.*
[321] *Id.* at § 15.
[322] *Id.* at § 16.

business.[323] The bill further provided that a corporation owning at least 90 percent of the stock of another corporation engaged in a similar business or a business incidental to the corporation, could file in the place where its original articles were filed, a certificate of ownership.[324] Assuming statutory compliance, a 100 percent merger of the two corporations would occur, with the parent assuming possession of all assets and liabilities of its subsidiary.[325] This provision essentially set forth the requirements of what we now know as a "short-form merger."[326] In fact, the first state "short-form merger" statute was not adopted until over a decade later.[327]

This bill authorized creditors and shareholders to petition a federal circuit court to appoint a receiver in the case of corporate insolvency.[328] The circuit courts also had the power to hear complaints regarding elections of directors.[329]

O. 1912 BILL—HOUSE OF REPRESENTATIVES—H.R. 26414

On August 24, 1912, two bills aimed at corporate formation were introduced. The first was entitled "a bill to authorize the formation and organization of corporations for the transaction and conduct of commerce among the several States and with the foreign nations."[330] This bill applied to all corporations formed "for the transaction and conduct of commerce."[331] The bill required that a verified application of at least five U.S. citizens and residents be provided to the Secretary of Commerce and

[323] *Id.* at § 19 ("[E]very corporation organized under this Act shall have power . . . [t]o purchase, hold, and dispose of the stocks, bonds, and other evidences of indebtedness of any corporation, except as prohibited by the existing law against monopolies and contracts in restraint of trade. . . .").

[324] *Id.* at § 39.

[325] *Id.* ("[A]ny corporation lawfully owning all or ninety per centum of the stock of any other corporation organized or engaged in business similar or incidental to that of the possessor corporation may file . . . a certificate of such ownership and of the resolution of the board of directors to merge such other corporation, and thereupon it shall acquire and become and be possessed of all the estate, properties, rights, privileges, and franchises of such other corporation, and they shall vest in and be held and enjoyed by it as fully and entirely and without change or diminution as the same were before held and enjoyed by such other corporation, and be managed and controlled by the board of directors of such possessor corporation, and in its name, but without prejudice to any liabilities of such other corporation or the rights of any creditors thereof; and the liabilities of such other corporation shall, by virtue of such merger, become the liabilities of such possessor corporation.").

[326] *Compare* 8 Del. Gen. Corp. Code § 253.

[327] Catherine L. Curran, *Shareholders' Right in Short Form Mergers: The New Delaware Formula*, 64 Marq. L. Rev 687, 692 (1981) (The first state short-form merger statute, compiled in 1924 N.Y. Laws ch. 441, was adopted in New York in 1924.). *See* Marc I. Steinberg, *Short-Form Mergers in Delaware*, 27 Del. J. Corp. L. 489 (2002).

[328] H.R. 18662, 62d Cong. § 41 (1912).

[329] *Id.* at § 42.

[330] H.R. 26414, 62d Cong. (1912).

[331] *Id.* at § 1.

Labor.[332] The Secretary was then required to make public the company's articles of association, with its bylaws.[333]

The bill required each purchaser and seller of stock to send notice of the transaction to the Secretary.[334] It required that each corporation have at least five directors, with each director holding at least a five percent stake in the company.[335] The corporation would be required to keep a detailed account of its transactions along with copies of all letters and communications sent or received by the business.[336] These were required to show the corporation's transactions and communications for at least the previous ten years.[337] These records were open to inspection by any stockholder or group thereof owning at least ten percent of the company's capital, by the Secretary of Commerce and Labor, and the U.S. Attorney General.[338]

This bill took a unique approach toward corporate formation. Instead of the incorporators or other insiders collecting the subscribed for stock, each corporation was assigned a collector to assist in assigning and dividing shares and classes of stock.[339] The collectors held all funds received for capital stock until the formation was complete.[340] Furthermore, the Secretary of Commerce and Labor was given significant control over how these shares were to be divided.[341] The bill allowed the Secretary to "divide subscriptions . . . into such classes as shall to him seem best likely to bring about the widest distribution of shares and afford opportunity of investment to the largest number of citizens, particularly of those of small means."[342] In this regard, it seems that the bill was designed not only to protect current investors, but also to encourage capital investment among the populace.

Once directors were elected, the collector delivered to them a certificate setting forth the company's articles of association.[343] In turn, the directors were to deliver that certificate to the Secretary of Commerce and Labor.[344] At that time, at least three-quarters of the directors were required to execute an affidavit stating that they

---

332 *Id.*

333 *Id.* at § 2.

334 *Id.* ("Each seller and purchaser of stock shall send a notice in writing of his sale or purchase to the treasurer of the company, to the Secretary of Commerce and Labor, and to the collector of internal revenue of the district in which the principal office of the company is located. . . .").

335 *Id.* at § 4. *See infra* notes 554–585 and accompanying text, for modern day relevance.

336 H.R. 26414, 62d Cong. § 5 (1912).

337 *Id.*

338 *Id.*

339 *Id.* at § 6.

340 *Id.*

341 *Id.*

342 *Id.*

343 *Id.* at § 9.

344 *Id.*

would conduct the business in good faith consistent with the terms of the corporation's articles of association.[345] After all of this was completed, the collector would turn over the funds subscribed by the stockholders to the directors.[346]

P. 1912 BILL—HOUSE OF REPRESENTATIVES—H.R. 26415

The second bill introduced that day was by Congressman Augustus P. Gardner of Massachusetts and was known as "a bill creating a United States Corporation Commission, and providing for incorporation under the laws of the United States."[347] The bill provided that all corporations and joint-stock associations engaged in "manufacturing, mining, or other commercial or industrial business" in interstate commerce whose business annually exceeded a set amount of dollars were required to become corporations under the laws of the United States.[348]

The bill called for the formation of a new agency, the "United States Corporation Commission."[349] The President was given power, with advice and consent of the Senate, to appoint the commissioners for the Commission.[350] Furthermore, the bill required that the commissioners be comprised of both Democrats and Republicans.[351]

The bill required any corporation organizing under the Act to file a statement with the Commission.[352] The statement was to set out the corporation's name, nature of

---

[345] *Id.*

[346] *Id.*

[347] H.R. 26415, 62d Cong. (1912).

[348] *Id.* at § 1. The exact dollar value of the business required was left blank when the bill was introduced; presumably it was to be filled in later.

[349] *Id.* at § 2. The bill does not explicitly state whether the United States Corporation Commission was to replace the existing Bureau of Corporations, but it is possible to presume such. *Cf.* the language of Federal Trade Commission Act at 15 U.S.C. § 41 (2012) ("A commission is created and established, to be known as the Federal Trade Commission (hereinafter referred to as the Commission), which shall be composed of five Commissioners, who shall be appointed by the President, by and with the advice and consent of the Senate. Not more than three of the Commissioners shall be members of the same political party. The first Commissioners appointed shall continue in office for terms of three, four, five, six, and seven years, respectively, from September 26, 1914, the term of each to be designated by the President, but their successors shall be appointed for terms of seven years, except that any person chosen to fill a vacancy shall be appointed only for the unexpired term of the Commissioner whom he shall succeed."). Although the text of H.R. 26415 does not provide for replacement of the Bureau of Corporations, it apparently would have had that effect in practice. For a discussion of the Bureau of Corporations and the Federal Trade Commission Act, *see supra* notes 17–23 & accompanying text.

[350] H.R. 26415, 62d Cong. § 2 (1912).

[351] *Id.* (once again there are blanks in the bill: "not more than ____ of the commissioners so appointed shall be from the same political party").

[352] *Id.* at § 3.

business, location, amount of capital stock, proposed number of officers and directors and their respective place of residence, proposed number of shareholders along with each shareholder's residence, amount of stock paid in, corporate assets, and liabilities.[353] After a satisfactory statement was submitted, the Commission would issue a charter and qualify the corporation to conduct business.[354]

The Commission was directed not to issue a charter authorizing any company to issue stock or bonds or other types of indebtedness that exceeded "the true value of its physical assets and the good will of its business."[355] In this valuation, "no account shall be taken of any control or monopoly which the said corporation may have in the trade and commerce or any part thereof, in any article or commodity."[356] In addition, the Commission, after a hearing and upon good cause, was authorized to "alter, amend, or repeal" the charter.[357]

Under this bill, the Commissioner was given substantial oversight power. No stock could be issued without approval of the Commission.[358] Any person who knowingly and willfully issued unapproved stock or a form of indebtedness was subject to a fine of up to $10,000, imprisonment of up to five years, or both.[359] Commission consent was to be obtained before a company could own, hold, or control any stock or debt in another corporation formed under the Act.[360] Likewise, absent Commission approval, the Act prohibited any corporation not organized under the Act from owning stock or debt of any corporation organized thereunder.[361] The bill also required officers, directors, and certain other fiduciaries to obtain Commission consent before serving in a like capacity of any other corporation organized under the Act or of any common carrier.[362]

The bill authorized the Commission to serve as a type of arbitration panel or administrative body in civil suits involving violation of the Act,[363] entitling any person who had allegedly been injured due to a violation to file a complaint setting forth the alleged facts of the violation.[364] The Commission would then investigate the matter and issue a final order.[365] These proceedings were to be done "without

353 *Id.*

354 *Id.* at § 4.

355 *Id.*

356 *Id.*

357 *Id.*

358 *Id.* at § 5.

359 *Id.*

360 *Id.* at § 7.

361 *Id.*

362 *Id.* at § 8. These fiduciaries included those serving as an officer, director, manager, trustee, or receiver. *Id.*

363 *See id.* at § 10.

364 *Id.*

365 *Id.*

the formal pleadings, rules of evidence, [or] proceedings applicable to ordinary proceedings in equity and trials at common law."[366] Additionally, the bill authorized the Commission to "award damages to any party aggrieved by the violation of any of the provisions of this Act."[367]

The bill granted the Commission broad subpoena power to compel the appearance of witnesses and production of documents as well as the authority to seek enforcement of any such subpoena through the order of a federal court.[368] A witness in such a proceeding was compelled to testify, even if his testimony would tend to incriminate him in a criminal proceeding, except that his testimony could be used only as evidence against the corporation and was inadmissible in a separate criminal trial.[369] Likewise, the Commission had access to all corporate accounts, records, and memoranda kept by corporations doing business under the Act.[370]

The bill required the Commission to issue a report regarding all matters investigated by it.[371] This provision gave the Commission power to issue cease-and-desist orders along with any other reasonable penalty.[372] Additionally, the Commission had the power to declare that a corporation was charging an unreasonable price for certain goods and to "recommend" a more "just" nondiscriminatory price.[373]

An appeal of a Commission decision was to be made within 90 days after an adverse Commission order and was to be filed in the federal district court where the corporation's principal office was located.[374] However, the Commission's finding of facts were to be "conclusive and binding," with the district court reviewing only questions of law.[375] The bill required that substantial deference be given to the

[366] *Id.*

[367] *Id.* at § 16.

[368] *See id.* at § 11. This subpoena power resembles that held today by the U.S. Securities and Exchange Commission. *See SEC v. Jerry T. O'Brien, Inc.*, 467 U.S. 735 (1984).

[369] H.R. 26415, 62d Cong. § 11 (1912) ("The claim that any such testimony or evidence may tend to criminate the person giving such evidence shall not excuse such witness from testifying, but such evidence shall not excuse such witness from testifying, but such evidence or testimony shall not be used against such person upon the trial of any criminal proceeding."). This provision raises Fifth Amendment concerns. *See United States v. Stringer*, 521 F.3d 1189 (9th Cir. 2008); *SEC v. Dresser Indus., Inc.*, 628 F.2d 1368 (D.C. Cir. 1980); *United States v. Scrushy*, 366 F. Supp. 2d 1134 (N.D. Ala. 2005). For a discussion on invoking the Fifth Amendment in parallel proceedings, *see generally* Marc I. Steinberg and Ralph C. Ferrara, *Securities Practice: Federal and State Enforcement* §§ 7:24–7:32 (2d ed. 2001 & 2017–2018 supp.).

[370] H.R. 26415, 62d Cong. § 12 (1912).

[371] *Id.* at § 14.

[372] *Id.* Today, the SEC has the authority to issue cease and desist orders. *See* § 8A of the Securities Act, 15 U.S.C. § 77h-1 (2012); § 21C of the Securities Exchange Act, 15 U.S.C. § 78u-3 (2012).

[373] H.R. 26415, 62d Cong. §14 (1912).

[374] *Id.* at § 15.

[375] *Id.*

Commission in such a review, with Commission decisions being overturned only upon a "single, distinct, and dominant proposition of law."[376]

The bill required corporations to submit annual reports to the Commission.[377] These reports were to include: the amount of capital stock issued and paid for; dividends paid; the amount of surplus, if any; number of stockholders; corporate debts; value of the corporation's property, franchises, and equipment; the number of employees and the salary paid to each class; employee accidents and the causes thereof; the amounts spent for improvements; earnings and operating expenses; amount of profit; and a "complete exhibit of the financial operations of the corporation," including an annual balance sheet.[378] Failure to issue annual reports would result in a $100 per day fine for every day after the deadline that such report had not been filed.[379] Furthermore, the Commission had power to require those corporations that failed timely to issue an annual report to file monthly and other periodical reports with the Commission.[380]

The bill included penalties for knowingly and willfully entering a false entry in any book or record.[381] A guilty party would be punished by a fine up to $5,000, imprisonment of up to three years, or both.[382]

Q. 1913 BILL—HOUSE OF REPRESENTATIVES—H.R. 2488

The next incorporation bill was known as "a bill to prescribe the conditions under which a corporation may engage in interstate commerce and to provide penalties for otherwise engaging in the same."[383] This bill, with certain exceptions, applied to all joint-stock companies, business trusts, estates, or any other form of "association or combination in the nature thereof used for business purposes."[384] The bill required corporations to file a certified copy of its certificate or articles of incorporation with the Bureau of Corporations within 30 days after adopting said articles.[385]

For the most part what was required in this filing was similar to those requirements found in other bills. For example, a corporation was not allowed to own stock

---

[376] *Id.*

[377] *Id.* at § 23.

[378] *Id.*

[379] *Id.*

[380] *Id.*

[381] *Id.* at § 24.

[382] *Id.*

[383] H.R. 2488, 63d Cong. (1913). For a discussion regarding the Bureau of Corporations, *see supra* notes 17–23 & accompanying text.

[384] H.R. 2488, 62d Cong. § 3 (1913). For example, enterprises that were common carriers or engaged in banking or insurance were excluded from the bill. *Id.*

[385] *Id.* at § 1.

in any other corporation.[386] The bill, however, allowed for a company to hold the stock of another corporation for a period of up to 90 days as collateral for a debt.[387] As another example, the bill provided that any excess capital over and above par value would be deemed a surplus of the corporation.[388] A company's surplus was not allowed to exceed 50 percent of the amount of the company's capital stock.[389]

Penalties for violation were fairly steep. The bill provided that "every corporation, association, or person violating this Act shall be subject . . . to a fine not exceeding ten per centum of its capital stock."[390] In the case of an individual, the punishment was a fine of up to $10,000.[391] If the violation was willfully made, "with intent to defraud or to create a monopoly or unfairly to stifle competition," the person would be subject to imprisonment of up to five years, plus the fine.[392]

R. 1913 BILL—HOUSE OF REPRESENTATIVES—H.R. 1890

The sixty-third Congress saw the introduction of "a bill to regulate the commerce of certain corporations, and for other purposes."[393] This bill applied to any corporation engaged in interstate commerce that was not subject to the Interstate Commerce Act, and whose gross receipts for 1911 or 1912 exceeded $5 million dollars.[394] The bill declared "every corporation subject to the provisions of this Act . . . to be a quasi-public agency."[395]

This bill gave the government significant regulatory power over corporate affairs. For instance, the bill prohibited any corporation from selling its products at a price that was "unjust, unfair, or unreasonable."[396] The bill also required that "every practice, method, means, system, policy, device, scheme, or contrivance used by any corporation . . . shall be just, fair, and reasonable, and not contrary to public policy. . . ."[397] Additionally, the bill would have prohibited discrimination against persons based on their "locality or section of the country. . . ."[398]

---

[386] *Id.*
[387] *Id.*
[388] *Id.*
[389] *Id.*
[390] *Id.* at § 5.
[391] *Id.*
[392] *Id.*
[393] H.R. 1890, 63d Cong. (1913).
[394] *Id.* at § 1.
[395] *Id.* at § 2.
[396] *Id.* at § 3.
[397] *Id.* at § 4.
[398] *Id.* at § 5.

The regulatory teeth to these pronouncements came from the creation of the Interstate Corporation Commission, which would have replaced the existing Bureau of Corporations.[399] The Commission was to consist of seven members, with not more than four coming from the same political party.[400] The members were to be appointed by the President, with the advice and consent of the Senate.[401] The bill gave the Commission expansive power to create and enforce regulations.[402] Like Congressman Gardner's bill,[403] this bill would have made all Commission decisions final and reviewable only for questions of law.[404]

The bill gave the Commission authority to initiate investigations into a company's affairs and records in order to determine whether the corporation violated any provision of the Act.[405] Furthermore, a corporation formed under the Act would be liable to any person injured because of a violation of the Act for double the amount of actual damages sustained by such person.[406] A person claiming to be injured could either submit a complaint to the Commission or to the Commerce Court,[407] except that such person could not bring a complaint in both arenas.[408] The bill provided that any corporation or officer, director, agent, trustee, lessee, or receiver who willfully violated the Act may be liable for a fine of up to $5,000 and imprisoned for up to two years.[409]

S. 1913 BILL—SENATE—S. 1617

Less than a month after the introduction of H.R. 1890 in the House, Senator Albert Cummins of Iowa introduced a "tamer" bill entitled "a bill to further regulate commerce among the states and with foreign nations."[410] The bill was intended to "create

---

[399] *Id.* at §§ 7–8.

[400] *Id.* at § 9.

[401] *Id.*

[402] *Id.* ("The commission is hereby authorized and empowered to make and establish rules and regulations not in conflict with the Constitution and laws of the United States to aid in the administration and enforcement of the provisions of this Act.").

[403] *See supra* notes 347–382 & accompanying text.

[404] H.R. 1890, 63d Cong. § 9 (1913).

[405] *Id.* at § 15.

[406] *Id.* at § 10. Reasonable attorney's fees also would be awarded. *Id.*

[407] The United States Commerce Court was a short-lived specialized court set up by the Mann-Elkins Act in 1910. It had jurisdiction to review decisions of the Interstate Commerce Commission. It existed for only three years and was dissolved in 1913. *See Commerce Court, 1910–1913*, FEDERAL JUDICIAL CENTER, http://www.fjc.gov/history/home.nsf/page/courts_special_com.html (last visited Oct. 2, 2015).

[408] H.R. 1890, 63d Cong. § 11 (1913).

[409] *Id.* at § 12.

[410] S. 1617, 63d Cong. (1913).

and maintain competitive conditions in commerce among the States and with foreign nations," and was to be construed liberally to accomplish this purpose.[411] The bill did not apply to common carriers or corporations with less than $5 million in capital.[412]

This bill did not require that a corporation register with the federal government; instead it prohibited a subject corporation from conducting business in interstate commerce if it engaged in proscribed conduct as set forth in the bill.[413] For example, the bill prohibited a corporation's officers and directors from serving in the same capacity for a competitive corporation.[414] Further, corporations with capital of $10 million or greater were prohibited from having directors or officers who also served as officers or directors of a banking corporation.[415] Corporations were forbidden from holding stock in other corporations, except for a three-month period as collateral for a debt.[416] Likewise, a corporation was prohibited from engaging in specified anticompetitive practices.[417]

A violation of any of the bill's provisions was a misdemeanor.[418] A violative corporation was subject to a fine not exceeding ten percent of its capital stock, whereas an individual could be punished with a fine not exceeding $10,000 and/or imprisonment of up to one year.[419]

T. 1913 BILLS—HOUSE OF REPRESENTATIVES—H.R. 11167 AND H.R. 11168

On December 12, 1913, two virtually identical bills were presented in the House by Congressman Augustus Stanley of Kentucky[420] and Congressman Daniel McGillicuddy of Maine.[421] These bills were both entitled "a bill to prescribe the conditions under which corporations may engage in interstate commerce, and for other

---

[411] *Id.* at § 1.

[412] *Id.* at § 2.

[413] *See id.* at § 3.

[414] *Id.*

[415] *Id.*

[416] *Id.*

[417] *Id.* (For example: (1) "For a period of two months or more it regularly and generally sells the product or products in which it deals or which it manufactures below actual cost for the purpose of inflicting injury upon a competitor"; and (2) "The amount of capital employed is so great as to destroy or prevent substantially competitive conditions in the general field of industry in which the business carried on belongs.").

[418] *Id.* at § 4.

[419] *Id.*

[420] *See* H.R. 11167, 63d Cong. (1913) (A version of this bill was reintroduced in the following year with virtually the same provisions. *See* H.R. 12123, 63d Cong. (1914).).

[421] *See* H.R. 11168, 63d Cong. (1913).

purposes."[422] Like S. 1617, these bills did not require that a corporation register with the federal government; rather, they set out requirements to be included in the charters of corporations seeking to engage in interstate commerce.[423]

The bills prohibited corporations from owning or holding stock in corporations engaged in similar business, except to be held for up to 90 days as collateral.[424] Corporations were also prohibited from owning stock in common carriers.[425] The bills further barred officers, directors, and employees from serving in any of those roles in a competing business or common carrier.[426] The bill also contained a sweeping provision that a subject corporation had and could exercise "only such powers as are necessary or are incidental to its business."[427]

The bills also contained books and records requirements. The corporate books were required to reflect "every transfer of stock or of any right or interest."[428] This had to be done within 30 days of the transaction.[429] A willful failure to disclose the transfer of stock in the books would result in forfeiture of said stock.[430]

In addition to the requirements of both bills, Congressman Stanley's bill required that stock transferred for property or services rendered reflect actual value.[431] This bill required specific proof of the value of said property or services to be filed in a public office, designated by law in the state where the corporation was formed.[432] Representative Stanley's bill prohibited a company from issuing bonds in a greater amount than the sum of its outstanding capital stock and surplus; it also prohibited directors and stockholders from converting their stock into bonds.[433] Additionally, Representative Stanley's bill provided that a corporation that violated the Act would be subject to a fine not exceeding ten percent of its capital stock or dissolution of its charter, whereas an individual could be punished by fine not exceeding $10,000.[434] In case of a willful violation, a person may be subject to such fine and imprisonment of up to five years.[435]

---

[422] Bills cited *supra* notes 420–421.

[423] H.R. 11167, at § 1; H.R. 11168 at § 1. For discussion of S. 1617, *see supra* notes 410–419 & accompanying text.

[424] H.R. 11167, *supra* note 420, at § 1; H.R. 11168, *supra* note 421, at § 1.

[425] *Id.*

[426] *Id.*

[427] *Id.* ("No corporation, association, or partnership, including the business of a holding company, . . . shall be or act as for a stockholder or member thereof, or receive or hold any such stock, right, interest, or trust therein.").

[428] *Id.*

[429] *Id.*

[430] *Id.*

[431] H.R. 11167 at § 1.

[432] *Id.*

[433] *Id.*

[434] *Id.*

[435] *Id.* Although the bills are identical in other regards, Congressman McGillicuddy's bill—H.R. 11168—lacked any provision regarding penalties.

U. 1914 BILL—SENATE—S. 4647

The next bill to be introduced came from Senator Knute Nelson of Minnesota, and was titled "a bill for the regulation of corporations engaged in interstate commerce."[436] Senator Nelson's bill required that all corporations engaged in interstate commerce that were not subject to regulation by the Interstate Commerce Commission obtain a license from the Secretary of the Department of Commerce.[437] The bill also gave the Secretary the power to inspect, supervise, and regulate all such corporations.[438]

In order to obtain a license, a corporation was to make a written application to the Secretary of the Department of Commerce. The application included the company's articles of association and bylaws.[439] The filing then had to be verified by an oath from the president, secretary, and treasurer of the corporation.[440] If the oath was found to be false or untrue, the person making it was guilty of perjury, and upon conviction, would be punished by a fine of up to $10,000, imprisonment of up to three years, or both.[441]

The bill required that a corporation's board of directors keep a "directors' book," which was to contain "a full, true and correct record of all acts and transactions of the board pertaining to the business and property of the corporation. . . ."[442] The directors' book was open to inspection during reasonable business hours to all stockholders and bondholders of the corporation.[443] Furthermore, an authenticated copy of that book had to be filed with the Department of Commerce.[444] Failure to keep the book would result in a fine up to $5,000, imprisonment of up to two years, or

---

[436] S. 4647, 63d Cong. (1914).

[437] *Id.* at §§ 2–3.

[438] *Id.* at § 2.

[439] *Id.* at § 4.

[440] *Id.*

[441] *Id.* The bill did not require that the oath be knowingly false or untrue; however, because one making a false oath would be deemed to be guilty of perjury, an alleged violator would have needed to make such an oath with knowledge of its falsity. *See* 18 U.S.C. § 1621 (2012) ("whoever—(1) having taken an oath before a competent tribunal, officer, or person, in any case in which a law of the United States authorizes an oath to be administered, that he will testify, declare, depose, or certify truly, or that any written testimony, declaration, deposition, or certificate by him subscribed, *is true, willfully and contrary to such oath states or subscribes any material matter which he does not believe to be true*; or (2) in any declaration, certificate, verification, or statement under penalty of perjury as permitted under section 1746 of title 28, United States Code, willfully subscribes as true any material matter which he does not believe to be true; is guilty of perjury and shall, except as otherwise expressly provided by law, be fined under this title or imprisoned not more than five years, or both") (emphasis added); *see also* Charles Doyle, Cong. Research Serv., 98-807 excerpted from RL34303, *Perjury under Federal Law: A Brief Overview* 1 (2014) (stating that perjury has required willfulness since the framing of the Constitution).

[442] *Id.* at § 5.

[443] *Id.*

[444] *Id.*

both.[445] Furthermore, directors were jointly and severally liable in a civil action for "all damages which *any person* may sustain in consequence of" their failure to keep such a book.[446]

The bill also required that the presiding officer and secretary of every meeting of stockholders keep (or cause to be kept) a "Stockholders' book" to reflect "a full, true, and correct record of all business transactions" taking place at such meetings.[447] The Stockholders' book must also reflect any vote made at each such meeting along with the number of shares of each shareholder voting in either the negative or affirmative.[448] The book was open to inspection, during reasonable business hours, to the company's officers, bondholders, and stockholders.[449] Like the directors' book, an authenticated copy of the Stockholders' book had to be filed with the Department of Commerce.[450] The corporation's president and secretary of a shareholder meeting who failed to keep a record in such Stockholders' book were subject to fine and imprisonment as well as joint and several liability in a civil action for damages brought by "any person" who sustained injury as a result of the defendants' violative conduct.[451]

A company seeking to issue or dispose of capital stock, bonds, or other instruments first had to obtain the approval of the Secretary of Commerce.[452] This involved submitting an application to the Secretary detailing, for example, the character, location, and value of the corporation's property, the volume and nature of its business, the current amount of outstanding capital stock, the dividend available for each class of stock, and the maturity of all bonds along with the interests rates paid thereupon.[453] Additionally, the application had to state the purpose for issuing or disposing of the securities.[454] Like the application for a license, this application had to be verified by oath of the president, secretary, and treasurer, with the same penalties applying to persons making a false oath.[455]

---

[445] *Id.*

[446] *Id.* (emphasis added).

[447] *Id.* at § 6.

[448] *Id.*

[449] *Id.*

[450] *Id.*

[451] *Id.*

[452] *Id.* at § 7 (stating that "no corporation licensed under and pursuant to . . . this Act shall . . . be permitted to issue or dispose of any capital stock, bonds, or other obligations or securities . . . without first securing the permission and authority of the Secretary of Commerce").

[453] *Id.*

[454] *Id.*

[455] *Id.*

The bill prohibited corporations from holding the securities of other corporations.[456] Had the bill been passed, existing corporations would have been given one year to divest themselves of all of their holdings in other corporations.[457] If divestment was not made voluntarily, the secretary could obtain a court order mandating such.[458] Likewise, officers and directors were barred from serving the same role in competing corporations; the penalty for such was a fine of up to $5,000, imprisonment for up to two years, or both.[459]

The bill required all subject corporations to submit annual reports to the Secretary of Commerce.[460] These reports were to reflect an accurate description of the company's business, financial condition, and income.[461] The Secretary had the power under this bill to request additional reports at his discretion.[462] These reports were to be certified by oath; a person making a false statement could face a punishment of a $5,000 fine, imprisonment of up to two years, or both.[463] The bill also gave the Secretary, and employees of his department, access to inspect all "books, records, reports, memoranda, and minutes" of subject corporations.[464] The Secretary could also call upon any competent court to compel the production of documents or testimony of witnesses.[465] The Attorney General was given power to prosecute violations of the Act.[466]

A number of bills introduced between 1903 and 1914 were aimed at creating a federal corporate license; others went further seeking mandatory federal incorporation of companies engaging in interstate commerce.[467] Ultimately, however, no such federal licensing or federal incorporation law passed in this time period or in the years since.[468] Perhaps realizing that it would be difficult to pry incorporation from the

---

456 *Id.* at § 8.
457 *Id.*
458 *Id.*
459 *Id.*
460 *Id.* at § 9.
461 *Id.*
462 *Id.*
463 *Id.*
464 *Id.*
465 *Id.*
466 *Id.* at § 10.
467 *See, e.g.,* H.R. 66, *supra* note 31; H.R. 10704, *supra* note 74; S. 6186, *supra* note 224.
468 *See* S. 2567, *infra* note 532.

hands of the states,[469] much of the subsequent legislation sought to allow state incorporation, while providing significant federal oversight over such corporations.[470]

III. Establishment of the Federal Trade Commission and Subsequent Legislative Proposals (1914–1930)

Although ultimately none of the bills discussed above were enacted, these efforts were not totally unrewarded. In 1914, Congress enacted the Federal Trade Commission Act which established the Federal Trade Commission (FTC) and addressed many of the concerns regarding anticompetitive behavior.[471] However, the establishment of the FTC did not quell interest in this subject. Many subsequent bills were offered to ascribe more power to the FTC or to further regulate commerce. A number of these bills sought to amend individual sections of the FTC Act, and thus were not comprehensive pieces of legislation like their predecessors.

A. 1917 BILL—HOUSE OF REPRESENTATIVES—H.R. 315

In 1917, Congressman Joseph Walsh of Massachusetts sought to amend the Clayton Antitrust Act with H.R. 315.[472] His amendment would have allowed any director of a corporation to become a director of up to two more corporations, "if such corporations are or shall have been heretofore, by virtue of their business and location of operation, competitors, so that the elimination of competition by agreement between them would constitute a violation of any of the provisions of any of the antitrust laws."[473] A director wishing to undertake these directorships would have to first obtain the consent of the newly established FTC.[474]

---

[469] *See* William Cary, *Federalism and the Corporate Law: Reflections Upon Delaware*, 83 Yale L. J. 663, 664 (1974) (States began deriving significant revenue from the issuance of corporate charters which led to the so called "race to the bottom.").

[470] *See, e.g.*, H.R. 315, *infra* note 471; S. 1612, *infra* note 510.

[471] *See generally* "An Act to create a Federal Trade Commission, to define its powers and duties, and for other purposes. . . ." H.R. 15613, 63d Cong. (1914).

[472] A bill to further amend section eight of an Act entitled "An Act to supplement existing laws against unlawful restraints and monopolies, and for other purposes," approved October fifteenth, nineteen hundred and fourteen. H.R. 315, 65th Cong. (1917) (The bill itself is barely two pages in length.). The bill generally did not apply to banks, trust companies, and common carriers.

[473] *Id.* at § 1.

[474] *Id.* My wonderful mother Phyllis Marblestone Steinberg was born May 14, 1917.

B. 1917 BILL—HOUSE OF REPRESENTATIVES—H.R. 4425

A bill seeking to amend the Federal Trade Commission Act was introduced by Congressman John Marvin Jones of Texas.[475] This bill made it unlawful to sell stock, bonds, or other securities without prior notice of sale to the FTC.[476] It also required that a report be filed detailing the amount of outstanding capital stock, dividends paid, surplus funds, number of stockholders, amount of debt, cost and value of all property and other holdings, "number of employees and *salaries paid [to] each*," earnings, receipts, expenses, and the profits for the preceding year.[477] Any subject person who failed to submit the notice of sale and report to the FTC would be fined $100 per each delinquent day.[478]

C. 1919 BILL—HOUSE OF REPRESENTATIVES—H.R. 1186

A bill introduced in 1919 by Congressman Henry Steele of Pennsylvania required that any corporation engaged in interstate commerce obtain a license from the FTC.[479] Generally, pursuant to this bill, the FTC had the authority to institute proceedings if it believed that the corporation was engaged in proscribed activity.[480] A corporation that was believed to be engaging in wrongful activity was entitled to a hearing before the Commission.[481] If the charge was upheld, the Commission would recommend adjustments to the enterprise's business.[482] A corporation that refused to comply with such adjustments was subject to revocation of its license.[483]

---

475 "A bill to amend an Act approved September twenty-sixth, nineteen hundred and fourteen, known as the Federal Trade Commission Act. . . ." H.R. 4425, 65th Cong. (1917).

476 *Id.* at § 6a.

477 *Id.* (emphasis added). Also, the bill provided that the FTC "may" issue to the subject corporation a certificate setting forth that such corporation was in compliance with the Act's provisions. *Id.*

478 *Id.* at § 6b.

479 "A Bill to confer certain additional powers upon the Federal Trade Commission, and for other purposes. . . ." H.R. 1186, 66th Cong., §§ 2–3, 5 (1919).

480 *Id.* at § 3 (such as conducting "an unlawful monopoly" or engaging "in unfair competition or unreasonable restraint of commerce").

481 *Id.* ("Whenever the Commission shall have reason to believe that any such licensee is conducting such interstate commerce as an unlawful monopoly, or in unfair competition or unreasonable restraint of commerce, or to the detriment of the public, it shall issue and serve upon such person a complaint stating its charges in that respect and . . . [t]hat person or persons so complained of shall have the right to appear at the place and time so fixed and show cause why an order should not be entered by the commission requiring such person or persons to cease and desist from the practices so charged in such complaint.").

482 *Id.*

483 *Id.*

D. 1919 BILL—SENATE—S. 2754

The next bill, introduced in 1919, was entitled "a bill to provide for licensing corporations engaged in interstate commerce and to prevent monopolies and undue restraint of trade."[484] This bill required all corporations, excluding common carriers, that engaged in interstate commerce and whose stock and assets equaled $10 million or more to obtain a certificate of license from the FTC.[485] Furthermore, the bill allowed any corporation engaged in interstate commerce with less than $10 million of assets to voluntarily apply for a license.[486] Any corporation licensed under this bill would not be allowed to carry on the business of discounting notes, receiving deposits, or issuing bills or notes for circulation as money.[487]

In order to obtain a certificate of license, a corporation had to file an application with the FTC stating, for example, its name, state of creation, date of creation, nature of business, amount of capital stock issued and outstanding, "the number of shares in which the capital stock is divided and the par value of such shares," the number of directors, and the post office addresses of the directors and executive officers.[488] In transmitting the application, the president and treasurer were required to make sworn statements attesting to the application's truthfulness.[489] The Commission then examined the application to determine whether the corporation was engaged in any unlawful restraint of trade or was holding a monopoly.[490] Upon a satisfactory investigation, the corporation would be issued a certificate of license and be given the right to engage in interstate and foreign commerce.[491]

In issuing the license, the FTC was to make a determination that no stock was issued except for cash or an equal value of property.[492] The Commission was to make its own assessment of the value of property and would not be bound by the judgment of the board of directors.[493] In order for the FTC to make this assessment, any corporation that exchanged stock for property was required to file a statement with the Commission including: a full description of the property; the number of shares issued as payment and their aggregate par value, if any; the names and addresses of the vendors of that property; whether or not any such vendors were also officers or

---

484 S. 2754, 66th Cong. (1919).
485 *Id.* at § 1.
486 *Id.*
487 *Id.* at § 6.
488 *Id.* at § 2.
489 *Id.*
490 *Id.* at § 3.
491 *Id.*
492 *Id.* at § 7.
493 *Id.*

directors of the corporation; and the terms of the agreement.[494] If the property was sold by an officer or director, the corporation was required to file all contracts held by such person pertaining to the purchase of said property.[495]

The bill allowed a corporation whose application for a certificate of license was refused to bring suit in a federal district court for review.[496] The court was given jurisdiction to review the Commission's decision based "*both on law and the facts.*"[497] This provision gave the court power to allow the corporation to continue in commerce while a suit was pending.[498] Upon a finding that the business of the corporation did not involve an undue restraint of trade or monopoly, the court was to issue an order requiring the FTC to grant said license.[499]

The bill included a general prohibition against corporations purchasing or holding stock in competing businesses.[500] However, a corporation seeking to engage in such conduct could apply to the FTC for approval. [501] The Commission would then examine the facts and circumstances surrounding the purchase to determine whether there was a significant risk that a monopoly or undue restraint on trade would be created.[502] Likewise, any increase in capital stock required pre-approval from the Commission.[503]

The bill required annual reports to be filed with the FTC.[504] The Commission could also require special reports when necessary to "secure a full and complete knowledge of the condition of [the] corporation."[505] Additionally, a report was to be filed with the FTC when a corporation declared a dividend.[506] A corporation that failed to timely make a report would be subject to a $100 per diem fine.[507] The bill gave the Commission power to inquire into a company's organization, conduct, and management in order to obtain necessary information.[508] Furthermore, it

---

[494] *Id.*
[495] *Id.*
[496] *Id.* at § 4.
[497] *Id.* (emphasis added).
[498] *Id.*
[499] *Id.*
[500] *Id.* at § 8.
[501] *Id.*
[502] *Id.* ("It shall thereupon be the duty of the Commission to inquire as to the facts and whether the purchase of said property *would tend to create a monopoly or to unduly restrain trade and commerce.*") (emphasis added).
[503] *Id.* at § 10.
[504] *Id.* at § 9.
[505] *Id.*
[506] *Id.*
[507] *Id.*
[508] *Id.* at § 12.

allowed a person complaining of unlawful conduct by a corporation to petition the Commission to engage in an investigation.[509]

E. 1921 BILL—SENATE—S. 1612

Two years later a bill was filed that would have also required corporations to register with the FTC.[510] This bill would have amended Section 6a of the Clayton Act to require that a corporation file a statement along with its articles of incorporation and bylaws with the Commission before it was allowed to issue stock, bonds, or other securities.[511] The provisions to be set forth in the statement included: the name and purpose of the corporation; its location; amount of capital stock; "the consideration for which stock had been and will be issued;" what the capital will be used for; a description of corporate assets and liabilities; the names of the promoters and underwriters involved in the sale; and copies of all promotion contracts and agreements.[512]

The bill also required a corporation offering securities to affix a legend on any prospectus, letter, or any advertisement for securities.[513] This legend was required to include the names of the promoters, fiscal agents, and underwriters of the corporation; the rate of commission and bonuses received from promoting, underwriting, or selling the securities; the net amount to be received by the sale; and a statement that information regarding the offering had been filed with the FTC.[514] The bill provided penalties for anyone who willfully violated the Act or willfully made a false statement in any of the required filings.[515] Such person would be guilty of a misdemeanor and subject to a fine of up to $5,000, imprisonment of not more than a year, or both.[516]

---

[509] *Id.* at § 13.

[510] "A bill to regulate the sale of bonds, stocks, and other evidences of interest in or indebtedness of corporations or associations in interstate commerce, and to amend an Act approved October 15, 1914, entitled 'An Act to supplement existing laws against unlawful restraints and monopolies, and for other purposes. . . .'" S. 1612, 67th Cong. § 1 (1921).

[511] *Id.* This amendment is excerpted in its entirety in Appendix I of this chapter.

[512] *Id.*

[513] *Id.*

[514] *Id.* The securities offering process, including the registration and disclosure regimen, was addressed in the Securities Act of 1933. *See generally* Marc I. Steinberg, *Securities Regulation* 221–341 (7th ed. 2017).

[515] S. 1612, 67th Cong. §1 (1921).

[516] *Id.*

F. 1930 BILL—SENATE—S. 2847

A bill introduced by Senator Smith Brookhart of Iowa in 1930 is the only bill since 1914 that proposed mandatory federal incorporation or licensing of interstate corporations.[517] The bill, entitled, "a bill to provide for the licensing of corporations engaged in interstate or foreign commerce," stated that it was unlawful for any corporation to engage in interstate commerce without obtaining a license from the FTC.[518] The bill required the filing of a statement of the corporation's capital investment, transactions made in interstate or foreign commerce, the gross and net earnings of the corporation, and the salaries of its managing officers.[519] Additionally, all corporations subject to the Act were required to issue annual reports including the same information.[520]

The bill required approval by the Commission of the managing officers' salaries.[521] Furthermore, under the bill, dividends were limited to five percent of capital investment and were required to be paid from net earnings.[522] Net earnings in excess of the amount authorized for dividends were required to be paid into a guaranty fund held by the United States.[523] In years where a corporation could not afford to pay a dividend, such dividend would be paid from its guaranty fund with the approval of the FTC.[524] Willful violation of the Act would result in a fine of up to $10,000, imprisonment of not more than five years, or both.[525]

G. 1930 BILL—HOUSE OF REPRESENTATIVES—H.R. 12810

In 1930, a bill was introduced to control the distribution of goods and wares.[526] This bill prohibited anyone from purchasing stock in corporations where such a purchase would exceed 49 percent "of the distribution of any line of goods, wares, merchandise, or other commodity, whether patented or unpatented, in interstate

---

[517] FTC Report, *supra* note 29, at 42.

[518] S. 2847, 71st Cong. § 1 (1930).

[519] *Id.*

[520] *Id.* at § 2.

[521] *Id.* at § 3. For a discussion of modern day "Say-on-Pay" provisions, *see* Modern Day Relevance, *infra* notes 559–561 & accompanying text; discussion Chapters 4, 5 herein.

[522] S. 2847, 71st Cong. § 3 (1930).

[523] *Id.* at §§ 3–4.

[524] *Id.* at § 3.

[525] *Id.* at § 5.

[526] "A bill providing for the prevention of monopolies and the control of the distribution of goods, wares, merchandise, and other commodities in interstate commerce: requiring affidavits in civil actions in United States courts that antitrust laws have not been violated, and for other purposes. . . ." H.R. 12810, 71st Cong. (1930).

commerce. . . ."[527] The bill also required annual reports to the Secretary of Commerce that set forth the corporation's amount of total distribution of any line of goods, wares, or other commodity by interstate commerce during the past year.[528] If a corporation was found to have violated these provisions, it could file an affidavit with the court that it did not willingly violate the Act.[529]

The concerns of some Senators and Congressmen were alleviated with the passage of the Securities Act[530] and Securities Exchange Act[531] in 1933 and 1934 respectively. However, advocates of pure federal incorporation were still left wanting more. While subsequent legislation has increased regulation of boardrooms, the concept of mandating federal licensing or federal incorporation fell out of favor and has not been seen since Senator Brookhart's bill in 1930.

IV. A Re-Emergence of Corporate Governance Legislative Proposals

In the period following the establishment of the SEC, the topic of corporate governance as a matter of federal legislation largely laid dormant until 1980, when Senator Howard Metzenbaum of Ohio introduced a bill designed to establish minimum standards of corporate governance.[532] The bill was designed to regulate officers and directors, who Senator Metzenbaum believed had been corrupted by self-interest and lax oversight.[533] Furthermore, he believed that the role of the shareholder had diminished, and wished to "expand the role of the shareholder in the corporate world."[534]

The bill was designed to apply to corporations engaged in or affecting interstate commerce that either:

> (A) had inventories, gross property, plant, and equipment which aggregated more than $100,000,000 and which comprised more than 10 per centum of the

---

527 *Id.* at § 1.

528 *Id.* at § 2.

529 *Id.* at § 3.

530 Codified at 15 U.S.C. § 77a et seq. (2012).

531 Codified at 15 U.S.C. § 78a et seq. (2012).

532 "A Bill to establish Federal minimum standards relating to composition of corporate boards, duties of corporate directors, audit and nomination committees, shareholders' rights, and for other purposes. . . ." S. 2567, 96th Cong. (1980).

533 126 Cong. Rec. 7989 (1980).

534 *Id.* at 7990.

total assets of the affected corporation, or (B) had $100,000,000 in totals sales or revenues, or (C) had 1,000,000,000 in total assets.[535]

The bill also allowed a corporation to be exempt from certain provisions if it was incorporated in a state that contained stricter or similar requirements to those set forth in the bill.[536] However, no corporation could opt out of Section 4 of the Act, relating to duties of directors.[537]

Section 4 codified a director's duty of loyalty.[538] It provided that "a director shall perform his duties as a director . . . in a manner such that the director does not use his corporate position to make a personal profit or gain other personal advantage."[539] The bill required a director to: disclose any material interest in a contract or transaction in which the corporation, directly or indirectly, is a party;[540] ascertain whether the proposed transaction is on "at least as favorable terms to the affected corporation as might be available from any other person or entity";[541] present business opportunities to the corporation that come to the director's attention due to her relation to the subject corporation, even if she could personally benefit therefrom;[542] and deal in confidence in all corporate matters, unless they are public knowledge.[543] The bill also federally mandated a duty of care requiring a director to act in the good faith best interests of the corporation "and with such care as an ordinarily prudent person in a like position would use under similar circumstances."[544]

Senator Metzenbaum believed that the way to build an accountable corporation was to require a majority of directors on the board to be independent, signifying that such an independent director does not have a significant economic or personal relationship with the subject corporation.[545] Therefore, the bill forbid the following persons from being deemed independent: any person who had been an officer or employee of the corporation, or its parent or subsidiaries, within the past five years; any person related to an executive officer of the corporation or its affiliates; any lawyer who earned over

---

[535] S. 2567, 96th Cong. § 3(a)(3) (1980).

[536] *Id.* at § 3(b)(2).

[537] *Id.* at § 3(b)(3).

[538] *Id.* at § 4(a).

[539] *Id.*

[540] *Id.* at § 4(a)(1).

[541] *Id.* at § 4(a)(2).

[542] *Id.* at § 4(a)(3).

[543] *Id.* at § 4(a)(4).

[544] *Id.* at § 4(b).

[545] *See Protection of Shareholder's Rights Act of 1980, Hearing on S. 2567, Before the Subcommittee on Securities of the S. Comm. On Banking, Housing, & Urban Affairs*, 96 Cong. 4–12 (Statement of Sen. Howard M. Metzenbaum).

$10,000 in fees from the corporation; any director, officer, or employee of any investment banking firm providing substantial services to the corporation; and any supplier of the corporation if the affected corporation's business represented more than one percent of such supplier's revenues or who received more than $5 million in revenues from that corporation.[546] Furthermore, none of the individuals described above were eligible to serve on the company's audit or nominating committee.[547]

To aid in enforcement, the bill included shareholders' actions.[548] This provision allowed a shareholder to enforce any provision of the Act by filing a civil action.[549] The action could be filed in the district where the act or transaction causing the alleged violation occurred or in any jurisdiction where the corporation transacted business.[550] A prevailing shareholder would be entitled to litigation costs, including attorney's fees.[551]

Although well intended, the bill and its ideas drew criticism from academics and practitioners alike, with a future SEC Chairman remarking that there was simply a lack of demand for this legislation among shareholders.[552] Likewise the then Chairman of the SEC, Harold M. Williams, while sharing Senator Metzenbaum's concerns regarding corporate governance, believed that enactment of the bill would be contrary to the best interests of the economy.[553] Perhaps before its time, Senator Metzenbaum's bill died in committee despite his efforts.

V. Modern Day Relevance

A. SUBSEQUENT LEGISLATION

Although all of the bills discussed above were not enacted, several of their provisions found their way into American corporate governance. For instance, many of the earliest bills sought to exclude directors from serving the same position at

---

546 S. 2567, 96th Cong. § 5(a)–(b) (1980).

547 *See id.* at §§ 6–7. Note that several of these concepts have been adopted today pursuant to the Sarbanes-Oxley Dodd-Frank Acts (*see infra* notes 554–578 and accompanying text, discussion Chapter 5 herein, as well as SEC and stock exchange rules (*see* Chapters 5, 6 herein)).

548 S. 2567, 96th Cong. § 10 (1980).

549 *Id.* at § 10(a).

550 *Id.* at § 10(b).

551 *Id.* at § 10(a).

552 *The Role of the Shareholder in the Corporate World: Hearings Before the Subcommittee on Citizens and Shareholders Rights and Remedies of the Committee on the Judiciary*, U.S. Senate, 95th Cong., 1st Sess. 59 (June 27, 28, 1977) (statement of David S. Ruder, Dean of the Northwestern University School of Law and subsequently Chairman of the SEC).

553 *Protection of Shareholders Rights Act of 1980, Hearings Before the Subcommittee on Securities of the Committee on Banking, Housing, and Urban Affairs*, U.S. Senate, 96th Cong. 6 (Nov. 18, 1980) (Statement of SEC Chairman Harold M. Williams).

competing corporations.[554] This provision was codified in the Clayton Act of 1914.[555] Specifically Section 19 of that Act states that:

> (1) No person shall, at the same time, serve as a director or officer in any two corporations (other than banks, banking associations, and trust companies) that are—
> (A) engaged in whole or in part in commerce; and
> (B) by virtue of their business and location of operation, competitors, so that the elimination of competition by agreement between them would constitute a violation of any of the antitrust laws; if each of the corporations has capital, surplus, and undivided profits aggregating more than $10,000,000 as adjusted pursuant to paragraph (5) of this subsection.
> (2) Notwithstanding the provisions of paragraph (1), simultaneous service as a director or officer in any two corporations shall not be prohibited by this section if—
> (A) the competitive sales of either corporation are less than $1,000,000, as adjusted pursuant to paragraph (5)[556] of this subsection;
> (B) the competitive sales of either corporation are less than 2 per centum of that corporation's total sales; or
> (C) the competitive sales of each corporation are less than 4 per centum of that corporation's total sales.[557]

Likewise, Senator Metzenbaum was concerned about directors who were not independent. Today, pursuant to the Sarbanes-Oxley Act and stock exchange regulation, a majority of directors serving on subject company boards must be independent and the audit and compensation committees must be comprised entirely of independent directors.[558]

---

[554] *See, e.g.,* S. 1377, 62d Cong., § 1 (1911).

[555] Prohibition of interlocking directorates between competing corporations under Section 8 of Clayton Act (15 U.S.C.A. § 19 (2012)), 60 A.L.R. Fed. 129, 1c (2015).

[556] 15 U.S.C. § 19(5) (2012)—"For each fiscal year commencing after September 30, 1990, the $10,000,000 and $1,000,000 thresholds in this subsection shall be increased (or decreased) as of October 1 each year by an amount equal to the percentage increase (or decrease) in the gross national product, as determined by the Department of Commerce or its successor, for the year then ended over the level so established for the year ending September 30, 1989. As soon as practicable, but not later than January 31 of each year, the Federal Trade Commission shall publish the adjusted amounts required by this paragraph."

[557] 15 U.S.C. § 19 (2012).

[558] *See* discussion Chapters 5, 6 herein; *The Role of the Shareholder in the Corporate World: Hearings Before the Subcommittee on Citizens' and Shareholders' Rights and Remedies of the Senate Committee on the Judiciary, 95th Cong., 1st Sess., pg. 5* (1977) ("The [Senate Advisory Committee on Corporate Governance] endorsed a number of specific reforms such as: At least a majority of the members of boards of directors of publicly-owned

One bill, introduced in 1930, required that the Commission of Corporations approve officers' salaries.[559] Although the United States has never adopted this rigid of a mandate, measures have been introduced designed to curtail excessive executive compensation. For instance, since the Dodd-Frank Wall Street Reform and Consumer Protection Act, shareholders must hold a non-binding vote, at least every three years, providing an advisory voice with respect to executive compensation.[560] Note that these votes are purely advisory and are not binding on the corporation.[561]

Another bill, introduced in 1912, required a subject corporation to submit an independent auditor's certification of such corporation's financial statements before its charter could be approved.[562] Almost 100 years later, auditors and audit committees became an important part of the Sarbanes-Oxley Act of 2002 (SOX).[563] SOX increases the independence requirements of auditors in order to curtail sweetheart deals and lax oversight.[564] Specifically, a firm performing a company's audit is forbidden from providing:

> bookkeeping or other services related to the accounting records or financial statements of the audit client; financial information systems design and implementation; appraisal or valuation services, fairness opinions, or contribution-in-kind reports; actuarial services; internal audit outsourcing services; management functions or human resources; broker or dealer, investment adviser, or investment banking services; legal services and expert services unrelated to the audit; and any other service that the Board determines, by regulation, is impermissible.[565]

---

corporations should be 'outside' directors or 'independent' of management. . . .") (statement of Senator Howard M. Metzenbaum).

[559] S. 2847, 71st Cong. § 3 (1930).

[560] Dodd-Frank Wall Street Reform Act § 951 (adding § 14A to the Securities Exchange Act of 1934); SEC Final Rules on Shareholder Approval of Executive Compensation and Golden Parachute Compensation, Securities Exchange Act Release No. 63768 (2011). Note that executive compensation must be extensively disclosed pursuant to SEC mandate. *See* Item 402 of SEC Regulation S-K, 17 C.F.R. § 229.402 (2017).

[561] *See* discussion Chapters 4, 5 herein; Randall S. Thomas, Alan R. Palmiter, and James F. Cotter, *Dodd-Frank's Say on Pay: Will It Lead to a Greater Role for Shareholders in Corporate Governance?*, 97 Cornell L. Rev. 1213, 1215 (2012).

[562] H.R. 17932, 62d Cong. § 53 (1912).

[563] *See generally* Sandra C. Vera-Munoz, *Corporate Governance Reforms: Redefined Expectations of Audit Committee Responsibilities and Effectiveness*, 62 J. Bus. Ethics 115 (2005). Note that the Sarbanes-Oxley Act established the Public Company Accounting Oversight Board (PCAOB), requiring that auditors of U.S. publicly-held enterprises be subject to independent and external oversight.

[564] Sarbanes-Oxley Act of 2002, Pub. L. No. 107-204, § 201(a), 116 Stat. 747 (2002).

[565] *Id.*

Likewise, SOX also required that auditors make periodic reports to the corporation's audit committee in regard to the company's accounting principles and treatment of financial information.[566]

SOX also includes heightened requirements for audit committee members. The Act requires that each director on the audit committee be independent, meaning that such director: does not "accept any consulting, advisory, or other compensatory fee from the issuer" or is not "an affiliated person of the issuer or any subsidiary thereof."[567] The term "affiliate person," although not defined in the Act, generally signifies one "who controls, is controlled by, or is under common control with (either directly or indirectly, through one or more intermediaries) such issuer."[568] In this regard, SOX provides comparable specific requirements for audit committees as S. 2567, introduced by Senator Metzenbaum in 1980.[569]

To date, the federal government has not codified a director's or officer's fiduciary duties. Nonetheless, several provisions of SOX have the effect of limiting an officer's or director's opportunity to breach.[570] For example, SOX generally prohibits directors and officers from drawing loans from the corporation,[571] sets forth SEC-favorable standards for officer and director bars,[572] institutes a provision by which the SEC can recover executive bonuses in the event of misconduct,[573] imposes

---

566 *Id.* at § 204(k).

567 *Id.* at § 301.

568 Marc I. Steinberg, *Understanding Securities Law* 483 (6th ed. 2014); SEC Rule 405, 17 C.F.R. § 230.405 (2017). *See generally* Alexander Poor and Michelle Reed, *The "Control" Quagmire: The Cumbersome Concept of "Control" for the Corporate Attorney,"* 44 Sec. Reg. L.J. 101 (2016).

569 *See* S. 2567, 96th Cong. § 3 (1980) (forbidding any person who had been an officer or employee of the corporation, or its parent or subsidiaries, in the past five years; any person related to an officer or director of the corporation or its affiliates; any lawyer who earned over $10,000 dollars in fees from the corporation; any director, officer, or employee of any investment banking firm providing substantial services to the corporation; any supplier of the corporation if the affected corporation's business represented more than one percent of the supplier's revenue or who received more than five million dollars in revenue from that corporation from being a member of the audit committee). For determination of whether a director is independent today, *see* the SEC definition at 17 C.F.R. § 229.407 (2017), and the New York Stock Exchange definition at NYSE Listed Company Manual Rule 303A.02; discussion Chapters 5, 6 herein.

570 *See generally* Lyman P.Q. Johnson and Mark A. Sides, *Corporate Governance and the Sarbanes-Oxley Act: The Sarbanes-Oxley Act and Fiduciary Duties*, 30 Wm. Mitchell L. Rev 1149 (2004).

571 Sarbanes-Oxley Act of 2002, Pub. L. No. 107-204, § 402(k) (2002) (providing an exception where the subject corporation transacts loans in the ordinary course of business and if the officer or director is extended the subject loan on the same terms as loans made to the general public).

572 Sarbanes-Oxley § 305; *see* Steinberg, *supra* note 568, at 178 (6th ed. 2014) ("SOX lowers the standard for barring individuals from being officers and directors of publicly held companies. Previously, a court had authority to bar a securities law violator from serving as a director or officer of a publicly-held enterprise who was found liable for securities fraud and held to be 'substantially unfit.' SOX lowers that standard to 'unfitness.'").

573 Sarbanes-Oxley Act § 304.

heightened disclosure requirements on reporting companies,[574] and mandates that public companies adopt internal controls to help ensure the accuracy of financial reporting.[575]

One of the ways in which several of the bills above attempted to induce officers to conduct business with adequate transparency was with the use of certifications.[576] Likewise, SOX includes provisions that require a subject company's CEO and CFO to sign the corporation's annual and quarterly SEC reports certifying the report's accuracy and attesting to the corporation's design and effectiveness of internal controls over financial reporting.[577] In addition to subjecting the company and certifying officers to a government enforcement action, material misrepresentations or nondisclosure contained in such reports can subject these persons to private liability under the securities laws.[578]

B. JUDICIAL ACTION

Several bills sought to impose a federal fiduciary duty of loyalty.[579] This is one area of state law that subsequent attention has been reluctant to bring within the confines of federal law. Even after the enactment of the Securities Act and Securities Exchange Act, many commentators observed that state law "inadequately protected shareholders from overreaching by management."[580] Because of this perceived shortcoming, some called for expansion of the general antifraud provisions, Section 10(b) of the Securities Exchange Act and SEC Rule 10b-5 promulgated thereunder, to include federal standards of corporate responsibility, with the SEC serving as a "watchdog for all corporate activity."[581] However, the Supreme Court declined

[574] *Id.* at § 408 (adopting a continuous reporting regime).

[575] *Id.* at § 404. *See* discussion Chapter 5 herein.

[576] *See, e.g.*, S. 6238, *supra* note 60, at § 7 (requiring sworn statements from all officers at the time of filing articles of association attesting that the company was solvent, was being carried on for legitimate purpose, and was not in restraint of trade); H.R. 17932, *supra* note 287, at § 9 (requiring the president, treasurer, and a majority of the directors to sign and swear, certifying to a true copy of the agreement of association); S. 6186, *supra* note 226, at § 18 (requiring an "oath of truthfulness," signed by the corporate treasurer and at least three directors, to accompany a corporation's annual reports).

[577] Sarbanes-Oxley Act of 2002, Pub. L. No. 107-204, §§ 302(a), 906 (2002).

[578] Certification of Disclosure in Companies' Quarterly and Annual Reports, 17 C.F.R. pts. 228, 229, 232, 240, 249, 270, and 274 at § II(b)(6) (2002), *available at* http://www.sec.gov/rules/final/33-8124.htm; discussion Chapter 5 herein.

[579] *See* S. 4874, 60th Cong. § 11 (1908), H.R. 66, 58th Cong. § 17, H.R. 473, 59th Cong. § 2. (This was mainly in the context of directors engaging in self-dealing in connection with a subject company's purchase of property.)

[580] *See* Ralph C. Ferrara and Marc I. Steinberg, *A Reappraisal of Santa Fe: Rule 10b-5 and the New Federalism*, 129 U. Pa. L. Rev. 263, 265 (1980) (sources cited therein).

[581] *Id.* at 269.

to extend the scope of Section 10(b) to encompass substantive fairness in *Santa Fe Industries v. Green*.[582]

Santa Fe involved the merger of the Kirby Lumber Corporation into its parent, Santa Fe Industries, Inc., which owned 96 percent of Kirby's stock. Availing itself of the Delaware short-form merger statute, under which a parent that owns at least 90 percent of a subsidiary's outstanding stock can absorb the subsidiary without being required to obtain approval by the shareholders of either corporation, Santa Fe informed the Kirby minority shareholders that they were now out of the picture, that they would receive $150 per share in cash, and that, if dissatisfied, they could seek appraisal in the Delaware courts.

The materials sent to the Kirby shareholders contained facts and figures that convinced the plaintiff, William Green, that his stock was actually worth at least $772 a share. Green did not claim that these materials were deceptive. Instead, his basic premise was that the gross undervaluation of the shares was itself a "fraud" within the meaning of that term as used in Rule 10b-5. Therefore, Green asserted that Santa Fe had committed a wrong under federal law, and that he was entitled to redress for that wrong.

The Supreme Court thoroughly rejected Green's contention, ruling that "the transaction was neither deceptive nor manipulative and therefore did not violate" Section 10(b) or Rule 10b-5.[583] Moreover, the Court made clear that a Section 10(b)/Rule 10b-5 claim requires some act of misrepresentation or nondisclosure.[584] Although recognizing the thorny problem of fiduciary self-dealing, the Court refused to extend the scope of the federal securities laws beyond the parameters of disclosure. As the Court reasoned, "there may well be a need for uniform federal fiduciary standards to govern mergers such as that challenged in this complaint. But those standards should not be supplied by judicial extension of § 10(b) and Rule 10b-5 to 'cover the corporate universe.'"[585]

VI. Conclusion

As seen in the foregoing discussion, the concept of federalizing corporate governance in the United States has been advocated, with varying degrees of vigor, for well over a century. This chapter focuses on the paths undertaken by legislative proponents in their quests to mandate federal regulation of corporations. Although the

---

582 *Santa Fe Indus., Inc. v. Green*, 430 US 462 (1977); Ferrara and Steinberg, *supra* note 580, at 272–77.

583 *Santa Fe Indus.*, 430 U.S. at 474.

584 *Id.* at 475–76.

585 *Id.* at 479–80. The Supreme Court's decision in *Santa Fe* also is discussed in Chapters 1, 3 herein.

extent of these requirements differed in the bills introduced, these bills all were directed at improving corporate governance practices that were perceived as being deficient. That none of these bills became law does not nullify their historical significance. They continue to play an ongoing role in the corporate governance dialogue. Indeed, a number of these provisions today are a part of the federal securities laws and self-regulatory organization regimen. Thus, the importance of these federal corporation governance efforts from long ago remain timely and relevant.

Appendix I

In the early part of the twentieth century there were numerous attempts to regulate corporations at the federal level. Although the objectives of these bills were similar, the methods used to achieve these objectives differed. Most bills were mandatory, yet others allowed for voluntary adherence. Likewise, while many bills called for registration or licensing at the federal level, some of the bills called for solely state chartering. Below is a compilation of some of the more interesting provisions from a number of the bills.

A. THE FIRST ATTEMPT—H.R. 66 (1903)

Representative Henry Palmer submitted in 1903 the first bill designed to provide a method for federal incorporation.[586] Many of the provisions of this first bill became staples in later attempts at federal incorporation.[587] Some relevant sections of this bill are included below along with the preamble.

> Whereas in article one, section eight, of the Constitution of the United States it is provided that the Congress shall have power to regulate commerce with foreign nations and among the Several States; and
>
> Whereas in the development of commerce of this nation with foreign nations and among the Several States a large proportion thereof has fallen into the hands of, and is now conducted by, corporations organized under the laws of the several States of the Federal Union; and
>
> Whereas it is for the interest of the people of the United States that corporations engaged in such commerce with foreign nations and among the several

[586] H.R. 66, 58th Cong. (1903). *See supra* notes 31–49 & accompanying text.

[587] Compare, for example, the provisions of the Taft-Wickersham bills excerpted below.

States should be directly accountable to the sovereign power of the Federal Government rather than to any one State: Therefore,

[SECTION 1] *Be it enacted by the Senate and House of Representatives of the United States of America in Congress assembled,* That corporations may be formed under the provisions of this Act for the purpose of engaging in commerce with the foreign nations or among the several States by the voluntary association of five or more persons in the manner mentioned herein, and when so formed each of them by virtue of its existence as such shall have the following powers, unless otherwise specially provided:

First. To have succession by its corporate name for the time stated in its charter and, when no period is limited thereby, perpetually, subject to the power of Congress to alter, revoke, or annul its charter whenever, in their opinion, it may be injurious to the citizens of the United States, in such manner, however, that no injustice shall be done to the incorporators.

Second. To maintain and defend judicial proceedings in any court.

Third. To make and use a common seal and alter the same at pleasure.

Fourth. To hold, purchase, and convey such real and personal estate, including stocks and bonds issued by other corporations, as the purposes of the corporation shall require, and all other property which shall have been in good faith mortgaged or conveyed to such corporation by way of security or in consideration of debts, or purchased at sale upon judgment or decree obtained for such debts, and to mortgage any such real or personal estate with franchises. The power to hold real and personal estate shall include the power to take the same by devise or bequest.

Fifth. To appoint and remove all necessary or proper officers and agents and to fix their compensation and define their powers and duties.

Sixth. To issue one or more classes of stock.

Seventh. To make by-laws consistent with the law fixing the number of its directors, and for its government, the regulation of its affairs, the management of its property, and for the certification and transfer of stock.

Eighth. To wind up or dissolve itself or be wound and be dissolved in the manner hereinafter mentioned.

Sec. 3. That the charter of an intended corporation shall be subscribed by five or more persons, all of whom must be citizens of the United States, and shall set forth:

First. The name of the corporation, which shall be such as to distinguish it from any other corporation chartered by or organized under the laws of the United States.

Second. The Countries and States in which its business is to be transacted.

Third. The county and States in which its principal office is to be located.

Fourth. The period, if any, limited for its existence.

Fifth. The names and residences of the subscribers and the number of shares subscribed by each.

Sixth. The number of its directors, and the names and residences of those who are chosen directors for the first year.

Seventh. The amount of the authorized capital stock which shall not be less than two thousand dollars, the number of shares in which the same is divided and the par value of each share, which shall not be less than twenty-five dollars, and if there be more than one class of stock, a description of the different classes with the terms on which they are respectively granted.

Eighth. The value of real and personal estate of which the corporation may become seized and possessed.

Ninth. The highest amount of indebtedness or liability which the corporation may at any time incur.

Tenth. Whether the private property of the stockholders, not subject by the provisions of this Act, shall be subject to the payment of corporate debts, and if so, to what extent.

Notice of the intention to apply for any such charter shall be inserted in one newspaper of general circulation, printed in the city of Washington, and in the county in which the principal office of the corporation is to be located for three weeks setting forth the names of the subscribers, the name of the proposed corporation, and the intention to make application therefore.

Sec. 4. That certificate of incorporation may also contain any provisions which the incorporators may choose to insert for the regulation of the business and for the conduct of the corporation, and any provisions creating, defining, limiting, and regulating the powers of the corporation, the direct[ors] and the stockholder[s], or any classes of the stockholders: *Provided,* that such provisions are not contrary to this Act or to the Constitution of the United States.

Sec. 5. That the said certificate of incorporation shall state, in addition to the requirements of section three, that ten per centum on the capital stock thereof has been paid in cash to the treasurer of the intended corporation, and shall set forth the name and residence of such treasurer. The same shall be sworn to and be acknowledged by at least three of the subscribers thereto before an officer authorized to take affidavits and acknowledgements, and shall be filed, together with proof of the publication of notice, as hereinbefore provided, in the office of the Secretary of the Department of Commerce and Labor, who shall examine the same; and if he shall find it conforms to law, and that all taxes which may be due upon the filing of the certificate under the provisions of the next succeeding section shall have been paid, he shall indorse thereon the word 'Approved,' with his name and official title, and shall thereupon record such certificate in a book kept by him for that purpose. He shall furnish a certified copy of every such certificate, and of his approval thereof, to the person filing the same, who shall forthwith file such certified copy in the recording office of the county in which the principal office of the corporation is situated, and the same shall be recorded in a book kept for that purpose by the recorder of deeds or officer exercising similar powers . . .

Sec. 11. That the business of every corporation created hereunder shall be managed by a board of not less than three directors, each of whom shall hold in his own right not less than ten shares of capital stock; they shall hold office until their successors are respectively elected and qualified; a majority of the directors shall constitute a quorum for the transaction of business; they shall be chosen annually by the stockholders at the time fixed by the by-laws and may fill any vacancy, however arising, in their board or in the offices of the company for the unexpired portion of the term; at least once in each year they shall make a full and detailed report of the financial condition of the corporation to its stockholders, which report shall be filed with the treasurer of the corporation and be subject to the inspection of the stockholders at all reasonable times. The members of the corporation may, at a meeting to be called for that purpose, determine, fix, or change the number of directors that shall thereafter govern its affairs and may divide the directors into one, two, or three classes, the terms of office of those of the first class to expire at the annual meeting next ensuing, of the second class one year thereafter, and of the third class two years thereafter; and at each annual election held after such classification directors shall be chosen for the full term, as the case may be to succeed those whose terms have expired.

B. S. 1612—AMENDMENT TO THE CLAYTON ACT (1921)

Following the creation of the Federal Trade Commission in 1914, many bills sought to give more power to the FTC. One such bill, introduced by Senator Arthur Capper in 1921, would have accomplished this goal by amending the Clayton Act of 1914 to broaden the FTC's power. The proposed amendment to the Clayton Act is excerpted in its entirety.

No person, firm, partnership, association, or corporation shall sell, or offer for sale, to the public in interstate commerce, bonds, stocks, or other evidences of interest in or indebtedness of any corporation or association (hereinafter described as securities) through the United States mails or any other medium of transportation whatsoever until such corporation or association shall file with the Federal Trade Commission at Washington, District of Columbia, a statement in the manner hereinafter provided, together with a copy of its articles of incorporation and by-laws, before any such securities are offered for sale. *Provided, however*, That this Act shall not apply to any corporation or association subject to the jurisdiction of the Interstate Commerce Commission under the provisions of the Transportation Act 1920 or of any corporation or association organized under the laws of one of the States of the United States for the purpose of engaging in public service in such State, if the issue or sale of securities shall be subject to the approval of a commission or other public authority of the state.

Said statement shall be made under oath before a notary public and be signed by the president, secretary, treasurer, or other chief financial officer, and a majority of the board of directors of such corporation or association, and shall contain the following namely:

(a) The names and addresses of the officers and directors of the corporation or association with a statement of the number of shares held by each and how the same were acquired;
(b) The purpose for which the corporation was organized and the general nature of its business;
(c) The location of its principal and branch offices and the States in which it is authorized to do business and the places at which it will transact business;
(d) The amount and plan of capitalization of the corporation or association;
(e) The consideration for which stock has been and will be issued;
(f) The purposes to which the proceeds of sales of stock will be devoted;
(g) A description of the property and assets and the amount and classes of liabilities of the corporation or association with the estimated value thereof;
(h) The names of the promoters, fiscal agents, and underwriters; the rate of commission, or commissions, and the amount of bonuses received and to be received by those promoting, consolidating, underwriting, or selling said securities; the net amount to be received from said sale by the issuing corporation or association, and to be actually issued in its business;
(i) Copies of all promotion contracts or agreements.

A copy of any statement filed pursuant to this Act, certified to by the secretary of the commission, shall be admissible in evidence in any court and in any action or proceeding with the same force and effect as if the original were produced.

Every person, firm, partnership, association, or corporation shall, in offering said securities for sale, print on the front page of any and all circulars, prospectuses, letters, and literature, and in the body of any advertisement describing or offering such securities for sale, in type larger than the type otherwise used, the names of the promoters, fiscal agents, and underwriters; the rate of commission, or commissions, and the amount of the bonuses received by those promoting, consolidation, underwriting, or selling said securities; the net amount to be received from said sale by the issuing corporation or association, and to be actually used in its business, and if said securities are not owned by the corporation which issued the same, a statement showing that fact and the name of the seller, together with a statement that information relating to the securities offered has been filed with the Federal Trade Commission at Washington, District of Columbia, and that the same is open to public inspection. In the event of an amendment to the Articles of Incorporation, the bylaws, or any other promotion contract or agreement, subsequent to the filing of a statement as heretofore provided in this section, a supplementary statement shall be filed showing said amendments.

Whoever shall willfully violate any of the provisions of this section or who shall willfully make any false or misleading statement in information required to be filed or set forth under the provisions of this Act, shall be guilty of a misdemeanor and upon conviction thereof shall be punished by a fine of not more than $5,000, or, if a natural person, by imprisonment for not more than one year, or both; and any officer, director, or agent of a corporation or association who knowingly participates in such violation or misstatement shall be punished by a like fine and imprisonment, or both.

There is hereby appropriated to the Federal Trade Commission for the fiscal year ending June 30, 1922, the sum of $50,000, or so much thereof as may be necessary, out of any moneys in the Treasury not otherwise appropriated, for purpose of this Act.

C. VOLUNTARY PRE-APPROVAL OF CONTRACTS—H.R. 19745 (1905)

Senator William Hepburn's proposed amendment to the Sherman Act would have allowed a subject corporation to file its contracts with the Commissioner of Corporations.[588] In other words, with certain exceptions, a corporation that prefiled a contract and had it approved by the Commissioner of Corporations could not later be prosecuted based on the terms of that contract.[589]

---

588 *See* H.R. 19745, 60th Cong. §10 (1908), *supra* notes 209–223 & accompanying text.

589 *Id.*

When this bill was introduced, Congressman Hepburn believed that enforcement of the Sherman Act had been rather lax in the 15 years following its enactment.[590] He felt that this was due in large part to the inferiority of federal prosecutors in comparison to big business defense lawyers.[591] Thus, this section took some of the burden off of the federal prosecutor and placed it in the hands of the Commissioner of Corporations to determine the legality of contracts. This was the only bill that allowed for contracts of subject corporations to be approved. If enacted, this bill would have significantly increased the role of the Bureau of Corporations, which at the time, was viewed as having little authority.[592] This provision is excerpted below.

> SEC. 10. That any corporation or association registered under this Act, and any person, not a common carrier under the provisions of the [Sherman Act] . . . , being a party to a contract or combination hereafter made, other than a contract or combination with a common carrier filed under section eleven of [the Sherman Act], may file with the Commissioner of Corporations a copy thereof, if the same be in writing, or if not in writing, statement setting forth the terms and conditions thereof, together with a notice that such a filing is made for the purpose of obtaining the benefit of the provisions of this section. Thereupon the Commissioner of Corporations, with the concurrence of the Secretary of Commerce and Labor, of his own motion and without notice or hearing, or after notice and hearing, as the Commissioner may deem proper, may enter an order declaring that in his judgment such contract or combination is in unreasonable restraint of trade or commerce among the several States or with foreign nations. If no such order shall be made within thirty days after the filing of such contract or written statement, no prosecution, suit, or proceeding by the United States shall lie under the first six sections of [the Sherman Act], for or on account of such contract or combination, unless the same be in unreasonable restraint of trade or commerce among the several States or with foreign nations; but the United States may institute, maintain, or prosecute a suit, proceeding, or prosecution under the first six sections of said Act for or on account of any such contract or combination hereafter made, of which a copy or written statement shall not have been filed as aforesaid, or as to which an order shall have been entered as above provided.[593]

---

[590] Staff of H.R. Comm. on the Judiciary, 57th–63rd Cong., Bills and Debates in Congress Relating to Trusts 1144-50 (Comm. Print 1914).

[591] *Id.* at 1137.

[592] *See* Introduction at p. 2.

[593] H.R. 19745, 60th Cong. § 10 (1908).

D. STATE REGISTRATION—H.R. 8883 (1904) AND S. 1377 (1911)

Most of the bills above called for subject corporations to register with the federal government in order to receive a license or charter. However, some bills called for corporations to register within the states where they conducted business.[594] For instance, S. 1377 required corporations to register with the state in which their principal place of business was located and stated that the corporation did not have "any express power to hold the stock of any other corporation or to do anything outside of the State or Territory of its incorporation which it is not permitted to do therein."[595] Thus, at a time when lawmakers were concerned over the increasing liberalization of the state corporate laws, Senator John Williams of Mississippi seemed content to keep corporate governance within the realm of the states.[596] Although this bill was not heavily debated, perhaps Senator Williams believed that, if companies were required to be licensed by the state in which they actually conducted business, these corporations would not flock to permissive states, such as Delaware and New Jersey, as they had done in the past.

Perhaps the most restrictive bill brought during this time period was H.R. 8883, introduced in 1904.[597] According to this bill, a corporation would be confined to doing business in the state where its principal place of business was located and could not do business outside of that state.[598] The bill stated that "a corporation is neither a citizen nor a person and is, therefore, not entitled to the privileges conferred by the constitutional doctrine of comity of the states."[599] Furthermore, corporations were barred from holding stock in other corporations operating outside of the state.[600]

E. VOLUNTARY FEDERAL INCORPORATION—TAFT-WICKERSHAM BILLS—H.R. 20142 AND S. 6186 (1910)

The Taft-Wickersham bills allowed for corporations to voluntarily avail themselves of the protection of the Act. President Taft may have believed that corporations would avail themselves to the definite rules of federal charters, as opposed to risking violation of the antitrust laws.[601] Several novel provisions of the bill are excerpted below.

---

594 *See* S. 1377, 62d Cong. (1911); H.R. 11167, 63d Cong. (1913); H.R. 11168, 63d Cong. (1913).

595 S. 1377, 62d Cong. § 1 (1911).

596 *See supra* notes 5–16 and accompanying text.

597 H.R. 8883, 58th Cong. (1904).

598 *Id.* at § 2.

599 *Id.* This bill raised constitutional concerns. *See supra* notes 57–59 and accompanying text.

600 *Id.* H.R. 8883, 58th Cong. §2 (1904).

601 Richard G. Handler and Thomas F. Liotti, *An Historical Survey of Federal Incorporation*, 1 Del. J. Corp. L. 370, 383 (1976).

SEC. 1. Any five or more persons, citizens of the United States, each of the age of twenty-one years or upward, may, upon complying with the requirements of this Act, form a corporation to engage in trade or commerce with foreign nations, or among the several States, or between a State or States and places subject to the jurisdiction of the United States, or between any Territories of the United States, or in and between any such Territory or Territories and any State or States and the District of Columbia or places under the jurisdiction of the United States, or between the District of Columbia and any State or States and foreign nations or places under the jurisdiction of the United States, or for all or any such kinds of trade and commerce.

SEC. 2. The person uniting to form such corporation shall make and subscribe Articles of Association, which shall specifically set forth: First, the name of the proposed corporation, with the addition of the words "national incorporation" as the last words thereof, which name shall be subject to the approval of the Commissioner of Corporations; second, the place in which the principal business office of the corporation is to be situated, designating the State, Territory, or District, and the particular county and city, town, or village; third, the object for which the proposed corporation is to be established, stating the general nature of the interstate or foreign trade or commerce which it is formed to carry on; fourth, the amount of the capital stock of the proposed corporation, which shall not be less than one hundred thousand dollars, and the amount with which it is to commence business, which shall not be less than ten thousand dollars, and whether or not any part of the capital stock is to be contributed in property other than money, and if so, the amount of such part; fifth, the number of shares into which the capital stock is to be divided and the par value, if any, of such shares, and if a portion of such shares are to have no par value, then specifying such portion; whether or not such shares are to be divided into classes, and if so, the amount of each class and a statement of the preferential and other special rights of each class; sixth, the number of directors, and if they are to be divided into two or more classes, the numbers of directors to constitute each class, and the terms of office of each class, respectively, and the names and post-office addresses of the directors for the first year and the name and post-office address of the treasurer of the corporation to serve until the election of officers for the first year; seventh, the period limited for the duration of the company, not to exceed fifty years; eighth, in case the corporation is formed for the purpose of acquiring the property and business of any existing corporation, the articles shall specify the amount of any indebtedness of such existing corporation, payment whereof is to be assumed by the new corporation, and what, if any, amount of such indebtedness is secured by mortgage or other lien upon the property to be so acquired; ninth, any other provision which the incorporators may choose to insert in the articles for the regulation of the business and conduct of the affairs of the corporation; and any provisions defining, limiting, and regulating the powers of the corporation, its officers, directors, or stockholders, or any class or classes of stockholders: *Provided*, that the provisions inserted pursuant to this clause ninth be approved by the Commission of Corporations as not inconsistent with this Act or any other Act of Congress; tenth, the fact that the articles are made to enable such persons to avail themselves of the advantages of this act; eleventh, the names and places of residence of the respective subscribers to the articles and the number of shares which each of them agrees to take in the corporation, which must not aggregate less than the amount specified in the articles as that with which the corporation is to commence business.

The Articles of Association shall be acknowledged by each subscriber before an officer authorized to take the acknowledgement of deeds for purposes of record at the place or places where they are so signed and acknowledged, and shall be authenticated by the seal of such officer and the certificate to his official character of the clerk of the court or county or other officer with whom his commission is required by law to be filed or recorded; and the Articles of Association so acknowledged and authenticated shall be transmitted to the Commissioner of Corporations.

SEC. 3. It shall be the duty of the Commissioner of Corporations to examine such articles, and if, in his opinion, they conform to the requirements of this Act and contain no provision which is contrary to any other Act of Congress, and if the name proposed to be adopted by such corporation is not the same as or so nearly resembling the name of another existing corporation organized under this Act, or by any other Act of Congress, or the name of any other corporation registered in the Bureau of Corporations pursuant to section four hereof, as to be calculated to deceive, he shall upon payment of the fees provided in this Act, file the said articles in his office and record the same in a book to be kept by him for the purpose, and upon proof satisfactory to him that the amount of the capital with which the corporation is to commence business has been paid in cash to the treasurer named in the articles, he shall thereupon issue a copy of said articles so filed, together with a certificate, under his hand and seal of office that incorporators have complied with all the provisions of law required to be complied with and have become and are a national corporation under the name and are authorized to have succession for the period specified in the articles of association. Such certificate, which is hereinafter described as the organization certificate, shall be in the form prescribed in

Schedule A of this Act, and thereupon and from the date of such certificate the said incorporators and their respective successor shall be and become a body corporate, having successor the period in said articles mentioned, and as such, and in the name designated therein shall have and may exercise the powers specified in this Act, and all powers necessary or proper to the effective exercise of the powers herein specifically granted.

SEC. 4. Any corporation existing under the laws of any State or Territory of the United States or the District of Columbia, upon the payment of a fee of five dollars may file in the Bureau of Corporations a duly certified copy of its charter, together with proof, by affidavit, of its president or vice-president and secretary or treasurer that it is engaged in business pursuant to such charter, specifying in such affidavit the location of its principal office and the principal places in which it is engaged in conducting its business.

The Commissioner of Corporations shall cause a book to be kept in his office to be called the "corporation name index," in which shall be entered the name, state in which incorporated, date of incorporation, and character of business of every corporation filing its charter in accordance with this section, and the date of such filing, and the commissioner shall on written request and on payment of a fee of one dollar furnish any person so requesting the same with the names of all corporations entered therein containing any word or words specified in such written request.

If, in the opinion of the commissioner, the Articles of Association transmitted to him for approval hereunder shall contain any provision at variance with this Act or any other Act of Congress, or if the name selected for said corporation shall be the same as the name of any other existing corporation engaged in the same or a similar business, and organized under this Act, or under any other Act of Congress, or which being organized under the laws of any State or Territory, shall have filed a copy of its charter in the Bureau of Corporations in compliance with this section, or so nearly resembling the same as to be calculated to deceive, the commissioner shall refuse to file said Articles of Association.

SEC. 5. Every corporation formed as herein provided shall have the following powers: First, to adopt and use a corporate seal and alter same at pleasure; second, to have succession for the period specified in its Articles of Association, unless it is sooner dissolved by the act of its shareholders owning two-thirds of its stock, or unless its existence is terminated by reason of some other provision of law; third, to acquire by grant, gift, purchase, devise, or bequest, and to hold and dispose of such property, real and personal, as the corporation shall require or find useful in its business, subject to such limitations as may be prescribed by law; fourth, to carry on the general kind of interstate or foreign trade and commerce specified in the Articles of Association, with the foreign nations or among the several States, or between a State or States and places subject to the jurisdiction of the United States, or in or between any such Territory or Territories and any State or States and the District of Columbia or places under the jurisdiction of the United States, or between the District of Columbia and any State or States or foreign nations or places under the jurisdiction of the United States, and to produce or manufacture in any State, Territory, or district any of the articles or commodities which are the subject of the interstate or foreign commerce carried on or proposed to be carried on by it; fifth, to sue and be sued, complain and defend in any court of law or equity, having jurisdiction, as fully as natural persons may do; sixth, to elect or appoint a board of directors and an executive committee, and by its board of directors to appoint a president, vice-president, secretary, treasurer, and other officers or agents, define their duties, prescribe their qualification, dismiss such officer or any of them at pleasure, and appoint others to fill their places; seventh, to make by-laws not inconsistent with this Act or any other Act of Congress for the management of its property, the regulation of its affairs, the transfer of its stock, and the calling of meeting of its members. Such by-laws may also fix the amount of stock which must be represented at meetings of stockholders to constitute a quorum, unless otherwise provided by law, but the holders of at least a majority of the stock shall be required to be present in person or by proxy to constitute a quorum for the transaction of business but a smaller number may be authorized to adjourn the meeting from time to time until a quorum shall be obtained. The by-laws shall also provide regulations for the issue of new certificates of stock in place of lost or destroyed certificates. By-laws shall be adopted by the stockholders, unless it is provided in the Articles of Association that the by-laws may be made by the board of directors, in which case by-laws may be so adopted, subject to alteration or repeal by the stockholders at their pleasure. By-laws adopted at a meeting of the stockholders shall control the action of the directors, but no by-laws shall be effective until two weeks after a copy of the same, duly certified by the secretary of the corporation . . . under its seal, shall have been filed in the Bureau of Corporations, unless such time shall be duly waived by writing, signed by the holders of all the stock and duly acknowledged in like manner as the articles of Association and filed with said by-laws in the Bureau of Corporations.

SEC. 8. *No Corporation formed pursuant to this Act shall purchase, acquire, or hold stock in any corporation, nor shall any corporation organized under this Act or under the laws of any State or foreign country for the purpose of or engaged in carrying on the like business to that of a corporation formed pursuant to this Act acquire or hold the stock of such last-mentioned corporation,*[602] and any attempted transfer of such stock contrary to this provision shall be null and void. No corporation formed pursuant to this Act shall, by any implication or construction, be deemed to possess the power of carrying on the business of discounting bills, notes, or other evidence of debt, or of receiving deposits or buying and selling bills of exchange, nor shall it issue bills, notes, or other evidence of debt for circulation as money.

SEC. 9. The business of every corporation organized hereunder shall be managed by its directors, who shall, respectively, be shareholders therein. They shall not be less than five in number, and except as hereinafter provided, they shall be chosen annually by the stockholders at the time and place provided in the by-laws, and shall hold office for one year, or until others are chosen and qualified in their stead; but by so providing in its Articles of Association or in Amended Articles adopted as herein provided, any corporation organized under this Act may classify its directors in respect to the time for which they shall severally hold office, the several classes to be elected for different terms: *Provided*, that no class shall be elected for a shorter period than one year or for a longer period than five years, and that the term of office of at least one class shall expire in each year. Any corporation having more than one kind of each stock may, by so providing in its Articles of Association, or in Amended Articles duly adopted, confer the right to choose the directors of any class, or a specified number of directors, upon the stockholders of any particular class or classes to the exclusion of the others. At least a majority of the directors shall, at all times, be citizens of the United States and bona fide residents therein.

The Articles of Association or any Amended Articles adopted as herein provided may provide that the powers of the board of directors shall be exercised by an executive committee, composed of not less than a majority of the whole number of directors, to be chosen by the votes of a majority of the whole board, which committee shall have and may exercise, except when the board is in session, all of the powers of the board, except such as are by this Act required to be exercised by the board of directors itself, and except the power to declare dividends; and may also provide that the members of the board of directors other than those constituting the executive committee shall not be liable in any respect except for the exercise of good faith and due diligence in respect to

[602] (Emphasis added). Note that even companies that were not registered under the Act were forbidden from merging with subject corporations.

matters brought before meetings of the board of directors and duly held and attended by them.

Appendix II

A. QUOTES OF THE COMMISSIONER OF CORPORATIONS, JAMES R. GARFIELD

James R. Garfield served as the Commissioner of Corporations from 1903 to 1907. He was an early proponent of federal incorporation. In the Commissioner's report to Congress in 1904, he specifically called for a federal franchise system. Commissioner Garfield stated:

> I therefore beg to suggest that Congress be requested to consider the advisability of enacting a law for the legislative regulation of interstate and foreign commerce under a license or franchise, which in general should provide as follows:
>
> (a) The granting of a Federal franchise or license to engage in interstate commerce.
> (b) The imposition of all necessary requirements as to corporate organization and management as a condition precedent to the grant of such franchise or license.
> (c) The requirement of such reports and returns as may be desired as a condition of the retention of such franchise or license.
> (d) The prohibition of all corporations and corporate agencies from engaging in interstate and foreign commerce without such federal franchise or license.
> (e) The full protection of the grantees of such franchise or license who obey the laws applicable thereto.
> (f) The right to refuse or withdraw such franchise or license in case of a violation of law, with appropriate right of judicial appeal to prevent abuse of power by the administrative officer.

This bureau [of Corporations] under the direction of the secretary of commerce and labor, affords the appropriate machinery for the administration of such a law.[603]

[603] FTC Report, *supra* note 29, at 5.

B. QUOTES OF ATTORNEY GENERAL GEORGE WICKERSHAM

After the introduction of the Taft-Wickersham bills in February 1910, Attorney General Wickersham defended his bill to the Senate Committee on Interstate Commerce, stating:

> No such comprehensive control over any one of the great industries which were dominated by those large aggregations of capital called "trusts" could have been attained but through the exercise of powers granted by the sovereign States . . . The problem was complicated by the dual nature of our Government. Concerted action by the States was impracticable—it may be said impossible. Efforts at control by one State were evaded, first by removal to another, then by the device of holding corporations.[604]

Speaking again in 1911, Attorney General Wickersham stressed the need for an administrative agency with oversight of corporations, stating:

> Moreover, unless Congress shall provide for the establishment of corporations drawing their life and powers only from the national Government and subject only to its control, or shall confer specific powers on State corporations which will enable them to carry on commerce away from the State of their creation without the interference of States into which they go, the present unsatisfactory condition of carrying on business in the different States by means of many different corporations owned or controlled by or through stock ownership by a parent company created by someone State will continue, and in the natural, normal, healthy, and legitimate growth of such business, questions of the application of the Sherman Law must arise which cannot be properly settled with the district attorney or the Department of Justice, but which should be dealt with by an administrative body having appropriate jurisdiction.[605]

C. QUOTES OF PRESIDENT WILLIAM HOWARD TAFT

Likewise, President Taft urged Congress to pass the Taft-Wickersham Bills on January 7, 1910, stating:

> I therefore recommend the enactment by Congress of a general law providing for the formation of corporations to engage in trade and commerce among the

---

[604] *Id.* at 8.
[605] *Id.*

States and with foreign nations, protecting them from undue interference by the States and regulating their activities so as to prevent the recurrence, under national auspices, of those abuses which have arisen under state control.

Such a national incorporation law will be opposed, first by those who believe that trusts should be completely broken up and their property destroyed. It will be opposed, second, by those who doubt the constitutionality of such a federal incorporation, and even if it is valid. It will be opposed, third, by those who will insist that a mere voluntary incorporation like this will not attract to its acceptance the worst of the offenders against the antitrust statute, and who will therefore propose instead of it a system of compulsory licenses for all Federal corporations engaged in interstate business.

If we would maintain our present business supremacy, we should give to industrial concerns an opportunity to reorganize and to concentrate their legitimate capital in a Federal corporation and to carry on their large business within the lines of the law.[606]

Appendix III

A. QUOTES FROM SENATOR HOWARD M. METZENBAUM'S OPENING STATEMENT, THE HEARING BEFORE THE SUBCOMMITTEE ON SECURITIES OF THE COMMITTEE ON BANKING, HOUSING, AND URBAN AFFAIRS

On November 19, 1980, Senator Howard Metzenbaum defended his bill before the Senate Committee on Banking, Housing, and Urban Affairs. Perhaps fearing that his bill would be viewed as too liberal, Senator Metzenbaum attempted to quell misconceptions about his bill. Senator Metzenbaum stated:

> I think there were something like 30 million investors in the stock market some years ago; now there are something like 25 million. Why? It means that there is a loss of confidence, concern about what kind of rights stockholders have in their corporations.
>
> There is nothing in the legislation that I propose that would solve the problems. It would be a step forward. That doesn't mean I think it is a step forward of the camel getting its nose under the tent; that Government is really going to move in on the corporations. That isn't the approach that I make.

[606] *Id.*

> All my bill does is to establish Federal minimum standards for the composition of corporate boards, duties, directors and shareholders' rights . . .
>
> That doesn't mean there couldn't be minimum standards for the composition of boards of directors, such as a majority being noncorporate personnel themselves. Really, my legislation is designed to make corporations more accountable to their shareholders and to the public.[607]

After his opening comments, Senator Metzenbaum presented a prepared statement outlining the provisions of his bill:

> There is widespread agreement in the business and wider community that reforms are necessary in the governance of the Nation's major corporations. There is not agreement, however, on the need for Federal legislation to bring about those essential reforms.
>
> In considering this question, we must answer two basic questions. First, do major and pressing problems exist? Second, is action in the form of legislation necessary to solve those problems in a timely manner? The answer to both those questions is yes.
>
> There is no doubt that we face major problems in the governance of our major corporations. In recent years, a corporate management style has appeared that is unresponsive to both shareholders and to the public interest.
>
> In a recent issue of Chief Executive, a magazine written by and for top corporate executives, Arnold Bernhard, research chairman of the Value Line Investment Survey, had this to say about today's corporations:
>
> "Management's self-interest now propels them to give first consideration to independent survival of the corporation itself, to their own salaries and bonuses, and to their standing in the communities where they live. The individual investor who put up the capital and took the risk to start the business is now being relegated to second class."
>
> . . . . [T]op corporate executives have all too often enriched themselves at the expense of the shareholders. For example, just a few months ago, the Wall Street Journal reported that the Playboy Enterprises, Inc. Audit Committee has asked Hugh Hefner and other top executives to repay $918,413 to the company

[607] *Protection of Shareholder's Rights Act of 1980, Hearing on S. 2567, Before the Subcommittee on Securities of the Senate Comm. On Banking, Housing, & Urban Affairs*, 96th Cong. 2-3 (Opening Statement of Sen. Howard M. Metzenbaum).

for "certain benefits" that were not "properly documented or approved." The SEC has documented scores of similar cases in which corporate executives have abused their corporate positions for personal gain—racing yachts, cars, home improvements, et cetera, and the Washington Post recently reported, with extensive documentation, how Mobil Corporation President William Tavoulareas put his son in a shipping venture that benefited handsomely from its relationship with Mobil. That arrangement catapulted the 24-year-old son from a $14,000 shipping clerk to a major owner of the Atlas Maritime Co., complete with a Rolls-Royce and luxurious homes in London and Long Island.

In theory, a major responsibility of a corporation's board of directors is to carefully monitor corporate policy in order to prevent abuses of this kind. But in fact, a very large number of corporate boards do not exercise meaningful oversight and control over management. "Directors," complained William O. Douglas as early as 1933, "do not direct."[608]

In a 1975 survey of 394 of the country's largest corporations, Korn/Ferry International—a New York executive recruiting firm—found that boards averaged only seven meetings per year. "In most large corporations," Korn/Ferry reported, "the board meetings have withered, through neglect, into a ritualized 1- to 3-hour ceremony with much of the time being consumed by a pro forma review of operations by the president or vice presidents and equally routine approvals of the capital appropriations that management wants."

Perhaps the best illustration of the failure of many corporate boards to exercise meaningful oversight and control over management is the Penn Central failure. At the time of the collapse in June 1970, Penn Central was the largest railroad in the country and the sixth largest industrial corporation overall. Within a 2-year period, shareholders watched their shares plummet from 86-1/2 to 2-3/4. A director who joined Penn Central in December 1969 gave the following, devastating description of board attitudes:

"They sat up there on the 18th floor in those big chairs with the (brass name) plates on them and they were a bunch of, well, I'd better not say it. The board was definitely responsible for the trouble. They took their fees and they didn't do anything. They didn't know the factual picture and they didn't try to find out."

---

[608] Note that William O. Douglas was appointed to the U.S. Supreme Court after his Chairmanship of the Securities and Exchange Commission. *See generally* William O. Douglas, *Go East Young Man* (1974).

In testimony before the Senate Commerce Committee a few years ago, former SEC Chairman Roderick Hills summed up the situation as follows:

"Too many boards are dominated by inside directors. Even where there are significant numbers of outsiders on a board, they are all too often old friends of the chief executive officer who would rather resign from the board than severely criticize or vote to oust their old friend."

And former AT&T Chairman John D. DeButts wrote recently in the Corporate Director:

"To strengthen the board of directors we must, first of all, get rid of the notion that the principal criterion for membership is compatibility."

Obviously, Mr. DeButts was responding to a very real problem. These examples raise the most basic questions related to the governance of the American corporation.

In June 1977, the Senate Subcommittee on Citizens and Shareholders Rights and Remedies, which I then chaired, held hearings on "The Role of the Shareholder in the Corporate World." Witness after witness spoke of the need to stop the erosion of standards of conduct for corporate management and to expand the role of the shareholder in the modern corporation. Testimony before other Congressional committees and before the Securities and Exchange Commission carried the same message . . .

In February of 1978, I appointed an advisory committee on corporate governance. Its 12 members represented many of the most prestigious and active names in American business, labor, and consumer activities—John D. DeButts, then chairman of the board of AT&T; Irving S. Shapiro, chairman of the board of DuPont; Douglas Fraser, president of the UAW; Mark Green, director of Congress Watch; A.A. Sommer, Jr., former member of the Securities and Exchange Commission; William Winpisinger, president of the International Association of Machinists and Aerospace Workers; William B. Batten, chairman of the New York Stock Exchange and former president of the J.C. Penney Co.; Prof. William L. Cary, chairman of the SEC from 1961 to 1964; Lewis D. Gilbert, a major spokesman for shareholders interests; John Bustamente, chairman of the First National Bank Association of Cleveland; Alice Tepper Marlin, founder and executive director of the Council of Economic Priorities; and George Aronoff, distinguished Cleveland attorney.

While divergent views were expressed by members of the committee regarding Federal legislation as a mechanism for effectuating change, the advisory committee agreed that improvements in corporate governance and corporate accountability are of great importance to the future of our economic system.

The committee endorsed a number of specific reforms such as: At least a majority of the members of boards of directors of publicly-owned corporations should be "outside" directors or "independent" of management; publicly-owned corporations should have an audit committee composed solely of independent directors; and publicly-owned corporations should have a nominating committee composed of a majority of independent directors....

Most corporations resist any Federal legislation and prefer to wait for the voluntary actions of the corporate community to make adjustments. Or, at a maximum, they prefer to leave all legislative decisions to the States. With all due respect to the advocates of laissez-faire and corporate voluntarism, I must confess that some of us have a more skeptical view of human nature.... This is not to say that there have not been changes and improvements, for there have been. Many major companies have brought outside directors onto the board. But history teaches that such voluntary reforms are likely to be short-lived, a response to passing pressures....

Just this month, for example, Hedrick and Struggles surveyed 13,000 of the nation's largest industrial and non-industrial concerns. Of the 487 who responded, 87.6 percent had boards on which outsiders were a majority. That sounds very good, until one looks a little closer. Many of these companies considered anyone not a present employee to be an outsider. Only 55 percent said they had a board with an "independent" outsider majority. Though we don't even know how "independent" was defined—did it include major suppliers or the firm's bankers, for example?—that's still only 55 percent of the 487 who responded. The other 813 may have been even worse. And there seems to be a regression here as well. For a while, there seemed to be a trend to keeping the company's lawyer off its board for the most obvious of reasons: how can one expect someone hired by a CEO to act critically and independently of that CEO? [Note that then SEC Chairman Harold M. Williams was particularly concerned about a subject company's inside or outside counsel serving also as a director of that corporation.[609]]

In a 1978 Korn/Ferry survey of 552 major corporations, the proportion of boards with the company's lawyer on them had dropped to 32.8 percent, still a very high figure. Last year, the figure turned upward to 35.1 percent—the first increase since 1973. One reason, according to Lester Korn, could be less SEC pressure. Nor can the problems be left solely to the States. State corporation

---

[609] *See* Harold M. Williams, *The Role of Inside Counsel in Corporate Accountability*, [1979–1980 Transfer Binder] Fed. Sec. L. Rep. (CCH) ¶ 82,318 (1979).

laws are designed primarily to enable management to operate with minimum interference. States have competed with each other in what has been called a race to the bottom, to develop a permissive, management-oriented body of law in order to attract corporations to domicile within their respective jurisdictions and provide corporate business. And the States know it.

A 1968 report of New Jersey's corporation law revision committees states:

"It is clear that the major protections to investors, creditors, employees, customers and the general public have come, and must continue to come, from Federal legislation and not from State corporation acts . . . [A]ny attempt to provide such regulations in the public interest through State incorporation acts and similar legislation would only drive corporations out of the State to more hospitable jurisdictions."

If voluntarism is uncertain and State reform is either unlikely or too time-consuming, why not rely upon the SEC instead of legislation? The simple answer is that the SEC does not now have the legislative authority to institute needed reform.

SEC jurisdiction—the 1933 and 1934 Securities Acts—relates primarily to the corporate securities distribution and trading process rather than to corporate governance. The principal purpose of these statutes is disclosure to permit investors to make informed investment decisions, and to permit shareholders to exercise their rights effectively and intelligently. That is simply not sufficient to achieve a more effective and responsive corporate governing structure.

The corporate shareholder thus finds that State laws often will not protect him, that the Federal securities laws apparently are not strong enough to do so, and that other laws are not broad enough. I therefore introduced S. 2567 (which prescribes minimum Federal standards to protect shareholders and to restore the sense of accountability that has been absent from too many of our major corporations, without reducing managerial efficiency). I believe that the best way to do that is to strengthen the role of the board of directors. Others would go much further. . . . I prefer instead to rely more on building a limited set of mechanisms to enable the good sense and honesty of American businessmen to operate in a manner that is creative, effective, and meaningful.

The only real way to accomplish this is to require that a majority of the board of major corporations be directors who do not have certain significant economic or personal relationships with the corporations they serve. As SEC Chairman Harold Williams put it:

"Independent directors perform a vital function for management. They provide a source of accountability and self-correction. They can serve management constructively by calling for management to examine decisions and actions in the light of new and different perspectives and asking hard questions . . ."

Hard questions might have prevented the Penn Central disaster, the slush funds, the illegal contributions, the foreign bribes, and the excessive corporate perks and compensation for insiders.[610]

The provision in the bill I introduced for an independent director majority does not go as far as some would go—they would require almost all board members to be outsiders. The bill reflects instead a widespread consensus. . . . Admittedly, the word "independent" is not easily defined. However, the categories set forth in the bill focus on those persons whose board service raises legitimate questions of independence. . . .

In line with that, investment bankers, commercial bankers, major suppliers and lawyers who do a certain amount of business with the corporation, among others, are not classified as independent directors in the bill. Nothing in this bill, of course, precludes them from serving on a corporate board—it is just that such persons cannot be in the majority.

The bill also requires all subject corporations to establish audit committees composed solely of independent directors. The audit committee would—in addition to other duties—have the sole authority to hire and dismiss the independent auditor, and to determine his compensation, subject to the approval of a majority of the outstanding shares of the corporation.

The value of independent audit committees is undisputed. The SEC first recommended audit committees as a means for improving financial disclosure in 1940. In 1939, the New York Stock Exchange endorsed the concept. Today, the Business Roundtable supports it. The New York Stock Exchange requires all listed companies to establish audit committees composed solely of independent directors, and the American Stock Exchange recommends the same thing for its listed companies.

But simply having an audit committee is not enough. Such a committee must responsibly perform some real, hard functions, and some do not. The bill therefore sets out some of the responsibilities of audit committees.

Nominating committees should also be independent. Corporate elections are usually won by the persons nominated by management. Also, the chief executive officer who traditionally selects the candidates for board membership, can intimidate would-be dissenters who wish to remain on the board and

---

[610] Then SEC Enforcement Director Stanley Sporkin played an instrumental role in the Commission's enforcement actions with respect to these practices and the enactment of the Foreign Corrupt Practices Act of 1977. *See* Symposium, *In Honor of Stanley Sporkin*, 43 Sec. Reg. L.J. No. 1 (2015).

who know he or she can deny them reappointment. The bill, therefore, requires that all subject corporations have a nominating committee composed solely of independent directors, with the responsibility for recommending nominees to fill board vacancies. Shareholders should be advised of the nominating committee's role and encouraged to submit recommendations to the committee. Properly implemented, this concept constitutes a significant step toward increasing shareholder participation in the corporate electoral process.

The bill also grants shareholders the right to nominate candidates for the board of directors, provided such candidates are supported by a specified number of shares outstanding at the time the candidate's name is sought to be placed in nomination. This provision will make proxy solicitations more open, and help put outside groups on a more equal footing with the inside management.

But simply giving shareholders the right to nominate directors is not enough. Shareholders must also have some electoral power. Cumulative voting is a mechanism that assures some stockholders, if they are sufficiently purposeful and cohesive, representation on the board of directors to an extent roughly proportionate to the size of their holdings. This is achieved by permitting each shareholder, acting alone or in concert with others, to cast the total number of his or her votes for a single candidate for election to the board, or to distribute such total among any number of such candidates.

Like all other provisions of this bill, the provision for cumulative voting does not create something new and unprecedented, but merely adopts the best of current practice. In ten States, cumulative voting is guaranteed in the State constitution, and in eleven States, cumulative voting is an absolute shareholder right by statute. A previous Congressional requirement for "fair, just and equitable suffrage" in the administration of the Public Utility Holding Company Act, has been interpreted to support the right of cumulative voting. . . .

The standard of care is taken from the Model Business Corporation Act which was written and approved by the American Bar Association's section on corporation, banking, and business law. It has been adopted in substance in more than 25 States and major portions have been followed in many others. Its enactment and uniform interpretation on a Federal level would be an important step toward protecting the basic rights of public investors, and adding a necessary uniformity to the way directors of national companies are supposed to act.

The duty of loyalty provision was taken from the Corporate Director's Guidebook. It is based on the single basic principle that a director should not use his corporate position to make a personal profit or gain other personal advantage.

Finally, the bill allows any shareholder of a subject corporation to enforce those provisions of the act not preempted by State law in Federal district court.

The court would have original but not exclusive jurisdiction of such actions, and the prevailing party would be allowed to recover reasonable litigation costs, including attorney's fees.

In closing, Mr. Chairman, let me point out that the proposed legislation reflects two important concerns: inflexible Federal regulation should not stifle the need for innovative, creative, and experimental reforms that often come only from the private sector itself or from the States. I believe that the standards in this bill are sufficiently modest so that efforts at such reform are not stifled, but encouraged. They are encouraged because States and companies are urged to go beyond these minimum standards on a voluntary basis.

The second concern is that small businesses not be unnecessarily burdened by this or any other legislation. In crafting the scope of this bill, we have therefore been quantitative as well as qualitative, sharply limiting the number of covered public corporations to about the 1,000 largest corporations, and not including any mutual insurance companies.

A final point. I do not delude myself into thinking that this bill will be promptly enacted, especially after the results of the recent election. But its time may well come, and soon. If we have another Penn Central, another wave of revelations about corporate misconduct, there may be such a revulsion that much harsher, less considered legislation will be hastily adopted.

I think that would be unfortunate.[611]

B. QUOTES OF THE ADVISORY COMMITTEE ON CORPORATE GOVERNANCE

Senator Howard Metzenbaum initiated the most recent attempt to impose widespread federal statutory standards of normative corporate fiduciary conduct. The Report of the Advisory Committee on Corporate Governance, appointed by Senator Metzenbaum, was issued in 1977. The Committee's Report is excerpted below.

The Committee agrees upon the following propositions:

1. Corporate governance and corporate accountability are of extraordinary importance, not only to the economy of the nation, but to its social well-being as well. Corporations are the creators of the bulk of the consumer and capital

---

[611] *Protection of Shareholder's Rights Act of 1980, Hearing on S. 2567, Before the Subcommittee on Securities of the S. Comm. On Banking, Housing, & Urban Affairs*, 96 Cong. 4-12 (Statement of Sen. Howard M. Metzenbaum). Indeed, the enactment of the Sarbanes-Oxley Act of 2002 and the Dodd-Frank Act of 2010 may be viewed as evidencing that Senator Metzenbaum's warning has become (to some extent) reality.

goods which have contributed to the prosperity and well-being of this nation. As such, they employ the overwhelming bulk of the employable population; they own vast amounts of the resources of the nation; their conduct can impact communities and masses of people in a profound manner. If they are inefficiently managed, then the nation may be denied goods at fair prices it might otherwise have; if they are managed in a manner indifferent to the demands and needs of their employees, they may create harsh hardships; if they are indifferent to the welfare of society, they may make life in our nation less rich and human. Events of recent years suggest that the general efficiency of the corporate community has, unfortunately, been accompanied by seeming indifference by some companies to the larger concerns of society and the expectations of that society with respect to proper and moral corporate conduct. If corporations are to function most efficiently and economically, and most satisfactorily in terms of society's broader needs, it is important that the respective rights, duties and needs of management, shareholders and others who have an interest in the consequences of corporate conduct be reasonably balanced through adequate mechanisms, procedures and practices, and through people who are sensitive to the needs for such a balance.

2. The most immediately available means of accomplishing changes conducive to more efficient and accountable conduct of corporate affairs is through a proper structure and quality of the board of directors. Among means which have been generally accepted as desirable, though not necessarily ultimate, mechanisms have been the inclusion on boards of a majority of directors who are "independent," the constitution of audit committees consisting solely of such "independent" directors, and nominating committees with at least a majority of such "independent" directors. Such audit committees would have significant responsibilities, including recommending the selection of, and a close working relationship with, the independent auditor and the monitoring of the corporation's internal control function and financial reporting practices. Nominating committees independent of management control would provide a mechanism for securing greater opportunity for shareholders to participate in the director election process.

There is no consensus concerning the proper definition of "independent." At a minimum the term should not embrace anyone employed by the corporation. In the estimation of many members of the Committee it should not include attorneys who do significant amounts of work for the corporation, former employees, suppliers or customers whose transactions with the corporation are significant, or investment or commercial bankers which serve the corporation. It is recognized that regardless of affiliations, past or present, the true test of the independence of a director is essentially his or her state of mind—willingness and ability to exercise independent judgment. . . . [I]t is also recognized that the ability to comprehend a corporation's affairs and its relationships to society, the ability to make incisive judgments on facts available, the ability to operate in a collegial manner with fellow directors are essential ingredients of a competent director. It is the conviction of the members of the Committee that all involved in the corporate process should take all reasonable measures to establish institutional arrangements and procedures to maximize the likelihood that directors are elected to boards who are competent to monitor management's conduct of the corporation's affairs, who are sensitive to the interests of employees, of the communities in which facilities are located, and of the shareholders, and who have a diversity of interests and backgrounds. While no process can assure that only persons with such characteristics will be elected as directors, a maturing combination of appropriate disclosure concerning nominees and the development of independent nominating committees will constitute a significant step toward the election of such persons. Statistical evidence indicates that the incidence of "independent" directors on the boards of publicly held corporations (especially larger ones) and audit and nominating committees constituted largely, if not wholly, of "independent" directors is mounting steadily, although in all areas the practices are far from uniform and there exists considerable diversity, largely related to the size of corporations. Independent auditors are, of course, mandated by the federal securities laws for all corporations with significant public ownership. The accounting profession and the Securities and Exchange Commission are engaged in a number of programs to strengthen the independence of such auditors. The members of the Committee also believe that shareholders should have the right to ratify the selection of the corporation's independent auditor and note the apparent increase in the incidence of this practice.

3. The members of the Committee agree that the foregoing trends are desirable, though there is disagreement about whether the simple continuation of them in response to present stimuli will accomplish sufficient corporate reform to satisfy critics of corporate governance and accountability. There is agreement upon the need for a continuation of these trends and agreement that, at least with respect to larger corporations, boards with majorities of outside directors and key committees consisting mostly or wholly of outside directors are desirable.

However, there is profound, but not unexpected, disagreement among members of the Committee concerning the means by which further change should be accomplished. Some members of the Committee previously filed separate statements of their views which are available on request. Some members of the Committee, largely identified with the management of large corporations, believe that federal legislation related to the governance of corporations is not necessary because the fundamental disclosure premise of the securities laws has provided and will continue to provide an effective and proper method of federal regulation of corporations. Moreover, corporations are subject to many other federal and state laws and constraints imposing substantial controls on their conduct. They also point out that the corporate community is now sufficiently animated and alerted that it may be relied upon to continue reforms that will, consistently with continuing economic efficiency, also serve well the larger community with which corporations are increasingly concerned, and which is increasingly concerned with the conduct of corporations.

Others, largely consumer, shareholder and labor representatives, believe that structural reforms of the board (which some members of the Committee regard as desirable, but less than is necessary to cure perceived ills in the conduct of corporations) can only be adequately achieved through legislation. These members of the Committee would have the Congress adopt legislation requiring such reforms as a minimum, and would go further to require other reforms ranging from a comprehensive federal incorporation or licensing law to a series of federal minimum standards. . . .

It has been suggested by some members of the Committee that on the basis of the Subcommittee's deliberations the Securities and Exchange Commission should be asked to study carefully the extent to which it has the power to adopt rules which would give shareholders the opportunity to nominate candidates for the board through the proxy machinery and to regulate the "going private" phenomenon. . . .[612]

The Committee, while in a sense feeling unfulfilled because of its inability to answer with one voice Senator Metzenbaum's question concerning what actions should be taken, nonetheless feels that the interchange of viewpoints has sensitized them to the need for constructive change and strengthened their capacities in their respective areas of endeavor to facilitate that change.[613]

---

[612] The SEC adopted going-private rules in 1979. *See* SEC Rule 13e-3, 17 C.F.R. § 240.13e-3 (2017); Securities Exchange Act Release No. 16075 (1979). These rules are discussed in Chapters 1, 3 herein. Pursuant to the Dodd-Frank Act of 2010, the Commission promulgated a rule entitling specified shareholders the right to nominate directors in the company's proxy statement (proxy access rule). *See* Rule 14a-11; Securities Exchange Act Release No. 62764 (2010). This rule was declared invalid by the U.S. Court of Appeals for the District of Columbia Circuit. *See Business Roundtable v. SEC*, 647 F.3d 1144 (D.C. Cir. 2011). This rule and its invalidation are addressed in Chapters 4, 5, 6 herein.

[613] Report of the Advisory Committee on Corporate Governance, Appointed by Senator Howard M. Metzenbaum (June 27, 1977).

3

THE SEC'S IMPACT ON THE FEDERALIZATION OF CORPORATE GOVERNANCE—A TRADITIONAL PERSPECTIVE

I. Introduction

Today with the enactment of the Sarbanes-Oxley Act of 2002 and the Dodd-Frank Act of 2010, along with implementing rules by the Securities and Exchange Commission (SEC) and the national stock exchanges, corporate governance is now within the purview of federal law to a significant degree. These developments are addressed in other chapters of the book.[1] Decades prior to the enactment of these seminal Acts in the twenty-first century, the SEC was active in its efforts to instill enhanced corporate governance standards. One historic example is the Commission's promulgation of the shareholder proposal rule in 1942—a rule that has been a key component of shareholder rights for 75 years.[2] Given the prominence of the shareholder proposal rule, Chapter 4 focuses on the adoption, implementation, and policy ramifications of this rule.

[1] *See* Chapters 1, 5, 6 herein.

[2] *See* Securities Act Release No. 3347 (1942) (adopting shareholder proposal rule); Patrick J. Ryan, *Rule 14a-8: Institutional Shareholder Proposals and Corporate Democracy*, 23 Ga. L. Rev. 97, 98 (1988) ("Since 1942, the Securities and Exchange Commission (SEC) has required corporate management to include shareholder proposals in its solicitation materials when management itself seeks shareholder voting proxies."); discussion Chapter 4 herein.

Of course, from a twentieth century perspective, the SEC generally did not have the statutory authority to mandate normative standards of corporate conduct.[3] Even today, unless a particular statute grants such authority,[4] the Commission ordinarily may not regulate substantive corporate conduct.[5] At times, the SEC's efforts to do so have been invalidated by the courts. Examples include the SEC's adoption of Rule 19c-4 that, with certain exceptions, barred national securities exchanges from listing stock of companies that disparately affected per share voting rights of shareholders,[6] and its more recent promulgation of Rule 14a-11 that, under specified conditions, allowed eligible shareholders to access the corporate proxy statement in order to nominate directors.[7] These rules were invalidated by the United States Court of Appeals for the District of Columbia Circuit[8] and are discussed elsewhere in this book.[9]

Nonetheless, under the guise of disclosure, the SEC has sought through the decades to impact the conduct of publicly-traded companies and their insiders. Indeed, as was stated by this author 35 years ago:

> Although the rationale underlying disclosure is not based primarily on influencing corporate internal affairs but rather on providing shareholders and the market place with sufficient information to make intelligent decisions and to be apprised of significant developments, there is little question that disclosure has a substantial impact on the normative conduct of corporations. In this

---

[3] *See, e.g., Santa Fe Indus., Inc. v. Green*, 430 U.S. 462 (1977).

[4] For example, pursuant to the Sarbanes-Oxley Act, a publicly-held company ordinarily may not make a loan to its executive officers and directors. *See* § 402 of the Sarbanes-Oxley Act, *adding*, § 13(k) to the Securities Exchange Act, 15 U.S.C. § 78m(k), discussed in Chapter 5 herein.

[5] *See Business Roundtable v. SEC*, 905 F.2d 406, 412 (D.C. Cir. 1990) (invalidating Rule 19c-4 and asserting that the Commission did not have the authority "to establish a federal corporate law by using access to national capital markets as its enforcement mechanism").

[6] *See* Securities Exchange Act Release No. 25891 (1988) (adopting Rule 19c-4). *See generally* Stephen M. Bainbridge, *The Short Life and Resurrection of SEC Rule 19c-4*, 69 Wash U. L.Q. 565 (1991). Today, particularly in connection with initial public offerings (IPOs), dual class capital structures having disparate rights are more frequent. *See* Blair Nicholas and Brandon Marsh, *One Share, No Vote*, The Advocate for Institutional Investors, at 6 (Summer 2017), *available at* www.blbglaw.com (stating that "the number of IPOs with multi-class structures is increasing [as] there were only 6 such IPOs in 2006, but that number more than quadrupled to 27 in 2015").

[7] *See* Securities Exchange Act Release No. 62764 (2010). *See generally* Christopher Takeshi Napier, Comment, *Resurrecting Rule 14a-11: A Renewed Call for Federal Access Reform, Justifications and Suggested Revisions*, 67 Rutgers L. Rev. 843 (2015).

[8] *Business Roundtable v. SEC*, 647 F.3d 1144 (D.C. Cir. 2011) (invalidating Rule 14a-11); *Business Roundtable v. SEC*, 905 F.2d 406 (D.C. Cir. 1990) (invalidating Rule 19c-4).

[9] *See* Chapters 4, 5, 6 herein.

> regard, the Commission's disclosure policies . . . have played a positive role in influencing the establishment of improved standards of conduct.[10]

As perceived by some critics, including a number of its Commissioners, the SEC should not seek to advance objectives that transcend its core mission of disclosure.[11] After the enactment of the Sarbanes-Oxley and Dodd-Frank Acts, this position appears outdated as these Acts expressly grant the Commission specified authority beyond the purview of its traditional disclosure mandate.[12] Nonetheless, even when viewed from the perspective of yesteryear, the SEC historically has invoked its disclosure regimen to significantly impact substantive conduct by corporations and their insiders. This practice continues today with the Commission actively enforcing the disclosure provisions[13] and, by doing so, inducing enhanced corporate governance practices.

This chapter examines several areas of disclosure where the Commission has impacted corporate governance. By way of example, these subjects include insider trading, qualitative materiality, the role of gatekeepers (such as outside directors, attorneys, and accountants), the implementation by subject companies of undertakings pursuant to SEC enforcement proceedings, and mergers and acquisitions. This chapter's focus is on the manner in which the SEC for well over 50 years has impacted corporate governance by means of its disclosure authority.

II. Insider Trading—Regulating Securities Trading by Corporate Fiduciaries and Their Tippees

Insider trading ought to be a fundamental aspect of state corporation law as such conduct implicates the duties of care and loyalty that corporate officers and

---

[10] Marc I. Steinberg, *Corporate Internal Affairs: A Corporate and Securities Law Perspective* 29 (1983). *See* Russell Stevenson, *Corporations and Information—Secrecy, Access and Disclosure* 81–82 (1980) ("Today, the disclosure requirements of the securities laws are used, in a variety of ways, for the explicit purpose of influencing a wide range of corporate primary behavior. . . ."); Elliott Weiss, *Disclosure and Corporate Accountability*, 34 Bus. Law. 575, 575 (1979) ("[O]ne of the central themes of the system by which large corporations are governed [is] that corporate decisionmaking is regulated through mandatory requirements rather than direct government intervention.").

[11] *See [SEC Commissioner] Paredes Questions Use of Securities Laws to Advance Goals Outside SEC Core Mission*, 45 Sec. Reg. & L. Rep. (BNA) 1432 (2013); *[SEC Commissioner] Gallagher Says SEC Should Defer to States on Corporate Governance Issues*, Fed. Sec. L. Rep. (CCH) No. 2564, No. 2567, at 1 (2013). *See generally* Roberta S. Karmel, *Is It Time for a Federal Corporation Law?*, 57 Brook. L. Rev. 55 (1991).

[12] *See* Chapters 5, 6 herein.

[13] *See* Marc I. Steinberg and Ralph C. Ferrara, *Securities Practice: Federal and State Enforcement* (2d ed. 2001 and annual supp.).

directors owe to their subject corporations and shareholders.[14] Yet, the states generally declined to set forth comprehensive principles proscribing this practice.[15] Indeed, even today in a number of states, impersonal stock market insider trading does not give rise to fiduciary liability.[16] This inaction by the states left a distinct gap that federal law has filled. As stated by the U.S. Court of Appeals for the Second Circuit, "a director's common law liability for trading on inside information has been largely mooted by the advent of a federal cause of action under § 10(b) and Rule 10b-5."[17]

A. SECTION 16 OF THE SECURITIES EXCHANGE ACT

The enactment of the Securities Exchange Act of 1934 principally was directed at the secondary trading markets.[18] Disclosure, rather than substantive fairness, was a

---

[14] *See Kahn v. Kolberg Kravis Roberts & Co.*, 23 A.3d 831, 838 (Del. 2011) (to implicate the duty of loyalty in this context, a plaintiff must establish that "(1) the corporate fiduciary possessed material nonpublic information; and (2) the corporate fiduciary used that information improperly by making trades because she was motivated, in whole or in part, by the substance of that information"); *Diamond v. Oreamuno*, 24 N.Y. 2d 494, 498–99, 248 N.E.2d 910, 912, 301 N.Y.S. 78, 81 (1969) (allowing derivative suit against inside traders based on unjust enrichment and alleged harm to the corporation, and stating "there can be no justification for permitting officers and directors . . . to retain for themselves profits . . . derived solely from exploiting information gained by virtue of their inside position as corporate officials").

[15] *See* Marc I. Steinberg and William Wang, *Insider Trading* § 15:2 (3d ed. Oxford University Press 2010) (Other than Delaware, New York, and a relatively small number of other states, the duty to abstain or disclose material information prior to trading only "attach[es] where the insider and the shareholder trade face-to-face; transactions conducted on anonymous exchanges apparently do not qualify."). For examples, *see Van Shaack Holdings, Ltd. v. Van Schaack*, 867 P.2d 892 (Colo. 1994); *Oliver v. Oliver*, 118 Ga. 362, 45 S.E. 232 (1903); *Hotchkiss v. Fischer*, 136 Kan. 530, 16 P.2d 531 (1932); *Buckley v. Buckley*, 230 Mich. 504, 202 N.W. 955 (1925); *Bailey v. Vaughan*, 178 W. Va. 371, 359 S.E.2d 599 (1987). *See also Strong v. Repide*, 213 U.S. 419, 434 (1909) (application of "special facts" doctrine in face-to-face transaction and holding that "under the circumstances detailed, there was a legal obligation on the part of the defendant to make these disclosures").

[16] *See, e.g., Freeman v. Decio*, 584 F.2d 186 (7th Cir. 1978) (applying Indiana law) (rejecting right of corporation to recover profits from insider trading, reasoning lack of corporate harm, concern with double liability, and more effective deterrent provided by federal securities law); *Schein v. Chasen*, 313 So. 3d 739, 746 (Fla. 1975) (opting not "to adopt the innovating ruling of the New York Court of Appeals in *Diamond* [and] adher[ing] to previous precedent established by the courts in this state that actual damage to the corporation must be alleged in the complaint to substantiate a stockholders' derivative action").

[17] *Treadway Companies, Inc. v. Care Corp.*, 638 F.2d 357, 375 n.35 (2d Cir. 1980). *See* Steinberg and Wang, *supra* note 15, at 1023 ("State law is rarely applied to stock market insider trading."); Stephen Bainbridge, *The Insider Trading Prohibition: A Legal and Economic Enigma*, 38 U. Fla. L. Rev. 35, 38 (1986) (stating that federal regulation with respect to insider trading "has, for all practical purposes, superseded" state law); Joel Seligman, *The New Corporate Law*, 59 Brook. L. Rev. 1, 1–2 (1993) (observing that "the state law applicable to insider trading has largely been ignored and has been generally displaced by such federal securities law staples as Rule 10b-5, Section 16 . . . and Rule 14e-3").

[18] *See, e.g., The "Work" of the SEC, available at* http:www.sec.gov/about/whatwedo.shtml (1997) (stating that the Securities Exchange Act "created the Securities and Exchange Commission . . . , empowers the SEC with broad authority over all aspects of the securities industry . . . , identifies and prohibits certain types of conduct

key focus of this legislation.[19] Yet, Congress elected to federalize an aspect of corporate governance by means of Section 16 of that Act.[20] Going beyond the reporting of an insider's trades in the subject security, the statute seeks to deter the misuse of corporate information by such insiders.[21] Section 16 attempts to accomplish this objective by:

- Requiring directors, officers, and shareholders who beneficially own more than 10 percent of a class of equity security of a subject company to report to the SEC and with the applicable securities exchange their stockholdings and transactions in such securities—Section 16(a).[22]

---

in the markets, ... provides the Commission with disciplinary powers ..., and empowers the SEC to require periodic reporting of information by companies with publicly-held securities").

[19] *See, e.g., Santa Fe Indus., Inc. v. Green*, 430 U.S. 462, 477–78 (1977) (This Court "repeatedly has described the fundamental purpose of the [Exchange] Act as implementing a philosophy of full disclosure; once full and fair disclosure has occurred, the fairness of the terms of the transaction is at most a tangential concern of the statute [namely, Section 10(b)]").

[20] 15 U.S.C. § 78p (2012).

[21] *See, e.g.*, Karl Okamoto, *Rereading Section 16(b) of the Securities Exchange Act*, 27 Ga. L. Rev. 183 (1992); Steven Thel, *The Genius of Section 16: Regulating the Management of Publicly-Held Companies*, 42 Hastings L.J. 393 (1991). *But see* Ellen Taylor, *Teaching an Old Law New Tricks: Rethinking Section 16*, 39 Ariz. L. Rev. 1315 (1997) (asserting that § 16(b) should be repealed by Congress).

[22] 15 U.S.C. § 78p(a) (2012). *See* Securities Exchange Act Release No. 18114, 4 Fed. Sec. L. Rep. (CCH) ¶ 26,062, at 19,063-6 (1981):

> Section 16(a) of the [Securities] Exchange Act provides that every person who is directly or indirectly the beneficial owner of more than 10 percent of any class of equity security (other than an exempted security) registered pursuant to Section 12 [of this Act], or who is an officer or director of the issuer of such security, shall file with the Commission an initial report disclosing the amount of all equity securities of such issuer of which he is a beneficial owner.... If the security is also listed on a national securities exchange, such ownership reports must also be filed with the Exchange.

See Securities Exchange Act Release No. 28869 (1991) (addressing the subsequent filing of ownership reports with respect to such insider's transactions in the securities).

With respect to the term "beneficial owner," Rule 16a-1(a)(2) defines the term as "any person who directly or indirectly, through any contract, arrangement, understanding, relationship or otherwise, has or shares direct or indirect pecuniary interest in the equity securities." 17 C.F.R. § 240.16a-1(a)(2) (2017). In ascertaining whether a person is a beneficial owner for purposes of Section 16, two key factors are: (1) whether the subject person has control over the securities, and (2) the subject person's ability to profit, directly or indirectly, from gains made from short-swing transactions. *See, e.g., Whiting v. Dow Chem. Co.*, 523 F.2d 680, 688 (2d Cir. 1975). Some courts, on the other hand, have applied a more restrictive analysis, focusing on whether the subject person is in a position to receive a direct pecuniary benefit from the transactions at issue. In this regard, the Seventh Circuit opined:

> [P]rofit realized by a corporate insider [under Section 16(b)] means direct pecuniary benefit to the insider.... [I]t is not enough that ties of affinity and consanguinity between the ... recipient and the insider make it likely that the insider will experience an enhanced sense of well-being as a result of the receipt, or will be led to reduce his gift-giving to the recipient.

CBI Indus., Inc. v. Horton, 682 F.2d 643, 646 (7th Cir. 1982).

- Requiring these insiders (i.e., directors, officers, and 10 percent shareholders) in an action brought by the corporation or a shareholder on such corporation's behalf to disgorge all profit[23] from "short-swing" transactions—purchases and sales or sales and purchases[24] of a subject equity security made within a six-month period.[25] Recovery is based on strict liability. In other words,

[23] "Profit" is interpreted very broadly under the statute. As summarized by this author:

> In view of the broad remedial nature of the statute, a strict formula for computing "profit realized" has been established. Such a formula is designed to "squeeze all possible profits out of stock transactions, and thus to establish a standard so high as to prevent any conflict between the selfish interest of a fiduciary officer, director, or stockholder and the faithful performance of his duty." ... The formula established matches the lowest price in with the highest price out, thus ensuring recovery of all possible profits. In fact, this formula can yield a profit when in actuality a loss has been suffered.

Marc I. Steinberg, *Securities Regulation: Liabilities and Remedies* § 4.01 n.12 (2017), *quoting, Smolowe v. Delendo Corp.*, 136 F.2d 231, 239 (2d Cir. 1943). *See Whittaker v. Whittaker Corp.*, 639 F.2d 516, 539 (9th Cir. 1981); *Morales v. Mylan Labs., Inc.*, 443 F. Supp. 778 (W.D. Pa. 1978).

[24] With respect to what may be viewed as "unorthodox" transactions, the pragmatic approach has been implemented to ascertain whether a "purchase" or "sale" within the meaning of the statute has occurred. As stated by the U.S. Supreme Court:

> In deciding whether borderline transactions are within the reach of the statute, the courts have come to inquire whether the transaction may serve as a vehicle for the veil which Congress sought to prevent—the realization of short-swing profits based upon access to inside information—thereby endeavoring to implement Congressional objectives without extending the reach of the statute beyond its intended limits.... [T]he prevailing view is to apply the statute only when its application would serve its goals.... [I]n interpreting the terms "purchase" and "sale," courts have properly asked whether the particular type of transaction is one that gives rise to speculative abuse.

Kern County Land Co. v. Occidental Petroleum Corp., 411 U.S. 582, 594–95 (1973) (citations omitted). *See, e.g., At Home Corp. v. Cox Commc'ns, Inc.*, 446 F.3d 403 (2d Cir. 2006); *Heublein, Inc. v. Gen. Cinema Corp.*, 722 F.2d 29 (2d Cir. 1983); *Tex. Int'l Airlines v. Nat'l Airlines, Inc.*, 714 F.2d 533 (5th Cir. 1983).

[25] Generally, a purchase or sale occurs when the subject insider becomes irrevocably committed to the transaction or when transfer of title occurs. *See Absolute Activist Value Master Fund Limited v. Ficeto*, 677 F.3d 60 (2d Cir. 2012). Not surprisingly, many issues are raised with respect to the proper construction of Section 16(b). SEC rules and court decisions have addressed many of these issues. *See, e.g., Credit Suissse Sec. (USA) LLC v. Simmonds*, 556 U.S. 221 (2012) (declining to adopt "open-ended" tolling with respect to § 16(b) claims, and dividing 4 to 4 whether equitable tolling applies to such claims); *Gollust v. Mendell*, 501 U.S. 115 (1991) (holding that provided the complainant beneficially owned a subject security of the issuer when the § 16(b) action is brought and maintains some financial interest in the litigation's outcome, standing to bring suit exists); *Foremost-McKesson, Inc. v. Provident Sec. Co.*, 423 U.S. 232, 250 (1975) (holding that "in a purchase-sale sequence, a beneficial owner [who is not an officer or director] must account for profits only if [he or she] was a beneficial owner [of greater than ten percent of such issuer's equity securities] before the purchase"); *Reliance Electric Co. v. Emerson Elec. Co.*, 404 U.S. 418 (1972) (holding that liability under § 16(b) of a beneficial shareholder (who is not an officer or director) ordinarily cannot be based on such person's sale of the subject securities that occurred after such person's ownership level was less than ten percent); *Merrill Lynch, Pierce Fenner and Smith v. Livingston*, 566 F.2d 1119 (9th Cir. 1978) (holding that determination of "officer" status under § 16 is based on an individual's functions and responsibilities within the company, not on the title held); *Feder v. Martin Marietta Corp.*, 406 F.2d 260 (2d Cir. 1969) (holding that a corporation, such as a parent company, may "deputize" one of its directors or another individual to serve as a director on another entity's board of directors); Securities Exchange Act Release No. 28869 (1991) (SEC release adopting rules under § 16). For

an irrebuttable presumption arises when a subject insider engages in such transactions. The insider's intent to profit from a trade that comes within the statute's reach need not be proven—Section 16(b).[26]

- Prohibiting subject insiders (namely, directors, officers, and 10 percent shareholders) from engaging in short-sale transactions in their corporation's equity securities—Section 16(c).[27]

Thus, Section 16(b) goes far beyond disclosure and directly regulates the substantive conduct of corporate fiduciaries. As Section 16(b)'s language clearly provides, the statute's objective is to "*prevent . . . the unfair use of information* which may be obtained by such beneficial owner [of greater than ten percent of a class of such issuer's equity securities], director, or officer by reason of his relationship to the issuer. . . ."[28] This federal statute, dating back to 1934 and, as elaborated upon by the SEC in its rulemaking function,[29] focuses on normative fiduciary conduct—the *unfair* use of confidential information by directors, officers, and large shareholders. This statute thus is of historical importance as it illustrates Congress's willingness, when deemed appropriate, to federalize key aspects of corporate governance normally perceived to be within the purview of state company law.[30]

---

further discussion on these issues, *see* Marc I. Steinberg and Daryl L. Landsdale, Jr., *The Judicial and Regulatory Constriction of Section 16(b) of the Securities Exchange Act of 1934*, 68 Notre Dame L. Rev. 33 (1992).

[26] *See, e.g., Whiting v. Dow Chem. Co.*, 523 F.2d 680, 687 (2d Cir. 1975) (stating that "the unwary who fall within [§ 16(b)'s] terms have no one but themselves to blame"); *Bershad v. McDonough*, 428 F.2d 693, 696 (7th Cir. 1970) (stating that a subject insider is "deemed capable of structuring his dealings to avoid any possibility of taint and therefore must bear the risks of any inadvertent miscalculation"). For treatises focusing on Section 16, *see, e.g.*, Arnold S. Jacobs, *Section 16 of the Securities Exchange Act* (2016); Peter J. Romeo and Alan L. Dye, *Section 16 Treatise* (2016).

[27] 15 U.S.C. § 78p(c) (2012). Generally, short-selling may be described as "the sale of a security that the seller does not own or that the seller owns but does not deliver." Ralph Janvey, *Short-Selling*, 20 Sec. Reg. L.J. 270, 271 (1992). *See Short-Selling in the Stock Market*, H.R. Rep. No. 102-414, at 8 (1992) (stating that many complaints concerning short-selling "have alleged that short-sellers, after establishing a major short position in a particular stock, have aggressively circulated false rumors about the company's financial condition, problems with its products, or the health or integrity of its officers in an effort to drive down the stock price").

[28] 15 U.S.C. § 78p(b) (2012) (emphasis supplied).

[29] *See, e.g.*, Securities Exchange Act Release No. 28869 (1991); Securities Exchange Act Release No. 37260 (1996); Securities Exchange Act Release No. 47809 (2003); Securities Exchange Act Release No. 64628 (2011).

[30] Another historic example is the role of independent directors of investment companies who are statutorily directed pursuant to the Investment Company Act of 1940 to adhere to specified obligations, including a number of which are fiduciary in nature. As set forth by the SEC Staff:

> The critical role of independent directors of investment companies is necessitated, in part, by the unique structure of investment companies. Unlike a typical corporation, a fund generally has no employees of its own. Its officers are usually employed and compensated by the fund's investment adviser, which is a separately owned and operated entity. The fund relies on its investment adviser and other affiliates—who are

B. EMERGENCE OF A BROAD FEDERAL INSIDER TRADING PROHIBITION—SECTION 10(b) AND RULE 10b-5

Compared to Section 16 of the Securities Exchange Act, Section 10(b) and Rule 10b-5 do not by their terms mention insider trading—or trading on material[31] nonpublic[32] information. Rather, these provisions proscribe deceptive and manipulative acts or practices in connection with the purchase or sale of a security.[33] When Professor William Cary began his tenure as Chairman of the SEC in 1961, he had a relatively short policy agenda.[34] Nonetheless, one key item was to rectify the position of state common law with respect to open-market insider trading. One striking example was a decision by the Massachusetts high court handed down three decades earlier

---

usually the very companies that sponsored the fund's organization—for basic services, including investment advice, administration, and distribution.

Due to this unique structure, conflicts of interest can arise between a fund and the fund's investment adviser. . . . In an effort to control conflicts of interest between funds and their investment advisers, Congress required that at least 40% of a fund's board be composed of independent directors. Congress intended to place independent directors in the role of "independent watchdogs," who would furnish an independent check upon the management of funds and provide a means for the representation of shareholder interests in fund affairs.

Independent directors play a critical role in policing the potential conflicts of interest between a fund and its investment adviser. The Act requires that a majority of a fund's independent directors: approve the fund's contracts with its investment adviser and principal underwriter; select the independent public accountant of the fund; and select and nominate individuals to fill independent director vacancies resulting from the assignment of an advisory contract. . . . Each of these duties and responsibilities is vital to the proper functioning of fund operations and, ultimately, the protection of fund shareholders.

SEC Interpretation: Matters concerning Independent Directors of Investment Companies, Investment Company Act Release No. 24083 (SEC Staff 1999). *See also SEC v. Capital Gains Research Bur., Inc.*, 375 U.S. 180 (1963) (addressing, inter alia, federal fiduciary standards for investment advisers to their clients).

[31] Generally, information is deemed material "if there is a substantial likelihood that a reasonable [investor] would consider it important in deciding how to invest." *Basic, Inc. v. Levinson*, 485 U.S. 224, 231 (1988). *Accord, Matrixx Initiatives, Inc. v. Siracusano*, 563 U.S. 27 (2011). With respect to information relating to prospective events that are contingent in nature, such as in the merger context, the materiality assessment focuses "upon a balancing of both the indicated probability that the event will occur and the anticipated magnitude of the event in light of the totality of the company activity." *SEC v. Tex. Gulf Sulphur Co.*, 401 F.2d 833, 849 (2d Cir. 1968) (en banc). *See* Steinberg and Wang, *supra* note 15, at § 4:2.

[32] *See SEC v. Mayhew*, 121 F.3d 44, 50 (2d Cir. 1997) (stating that information becomes public when there is broad dissemination to the investing public without favoring any person or group or when, although relatively few persons are aware of the subject information, trading on the basis of such information has caused such information to be fully impounded into the particular security's market price). *See* Steinberg and Wang, *supra* note 15, at § 4:3.

[33] *See* 15 U.S.C. § 78j(b) (2012); 17 C.F.R. § 240.10b-5 (2017); *Santa Fe Indus., Inc. v. Green*, 430 U.S. 462, 473 (1977) ("The language of § 10(b) gives no indication that Congress meant to prohibit any conduct not involving manipulation or deception. Nor have we been cited to any evidence in the legislative history that would support a departure from the language of the statute.").

[34] *See* Donald C. Langevoort, *Rereading Cady, Roberts: The Ideology and Practice of Insider Trading Regulation*, 99 Colum. L. Rev. 1319 (1999), *citing* Joel Seligman, *The Transformation of Wall Street*, 344–45 (2d ed. 1995).

opining that open-market insider trading did not constitute common law fraud.[35] Chairman Cary's position was that it is "shocking for business executives to personally profit from their inside information about the corporations they managed [and] that those actions were likely to reduce public confidence . . . in the markets."[36]

Addressing this failure by the states to prohibit insider trading in the impersonal stock exchange context, the SEC handed down its administrative decision in *In re Cady, Roberts & Company*.[37] In an opinion authored by Chairman Cary, the SEC federalized the law of insider trading by treating the exchange-based conduct present in that proceeding as securities fraud. The importance of the proceeding was well recognized by the Commission as the decision starts off by stating: "This is a case of first impression and one of signal importance in our administration of the Federal securities acts."[38] The Commission thereafter opined that "insiders [namely, officers, directors, and controlling stockholders] must disclose material facts which are known to them by virtue of their position but which are not known to persons with whom they deal and which, if known, would affect their investment judgment."[39] This obligation, as set forth in *Cady, Roberts*, rests on two principal rationales: "first, the existence of a relationship giving access, directly or indirectly, to information intended to be available only for a corporate purpose and not for the personal benefit of anyone, and second, the inherent unfairness involved where a party takes

[35] *Goodwin v. Agassiz*, 283 Mass. 358, 362–63, 186 N.E. 659, 661 (1933) (distinguishing when an insider trades on an impersonal stock exchange and one "where a director personally seeks a stockholder for the purpose of buying his shares without making disclosure," and suggesting that liability would ensue only in such face-to-face transactions). *See* Henry Manne, *Insider Trading and the Stock Market* 22 (1966) (commenting that no common law decision was found finding an insider liable for failing to disclose material nonpublic information where the transaction occurred on an impersonal stock exchange); Langevoort, *supra* note 34, at 1319 (discussing the importance of the *Goodwin* decision to Chairman Cary); Joel Seligman, *The Reformulation of Federal Securities Law concerning Nonpublic Information*, 73 Geo. L.J. 1083, 1101 (1985) ("There was no cause of action for transactions effected through 'impersonal' stock markets.").

[36] *Fair To All People: The SEC and the Regulation of Insider Trading, In the Matter of Cady, Roberts & Company*, SEC Historical Society, *available at* www.sechistorical.org (2006). *See* Langevoort, *supra* note 34, at 1320 (stating that "Cary's speeches and writings during and after his chairmanship leave little doubt that he believed that state corporate law was moribund, perhaps even corrupt").

[37] 40 S.E.C. 907 (1961).

[38] *Id.* at 907 (also stating that "the securities acts may be said to have generated a wholly new and far-reaching body of federal corporation law"—*id.* at 910).

[39] *Id.* at 910. In its opinion, the Commission made clear its rejection of state common law, including the "special facts" doctrine. The Commission opined:

> Respondents . . . assert that they made no express representations and did not in any way manipulate the market, and urge that in a transaction on an exchange there is no further duty such as may be required in a "face-to-face" transaction. We reject this suggestion. It would be anomalous indeed if the protection afforded by the anti-fraud provisions were withdrawn from transactions effected on exchanges, primary markets for securities transactions. . . . Consequently, any sales by the insider must await disclosure of the information.

Id. at 912.

advantage of such information knowing it is unavailable to those with whom he is dealing."[40] Thus, the SEC adopted the disclose or abstain rule: a subject insider must refrain from trading in the subject securities until adequate information has been disseminated to the securities marketplace.[41]

In the aftermath of *Cady, Roberts*, there was uncertainty regarding its precedential value. The matter was an administrative ruling, not a federal court decision.[42] Neither the language of the federal securities laws, including Section 10(b), nor the accompanying legislative history commanded that an expansive insider trading prohibition be recognized.[43] Yet, a few years thereafter, the SEC instituted its famous enforcement action in *Texas Gulf Sulphur*,[44] resulting in the Second Circuit's embracement of *Cady, Roberts*. For all practical purposes, within a decade, the Commission's decision in *Cady, Roberts* was instrumental in creating a federal insider trading prohibition in the impersonal stock market context.

In *Texas Gulf Sulphur*, the U.S. Court of Appeals for the Second Circuit embraced the broad "disclose or abstain" rule advanced by the SEC. Reasoning that Section 10(b) and Rule 10b-5 were designed to help ensure that "all investors trading on impersonal exchanges have relatively equal access to material information [and that investors] should be subject to identical market risks,"[45] the court espoused an expansive parity-of-information principle: "[A]nyone in possession of material inside information must either disclose it to the investing public, or if he is disabled from disclosing it in order to protect a corporate confidence, or he chooses not to do so, must abstain from trading in or recommending the securities concerned while

[40] *Id.* at 911, *citing*, 3 Louis Loss, *Securities Regulation* 1450–51 (2d ed. 1961). In an accompanying footnote, the Commission stated: "A significant purpose of the [Securities] Exchange Act was to eliminate the idea that the use of inside information for personal advantage was a normal emolument of corporate office." 40 S.E.C. at 911 n.15.

[41] *See Fair to All People, supra* note 36 ("Cary's administrative opinion announced what became known as the 'disclose or abstain rule,' whereby an insider in possession of material nonpublic information must disclose such information before trading, or if disclosure be impossible or improper, must abstain from trading in that company's stock."); Joel Seligman, *The Transformation of Wall Street—A History of the Securities and Exchange Commission and Modern Corporate Finance* 345 (1982) (discussing SEC expansion of § 10(b) in *Cady, Roberts* to proscribe insider trading in the impersonal stock market context).

[42] *See* Stephen M. Bainbridge, *Who Was the First Person the SEC Found to Have Violated the Insider Trading Laws?, available at* ProfessorBainbridge.com (Nov. 3, 2014).

[43] *Id. See Recent Decision*, 48 Va. L. Rev. 398, 403–04 (1962) (stating that "in view of the limited resources of the Commission, the unfortunate existence of more positive and reprehensible forms of fraud, and the inherent problems concerning proof and evidence adhering to any controversy involving a breach of duty of disclosure, there is little prospect of excessive litigation evolving pursuant to [the SEC's decision in *Cady, Roberts*]"). *See also* Stephen M. Bainbridge, *Incorporating State Law Fiduciary Duties into the Federal Insider Trading Prohibition*, 52 Wash. & Lee L. Rev. 1189 (1995).

[44] *SEC v. Tex. Gulf Sulphur*, 401 F.2d 833 (2d Cir. 1968), *cert. denied sub nom. Coates v. SEC*, 394 U.S. 976 (1969).

[45] 401 F.2d at 848.

such information remains undisclosed."[46] Subsequent decisions handed down by the appellate courts, although apparently retreating from the parity-of-information principle, embraced the access approach: "Anyone—corporate insider or not—who regularly receives material nonpublic information may not use this information to trade in securities without incurring an affirmative duty to disclose."[47]

Clearly, these more expansive principles have been rejected by the U.S. Supreme Court;[48] nonetheless, the federalization of the insider trading prohibition remains entrenched. Although critics may be dismayed that the Supreme Court has confined the reach of the securities laws in general,[49] and more particularly, in the insider trading context,[50] it should not be slighted that the Court has recognized that illegal insider trading comes within the purview of Section 10(b) and Rule 10b-5.[51] And, in so holding, the Court approvingly quoted from the SEC's decision in *Cady, Roberts*.[52]

As interpreted by the U.S. Supreme Court, insider trading liability under Section 10(b) and Rule 10b-5 is based on an insider's breach of fiduciary duty or relationship of trust and confidence. That duty may be owed to the subject company's shareholders on the other side of the transaction ("classical" theory)[53] or to the source of

---

[46] *Id.* at 849. Interestingly, the parity-of-information principle has been adopted by a number of foreign countries. *See, e.g.*, Directive 2014/57/EU of the European Parliament and of the Council (16 April 2014). For further discussion on this Directive, *see* Chapter 7 herein.

[47] *United States v. Chiarella*, 588 F.2d 1358, 1365 (2d Cir. 1978), *rev'd*, 445 U.S. 222 (1981).

[48] *See infra* notes 53–57 and accompanying text.

[49] This author is among the critics, at least with respect to certain of the Supreme Court's decisions. *See* Marc I. Steinberg, *The Ramifications of Recent U.S. Supreme Court Decisions on Federal and State Securities Regulation*, 70 Notre Dame L. Rev. 489 (1995).

[50] *See, e.g.*, Allison Anderson, *Fraud, Fiduciaries, and Insider Trading*, 10 Hofstra L. Rev. 341, 376 (1982) (stating that, with respect to the *Chiarella* decision: "This is not a Supreme Court construing a complicated federal statutory scheme with wisdom, craft, and candor; this is a first-year Torts class on a bad day.").

[51] *See, e.g.*, *Chiarella v. United States*, 445 U.S. 222 (1980):

> Thus, administrative and judicial interpretations have established that silence in connection with the purchase or sale of securities may operate as a fraud actionable under § 10(b) despite the absence of statutory language or legislative history specifically addressing the legality of nondisclosure. But such liability is premised upon a duty to disclose arising from a relationship of trust and confidence between parties to a transaction. Application of a duty to disclose prior to trading guarantees that corporate insiders, who have an obligation to place the shareholder's welfare before their own, will not benefit personally through fraudulent use of material, nonpublic information.

Id. at 230. *See* Roberta S. Karmel, *Prosecution of Tippees Affirmed in* Salman v. United States, 45 Sec. Reg. L.J. 195, 199 (2017) (stating that "given the push back of Justice Scalia and some other judges against insider trading cases, it is important that the Supreme Court [in *Salman v. United States*, 137 S. Ct. 420 (2016)] unanimously approved insider trading prosecutions pursuant to Section 10(b) of the Exchange Act and Rule 10b-5 against remote tippees").

[52] 445 U.S. at 242, *quoting*, *Cady, Roberts & Co.*, 40 S.E.C. 907 (1961).

[53] *See Chiarella v. United States*, 445 U.S. at 222, 230 (1980) (opining that silence may give rise to § 10(b) liability where a duty to disclose exists "arising from a relationship of trust and confidence between parties to a

the information ("misappropriation" theory).[54] The parity of information and equal access theories have been rejected.[55] In the tipper-tippee setting, liability is incurred when the inside tipper conveys the information to the tippee for personal gain or as a gift.[56] Rather ironically, in formulating principles of insider trading liability under federal law, the Supreme Court has applied state law principles of fiduciary duty to determine the parameters of federal disclosure obligations.[57] These Supreme Court decisions and their impact have been analyzed by me in several other books.[58] Suffice it to say, although the Supreme Court has narrowed the scope of the insider trading prohibition, the legacy of *Cady, Roberts* and *Texas Gulf Sulphur* comprises

---

transaction"). In *Dirks v. SEC*, 463 U.S. 646 (1983), the Supreme Court recognized that temporary insiders may be treated the same as directors and officers under certain circumstances:

> Under certain circumstances, such as where corporate information is revealed legitimately to an underwriter, accountant, lawyer, or consultant working for the corporation, these outsiders may become fiduciaries of the shareholders. The basis for recognizing this fiduciary duty is not simply that such persons acquired nonpublic corporate information, but rather that they have entered into a special confidential relationship in the conduct of the business of the enterprise and are given access to information solely for corporate purposes. When such a person breaches his fiduciary relationship, he may be treated more properly as a tipper than a tippee. For such a duty to be imposed, however, the corporation must expect the outsider to keep the disclosed nonpublic information confidential, and the relationship at least must imply such a duty.

Id. at 677 n.14.

[54] *See United States v. O'Hagan*, 521 U.S. 642, 652 (1997) (adopting the misappropriation theory, which provides that "a person commits fraud 'in connection with' a securities transaction, and thereby violates § 10(b) and Rule 10b-5, when he misappropriates confidential information for securities trading purposes, in breach of a duty owed to the source of the information").

[55] *Chiarella*, 445 U.S. at 232–33.

[56] *See United States v. Salman*, 137 S. Ct. 420 (2016); *Dirks v. SEC*, 463 U.S. 646 (1983). As the Court more recently stated in the *Salman* decision: "By disclosing confidential information as a gift to his brother with the expectation that he would trade on it, Maher [the 'inside' tipper] breached his duty of trust and confidence to [his employer] Citigroup and its clients—a duty Salman acquired, and breached himself, by trading on the information with full knowledge that it had been improperly disclosed." 137 S. Ct. at 428.

Nonetheless, the fact remains that *Dirks* rejected the law of tipper-tippee liability that had been embraced by the lower federal courts—namely, that a tippee stood in the shoes of her tipper: if the tipper could not legally engage in the subject transaction, then generally neither could the tippee. *See, e.g., Elkind v. Liggett & Myers, Inc.*, 635 F.2d 156 (2d Cir. 1980).

[57] *See* Marc I. Steinberg and William E. Kaulbach, *The Supreme Court and the Definition of "Security": The "Context" Clause, "Investment Contract" Analysis, and Their Ramifications*, 40 Vand. L. Rev. 489, 538 (1987) (asserting that, in *Chiarella* and *Dirks*, the Supreme Court's "reliance on state law based principles of fiduciary duty is misplaced [and that] Congress clearly intended the federal securities laws to offer greater protection than state law provides").

[58] *See, e.g.*, Marc I. Steinberg, *Securities Regulation* §§ 12.01–12.08 (7th ed. 2017); Marc I. Steinberg, *Securities Regulation: Liabilities and Remedies*, §§ 3.01–3.06 (2017); Marc I. Steinberg, *Understanding Securities Law* 383–94 (6th ed. 2014); Marc I. Steinberg, *International Securities Law—A Contemporary and Comparative Analysis*, 109–12 (1999); Marc I. Steinberg and William K.S. Wang, *Insider Trading* (3d ed. Oxford Univ. Press 2010).

the foundation for the federalization of this important component of corporate governance.[59]

C. THE SEC'S ACTIVISM IN THE INSIDER TRADING CORPORATE GOVERNANCE CONTEXT

Acting pursuant to its rule-making authority, the SEC has expanded the parameters of the insider trading prohibition. Frequently, the Commission has undertaken this course of action when faced with adverse Supreme and lower court decisions. By exercising its authority in this manner, the SEC effectively has further entrenched the federalization of insider trading. For purposes of illustration, three examples follow.

1. Tender Offer Insider Trading—A Return to Yesteryear

Greatly disappointed by the U.S. Supreme Court's decision in *Chiarella*, which rejected both the parity-of-information and access approaches that had been adopted by the lower courts,[60] the SEC searched for a meaningful avenue to ameliorate the impact of that decision. Focusing on Section 14(e) of the Securities Exchange Act,[61] the federal antifraud statute that proscribes fraudulent, deceptive, or manipulative acts or practices in connection with a tender offer,[62] the Commission promulgated an expansive insider trading prohibition confined to the tender offer setting. Viewed as

---

[59] In celebration of the 50th anniversary of the U.S. Court of Appeals for the Second Circuit's en banc decision in *Texas Gulf Sulphur*, the *SMU Law Review* will publish a Symposium Issue. *See* 71 SMU L. Rev. No. 2 (2018). For an insightful article on *Texas Gulf Sulphur* and its ramifications, *see* Alan M. Weinberger, *Forever Young:* Texas Gulf Sulphur *Rules at Fifty*, 45 Sec. Reg. L.J. 23 (2017).

[60] *See* cases cited *supra* notes 44–47; Stephen M. Bainbridge, *Insider Trading Regulation: The Path Dependent Choice between Property Rights and Securities Fraud*, 52 SMU L. Rev. 1589, 1594–98 (1999) (discussing a number of the pre-*Chiarella* lower court and SEC decisions focusing on insider trading); Michael Dooley, *Enforcement of Insider Trading Restrictions*, 66 Va. L. Rev. 1, 74–83 (1980) (listing all insider trading cases brought by the SEC after *Texas Gulf Sulphur*).

[61] 15 U.S.C. § 78n(e) (2012) (providing that "it shall be unlawful for any person to make any untrue statement of a material fact or omit to state any material fact necessary in order to make the statements made, in the light of the circumstances under which they are made, not misleading, or to engage in any fraudulent, deceptive, or manipulative acts or practices, in connection with any tender offer. . . .").

[62] *See id.*; *Schreiber v. Burlington Northern, Inc.*, 472 U.S. 1 (1985) (interpreting the scope of § 14(e) and confining the statute's reach to that of adequacy of disclosure). The term "tender offer" may be defined as "a means frequently used to acquire control of a corporation characterized by active solicitation to purchase a substantial percentage of the target's stock from the target's shareholders at a premium over the market price, offered for a limited period of time and that may be contingent upon the tender of a specific number of shares." Marc I. Steinberg, *Understanding Securities Law* 501 (6th ed. 2014).

perhaps the foremost context in which exorbitant insider trading profits are made,[63] the SEC perceived that it had the authority under Section 14(e)'s delegation of rule-making authority to adopt the far-reaching prohibition that is contained in Rule 14e-3.[64] The SEC's vision of the legitimacy of its authority with respect to Rule 14e-3's promulgation thus far has proven accurate as the Supreme Court in *O'Hagan*, under the facts presented at bar, subsequently upheld the provision's validity.[65]

Eliminating the breach of fiduciary duty (or relationship of trust and confidence) element that the Supreme Court required as an essential condition of insider trading liability under Section 10(b) and Rule 10b-5,[66] the SEC's promulgation of Rule 14e-3 returned to the legal principles that it had embraced in days of yesteryear—namely, the parity-of-information approach enunciated in *Cady, Roberts* and *Texas Gulf Sulphur*.[67] With certain exceptions, Rule 14e-3 prohibits any person who possesses material information relating to a tender offer from trading on or tipping

---

[63] *See Fair to All People: The SEC and the Regulation of Insider Trading—Rule 14e-3 and the Misappropriation Theory*, SEC Historical Museum, *available at* www.sechistorical.org (2006).

[64] *Id.* (stating that "[d]espite Justice Powell's reprimand [in *Chiarella*] about expansive rulemaking outside of the common law of fraud, Rule 14e-3 is not premised on a breach of fiduciary duty [and moreover] Rule 14e-3 was the SEC's institutional response to the *Chiarella* judicial roadblock that had effectively limited the Commission's interpretation of Rule 10b-5"); Thomas C. Newkirk and Melissa A. Robertson, *Speech by SEC Staff: Insider Trading—A U.S. Perspective*, Presented Before the 16th International Symposium on Economic Crime, Jesus College, Cambridge, England (Sept. 19, 1998) (stating that Rule 14e-3's purpose "was to remove the *Chiarella* duty requirement in the tender offer context—where insider trading was most attractive and easily disruptive"). With respect to the SEC's rule-making authority, Section 14(e), 15 U.S.C. § 78n(e), provides: "The Commission shall, for the purposes of this subsection, by rules and regulations, define and prescribe means reasonably designed to prevent, such acts and practices as are fraudulent, deceptive, or manipulative."

[65] *See United States v. O'Hagan*, 521 U.S. 642 (1997), where the Supreme Court held:

> Rule 14e-3(a), *as applied to cases of this genre*, qualifies under § 14(e) as a "means reasonably designed to prevent" fraudulent trading on material, nonpublic information in the tender offer context. A prophylactic measure, because its mission is to prevent, typically encompasses more than the core activity prohibited.... We hold, accordingly, that under § 14(e), the Commission may prohibit acts not themselves fraudulent under the common law or § 10(b), if the prohibition is "reasonably designed to prevent... acts and practices [that] are fraudulent."

Id. at 672–73 (emphasis supplied and quoting 15 U.S.C. § 78n(e) (2012)). On remand, the Eighth Circuit upheld the government's invocation of Rule 14e-3 in that case. *See United States v. O'Hagan*, 139 F.3d 641, 650 (8th Cir. 1998). For further discussion, *see* Steinberg and Wang, *supra* note 15, at § 9:3.

[66] *See, e.g., Chiarella*, 445 U.S. at 230 (holding that "silence in connection with the purchase or sale of securities may operate as a fraud actionable under § 10(b)... [but] such liability is premised upon a duty to disclose arising from a relationship of trust and confidence between parties to a transaction"); discussion *supra* notes 48–57 and accompanying text.

[67] *See* discussion *supra* notes 37–47 and accompanying text. As stated by the Second Circuit in *Texas Gulf Sulphur*, "anyone in possession of material inside information must either disclose it to the investing public, or if he is disabled from disclosing it in order to protect a corporate confidence, or he chooses not to do so, must abstain from trading in or recommending the securities concerned while such information remains undisclosed." 401 F.2d at 849.

that information if such person "knows or has reason to know the information is nonpublic and was received directly or indirectly from the offeror, the subject [e.g., target] corporation, any of their affiliated persons, or any person acting on behalf of either [the offeror or the target]."[68] The Rule also applies lower court case law handed down prior to the Supreme Court's decision in *Dirks*,[69] thereby containing an expansive anti-tipping provision.[70] With certain exceptions, the knowing conveying of material nonpublic information by a tipper is proscribed by Rule 14e-3.[71] Significantly, the recipient-tippee incurs liability under Rule 14e-3 by trading on such material nonpublic information irrespective of whether the subject tipper breached a fiduciary duty or a relationship of trust and confidence.[72]

Through SEC activism, the insider trading prohibition in the tender offer setting has an expansive reach. Unfortunately, this disparate treatment between tender offers and insider trading that occurs in other contexts is problematic. For example, if a subject transaction is structured as a merger, only Section 10(b) and Rule 10b-5 would apply.[73] On the other hand, if a tender offer is deemed to serve as a more suitable acquisition form to attain the desired objectives, then Rule 14e-3 applies along

[68] Marc I. Steinberg, *Securities Regulation* 969 (7th ed. 2017). Notably, Rule 14e-3 provides for certain exceptions with respect to sales to the offeror and to specified activities engaged in by multiservice financial institutions. *See* Rule 14e-3(c), 17 C.F.R. § 240.14e-3(c) (2017). *See generally* SEC Division of Market Regulation, *Broker-Dealer Policies and Procedures Designed to Segment the Flow and Prevent the Misuse of Material Nonpublic Information*, [1989–1990 Transfer Binder] Fed. Sec. L. Rep (CCH) ¶ 84,520 (1990); Theodore A. Levine, et al., *Multiservice Securities Firms: Coping with Conflicts in a Tender Offer Context*, 23 Wake Forest L. Rev. 41 (1988); Marc I. Steinberg and John Fletcher, *Compliance Programs for Insider Trading*, 47 SMU L. Rev. 1783 (1994).

[69] *See, e.g., Elkind v. Liggett & Myers, Inc.*, 635 F.2d 156, 167 (2d Cir. 1980) (imposing liability under § 10(b) based on unlawful trading when recipient-tippee was conveyed material nonpublic information by loose-lip corporate executive).

[70] *See* Rule 14e-3(d), 17 C.F.R. § 240.14e-3(d) (2017). The anti-tipping proscription does not extend to certain communications, such as communications made to persons involved in the financing of the takeover bid or to specified persons "involved in the planning, financing, preparation, or execution of the activities of the issuer with respect to such tender offer." Rule 14e-3(d)(1). Rule 14e-3 also is not intended to encompass casual social discourse that is in good faith. *See* Securities Exchange Act Release No. 17120, [1980 Transfer Binder] Fed. Sec. L. Rep. (CCH) ¶ 82,646, at 83,463 (1980).

[71] *See* discussion *supra* note 70.

[72] *See* sources cited *supra* note 64. Indeed, the absence of such a requirement was observed by the U.S. Supreme Court in *O'Hagan*. In upholding the validity of Rule 14e-3 in the case at bar, the Court observed: "The SEC . . . placed in Rule 14e-3(a) a 'disclose or abstain from trading' command that does not require specific proof of a breach of fiduciary duty." 521 U.S. at 645.

[73] At times, the SEC has invoked Section 17(a)(3) of the Securities Act, 15 U.S.C. § 77q(a)(3), in the insider trading context when the nonpublic information is adverse, thereby precipitating a drop in the market price of the subject security. *See, e.g., In re Bolan*, 2015 SEC LEXIS 2201 (SEC 2015). *See generally* Marc I. Steinberg and Abel Ramirez, Jr., *The SEC's Neglected Weapon: A Proposed Amendment to Section 17(a)(3) and the Application of Negligent Insider Trading*, 19 U. Pa. J. Bus. L. 239 (2017).

with Section 10(b) and Rule 10b-5.[74] The result is that in the tender offer setting a far wider liability net exists. Hence, the liability of an alleged insider trader, tipper, or tippee may depend on the form of the subject transaction, with respect to which the alleged violator may have been unaware.[75] Such disparity in treatment without adequate justification cannot be reconciled with market integrity, investor protection, or fundamental principles of fair treatment among similarly-situated actors.[76]

2. Regulation FD—Solving the "Loose-Lip" Executive Dilemma

Prior to the U.S. Supreme Court's decision in *Dirks*, the law of tipper-tippee liability under Section 10(b) and Rule 10b-5 was relatively clear: namely, if the tipper could not trade, neither could the tippee who knowingly received the material nonpublic information. In other words, the tippee stood in the shoes of its tipper and, upon receiving material nonpublic information, was subject to the disclose or abstain rule.[77] Although this doctrine generally remains good law after the SEC's promulgation of Rule 14e-3 in the tender offer setting,[78] the Supreme Court's decision in *Dirks*[79] drastically curtailed the scope of tipper-tippee liability under Section 10(b) and Rule 10b-5. In that case, and a more recent decision in *Salman v. United States*,[80] the Supreme Court embraced a far more narrow theory of liability dependent on whether the tipper breached his fiduciary duty:

> [T]he test is whether the insider personally will benefit, directly or indirectly, from his disclosure. Absent some personal gain, there has been no breach of

---

[74] For example, under Delaware law, once a parent corporation owns 90 percent or more of its subsidiary stock, a short-form merger may be effected, with appraisal (absent fraud or illegality) being a minority shareholder's sole remedy. *See* Del. Corp. Code § 253 (2011); *Glassman v. Unocal Exploration Corp.*, 777 A.2d 242 (Del. 2001). In order to avoid the "entire fairness" inquiry (*see, e.g., Weinberger v. UOP, Inc.*, 457 A.2d 701 (Del. 1983)), a parent corporation may opt to pursue a tender offer with the objective of reaching the 90 percent ownership threshold. Once that objective is met, a short-form cash-out merger is consummated.

[75] A clear example is *SEC v. Switzer*, 590 F. Supp. 756 (W.D. Okla. 1984), where Coach Barry Switzer overheard a conversation between a corporate executive and his wife regarding a prospective merger. Neither the executive nor his wife was aware of Coach Switzer's presence. Because the deal was structured as a merger, only Section 10(b) and Rule 10b-5 applied. As a result, no liability was incurred as the tipper did not convey the material inside information to Coach Switzer for financial gain or as a gift. On the other hand, if the deal had been structured as a tender offer, clear liability exposure would have existed as Coach Switzer knew that he had received material nonpublic information from an inside source. (Coach Switzer is the former football coach of the Dallas Cowboys and of the University of Oklahoma.)

[76] I have made this point in a number of my other writings. *See, e.g.*, Marc I. Steinberg, *Insider Trading Regulation—A Comparative Analysis*, 37 Int'l Law. 153, 160 (2003).

[77] *See, e.g., Elkind v. Liggett & Myers, Inc.*, 635 F.2d 156 (2d Cir. 1980).

[78] *See* discussion *supra* notes 68–76 and accompanying text.

[79] 463 U.S. 646 (1983).

[80] 137 S. Ct. 420 (2016).

> duty to shareholders. And absent a breach by the insider, there is no derivative breach [by the tippee].[81]

This personal benefit may be established by the insider's receipt of pecuniary gain or enhancement to reputation that will impact future earnings.[82] The requisite benefit also may be shown by the insider's gift of nonpublic information to the recipient: "The tip and trade resemble trading by the insider himself followed by a gift of the profits to the recipient."[83]

That the making of a gift satisfies the personal benefit test for tipper-tippee liability was reaffirmed more recently by the Supreme Court in its 2017 decision in *Salman*. There, the Court held that the defendant violated Section 10(b) and Rule 10b-5 when he traded on material confidential information knowing that the subject information had been conveyed in breach of the tipper's obligation to his employer and his employer's clients: "By disclosing confidential information as a gift to his brother with the expectation that he would trade on it, Maher [the 'inside' tipper] breached his duty of trust and confidence to [his employer] Citigroup and its clients—a duty [the tippee] Salman acquired, and breached himself, by trading on the information with full knowledge that it had been improperly disclosed."[84]

As perceived by the SEC, *Dirks* left a large void with respect to improper tipping—namely, the situation involving the "loose lip" executive. Lower court case law prior to *Dirks* prohibited the tippee from trading on the material nonpublic information or improperly conveying such information to others, as the tippee stood in the shoes of her tipper.[85] After *Dirks*, however, receipt of personal benefit by the insider-tipper or conveyance of a gift by such insider is required to be shown.[86] What ensued,

---

[81] 463 U.S. at 662.

[82] *Id.* at 663. *See also United States v. McDermott*, 277 F.3d 240 (2d Cir. 2002); *SEC v. Maio*, 51 F.3d 623 (7th Cir. 1995); *SEC v. Musella*, 678 F. Supp. 1060 (S.D.N.Y. 1988).

[83] 463 U.S. at 664. *See United States v. Blackwell*, 459 F.3d 739 (6th Cir. 2006); *SEC v. Thayer*, 84 Civ. 0066 (S.D.N.Y. 1984).

[84] *Salman v. United States*, 137 S. Ct. 420, 428 (2017). Language in *Dirks* sets forth that the tippee knew or should have known of the insider's breach. *See* 463 U.S. at 660 ("Thus, a tippee assumes a fiduciary duty to the shareholders of a corporation not to trade on material nonpublic information only when the insider has breached his fiduciary duty to the shareholders by disclosing the information to the tippee and the tippee knows or should know that there has been a breach."). On the other hand, language in *Salman* makes clear that the tippee's knowledge must be proven. *See* 137 S. Ct. at 427, 428. *Salman* was a criminal case; therefore, knowledge clearly was required. In any event, because Section 10(b) is a fraud statute, requiring scienter (*see Aaron v. SEC*, 446 U.S. 680 (1980), *Ernst & Ernst v. Hochfelder*, 425 U.S. 185 (1976)), the defendant tippee's knowledge (knowing or reckless misconduct) should be the appropriate culpability standard. *See* Marc I. Steinbeg, *Securities Regulation: Liabilities and Remedies* § 3.04[1] (2017); Marc I. Steinberg and Ralph C. Ferrara, *Securities Practice: Federal and State Enforcement* § 2:8 (2d ed. 2001 and 2017–2018 supp.).

[85] *See, e.g., Elkind v. Liggett & Myers, Inc.*, 635 F.2d 156 (2d 1980) ("loose-lip" executive).

[86] *See* discussion *supra* notes 79–84 and accompanying text.

according to the Commission and others, was an onslaught of selective disclosure by companies (through their spokespersons) to financial analysts—allegedly with the objective of currying favor with such analysts.[87] Although the Commission on occasion instituted enforcement actions seeking to bring such conduct within the realm of *Dirks*,[88] this approach proved problematic.[89]

This practice persisted for several years until it drew the ire of SEC chairman Arthur Levitt at the beginning of the century.[90] Such selective disclosure practices, as observed by Chairman Levitt, benefitted market professionals to the detriment of ordinary investors, defying "principles of integrity and fairness."[91] Responding to this perceived unfairness, the Commission promulgated Regulation FD (Fair Disclosure),[92] thereby effectively filling the gap left open by *Dirks*. The Regulation's fundamental premise is that "when an issuer, or person acting on its behalf, discloses material nonpublic information to [selective] persons, . . . it must make public disclosure of that information."[93] Hence, by engaging in rule-making outside the realm

[87] *See, e.g.*, Fred Barbash, *Companies, Analysts a Little Too Cozy*, Wash. Post, Oct. 31, 1999, at H1 (reporting that analysts were basing their recommendations to an increasing degree on information procured by means of selective disclosure made by corporate insiders rather than by undertaking independent research).

[88] *See, e.g.*, *SEC v. Stevens*, Securities Litigation Release No. 12813, 1991 SEC LEXIS 451 (1991) (settlement whereby subject corporation's CEO allegedly received a "direct, tangible benefit to his status as a corporate manager" through his selective disclosure of material nonpublic information to analysts).

[89] *See* Marc I. Steinberg and Jason B. Myers, *Lurking in the Shadows: The Hidden Issues of the Securities and Exchange Commission's Regulation FD*, 27 J. Corp. L. 173, 177 (2002) ("Given the absence of any personal benefit, the Supreme Court's holding in *Dirks* ordinarily foreclosed any liability to the insider who selectively disclosed material nonpublic information as well as any tippee liability to the analyst who recommended trading in the company's stock to clients [and, in addition,] the analyst ordinarily did not incur liability under *O'Hagan*'s misappropriation theory because no obligation was owed by the analyst to the issuer to keep the information confidential.").

[90] Mr. Levitt served as SEC Chairman from 1993 to 2001, the longest serving chairman in the Commission's history.

[91] Michael Schroeder and Randall Smith, *Disclosure Rule Cleared by the SEC*, Wall St. J., Aug. 11, 2000, at C1.

[92] *See Selective Disclosure and Insider Trading*, Securities Exchange Act Release No. 43154, 2000 SEC LEXIS 1672 (2000).

[93] *Id.* As the Commission summarized in the adopting Release:

> *Regulation FD (Fair Disclosure)* is [an] issuer disclosure rule that addresses selective disclosure. The regulation provides that when an issuer, or person acting on its behalf, discloses material nonpublic information to certain enumerated persons (in general, securities market professionals and holders of the issuer's securities who may well trade on the basis of the information), it must make public disclosure of that information. The timing of the required public disclosure depends on whether the selective disclosure was intentional or non-intentional; for an intentional selective disclosure, the issuer must make public disclosure simultaneously; for a non-intentional disclosure, the issuer must make public disclosure promptly. Under the regulation, the required public disclosure may be made by filing or furnishing a Form 8-K, or by another method or combination of methods that is reasonably designed to effect broad, non-exclusionary distribution of the information to the public.

of Section 10(b), the Commission wisely opted to chart an approach that largely remedied its concerns with *Dirks* without contravening Supreme Court authority.[94] In this manner, the SEC federalized the insider trading prohibition (albeit pursuant to Regulation FD) with respect to unlawful tipping to a degree that the Supreme Court did not envision.[95]

3. The Sanctity of Family Relationships

As discussed above, the misappropriation theory is premised upon the subject trader's breach of fiduciary duty or breach of a relationship of trust and confidence to the source of the information.[96] In a surprising decision, the Second Circuit, in a case involving the government's attempted invocation of the misappropriation theory, held that marriage constitutes neither a fiduciary relationship nor a relationship of trust and confidence.[97] Although a number of courts declined to follow the Second

---

[94] Note that Regulation FD does not give rise to a private right of action. Further, seeking to help ensure the Regulation's validity, Regulation FD provides that Section 10(b) liability does not arise "solely" due to an issuer's failure to adhere to the Regulation. *Id.*

[95] The SEC episodically has brought enforcement actions for violations of Regulation FD by subject issuers, insiders, and company spokespersons. *See, e.g.*, *SEC v. Flowserve Corp.*, 37 Sec. Reg. & L. Rep. (BNA) 556 (D.D.C. 2005); *SEC v. Schering-Plough Corp.*, 35 Sec. Reg. & L. Rep. (BNA) 1479 (D.D.C. 2003); *In the Matter of Secure Computing Corp.*, Securities Exchange Act Release No. 46895 (2002). On the other hand, at times, the Commission has been criticized for its overzealous invocation of Regulation FD in its enforcement actions. For example, in *SEC v. Siebel Sys., Inc.*, 384 F. Supp. 2d 694 (S.D.N.Y. 2005), the court dismissed the Commission's action alleging Regulation FD violations and expressed its displeasure:

> The SEC . . . scrutinized, at an extremely heightened level, every particular word used in the statement, including the tense of verbs and the general syntax of each sentence. No support for such an approach can be found in Regulation FD. . . . Such an approach places an unreasonable burden on a company's management and spokespersons to become linguistic experts, or otherwise live in fear of violating Regulation FD should the words they use later be interpreted by the SEC as connoting even the slightest variance from the company's public statements.
>
> . . . .
>
> Applying Regulation FD in an overly aggressive manner cannot effectively encourage full and complete public disclosure of facts reasonably deemed relevant to investment decision making. It provides no clear guidance for companies to conform their conduct in compliance with Regulation FD. Instead, the enforcement of Regulation FD by excessively scrutinizing vague general statements has a potential chilling effect which can discourage, rather than encourage, public disclosure of material information.

[96] *See United States v. O'Hagan*, 521 U.S. 642, 652–53 (1997) (stating that "the misappropriation theory outlaws trading on the basis of nonpublic information by a corporate 'outsider' in breach of a duty owed not to a trading party, but to the source of the information"); discussion *supra* note 54 and accompanying text.

[97] *United States v. Chestman*, 947 F.2d 551 (2d Cir. 1991) (en banc), *cert. denied*, 503 U.S. 1004 (1992). *See id.* at 571 (stating that "Keith's status as Susan's husband could not itself establish fiduciary status" and that no relationship of trust and confidence existed between the husband and wife as "[s]uperiority and reliance did not mark this relationship. . . .").

Circuit's decision,[98] the SEC proactively engaged in its rule-making function to bring certainty to this area—and resolving the matter to the Commission's liking. In adopting Rule 10b5-2, the SEC set forth three nonexclusive situations when a subject person is deemed to have a relationship of trust and confidence for purposes of the misappropriation theory under Section 10(b) and Rule 10b-5.[99] As enunciated by the Commission, such a duty of trust and confidence exists when:

> [1] A person agrees to maintain information in confidence.
>
> [2] Two people have a history, pattern, or practice of sharing confidences such that the recipient of the information knows or reasonably should know that the person communicating the material nonpublic information expects that the recipient will maintain its confidentiality. This is a "facts and circumstances" test based on the expectation of the parties in light of the overall relationship.
>
> [3] A person receives or obtains material nonpublic information from certain enumerated close family members: a spouse, parents, children, and siblings. An affirmative defense permits the person receiving or obtaining the information to demonstrate that under the facts and circumstances of that family relationship, no duty of trust or confidence existed.[100]

In promulgating Rule 10b5-2, the Commission included not only close family members but also other personal relationships. Indeed, in a striking expansion, the Rule encompasses even persons who may be strangers—namely, its inclusion of persons subject to nondisclosure agreements.[101] In this manner, the SEC transformed a contractual arrangement into a relationship of trust and confidence. Indeed, parties often enter into nondisclosure agreements because they do not trust the other party to maintain the confidentiality of the subject information. Whether this aspect of Rule 10b5-2 will be upheld by the courts has not yet been resolved.[102] For our

---

[98] *See, e.g., SEC v. Yun*, 327 F.3d 1263, 1272–73 (11th Cir. 2003) (stating that "a spouse who trades in breach of a reasonable and legitimate expectation of confidentiality held by the other spouse sufficiently subjects the former to insider trading liability").

[99] 17 C.F.R. § 240.10b5-2 (2017).

[100] Securities Exchange Act Release No. 43154, [2000 Transfer Binder] Fed. Sec. L. Rep. (CCH) ¶ 86,319, at 83,686–87 (2000).

[101] *See* Rule 10b5-2(b)(1), 17 C.F.R. § 240.10b5-2(b)(1) (2017) (providing that a duty of trust and confidence exists "[w]henever a person agrees to maintain information in confidence").

[102] *See SEC v. Cuban*, 634 F. Supp. 2d 713, 730–31 (N.D. Tex. 2009), *rev'd on other grounds*, 620 F.3d 551 (5th Cir. 2010) ("Because Rule 10b5-2(b)(1) attempts to predicate misappropriation theory liability on a mere confidentiality agreement lacking a non-use component, the SEC cannot rely on it to establish Cuban's liability under the misappropriation theory."); *United States v. Kim*, 184 F. Supp. 2d 1006, 1015 (N.D. Cal. 2002) (stating that "an express agreement can provide the basis for misappropriation liability only if the express agreement sets forth a relationship with the hallmarks of a fiduciary relationship").

purposes, however, the SEC's adoption of this far-reaching Rule is consistent with the Commission's quest to federalize the insider trading proscription, at times to the greatest extent practicable.[103]

III. Qualitative Materiality—Seeking to Impact Normative Fiduciary Conduct Through the Guise of Disclosure

Self-dealing by corporate directors and officers implicates the duty of loyalty under state corporate law.[104] Yet, such conduct ordinarily becomes known to shareholders by means of the disclosure requirements of the federal securities laws and SEC regulations adopted pursuant thereto. For example, SEC Regulation S-K requires executive compensation to be disclosed for a company's chief executive officer (CEO), chief financial officer (CFO), and the three most highly paid executive officers other than the CEO and CFO.[105] Transactions between a subject company and any of its

---

[103] *See* Bainbridge, *supra* note 60, at 1597, where Professor Bainbridge asserted:

> Insider trading was an ideal target for federalization. Rapid expansion of the federal insider trading prohibition purportedly demonstrated the superiority of federal securities law over state corporate law. Because the states had shown little interest in insider trading for years, federal regulation demonstrated the modernity, flexibility, and innovativeness of the securities laws. The SEC's prominent role in attacking insider trading thus placed it in the vanguard of the movement to federalize corporate law and ensured that the Commission would have a leading role in any system of federal corporations law.

Id.

Another example where the SEC acted proactively to expand insider trading liability involved the "use" versus "possession" standard. Historically, the SEC's position generally was that the mere possession of material nonpublic information is adequate for insider trading liability under Section 10(b). This position evidently was accepted by the Second Circuit. *See United States v. Teicher*, 987 F.2d 112, 120 (2d Cir. 1993). On the other hand, a number of other appellate courts held that proof of use of the subject information was required under Section 10(b). *See United States v. Smith*, 155 F.3d 1051 (9th Cir. 1998); *SEC v. Adler*, 137 F.3d 1325 (11th Cir. 1998). Reacting to these decisions, the SEC adopted Rule 10b5-1, 17 C.F.R. § 240.10b5-1, which provides an "awareness" standard. Hence, under Rule 10b5-1, the applicable standard is whether the trader was "aware" of the subject material nonpublic information at the time that the purchase or sale occurred. In addition, Rule 10b5-1 generally provides an affirmative defense if the specified transactions were engaged in pursuant to a preexisting contract, plan, or instruction that is specific and binding. *See* Securities Exchange Act Release No. 43154 (2000); Allan Horwich, *The Origin, Application, Validity, and Potential Misuse of Rule 10b5-1*, 62 Bus. Law. 913 (2007). This proactive rule-making by the Commission serves as another example of the SEC seeking to implement a more expansive federalization of insider trading than what a number of courts had determined. For discussion critical of the current approach under the federal securities laws with respect to insider trading, *see* Chapter 7 herein.

[104] *See, e.g., Marciano v. Nakash*, 535 A.2d 400 (Del. 1987); *Aronson v. Lewis*, 473 A.2d 805 (Del. 1984); *State ex rel. Hayes Oyster Co. v. Keypoint Oyster Co.*, 391 P.2d 979 (Wash. 1964); *Remillard Brick Co. v. Remillard-Dandini Co.*, 241 P.2d 66 (Cal. App. 1952). Self-dealing may be defined as the fiduciary receiving a financial benefit to the detriment of the corporation and collectively its shareholders. *See Sinclair Oil Corp. v. Levien*, 280 A.2d 717 (Del. 1971).

[105] Regulation S-K, Item 402(a)(3), 17 C.F.R. § 229.402(a)(3) (2017).

executive officers or directors (as well as any immediate family member) also must be disclosed, provided that the amount involved is greater than $120,000.[106] In addition, SEC Regulation S-K mandates disclosure of a director's or executive officer's involvement in specified legal proceedings, including, for example, criminal prosecutions, securities regulatory proceedings, and civil actions wherein the fiduciary was found liable of fraud in connection with a business entity.[107] Regulation S-K also calls for other pertinent information impacting an executive officer's or director's integrity or competency, such as such person's: involvement in bankruptcy proceedings,[108] business experience,[109] and family relationships with any other director or executive officer.[110]

The Commission's historical focus on requiring disclosure of information relating to a director's or executive officer's integrity or competency dates back to the mid-1960s. In the *Franchard Corporation* proceeding,[111] an opinion authored by Chairman Cary, the company's registration statement neglected to disclose the diversion of corporate funds for the benefit of the company's CEO. Finding that this omission rendered the representations contained in the registration statement materially misleading, the Commission concluded that such self-dealing was material to investors as it was "germane to an evaluation of the integrity of management."[112] The *Franchard* proceeding established the principle that has been recognized by the federal courts that management self-dealing is required to be disclosed to shareholders, as such conduct "demonstrates a betrayal of trust to the corporation and shareholders and the director's essential unfitness for corporate stewardship."[113]

---

[106] Regulation S-K, Item 404, 17 C.F.R. § 229.404 (2017).

[107] Regulation S-K, Item 401(f), 17 C.F.R. § 229.401(f) (2017).

[108] Regulation S-K, Item 402(f)(1), 17 C.F.R. § 229.401(f)(1) (2017).

[109] Regulation S-K, Item 401(e)(1), 17 C.F.R. § 229.401(e)(1) (2017).

[110] Regulation S-K, Item 401(d), 17 C.F.R. § 229.401(d) (2017). Depending on the circumstances, courts may require greater disclosure than that called for by SEC rules and regulations, including Regulation S-K. *See, e.g.*, *Maldonado v. Flynn,* 597 F.2d 789 (2d Cir. 1979):

> Since self-dealing presents opportunities for abuse of a corporate position of trust, the circumstances surrounding corporate transactions in which directors have a personal interest are directly relevant to a determination of whether they are qualified to exercise stewardship of the company. . . . For this reason Rule 14a-9 specifically sets out minimum standards and, *going beyond the Rule,* it has been recognized that shareholders are entitled to truthful presentation of factual information impugning the honesty, loyalty or competency of directors in their dealings with the corporation to which they owe a fiduciary duty.

Id. at 796 (emphasis supplied).

[111] *In re Franchard Corp.*, 42 S.E.C. 163, [1964–1966 Transfer Binder] Fed. Sec. L. Rep. (CCH) ¶ 77,113 (1964).

[112] 42 S.E.C. at 172, [1964–1966 Transfer Binder] Fed. Sec. L. Rep. (CCH) ¶ 77,113, at 82,043 (also commenting that the "quality" of executive officers is of "cardinal importance" to investors).

[113] *Gaines v. Haughton,* 645 F.2d 761, 779 (9th Cir. 1981). For cases holding that management self-dealing must be disclosed to shareholders, *see, e.g.*, *Maldonado v. Flynn*, 597 F.2d 789, 796 (2d Cir. 1979) ("Since self-dealing presents opportunities for abuse of a corporate position of trust, the circumstances surrounding corporate

Nonetheless, not all misconduct or other questionable conduct by executive officers or directors must be disclosed. For example, one appellate court has held that a CEO's fabrication of his educational background representing that he had a college degree was not material to investors.[114] As another example, courts have held that, so long as not economically material, a company need not disclose unethical or uncharged criminal conduct by an executive officer or director.[115] Hence, even though a good amount of information relating to the integrity and competency of directors and executive officers must be disclosed, the fact remains that (unless economically material) certain unethical conduct need not be disclosed.[116]

Nonetheless, the important point for purposes of our discussion is that disclosure of qualitative materiality, embraced by the SEC over 50 years ago, has a positive role with respect to improving standards of normative conduct. As SEC Chairman Manuel F. Cohen (1964–1969) reflected, "if specific facts as to the independence, [integrity,]

---

transactions in which directors have a personal interest are directly relevant to a determination of whether they are qualified to exercise stewardship of the company."); *SEC v. Kovzan*, 43 Sec. Reg. & L. Rep. (BNA) 1663 (D. Kan. 2011) (failure to disclose company's payment of more than $1 million in perquisites to former CEO actionable); *SEC. v. Savino*, [2005–2006 Transfer Binder] Fed. Sec. L. Rep. (CCH) ¶ 93,705 (S.D.N.Y. 2006) (alleged failure by company to disclose kickbacks to fiduciary held actionable); *SEC v. Tyson Foods Inc.*, 37 Sec. Reg. & L. Rep. (BNA) 774 (D.D.C. 2005) (settlement alleged that company failed to disclose perquisites received by its former chairman); *SEC v. Kalvex, Inc.*, 425 F. Supp. 310, 315 (S.D.N.Y. 1975) (failure to disclose self-dealing by director held material as "the undisclosed facts might have led a reasonable stockholder to question the integrity of [the director] and his ability to discharge his fiduciary obligations"). *But see Rok v. Identiv*, [2016–2017 Transfer Binder] Fed. Sec. L. Rep. (CCH) ¶ 99,491 (N.D. 2017) (among other holdings, dismissing complaint on basis that allegedly improper personal benefit that executive received was relatively small). For further discussion, *see* Ralph C. Ferrara, Richard M. Starr, and Marc I. Steinberg, *Disclosure of Information Bearing on Management Integrity and Competency*, 65 Nw. U. L. Rev. 555 (1981).

114 *Greenhouse v. MCG Capital Corp.*, 392 F.3d 650 (4th Cir. 2004). *But see* Floyd Norris, *Radio Shack Chief Resigns after Lying*, N.Y. Times, Feb. 21, 2006, at C1 (reporting that company's CEO resigned after "revelation that he had lied to the company about his education by claiming two college degrees when he had none").

115 *See, e.g., Gaines v. Haughton*, 645 F.2d 761, 779 (9th Cir. 1981) (unless self-dealing or SEC mandated disclosure, no duty to disclose unethical or uncharged criminal conduct by director or executive officer); *In re Axis Capital Holdings Ltd. Sec. Litig.*, 456 F. Supp. 2d 576, 587 (S.D.N.Y. 2006) (stating that "the obligation to disclose uncharged illegal conduct will not arise from the materiality of this information alone [but rather] arises when it is necessary to disclose this conduct under the terms of a statute or regulation or . . . to prevent statements the corporation does make from misleading the public"). *See also* SEC Memorandum as Amicus Curiae in *Gaines v. Haughton* (seeking rehearing) (asserting that plaintiff's allegations that "certain of Lockheed's officers and directors knew and participated in substantial and pervasive illegal practices . . . are not so obviously unimportant to a reasonable shareholder's evaluation of the fitness of nominees to serve as directors that they may be dismissed as a matter of law [and that such] alleged practices raise substantial questions regarding the character and integrity of the officers relevant to their management of the corporation which shareholders might well consider important").

116 *See generally* Geeyoung Min, *The SEC and the Courts' Cooperative Policing of Related Party Transactions*, 2014 Colum. Bus. L. Rev. 663 (2014) ("cast[ing] doubt on the effectiveness of the current regulation of related party transactions [and opining that the] ambiguity of the federal securities regulations leaves too much room for manipulation").

and diligence of directors . . . are required to be openly discussed, . . . progress will indeed occur."[117] In this regard, the mandatory disclosure of an unsavory contemplated self-dealing transaction that would arouse the ire of activist shareholders may induce the subject company's board of directors to refrain from engaging in the transaction.[118] Likewise, that disclosure must be made that a prospective candidate for election as a director was found liable in a state court action for fraud in connection with a closely-held corporation may dissuade the board of directors from pursuing that nomination.[119] In such instances, the SEC's disclosure regimen, as interpreted and buttressed by the federal courts, substantively impacts corporate governance practices.[120]

IV. Rebounding from a Failed Attempt to Create Federal Minimum Standards

Chapter 2 of this book discusses the many legislative proposals to enact a federal corporation law or mandatory federal minimum standards. Until the enactment of the

[117] Manuel F. Cohen, *S.E.C. Power to Regulate Corporate Internal Affairs through Disclosure*, in *Standards for Regulating Corporate Internal Affairs* 292 (D. Fischel ed. 1981).

[118] *See* Regulation S-K, Item 404, 17 C.F.R. § 229.404 (2017).

[119] *See* Regulation S-K, Item 401(f)(7)(iii), 17 C.F.R. § 229.401(f)(7)(iii) (2017).

[120] This point was made by me in a book published 35 years ago. *See* Marc I. Steinberg, *Corporate Internal Affairs—A Corporate and Securities Law Perspective* 28–39 (1983).

Note that qualitative materiality focusing on management integrity and competency is to be distinguished from qualitative economic materiality. For example, SEC Staff Accounting Bulletin (SAB) 99, 64 Fed. Reg. 45150 (1999), recognizes that a company should not solely rely on quantitative benchmarks (such as 5 percent in making its materiality determinations). In SAB 99, the SEC staff set forth a list of factors that may have the effect of causing a seemingly small quantitative misstatement of a financial statement item to be deemed material. As set forth in SAB 99, these factors are:

- Whether the misstatement arises from an item capable of precise measurement or whether it arises from an estimate and, if so, the degree of imprecision inherent in the estimate;
- Whether the misstatement masks a change in earnings or other trends;
- Whether the misstatement hides a failure to meet analysts' consensus expectations for the enterprise;
- Whether the misstatement changes a loss into income or vice versa;
- Whether the misstatement concerns a segment or other portion of the registrant's business that has been identified as playing a significant role in the registrant's operations or profitability;
- Whether the misstatement affects the registrant's compliance with regulatory requirements;
- Whether the misstatement affects the registrant's compliance with loan covenants or other contractual requirements;
- Whether the misstatement has the effect of increasing management's compensation—for example, by satisfying requirements for the award of bonuses or other forms of incentive compensation; and
- Whether the misstatement involves concealment of an unlawful transaction.

Id. Generally, SAB 99 has received judicial approbation. *See, e.g., Litwin v. Blackstone Group, L.P.*, 634 F.3d 706 (2d Cir. 2011); *Ganino v. Citizens Utilities Co.*, 228 F.3d 154 (2d Cir. 2000). *See generally* Clarissa Hodges, *The Qualitative Considerations of Materiality: The Emerging Relationship between Materiality and Scienter*, 30 Sec. Reg. L.J. 4 (2002).

Sarbanes-Oxley Act of 2002, all of these efforts failed. In the 1970s, one such effort was initiated by means of Section 10(b) of the Securities Exchange Act and Rule 10b-5 promulgated thereunder by the SEC. Stated succinctly, the plaintiff alleged in *Santa Fe Industries, Inc. v. Green*[121] that the monetary consideration that he received for his shares in connection with a short-form merger was grossly deficient and thereby constituted constructive fraud within the scope of Section 10(b).[122] The U.S. Court of Appeals for the Second Circuit agreed, holding that neither misrepresentation nor nondisclosure was required to be shown.[123] The Supreme Court reversed. The Court reasoned that Section 10(b)'s statutory language, its legislative history, the federal securities law objective of effectuating adequacy of disclosure, and the focus of state corporation law on fiduciary standards for directors and officers signified that breaches of fiduciary duty, absent deficiency in disclosure, do not come within Section 10(b) and Rule 10b-5.[124]

Hence, the Supreme Court recognized that affirming the Second Circuit's holding would bring within Section 10(b) and Rule 10b-5 "a wide variety of corporate conduct traditionally left to state regulation."[125] While recognizing that a need may exist for the adoption of uniform federal fiduciary standards to govern management self-dealing in certain contexts, these standards, the Court reasoned, "should not be supplied by judicial extension of § 10(b) and Rule 10b-5 to cover the corporate universe."[126] The Court thus rejected the attempt to create a federal minimum standards regime by means of Section 10(b) and Rule 10b-5 whereby fiduciary misconduct involving self-dealing (in connection with the purchase or sale of a security) would come within the purview of federal law. The *Santa Fe* decision thus is clearly significant. Had the Supreme Court upheld the Second Circuit's embracement of "constructive fraud," such self-dealing transactions would have become part of the federal securities law landscape.[127]

---

[121] 430 U.S. 462 (1977).

[122] *Id.* at 466–67.

[123] *Green v. Santa Fe Indus., Inc.*, 533 F.2d 1283, 1292 (2d Cir. 1976), *rev'd*, 430 U.S. 462 (1977). The Second Circuit held:

> Whether full disclosure has been made is not the critical inquiry since it is the merger and the undervaluation which constitutes the fraud, and not whether or not the majority determines to lay bare their real motives. If there is no valid corporate purpose for the merger, then even the most brazen disclosure of that fact to the minority shareholders in no way mitigates the fraudulent conduct.

[124] 430 U.S. at 473, 477–79 (also expressing concern that expanding Section 10(b) to encompass fiduciary self-dealing violations would pose a danger of "vexatious litigation"). *Id.* at 478–79.

[125] *Id.* at 478.

[126] *Id.*

[127] *See* Ralph C. Ferrara and Marc I. Steinberg, *A Reappraisal of Santa Fe: Rule 10b-5 and the New Federalism*, 129 U. Pa. L. Rev. 263 (1980).

A. THE SEC'S RESPONSE—DISCLOSURE OF "FAIRNESS"

In response to *Santa Fe*, the SEC adopted Rule 13e-3 under the Securities Exchange Act.[128] Under the guise of disclosure, the Commission requires that in a going-private transaction[129] the subject issuer disclose material facts regarding the transaction, including whether it "reasonably believes that the Rule 13e-3 transaction is fair or unfair to unaffiliated security holders" and the "material factors" upon which such belief is based.[130] Failure to adequately disclose or the providing of materially false information in this context gives rise to SEC enforcement action as well as private litigation under the federal securities laws.[131] Thus, although *Santa Fe* precluded Section 10(b) from being applied with respect to the substantive fairness of a going-private transaction, Rule 13e-3 indirectly accomplishes this result to a significant degree by means of its rigorous disclosure mandates. Through its rule-making authority, the SEC, in practical effect, has improved the process by which going-private transactions are effectuated.[132] This activism has proven beneficial to minority shareholders and the enhancement of corporate governance standards.

B. RECOGNITION OF A FEDERAL CLAIM BASED ON STATE LAW

Unrelated to SEC activism, the *Santa Fe* decision precipitated a new line of cases that premised a Section 10(b) cause of action on the availability of a state law remedy. This line of cases arose from the *Santa Fe* Court's statement that the defendant company's failure to provide the minority shareholders with advance notice of the merger did not constitute a material nondisclosure.[133] The Supreme Court

---

[128] 17 C.F.R. § 240.13e-3 (2017).

[129] Stated generally, a going-private transaction involves the undertaking of a merger or other transaction whereby a publicly-traded company becomes privately-held and its shareholders are cashed-out.

[130] *See* Rule 13e-3, 17 C.F.R. § 240.13e-3, SEC Schedule 13E-3, Item 8 (2017); SEC Regulation M-A, Item 1014.

[131] *See, e.g., Howing Co. v. Nationwide Corp.*, 826 F.2d 1470 (6th Cir. 1987); *In the Matter of FSC Corp.*, 22 SEC Docket 1374 (SEC 1981). *See generally* Ndiva Kofele-Kale, *Some Unfinished Business, Some Unresolved Issues: Section 13(e) and the Going-Private Rules after* Howing, 20 Toledo L. Rev. 625 (1989). Note that the U.S. Supreme Court has held that under certain conditions statements of belief or opinion constitute statements of fact, thereby being actionable under the federal securities laws. *See Omnicare, Inc. v. Laborers District Council Constr. Indus. Pension Fund*, 135 S. Ct. 1318 (2015); *Virginia Bankshares, Inc. v. Sandberg*, 501 U.S. 1083 (1991). For further discussion, *see* James D. Cox, *"We're Cool" Statements after* Omnicare*: Securities Fraud Suits for Failures to Comply with the Law*, 68 SMU L. Rev. 715 (2015); Harvey Gelb, *Implied Private Actions Under SEC Rules 14a-9 and 10b-5: The Impact of* Virginia Bankshares, Inc. v. Sandberg, 76 Marq. L. Rev. 363 (1993); Marc I. Steinberg and William A. Reece, *The Supreme Court, Implied Rights of Action, and Proxy Regulation*, 54 Ohio St. L.J. 67 (1993).

[132] Of course, state corporation law, particularly Delaware law, also has played an instrumental role with respect to improving the plight of minority shareholders in going-private transactions. *See, e.g., Kahn v. M & F Worldwide Corp.*, 88 A.3d 635 (Del. 2014); *Weinberger v. UOP, Inc.*, 457 A.2d 701 (Del. 1983).

[133] 430 U.S. at 474 n.14.

reasoned that, under Delaware law as it existed at that time, the plaintiffs "could not have enjoined the merger because an appraisal proceeding [was] their sole remedy in the Delaware courts for any alleged unfairness in the terms of the merger."[134] Subsequent to *Santa Fe*, Delaware expanded plaintiffs' remedies in long-form mergers, permitting suits alleging breach of fiduciary duty in both actions for injunctive relief seeking to enjoin the subject merger as well as for damages after such merger was consummated.[135]

Seizing upon this new approach by the Delaware courts, complainants alleged that adequate disclosure would have enabled them to pursue corrective steps to avoid financial loss, namely, obtaining a state court injunction preventing the completion of the contemplated merger. Failure to disclose the requisite information or conveying materially false information, plaintiffs alleged, constituted deception actionable under Section 10(b) and Rule 10b-5. This federal right to information extended beyond the merger context to encompass any corporate transaction involving the purchase or sale of securities that plaintiffs could have successfully challenged under applicable state law—had they been adequately informed of the facts. After *Santa Fe*, with a number of caveats,[136] several appellate courts have embraced a federal right of action premised on this line of reasoning,[137] known as the "*Goldberg*" rationale.[138]

---

[134] *Id.*

[135] *See, e.g.*, *Weinberger v. UOP, Inc.*, 457 A.2d 701 (Del. 1983); *Singer v. Magnavox Co.*, 380 A.2d 969 (Del. 1977). Note, however, that subsequently the Delaware Supreme Court held that, absent fraud or illegality, appraisal is a minority shareholder's exclusive remedy in a short-form merger. *See Glassman v. Unocal Exploration Corp.*, 777 A.2d 242 (Del. 2001). These Delaware cases are examined by the author in Marc I. Steinberg, *Short-Form Mergers in Delaware*, 27 Del. J. Corp. L. 489 (2002); Marc I. Steinberg and Evalyn N. Lindahl, *The New Law of Squeeze-Out Mergers*, 62 Wash. U. LQ. 351 (1984).

[136] These caveats, for example, include: (1) Only objective facts are required to be disclosed. Undisclosed motivation is not sufficient to state a federal claim. *See Virginia Bankshares, Inc. v. Sandberg*, 501 U.S. 1083, 1096 (1991); (2) Plaintiffs must prove more than injunctive relief *may* have been available. Rather, depending on the appellate court, the plaintiff must establish the requisite level of likelihood of success. *Compare Kidwell ex rel. Penfold v. Meikle*, 597 F.2d 1273, 1294 (9th Cir. 1979) (requiring proof of success in state court action), *with Ala. Farm Bur. Mut. Casualty Co. v. Am. Fidelity Life Ins. Co.*, 606 F.2d 606, 612 (5th Cir. 1979) (requiring "a showing that state law remedies were available and that the facts shown must make out a prima facie case for relief"), *with Healey v. Catalyst Recovery, Inc.*, 616 F.2d 641, 647 (3d Cir. 1980) (requiring that the plaintiff "demonstrate that at the time of the misrepresentation or omission, there was a reasonable probability of ultimate success in securing an injunction had there been no misrepresentation or omission"); and (3) When shareholder approval of a subject transaction is not required under state law, adequate disclosure to a requisite number of disinterested directors is deemed equivalent to such disclosure to shareholders. *See, e.g.*, *Maldonado v. Flynn*, 597 F.2d 789 (2d Cir. 1979).

[137] *See Goldberg v. Meridor*, 567 F.2d 209 (2d Cir. 1978); cases cited *supra* note 136. *See also*, *Wilson v. Great Am. Ind., Inc.*, 979 F.2d 924 (2d Cir. 1992); *Madison Consultants v. FDIC*, [1982–1983 Transfer Binder] Fed. Sec. L. Rep. (CCH) ¶ 99,239 (2d Cir. 1983).

[138] *Goldberg v. Meridor*, 567 F.2d 209 (2d Cir. 1978). For further discussion, *see* Marc I. Steinberg, *Securities Regulation: Liabilities and Remedies* § 8.05 (2017).

Hence, the *Goldberg* rationale posits that, although unfairness alone does not give rise to a Section 10(b) claim, such a claim may be asserted under certain conditions when unfairness is coupled with deficient disclosure. Accordingly, what is striking about the *Goldberg* rationale is that federal courts assess the availability of *state* remedies in order to determine whether a *federal* right of action exists. Thus, in this context, the viability of a Section 10(b) claim is dependent upon the applicable state law.[139] Such an approach indeed is novel. For our purposes, the *Goldberg* rationale provides an unusual situation where the recognition of a federal claim looks to a significant degree to state law aspects of corporate governance.[140]

V. The Federal Tender Offer Regimen—Composing the Rule Book

The legitimacy of defensive tactics in tender offers[141] comes within the purview of state company law.[142] Perceiving that state courts unduly favored target boards of directors, plaintiffs sought to invoke Section 14(e) of the Securities Exchange Act, the federal antifraud provision in the tender offer context, as a means to challenge the defensive maneuvers undertaken.[143] The rationale frequently invoked was that certain defensive tactics, the practical effect of which precluded shareholders from tendering their stock in response to a takeover bid, were manipulative within the meaning of Section 14(e).[144] In *Schreiber v. Burlington Northern, Inc.*,[145] the U.S. Supreme Court rejected this rationale. Echoing its reasoning in *Santa Fe*,[146] the Court held: "all three species of misconduct listed in Section 14(e), i.e., fraudulent,

---

139 *See* cases cited *supra* notes 136–137. On the other hand, the Seventh Circuit has rejected the *Goldberg* rationale. *See Isquith v. Caremark Int'l Inc.*, 136 F.3d 531, 534 (7th Cir. 1998) (stating that "*Goldberg* would allow every complaint about the mismanagement of a corporation that issues securities subject to federal securities law to be shoehorned into federal court on the theory that management had defrauded the shareholders by concealing the mismanagement"), *citing, LHLC Corp. v. Cluett, Peabody & Co.*, 842 F.2d 928, 931–32 (7th Cir. 1988); *Harris Trust & Savings Bank v. Ellis,* 810 F.2d 700, 704 (7th Cir. 1987).

140 The U.S. Supreme Court has raised but has not resolved the validity of this rationale. *See Virginia Bankshares, Inc. v. Sandberg*, 501 U.S. 1083, 1106–08 (1991). *See* Marc I. Steinberg, *Understanding Securities Law* 272–76 (6th ed. 2014); Steinberg, *supra* note 138, at § 8.05. *See generally* Mark J. Loewenstein, *The Supreme Court, Rule 10b-5 and the Federalization of Corporate Law*, 39 Ind. L. Rev. 17 (2005).

141 The term "tender offer" is defined in note 62 *supra*.

142 *See, e.g., Schreiber v. Burlington N., Inc.* 472 U.S. 1 (1985); *MacAndrews & Forbes Holdings v. Revlon*, 506 A.2d 173 (Del. 1986); *Unocal Corp. v. Mesa Petroleum*, 493 A.2d 946 (Del. 1985).

143 15 U.S.C. § 78n(e) (2012).

144 This argument met with some success. *See, e.g., Mobil Corp. v. Marathon Oil Co.*, 669 F.2d 366 (6th Cir. 1981) (holding that target company's grant to competing bidder of attractive options was manipulative and therefore prohibited under § 14(e)).

145 472 U.S. 1 (1985).

146 *Santa Fe Indus., Inc. v. Green*, 430 U.S. 462 (1977). *See* discussion *supra* notes 121–140 and accompanying text.

deceptive or manipulative . . . are directed at failure to disclose."[147] In so holding, the Court relegated the legitimacy of defensive tactics to state corporation law.

Irrespective of the Supreme Court's decision in *Schreiber*, the SEC found a way to overturn the Delaware Supreme Court with respect to the invocation of one particular defensive tactic. In *Unocal v. Mesa Petroleum Co.*,[148] the Delaware Supreme Court upheld the target company's use of a discriminatory issuer tender offer, excluding the hostile shareholder-bidder from participating in the issuer's tender offer.[149] Responding to the *Unocal* decision, the SEC promulgated rules requiring that both issuer and third-party tender offers must remain open to all shareholders, and that the best price paid to a tendering shareholder must be paid to any other shareholder tendering its shares.[150] The Commission's proactive rule-making signifies that discriminatory tender offers for shares of publicly-held companies no longer are an available defensive strategy.

Moreover, it is clear that federal legislation as well as the SEC's tender offer rules encompass not only issues relating to disclosure and deceptive practices but extend also to the process by which tender offers are "played." In addition to the "all holders" and "best price" rules discussed above, examples include: setting the time period that a tender offer must remain open,[151] establishing the bidder's obligation in an oversubscribed partial tender offer to purchase the shares tendered on a pro rata basis,[152] entitling a shareholder to withdraw shares tendered during the entire time

[147] 472 U.S. at 8.

[148] 493 A.2d 946 (Del. 1985).

[149] *Id.* at 958 (concluding that "there was directorial power to oppose the Mesa tender offer, and to undertake a selective stock exchange made in good faith and upon a reasonable investigation pursuant to a clear duty to protect the corporate enterprise").

[150] 17 C.F.R. §§ 240.13e-4, .14d-10 (2017). Rule 13e-4(f)(8) provides: "No issuer or affiliate shall make a tender offer unless: (i) The tender offer is open to all security holders of the class of securities subject to the tender offer; and (ii) The consideration paid to any security holder for securities tendered in the tender offer is the highest consideration paid to any other security holder for securities tendered in the tender offer." *See* Securities Exchange Act Release No. 23421 (1986). In that Release, the Commission stated:

> [M]any commentators have asserted that the Commission's authority under this provision is limited to regulating disclosure. It is clear, however, that in adopting the Williams Act, Congress granted to the Commission broad rulemaking authority in section 13(e) to determine the most appropriate regulatory scheme for issuer tender offers, and that the exercise of this authority could include adoption of substantive regulations. . . .

Id. 1986 WL 703866 at *6.

[151] Rule 14e-1, 17 C.F.R. § 240.14e-1 (2017) (providing a tender offer must remain open for a minimum of 20 business days). For an issuer tender offer for non-convertible debt securities, the SEC staff allows these offers to be open for five business days. *See* SEC No-Action Letter, Cahill Gordon & Reindel LLP (Jan. 23, 2015).

[152] Rule 14d-8, 17 C.F.R. § 240.14d-8 (2017) (extending the proration period from the statutory 10-calendar-day period in § 14(d)(6) to the entire period of the tender offer). *See* Peter Brennan, *SEC Rule 14d-8 and Two-Tier Offers*, in *Tender Offers: Developments and Commentaries* 109 (M. Steinberg ed. 1985).

of the initial tender offer period,[153] and authorizing bidders in third-party tender offers to have a subsequent offering period during which shareholders may not withdraw the shares they tendered.[154] Undoubtedly, the SEC tender offer rules, expanding upon the federal statutory framework, significantly affect the manner in which tender offers are conducted.

VI. The SEC's Impact on Corporate Governance by Means of "Undertakings"

For several decades, the SEC has procured meaningful ancillary relief and undertakings impacting corporate governance. By doing so, the Commission has enhanced the efficacy and integrity of corporate mechanisms, at times dramatically. Commencing at least from the 1970s, in SEC enforcement actions,[155] far-reaching orders have been procured.[156] By way of example, a subject company has been required to: restructure

---

[153] Rule 14d-7, 17 C.F.R. § 240.14d-7 (2017) (extending the withdrawal period from the statutory seven-calendar-day period in § 14(d)(5) to the entire initial offering period).

[154] Rule 14d-11, 17 C.F.R. § 240.14d-11 (2017). This subsequent offering period must be at least three business days. The bidder must offer "the same form and amount of consideration to security holders in both the initial and subsequent offering period." *Id.*

[155] Ordinarily, SEC enforcement actions are settled pursuant to the consent negotiation process whereby the subject defendant neither admits nor denies the allegations set forth in the Commission's complaint. This manner of adjudicating cases reached its zenith in the era of SEC Enforcement Director Stanley Sporkin who subsequently served as General Counsel of the Central Intelligence Agency and as a federal district court judge. As recently explained by former SEC Enforcement Director Bill McLucas and his coauthors:

> Over the last 40 years, the Commission's standard approach has been to permit defendants to enter into a settlement without admitting or denying the allegations against them (i.e., on a "neither admit nor deny" basis). This approach has historically allowed the Commission to achieve substantial relief in settled enforcement actions that often approaches the relief available in litigation, without expending the resources required to litigate or incurring the risk of losing and obtaining no relief. For settling defendants, notwithstanding the neither-admit-nor-deny formulation, the public typically infers wrongdoing, which the defendants are prohibited from denying.

William B. McLucas, et al., *"Neither Admit Nor Deny" Settlements from the Stanley Sporkin Era: Wise Policy or Outdated Enforcement Notion?*, 43 Sec. Reg. L.J. 29 (2015).

[156] The SEC's Volunteer Program in which approximately 450 corporations conducted internal investigations with respect to illicit or foreign payments in the early 1970s and that culminated with the enactment of The Foreign Corrupt Practices Act of 1977 proved to be an important development impacting the undertaking of meaningful corporate governance measures. *See* Senate Committee on Banking, Housing and Urban Affairs, 94th Cong., 2d Sess., Report of the Securities and Exchange Commission on Questionable and Illegal Corporate Payments Practices (Comm. Print 1976); Thomas O. Gorman, *The Origins of the FCPA: Lessons for Effective Compliance and Enforcement*, 43 Sec. Reg. L.J. 43, 53 (2015) ("The Volunteer Program was a step toward repairing and strengthening corporate self-governance under the supervision of the board of directors and its independent directors and outside auditors and counsel.").

its board of directors,[157] appoint independent directors,[158] retain special independent legal counsel to investigate and report,[159] appoint independent consultants,[160] and retain an independent monitor.[161] Moreover, for several years prior to being granted express statutory authority,[162] the SEC procured orders removing or barring subject persons from serving as corporate officers or directors of publicly-held companies.[163]

An SEC enforcement action that highlights the expansive relief that the Commission procured nearly four decades ago is the *Occidental Petroleum Corp.*

---

[157] *See, e.g., SEC v. Mattel*, [1974–1975 Transfer Binder] Fed. Sec. L. Rep. (CCH) ¶ 94,807 (D.D.C. 1974). For an article addressing the relief that the SEC procured in the *Mattel* proceeding, *see* Robert J. Malley, *Far-Reaching Equitable Remedies under the Securities Act and the Growth of Federal Corporate Law*, 17 Wm. & Mary L. Rev. 47, 49 (1975) (among other undertakings, requiring Mattel "to maintain an executive committee of the board of directors, ... the majority of whom at all times would be unaffiliated directors [as well as] two additional committees were ordered to be established and maintained, [namely,] ... a financial controls and audit committee ... [comprised of] three independent directors [who] were to exercise all voting power on matters before the committee [and] a fourth member, who was permitted to be a Mattel designee, was without voting rights [and] a litigation and claims committee consisting of three unaffiliated directors. ...").

[158] *See, e.g., SEC v. Mattel*, [1974–1975 Transfer Binder] Fed. Sec. L. Rep. (CCH) ¶ 94,807 (D.D.C. 1974) (requiring company to appoint independent directors who would constitute a majority of its board of directors, with such directors being "satisfactory" both to the SEC and the company).

[159] *See, e.g., SEC v. Lockheed Aircraft Corp.*, [1975–1976 Transfer Binder] Fed. Sec. L. Rep. (CCH) ¶ 95,509 (D.D.C. 1976). *See generally* Samuel H. Gruenbaum and Martin A. Oppenheimer, *Special Investigative Counsel: Conflicts and Roles*, 33 Rutgers L. Rev. 965 (1981).

[160] *See, e.g., SEC v. Occidental Petroleum Corp.*, [1980 Transfer Binder] Fed. Sec. L. Rep. (CCH) ¶ 82,622 (SEC 1980) (ordering, inter alia, appointment of new director "satisfactory" to the SEC and retention of an independent consulting firm).

[161] *See, e.g., id.* (although not called a monitor, independent director appointed to recommend procedures focusing on company's disclosure obligations with respect to its environmental matters); *In re JH Partners, LLC*, [2015–2016 Transfer Binder] Fed. Sec. L. Rep. (CCH) ¶ 81,158 (SEC 2015) (ordering retention of independent compliance monitor).

[162] The SEC received this express statutory authority to bar an individual from serving as an officer or director of a publicly-held company pursuant to the Securities Enforcement Remedies and Penny Stock Reform Act of 1990. *See* § 20(d) of the Securities Act, 15 U.S.C. § 77t(e) (2012); § 21(d)(2) of the Securities Exchange Act, 15 U.S.C. § 78u(d)(2) (2012). The Sarbanes-Oxley Act lessened the standard for such bars from "substantial unfitness" to that of "unfitness." *See* § 305 of the Sarbanes-Oxley Act. *See generally* Marc I. Steinberg and Ralph C. Ferrara, *Securities Practice: Federal and State Enforcement* § 6:18 (2d ed. 2001 and 2017–2018 supp.).

[163] *See, e.g., SEC v. Florafax Int'l, Inc.*, SEC Litigation Release No. 10617, 31 SEC Docket 1038 (N.D. Okla. 1984); *SEC v. Techni-Culture, Inc.*, 1974 WL 385 (D. Ariz. 1974). *See also SEC v. Posner*, 16 F.3d 520 (2d Cir. 1994). The Second Circuit stated:

> The Posners seem to be shocked by what they see as the draconian remedy of eternal boardroom banishment. We intend our affirmance ... as a sharp warning to those who violate the securities laws that they face precisely such banishment. Of course, as the SEC points out, such bar orders are imposed routinely by consent decree.

Id. at 522.

Matter.[164] In that case, the SEC brought suit against Occidental Petroleum (Oxy) alleging that the company did not disclose several material facts relating to, inter alia, "Oxy's discharge of chemical or toxic wastes into the environment; . . . the status of Oxy's negotiations with Libya concerning the financial arrangement pursuant to which Oxy operated in Libya; and signed, undated letters of resignation which were submitted by certain nominees to Oxy's Board of Directors at the request of Dr. Armand Hammer, the Chairman of the [Oxy] Board."[165] In settling the proceeding, Oxy agreed to undertake significant remedial measures. One such measure was Oxy designating a director who was "satisfactory" to the SEC, who was charged with responsibility for: preparing an environmental report in which procedures were to be recommended to the Oxy board of directors to ensure that timely and accurate disclosure would be made with respect to the company's environmental matters, reasonably determining the potential costs that the company would be required to incur during the subsequent three years in order to make its facilities compliant with government requirements, ascertaining the maximum civil penalties that may be levied on Oxy for its violations of environmental laws and regulations and describing third-party claims against the company based on its violation of environmental laws and regulations.[166] Pursuant to the settlement, the SEC had the discretion to

---

[164] *In the Matter of Occidental Petroleum Corp.*, Securities Exchange Act Release No. 16950, [1980 Transfer Binder] Fed. Sec. L. Rep. (CCH) ¶ 82,622 (SEC 1980). In light of its prominence, this proceeding has been contained in the author's law school textbook through all seven editions. *See* Marc I. Steinberg, *Securities Regulation* 928 (1986); Marc I. Steinberg, *Securities Regulation* 1182 (7th ed. 2017).

[165] [1980 Transfer Binder] Fed. Sec. L. Rep. (CCH) ¶ 82,622, at 83,348.

[166] *Id.* at 83,356 (also providing, *id.* at 83,357, that: "Oxy will cooperate fully with the director by permitting him to review such documents and interview such employees of Oxy as he deems relevant in the preparation of the Report. Further, the director will have authority to retain experts whom he determines are reasonably necessary to complete the Report.").

Disclosure as to environmental matters remains a pertinent subject of the SEC disclosure regimen. A relatively recent example focuses on the impact of climate change matters on a subject company. *See* Commission Guidance Regarding Disclosure Related to Climate Change, Securities Exchange Act Release No. 9106 (2010) (providing that "[t]his release outlines our view with respect to our existing disclosure requirements as they apply to climate change . . . and is intended to assist companies in satisfying their disclosure obligations under the federal securities law and regulations").

An area where the Commission has been subject to criticism for declining to require more substantive disclosure is with respect to a subject company's operations in sanctioned countries (i.e., State Sponsors of Terrorism). With respect to this subject, Professor Amy Westbrook has asserted:

> If information about a company's operations in or with the Sanctioned Countries is important to investors, then the U.S. federal securities laws should be enforced by requiring companies to disclose it. Yet the research . . . shows that the majority of companies are not providing any disclosure. . . . [I]t is still nearly impossible for investors to find the information they need from publicly available sources, including the SEC. In short, very little information is effectively disclosed.

Amy Deen Westbrook, *What's in Your Portfolio?, U.S. Investors Are Unknowingly Financing Sponsors of Terrorism*, 59 DePaul L. Rev. 1151, 1218 (2010).

"consult" with the director and be provided access to documents that were used in the preparation of the environmental report. In addition, the director was charged with utilizing the company's senior environmental official as well as an independent consulting firm, each of whom was to be "satisfactory" to the Commission.[167] With respect to the signed undated letters of resignation that Dr. Hammer received from director-nominees, Oxy was required to make appropriate disclosure of a change in its policy.[168]

That a New York Stock Exchange company in the late 1970s had its nominees sign undated letters of resignation is surprising and perhaps shocking. By invoking its authority enforcing the securities laws' adequacy-of-disclosure mandate, the SEC in *Oxy* attained a meaningful measure of remediation with respect to the company's environmental practices as well as corporate governance policies. This proceeding as well as others instituted by the Commission over four decades ago exemplify the SEC's impact on enhancing compliance with the law in areas outside of the securities laws as well as inducing improved standards of corporate governance.

---

[167] [1980 Transfer Binder] Fed. Sec. L. Rep. (CCH) ¶ 82,622, at 83,357. In this regard, the Settlement also provided:

> [1] Within 10 months of the date of the issuance of this Order, or such later date as the staff of the Commission and Oxy may agree, the director shall complete the report and submit it to the Board of Directors of Oxy.
>
> [2] Within 10 days of the submission of the report to the Board of Directors, Oxy will transmit copies thereof to the Commission and, within 30 days of such submission, to file with the Commission on Form 8-K a description thereof and a summary of the principal conclusions and recommendations.
>
> [3] In connection with the recommendations of the director, the Board of Directors of Oxy will review them within 45 days of their receipt and adopt and implement such of the recommendations as it reasonably believes necessary or appropriate.
>
> [4] Within 60 days of the submission of the report to the Board of Directors, Oxy will file with the Commission on Form 8-K a description of the actions taken by the Board of Directors, if any, with respect to the recommendations of the director.

[168] *Id.* (also providing that Oxy "will make appropriate disclosure of a change in its policy that neither Oxy nor any officer, director or employee of the company will request or receive any written or oral agreement, assurance or promise of any kind from any nominee to, or member of, Oxy's Board of Directors as it now is or may in the future be constituted. . . ."). In the Release setting forth the Settlement, the SEC reasoned:

> Full disclosure of the conditions under which persons stand for election to the Board of Directors of a corporation is important in order to enable shareholders and the investing public to understand the present circumstances under which a corporation is directed and the potential for changes in such direction in the future. Shareholders expect that the directors they elect will serve and function for the full elected term. Accordingly, any understandings or arrangements, whether oral or written, under which a director may not be able to do so, or pursuant to which the director's functions or term may be limited, should be fully disclosed.

Id. at 83,356.

VII. SEC Enforcement Actions Against Officers and Directors

To some degree, the SEC has sought to enhance corporate governance practices by means of enforcement actions against executive officers and directors. Actions instituted against executive officers are far more frequent than those against outside ("independent") directors.[169] In this regard, with some frequency, the SEC has invoked its authority barring officers and directors (normally, directors who also serve as executive officers) from serving in these capacities in any publicly-held company.[170] A high profile case in this context was the Commission's enforcement action against Angelo Mozilo, the former CEO and chairman of the board of directors of Countrywide Financial Corporation. In settling that proceeding, in addition to agreeing to money penalties and disgorgement amounting to over $67 million, Mr. Mozilo was permanently barred from serving as a director or officer of any publicly-held company.[171]

On occasion, the SEC has brought enforcement actions against outside directors. In a Section 21(a) Report of Investigation[172] issued over four decades ago, the Commission focused on the performance of the subject company's outside directors, asserting that they "did not play any significant role in the direction of [the] company's affairs even though they possessed considerable business experience and sophistication."[173] Addressing the obligations of officers and directors in the disclosure process, the SEC's language in a subsequent Section 21(a) proceeding likewise

---

[169] *See, e.g., SEC v. Delphi Corp.*, 2012 WL 6600324 (6th Cir. 2012) (affirming liability of chief accounting officer for accounting improprieties); *SEC v. Todd*, 642 F.3d 1207 (9th Cir. 2011) (reinstating jury verdict that corporate officers committed securities fraud); *Greenberg Former AIG Top Exec. Agrees to Pay $15M to Settle Accounting Claims*, 41 Sec. Reg. & L. Rep. (BNA) 1503 (S.D.N.Y. 2015) (CEO's alleged misconduct related to company's improper accounting); cases cited in Marc I. Steinberg and Forrest C. Roberts, *Laxity at the Gates: The SEC's Neglect to Enforce Control Person Liability*, 11 U. Va. L. & Bus. Rev. 201, 231 (2017); discussion in Chapter 7 herein.

[170] *See, e.g., SEC v. Bankowsky*, 716 F.3d 45 (2d Cir. 2013); *SEC v. Jasper*, 678 F.3d 1116 (9th Cir. 2012); *SEC v. Patel*, 61 F.3d 137 (2d Cir. 1995).

[171] *See SEC v. Mozilo*, No. CV 09-3994, 2010 WL 3656068 (C.D. Cal. Sept. 16, 2010) (payment of $22.5 million in penalties, $45 million of disgorgement, and officer and director bar). *See also* SEC Press Release, *Former CEO Angelo Mozilo to Pay Largest-Ever Financial Penalty Against a Public Company's Senior Executive* (Oct. 15, 2010), https://www.sec.govnewspress/2010/2010-197.htm (then SEC Enforcement Director, Robert Khuzami, stating that "Mozilo's record penalty is the fitting outcome for a corporate executive who deliberately disregarded his duties to investors by concealing what he saw from inside the executive suite").

[172] Generally, pursuant to Section 21(a) of the Securities Exchange Act, 15 U.S.C. § 78u(a), the Commission may issue a Report of Investigation. Although disciplinary action is not imposed pursuant to such a Report, this vehicle enables the SEC to present its position with respect to the conduct at issue, thereby providing public notice of its enforcement position on a particular subject.

[173] *In the Matter of Stirling Homex*, Securities Exchange Act Release No. 11516, 7 SEC Docket 298, 300 (1975).

rings somewhat of a corporate governance theme, "emphasiz[ing] the affirmative responsibilities of corporate officers and directors to ensure that the shareholders who they serve receive accurate and complete disclosure of information required by the . . . federal securities laws."[174] In a more recent action against outside directors who served as audit committee members, the SEC alleged that, through their "willful blindness to red flags signaling fraud," these directors facilitated senior management's fraudulent conduct. In settling the action, the defendant outside directors agreed to be enjoined, disgorge ill-gotten gains, pay money penalties, and be subject to officer and director bars.[175] While, as stated by one source, "outside directors are rarely charged in SEC corporate fraud actions,"[176] the above proceeding and a relatively small number of other enforcement actions[177] illustrate that the Commission, on occasion, will institute suit against outside directors based on their allegedly deficient conduct.[178]

Hence, SEC enforcement actions against executive officers and directors, although primarily directed at alleged deficient disclosure practices, have sought to address: executive officer misconduct, inadequate internal controls, and outside director failure of oversight. As discussed in Chapter 7 herein, the Commission's reluctance to pursue corporate fiduciaries of large publicly-held companies consistent with its statutory authority is subject to criticism. Nonetheless, when instituted,

---

[174] *In the Matter of W.R. Grace & Co.*, Securities Exchange Act Release No. 39157 (1997):

> Officers and directors who review, approve, or sign their company's proxy statements or periodic reports must take steps to ensure the accuracy and completeness of the statements contained therein, especially as they concern those matters within their particular knowledge or expertise. To fulfill this responsibility, officers and directors must be vigilant in exercising their authority throughout the disclosure process.

[175] *See SEC v. Krantz*, SEC Litigation Release No. 22154 (Nov. 15, 2011).

[176] Latham & Watkins LLP, *SEC v. Krantz: Liability of Outside Directors in SEC Enforcement Actions*, Lexology (Mar. 10, 2011). *See* Todd S. Fishman, *The SEC's Renewed Focus on Gatekeepers*, 49 Rev. Sec. & Comm. Reg. 219, 220 (2016) (stating that SEC enforcement actions against directors are "not frequent").

[177] *See, e.g.*, *SEC v. Gupta*, SEC Litigation Release No. 21451 (Mar. 10, 2010) (settlement whereby former chairman of company's audit committee consented to imposition of an injunction, money penalty, and five-year bar from serving as an officer or director of a publicly-held company); *SEC v. Chancellor Corp.*, SEC Litigation Release No. 19177 (Apr. 11, 2005) (in settled case involving alleged financial fraud, outside director agreed to injunction, money penalty, and officer and director bar); *SEC v. Marchese*, Securities Exchange Act Release No. 47732, 2003 WL 1940244 (2003) (settlement whereby outside director who served as an audit committee member agreed to cease-and-desist order, with the Commission asserting that the director "completely failed to exercise any oversight over [the company's] financial reporting, exercising no care to ensure that the company had appropriate internal controls and that its financial records were accurate").

[178] A number of SEC enforcement actions have involved outside directors who allegedly violated the insider trading prohibitions. *See, e.g.*, *SEC v. Hollier*, SEC Litigation Release No. 21883 (Mar. 14, 2011). These cases should not be viewed as focused on outside directors as any person, irrespective of position, who violates the insider trading laws is subject to government enforcement action.

SEC enforcement proceedings against officers and directors constitute another example of the Commission's role in the federalization of corporate governance.

VIII. Focusing on "Gatekeepers"—Accountants and Attorneys

For several decades, the SEC has focused on the role of "gatekeepers," particularly accountants and attorneys, in the disclosure process. Indeed, as astutely recognized by the eminent Judge Henry Friendly over 50 years ago: "In our complex society, the accountant's certificate and the lawyer's opinion can be instruments for inflicting pecuniary loss more potent than the chisel or the crowbar."[179] Stated in somewhat different terms in an enforcement proceeding of similar vintage: the securities attorney "works in his office where he prepares prospectuses, proxy statements, opinions of counsel, and other documents that we, our staff, the financial community, and the investing public must take on faith."[180]

Accordingly, accountants and attorneys are "gatekeepers."[181] They function as intermediaries who, in the corporate governance context, enhance shareholder interests through their professional conduct of assessing, verifying, or certifying material aspects of an investment, transaction, or other event.[182] In many circumstances, gatekeepers have the wherewithal to detect and deter fraud and other improper conduct.[183] Unfortunately, all too often, gatekeepers fail in this important task.

---

[179] *United States v. Benjamin*, 328 F.2d 854, 863 (2d Cir. 1964). *See id.* (also recognizing that Congress "could not have intended that men holding themselves out as members of these ancient professions should be able to escape criminal liability on a plea of ignorance when they have shut their eyes to what was plainly to be seen or have represented a knowledge they knew they did not possess").

[180] *In re Fields*, [1972–1973 Transfer Binder] Fed. Sec. L. Rep. (CCH) ¶ 79,407 (SEC 1973), *aff'd without opinion*, 495 F.2d 1075 (D.C. Cir. 1974). *See id.* at 83,174 n.20 (stating that the Commission, with its limited resources, "is peculiarly dependent on the probity and diligence of the professionals who practice before it").

[181] *See, e.g., Lawson v. FMR, LLC*, 134 S. Ct. 1158, 1170–71 (2014) (quoting S. Rep. No. 107-146, at 2 (2002)) ("Emphasizing the importance of outside professionals as 'gatekeepers who detect and deter fraud,' the Senate Report concludes: 'Congress must reconsider the incentive system that has been set up that encourages accountants and lawyers who come across fraud in their work to remain silent.'"). *See generally* Stephen Choi, *Market Lessons for Gatekeepers*, 92 Nw. U.L. Rev. 916 (1998); John C. Coffee, Jr., *The Attorney as Gatekeeper: An Agenda for the SEC*, 103 Colum. L. Rev. 1293 (2003); Reinier H. Kraakman, *Corporate Liability Strategies and the Costs of Legal Controls*, 93 Yale L.J. 857 (1984); Fred Zacharias, *Lawyers as Gatekeepers*, 41 San Diego L. Rev. 1387 (2004).

[182] *See* Marc I. Steinberg and James Ames, *From the Regulatory Abyss: The Weakened Gatekeeping Incentives Under the Uniform Securities Act*, 35 Yale L. & Pol. Rev. 1, 4–5 (2016); sources cited note 181 *supra*.

[183] *See Lawson*, 134 S. Ct. at 1170–71 (emphasizing the important function that accountants and attorneys perform in detecting and deterring fraud); Steinberg and Ames, *supra* note 182, at 5 (stating that "gatekeepers may function to reduce the risk of harm to investors by refusing to provide services [and that] the gatekeeper's position as the red or green light to the consummation of securities transactions is often superior to the after-the-fact remedies provided by investor lawsuits and government enforcement proceedings"); *Developments in*

With frequency, corporate scandals (such as Enron, Tyco, WorldCom, Adelphia, Global Crossings, and Mortgages, Ltd.[184]) involved professional gatekeepers who did not adequately respond,[185] thereby contributing to huge investor financial losses and hardship.[186] As Judge Stanley Sporkin lamented in *Lincoln Savings and Loan Association*:[187]

> Where were these professionals, a number of whom are now asserting their rights under the Fifth Amendment, when these clearly improper transactions were being consummated? Why didn't any of them speak up or disassociate themselves from the transactions? Where also were the outside accountants and attorneys when these transactions were effectuated? What is difficult to understand is that with all the professional talent involved (both accounting and legal), why at least one professional would not have blown the whistle to stop the overreaching that took place in this case.[188]

As Judge Sporkin's critique implies, the courts, like the SEC, have recognized the important function of gatekeepers in enhancing law compliance and the integrity of the securities markets.[189] Not surprisingly, when gatekeepers allegedly fail in

---

the Law: Corporations and Society, 117 Harv. L. Rev. 2169, 2245 (2004) ("By withholding his or her support (such as a lawyer's opinion letter or an accountant's certification), the professional gatekeeper may be able to prevent the fraud.").

[184] In each of these situations of large-scale fraud and other misconduct, accountants and lawyers allegedly did not adequately perform their gatekeeping functions. *See, e.g.*, *In re WorldCom, Inc. Sec. Litig.*, 346 F. Supp. 2d 628 (S.D.N.Y. 2004) (underwriter's assertion that it was entitled to rely on accountant's comfort letters for subject company's unaudited interim financial statements); *In re Enron Corp. Sec., Derivative & ERISA Litig.*, 235 F. Supp. 2d 549 (S.D. Tex. 2002) (law firm and accounting firm sued for alleged violations that enabled the scandal to continue); *Facciola v. Greenberg Traurig LLP*, 2011 WL 2268950 (D. Ariz. 2011) (two major law firms and an accounting firm sued for alleged violations in debacle that resulted in investors incurring hundreds of millions of dollars in losses).

[185] *See* Christine E. Earley, et al., *Some Thoughts on the Audit Failure at Enron: The Demise of Anderson, and the Ethical Climate of Public Accounting Firms*, 35 Conn. L. Rev. 1013 (2014); Steinberg and Ames, *supra* note 182, at 5–6; cases cited note 184 *supra*.

[186] *See* discussion in Steinberg and Ames, *supra* note 182, at 4–7.

[187] *Lincoln Savings & Loan Association v. Wall*, 743 F. Supp. 901 (D.D.C. 1990). Judge Sporkin previously served as SEC Enforcement Director and CIA General Counsel. *See generally* Symposium, *In Honor of Stanley Sporkin*, 43 Sec. Reg. L.J. No. 1 (2015).

[188] 743 F. Supp. 2d at 920.

[189] *See, e.g.*, *SEC v. Spectrum, Ltd.*, 489 F.2d 535, 536 (2d Cir. 1973) (stating that "the legal profession plays a unique and pivotal role in the effective implementation of the securities laws [and that] the smooth functioning of the securities markets will be seriously disturbed if the public cannot rely on the expertise proffered by an attorney when he renders an opinion on such matters"); *United States v. Benjamin*, 328 F.2d 854, 863 (2d Cir. 1964) (recognizing harm that can be caused to investors and the securities markets by noncompliant accountants and attorneys); *In re Parmalat Sec. Litig.*, 375 F. Supp. 2d 278, 289 (S.D.N.Y. 2005) (asserting

their gatekeeping tasks, they may be subject to private litigation[190] as well as government enforcement actions.[191] In this regard, the SEC for well over four decades has instituted enforcement proceedings against accountants and attorneys who allegedly engaged in violations of the federal securities laws as well as SEC rules.[192] In instances, where the government has utilized its enforcement authority effectively, more vigorous gatekeeping practices have been instituted—contributing, with some frequency, to the enhancement of law compliance by corporate clients of these gatekeepers as well as the implementation of improved corporate governance practices by these companies.[193]

After the enactment of the Sarbanes-Oxley Act of 2002,[194] the SEC has continued to institute enforcement actions against accountants and attorneys.[195] With

that "independent auditors serve a crucial role in the functioning of world capital markets because they are reputational intermediaries [and that] [i]n certifying a company's financial statements, their reputations for independence and probity signal the accuracy of the information disclosed by the company. . . .").

[190] *See, e.g.*, cases cited note 184 *supra*.

[191] *See, e.g.*, cases cited note 189 *supra*.

[192] *See, e.g.*, *SEC v. Fehn*, 97 F.3d 1276 (9th Cir. 1996); *Checkowsky v. SEC*, 23 F.3d 452 (2d Cir. 1994); *Touche Ross & Co., v. SEC*, 609 F.2d 570 (2d Cir. 1979); *SEC v. Coven*, 581 F.2d 1020 (2d Cir. 1978); *SEC v. Spectrum, Ltd.*, 489 F.2d 535 (2d Cir. 1973).

[193] *See In re Keating, Muething & Klekamp*, Securities Exchange Act Release No. 15982, [1979 Transfer Binder] Fed. Sec. L. Rep. (CCH) ¶ 82,124, at 81,989 (SEC 1979) (in settlement, ordering law firm to adopt, maintain, and implement "procedures which are reasonably designed to insure that respondent has adequate procedures"); proceedings cited in notes 207–212 *infra*. *See also Kirschner v. KPMG LLP*, 938 N.E. 2d 941, 963 (N.Y. 2010) (Ciparick, J., dissenting) (observing the significant policy concerns with respect to gatekeeping incentives and warning that immunizing subject gatekeepers "invites [such] gatekeepers 'to neglect their duty to ferret out fraud by corporate insiders. . . .' "), *quoting*, Adam Pritchard, *O'Melveny Myers v. FDIC: Imputation of Fraud and Optimal Monitoring*, 4 Sup. Ct. Econ. Rev. 179, 192 (1995).

[194] The corporate governance aspects of the Sarbanes-Oxley Act are addressed in Chapters 5 and 6 herein.

[195] *See generally* Marc I. Steinberg, *Attorney Liability After Sarbanes-Oxley* §§ 4.01–4.05 (2017); W. Hardy Callcott and Abigail Slonecker, *A Review of SEC Actions Against Lawyers*, 42 Rev. Sec. & Comm. Reg. 71 (2009); Louis Lowenfels, Alan Bromberg, and Michael Sullivan, *SEC Actions Against Lawyers Post Sarbanes-Oxley: A Reasoned Approach or an Assault Upon the Practicing Securities Bar?*, 41 Sec. Reg. & L. Rep. (BNA) 1739 (2009); Frank Razzano, *Is the SEC Targeting Lawyers?*, 35 Sec. Reg. L.J. 4 (2008); Manning Warren, *Revenue Recognition and Corporate Counsel*, 56 SMU L. Rev. 885 (2003); Lisa Wood and Matthew Miller, *Recent Trends in SEC Enforcement Actions Against Auditors*, 50 Rev. Sec. & Comm. Reg. 1 (2017). As stated by then SEC Enforcement Director Andrew Ceresney:

> A common thread throughout the [Division's enforcement] priority areas . . . is an emphasis on the importance of gatekeepers to our financial system: attorneys, accountants, fund directors, board members, transfer agents, broker-dealers, and other industry professionals who play a critical role in the functioning of the securities industry. Gatekeepers are integral to protecting investors in our financial system because they are best positioned to detect and prevent the compliance breakdowns and fraudulent schemes that cause investor harm. When gatekeepers fail to live up to their responsibilities, the Division has held—and will continue to hold—them accountable.

Oversight of the SEC's Division of Enforcement: Hearing Before the Subcommittee on Capital Markets and Government Sponsored Enterprises of the House Committee on Financial Services, 114th Cong. 7 (2015) (statement of Andrew Ceresney, Director, Division of Enforcement, SEC).

respect to attorneys, the Commission has focused on legal counsel's alleged misconduct in connection with: the issuance of opinion letters,[196] drafting client offering documents or SEC filed reports,[197] advising the corporate client's executive officers or board of directors as to disclosure matters,[198] and acquiescing in the client's non-compliant conduct.[199] In addition, in the brokerage firm setting (including firms whose common stock is publicly traded), in-house lawyers[200] have been subject to SEC enforcement proceedings due to their alleged inadequate supervision of miscreant firm employees.[201]

The SEC's oversight of the accounting and legal professions is highlighted by Rule 102(e) of the Commission's Rules of Practice,[202] which provides the SEC with the

---

[196] *See, e.g., SEC v. Zenergy*, 141 F. Supp. 3d 846 (N.D. Ill. 2015); *SEC v. Luna*, [2014 Transfer Binder] Fed. Sec. L. Rep. (CCH) ¶ 98,015 (D. Nev. 2014); *SEC v. Greenstone Holdings, Inc.*, [2013 Transfer Binder] Fed. Sec. L. Rep. (CCH) ¶ 97,556 (S.D.N.Y. 2013).

[197] *See, e.g., SEC v. Frank*, 388 F.2d 486 (2d Cir. 1968); *SEC v. Yuen*, SEC Litigation Release No. 18530 (C.D. Cal. 2005); *In re Isselmann*, Securities Exchange Act Release No. 50428 (2004).

[198] *See, e.g., SEC v. Fehn*, 97 F.3d 1276 (9th Cir. 1996); *SEC v. Coven*, 581 F.2d 1020 (2d Cir. 1978); *In re Feldman*, Securities Act Release No. 7014 (1993).

[199] *See, e.g., In re Tamman*, Securities Exchange Act Release No. 69746 (2013); *SEC v. Fisher*, 2008 WL 3006149 (E.D. Mich. 2008); *In re Stichta*, Securities Exchange Act Release No. 41132 (1999). With respect to SEC enforcement actions against auditors, *see* proceedings discussed in Wood and Miller, note 195 *supra*.

[200] With respect to the many issues implicating an attorney's role as inside counsel, *see generally* Marc I. Steinberg and Stephen B. Yeager, *Inside Counsel—Practices, Strategies, and Insights* (2015); E. Norman Veasey and Christine T. Di Guglielmo, *Indispensable Counsel—The Chief Legal Officer in the New Reality* (2012).

[201] *See In the Matter of Urban*, Securities Exchange Act Release No. 66259 (2012) (dismissing enforcement proceedings against Mr. Urban who, as general counsel of Ferris, Baker, Watts, was charged by the SEC staff with failure to supervise a miscreant broker who allegedly was under his supervision); *In re Gutfreund*, [1992 Transfer Binder] Fed. Sec. L. Rep. (CCH) ¶ 85,067 (SEC 1992) (Section 21(a) Report). In the *Gutfreund* proceeding, the SEC issued a Section 21(a) Report with respect to Salomon's chief legal officer, asserting:

> In this case, serious misconduct involving a senior official of a brokerage firm was brought to the attention of the firm's chief legal officer. That individual was informed of the misconduct by other members of senior management in order to obtain his advice and guidance, and to involve him as part of management's collective response to the problem. Moreover, in other instances of misconduct, that individual had directed the firm's response and had made recommendations concerning appropriate disciplinary action, and management had relied on him to perform those tasks.
>
> Given the role and influence within the firm of a person in a position such as [the CLO] and the factual circumstances of this case, such a person shares in the responsibility to take appropriate action to respond to the misconduct. Under those circumstances, we believe that such a person becomes a "supervisor" for purposes of Sections 15(b)(4)(E) and 15(b)(6) [of the Securities Exchange Act]. As a result, that person is responsible, along with the other supervisors, for taking reasonable and appropriate action. It is not sufficient for one in such a position to be a mere bystander to the events that occurred.

Id. at 83,609. *See* Lorelee Dodge, *The Definition of "Supervisor":* Urban *Muddies the Water*, 40 Sec. Reg. L.J. 117 (2012); Ralph Janvey, *The Feuerstein Report of Investigation: Supervisory Responsibilities of Legal and Compliance Officers of Brokerage Firms*, 21 Sec. Reg. L.J. 166 (1993).

[202] The Rule now has been codified in Section 4C of the Securities Exchange Act, 15 U.S.C. § 78dC.

authority to suspend or bar any such professional for improper or unethical professional conduct.[203] This Rule was codified by Congress pursuant to the Sarbanes-Oxley Act of 2002.[204] Under Rule 102(e), the SEC has broad authority to suspend or bar a subject professional.[205] Indeed, with respect to accountants, the Commission may take such disciplinary action based upon negligence.[206]

In Rule 102(e) disciplinary proceedings, the SEC at times has ordered that the subject firm perform specified undertakings. For example, in the accounting firm context, the Commission ordered the subject firm to expend a minimum of $1 million for fraud-detection training for its personnel.[207] In a number of other proceedings, the

---

[203] Prior to its codification pursuant to the Sarbanes-Oxley Act, Rule 102(e)'s (then Rule 2(e)'s) validity was challenged. In an important decision, the U.S. Court of Appeals for the Second Circuit upheld the Rule's validity in *Touche Ross & Co. v. SEC*, 609 F.2d 570 (2d Cir. 1979). In so doing, the court reasoned:

> The role of the accounting and legal professions in implementing the objectives of the disclosure policy has increased in importance as the number and complexity of securities transactions has increased. By the very nature of its operations, the Commission, with its small staff and limited resources, cannot possibly examine, with the degree of close scrutiny required for full disclosure, each of the many financial statements which are filed. Recognizing this, the Commission necessarily must rely heavily on both the accounting and legal professions to perform their tasks diligently and responsibly. Breaches of professional responsibility jeopardize the achievement of the objectives of the securities laws and can inflict great damage on public investors.

Id. at 581.

[204] *See* § 4C of the Securities Exchange Act, 15 U.S.C. § 78d(C) (2012).

[205] Under Rule 102(e), the Commission may censure, suspend, or bar a professional "the privilege of appearing or practicing" before the SEC if such person "is found by the Commission, after notice and opportunity for hearing in the matter—(1) not to possess the requisite qualifications to represent others; (2) to be lacking in character or integrity or to have engaged in unethical or improper professional conduct; or (3) to have willfully violated, or willfully aided and abetted the violation of, any provision of the securities laws or the rules and regulations thereunder."

[206] See § 4C(b) of the Securities Exchange Act, 15 U.S.C. § 78d(C)(b) (2012):

> With respect to any registered public accounting firm or associated person, for purposes of this section, the term "improper professional conduct" means—
>
> (1) Intentional or knowing conduct, including reckless conduct, that results in a violation of applicable professional standards; and
> (2) Negligent conduct in the form of—
>   (A) a single instance of highly unreasonable conduct that results in a violation of applicable professional standards in circumstances in which the registered public accounting firm or associated person knows, or should know, that heightened scrutiny is warranted; or
>   (B) repeated instances of unreasonable conduct, each resulting in a violation of applicable professional standards, that indicate a lack of competence to practice before the Commission.

See Dearlove v. SEC, 573 F.3d 801 (D.C. Cir. 2009) (upholding Commission's finding of improper conduct against accountant in first litigated proceeding invoking negligence standard under the statute and rule).

[207] *See In the Matter of Grant Thornton LLP*, Securities Exchange Act Release No. 50148 (2004) (pursuant to settlement, also ordering that the firm be censured, pay a $1.5 million money penalty, and disgorge specified improper gains).

SEC has ordered that the subject accounting firm implement more extensive substantive undertakings, including, for example, with respect to such firm's clients that are deemed to have significantly greater than normal audit risk: the use of forensic specialists; the requirement that partners satisfying specified qualifications be appointed as special review partners to oversee audits of such high risk clients; the completion by such firm's audit professionals of training for fraud detection; and the retention of "an independent consultant not unacceptable to the staff of the Commission, to review [such accounting firm's] compliance with the undertakings [ordered]."[208]

Rarely has the SEC ordered comparable undertakings for law firms. Perhaps the best known is the *Keating, Muething & Klekamp* proceeding.[209] There, pursuant to settlement, the Commission found that the law firm did not comply with its professional obligations in preparing its client's SEC filings, because it failed "to make sure that disclosure documents filed with the Commission include all material facts

[208] *See, e.g., In the Matter of Deloitte & Touche LLP*, Securities Exchange Act Release No. 51606 (2005) (serving as Adelphia's independent auditor). In settling the Rule 102(e) proceeding, for audits of publicly-held corporations placed in Deloitte's Risk Management Program, the firm agreed to, among other measures, the following undertakings:

> [1] Knowledgeable and experienced partners shall be appointed as Special Review Partners to oversee the planning and design of audit procedures for audit risks that have been identified in the planning stage of the audit, and these audit procedures will be specifically tailored to the particular audit risks identified in connection with the audit.
>
> [2] Deloitte will utilize Deloitte forensic specialists in the planning stage of audits of all clients in the Risk Management Program.
>
> [3] Prior to the issuance of a Report of an Independent Public Accountant, the Engagement Partner will be responsible for the preparation of a [comprehensive] written memorandum. . . .
>
> [4] The Engagement Partner and the Special Review Partner will review any significant issues arising during the audit to determine whether it is appropriate under the circumstances to consult with Deloitte's National Office about the issue. If consultation over such an issue occurs, the engagement team will ensure that the audit workpapers document any such consultation involving Deloitte's National Office.
>
> [5] Within 24 months from the date of this order, Deloitte will take reasonable steps to ensure that all Deloitte audit professionals have completed 8 hours of training on: (a) fraud detection; and (b) operation of, and an auditor's responsibilities under, Section 10A of the Exchange Act, based upon training materials approved by an individual or organization not unacceptable to the staff of the Commission. Training will include techniques in detecting or responding to possible fraud by audit clients, or by employees, officers or directors of audit clients.
>
> [6] Within ten days of the date of this Order, Deloitte shall distribute copies of the Order to all audit professionals.
>
> [7] Eighteen months from the date of this Order, Deloitte will retain, at its own expense, an independent consultant not unacceptable to the staff of the Commission, to review Deloitte's compliance with the undertakings set forth in this Section. The consultant will, within 120 days of commencing his/her review, provide a report of the results of that review to the staff of the Commission. . . .

[209] *In re Keating, Muething & Klekamp*, Securities Exchange Act Release No. 15982, [1979 Transfer Binder] Fed. Sec. L. Rep. (CCH) ¶ 82,124 (1979).

about a client of which it has knowledge as a result of its legal representation of the client."[210] The firm agreed to adopt, maintain, and implement "procedures" reasonably designed to ensure that its professional responsibilities were met.[211] In another proceeding, the Commission went further where, pursuant to settlement, the subject law firm agreed to implement specified internal procedures.[212]

In a number of disciplinary proceedings involving attorneys and accountants, the Commission also has focused on the subject of client fraud—namely, the obligations of a subject accountant or attorney when he or she is aware that a corporate client's SEC disclosure documents are materially false due to the misconduct of such corporation's officers or directors.[213] With respect thereto, the proceeding that is the most

---

[210] *Id.*, [1979 Transfer Binder] Fed. Sec. L. Rep. (CCH) ¶ 82,124, at 81,988. For a more recent example where knowledge of an agent of a law firm was attributable to the law firm itself, thereby giving rise to liability exposure, *see Cromeans v. Morgan Keegan & Co., Inc.*, 69 F. Supp. 3d 934, 939–40 (W.D. Mo. 2014) (stating that a "corporate entity can obtain knowledge only through its agents and, under the well-established rules of agency, the knowledge of agents obtained in the course of their employment is imputed to the [subject enterprise and that, accordingly,] the fact that the lawyer making the false statement did not know it was false does not show that [the law firm] Armstrong Teasdale lacked knowledge of the false statement").

[211] [1979 Transfer Binder] Fed. Sec. L. Rep. (CCH) ¶ 82,124, at 81,989 (ordering the firm to implement additional procedures and, for a period of 60 days, not to accept any legal engagement from a prospective new client that involved SEC filings). Note that, with respect to the practice of law in the corporate and securities area, important points from this proceeding include:

> First, and foremost, is that members of a firm should communicate with one another when preparing clients' filings with the Commission.... The second point that can be learned from this case is that a firm should have an internal procedural system which is designed to assure that the knowledge of individual members of the firm, with respect to material matters of a client, is communicated to the people in the firm who are responsible for preparing disclosure documents.

Marc I. Steinberg and Ralph C. Ferrara, *Securities Practice: Federal and State Enforcement* § 4:36 (2d ed. 2001).

[212] *See In re Ferguson*, Securities Act Release No. 5523 (1974), where the internal procedures adopted by the law firm included:

> (1) Every two weeks, members of the firm meet and discuss all of their active cases. Affirmative approval of each partner is required before the issuance of any legal opinion. (2) The firm will undertake an appropriate investigation in connection with acting as bond counsel including, among other things, obtaining independently-audited financial statements and inquiring into the background of the various parties connected with the offering.... (3) An appropriate "engagement letter" will be sent to all interested parties, emphasizing that the firm's duty is to the issuer and bondholders.... (4) The firm will require that it receive independently-audited financial statements, representation from appropriate interested persons concerning the accuracy and completeness of the statements about them in any offering circulars, and a statement from counsel for any lessee or guarantor that such counsel has reviewed the offering circular and is aware of no inaccuracies therein. (5) Partners and associates of the firm will attend, at least annually, municipal bond workshops and seminars.

[213] *See, e.g.*, Meredith Brown, *Counsel with a Fraudulent Client*, 17 Rev. Sec. Reg. 909 (1984); Samuel H. Gruenbaum, *Clients' Frauds and Their Lawyers' Obligations*, 68 Geo. L.J. 191 (1979); Marc I. Steinberg, *Attorney Liability for Client Fraud*, 1991 Colum. Bus. L. Rev. 1 (1991).

significant is *In the Matter of Carter and Johnson*.[214] Although declining to hold the subject attorneys liable in that proceeding, the Commission enunciated standards of professional conduct when an attorney renders correct disclosure advice that a corporate fiduciary refuses to follow. Addressing the steps that legal counsel should take in this situation, the SEC stated that such steps may include: enlisting the aid of other corporate officers, approaching one or more directors, notifying the board of directors, and resigning from the engagement.[215] In short, when faced with this dilemma, the attorney's continued advisory role violates professional standards unless she takes prompt steps to end the client's noncompliance.[216] If these steps prove unsuccessful, legal counsel's practical recourse may be to resign from the engagement rather than being deemed to be co-opted into the client's illegal scheme.[217] As discussed in Chapter 7 herein, in 2003, the SEC elaborated upon legal counsel's obligations in the client fraud context by promulgating its Standards of Professional Conduct.[218]

---

[214] [1981 Transfer Binder] Fed. Sec. L. Rep. (CCH) ¶ 82,847 (SEC 1981).

[215] *Id.* at 84,172–73. The proceeding did not raise the question of whether legal counsel had an obligation to "blow the whistle," thereby publicly disclosing the client's confidences and secrets. This subject is addressed in Chapter 7 herein.

[216] As subsequently elaborated upon by the American Bar Association's Model Rules of Professional Conduct and the SEC's Standards of Professional Conduct, adopted in 2003, other steps may be taken, including the procurement of a second opinion, referral to the chief legal officer, and revelation of confidential information related to the representation to the extent the lawyer reasonably believes is necessary to prevent or rectify the misconduct. *See* discussion in Chapter 7 herein.

[217] [1981 Transfer Binder] Fed. Sec. L. Rep. (CCH) ¶ 82,847, at 84,169–73. The Commission stated:

> Resignation is one option, although we recognize that other considerations, including the protection of the client against foreseeable prejudice, must be taken into account in the case of withdrawal. A direct approach to the board of directors or one or more individual directors or officers may be appropriate; or he may choose to try to enlist the aid of other members of the firm's management. What is required, in short, is some prompt action that leads to the conclusion that the lawyer is engaged in efforts to correct the underlying problem, rather than having capitulated to the desires of a strong-willed but misguided client.

Id. at 84,169–70. In this regard, where the client continues to use the attorney's work product (such as a securities offering document) that the attorney at that time discovers is materially false, resignation alone may not be sufficient. In such circumstances, a "noisy withdrawal" may be required. *See* American Bar Association, Model Rules of Professional Conduct, Rule 1.2 cmt. 10, Rule 4.1 cmt. 3; American Bar Association, Committee on Ethics and Professional Responsibility, Formal Opinion No. 92-366 (1992); discussion in Chapter 7 herein.

For law journal articles discussing the *Carter Johnson* proceeding as well as other Rule 102(e) proceedings and their ramifications, *see, e.g.*, Daniel Goelzer and Susan Wyderko, *Rule 2(e) Securities and Exchange Commission Discipline of Professionals*, 85 Nw. U. L. Rev. 652 (1991); Samuel H. Gruenbaum, *The SEC's Use of Rule 2(e) to Discipline Accountants and Other Professionals*, 56 Notre Dame L. Rev. 820 (1980); Simon Lorne and W. Hardy Callcott, *Administrative Actions Against Lawyers Before the SEC*, 50 Bus. Law. 1293 (1995); Ann Maxey, *SEC Enforcement Actions Against Securities Lawyers: New Remedies vs. Old Policies*, 22 Del. J. Corp. L. 537 (1997); Mark Sargent, *Lawyers in the Perfect Storm*, 43 Washburn L.J. 1 (2003).

[218] *See* 17 C.F.R. § 205 (2017); Securities Exchange Act Release No. 47276 (2002). These rules were adopted in order to implement the directive set forth in Section 307 of the Sarbanes-Oxley Act. To date, the SEC has not invoked these Standards in a disciplinary proceeding. *See* discussion in Chapter 7 herein.

Although largely premised on a disclosure rationale, the SEC's disciplinary proceedings against accountants and attorneys have impacted internal procedures and practices of professional firms. Requiring and enforcing applicable standards in this context, the Commission facilitates law-compliant behavior by accounting and law firms as well as by their clients. More than the laudable objective of disclosure is involved here; namely, adherence to requisite professional norms promotes compliance with the law. Law-compliant behavior serves as a solid foundation for the development and effective implementation of sound corporate governance practices.

IX. Conclusion

At times, the Sarbanes-Oxley Act of 2002 and the Dodd-Frank Act of 2010 are portrayed as initiating the federalization of corporate governance—at least, to a significant degree.[219] This chapter puts that proposition in its historical context.[220] As seen from the discussion herein, for several decades, Congress and the SEC have federalized aspects of corporate governance that otherwise would have been within the sole purview of state company law. Acting in this fashion, federal measures encompassing such matters as insider trading, management self-dealing, going-private transactions, tender offers, and shareholder proposals have provided greater protection for shareholders—as well as for the implementation of enhanced corporate governance practices—than would have been the situation if the respective states were the sole governors. Hence, the federalization of corporate governance did not begin at the beginning of the twenty-first century. Rather, it has been a process that, although at times has stalled, has received congressional approbation since the enactment of the Securities Exchange Act of 1934.[221]

[219] *See* discussion in Chapters 4, 5, and 6 herein.

[220] The SEC's shareholder proposal rule is the focus of Chapter 4.

[221] As discussed earlier in this chapter, such approbation may be viewed as commencing with the enactment of Section 16 of the Securities Exchange Act. *See supra* notes 18–30 and accompanying text. Moreover, congressional efforts to federalize corporate governance commenced over a century ago. *See* discussion Chapters 2, 8 herein.

4

THE SEC'S SHAREHOLDER PROPOSAL RULE AND RELATED DEVELOPMENTS

I. Introduction

Traditionally, state law has regulated the internal affairs of corporations.[1] With certain exceptions,[2] a corporation is managed by, or is managed under the direction of, its board of directors.[3] Accordingly, a subject company's board of directors is tasked with such matters as determining and monitoring the business decisions,

[1] The internal affairs doctrine generally applies the law of the subject company's state of incorporation to determine the relations among the company, its directors and officers, and its shareholders. *See, e.g., CTS Corp. v. Dynamics Corp. of Am.*, 481 U.S. 69 (1987). *See generally* Richard Buxbaum, *The Threatened Constitutionalization of the Internal Affairs Doctrine in Corporate Law*, 75 Cal. L. Rev. 29 (1987).

[2] For example, corporations comprised of few shareholders (close corporations) may elect to dispense with a board of directors and have the company managed directly by the shareholders pursuant to a unanimous shareholder agreement. *See, e.g.*, Model Bus. Corp. Act § 7.32 (2016).

[3] Del. Code Ann. tit. 8, §141(a) (2011) ("The business and affairs of every corporation organized under this chapter shall be managed by or under the direction of a board of directors. . . .); Model Bus. Corp. Act § 8.01(b) (2011) ("All corporate powers shall be exercised by or under the authority of the board of directors of the corporation, and the business and affairs of the corporation shall be managed by or under the direction, and subject to the oversight, of its board of directors. . . .").

strategies, acquisitions (and divestitures), succession planning, and law compliance of the enterprise.[4]

Within the corporate governance framework, state corporation law grants shareholders certain specified voting[5] and other rights.[6] For example, shareholders have the right to vote with respect to: the election (or removal) of directors, eligible shareholder proposals, certain fundamental corporate changes (e.g., specified business combinations), and amendment of the articles of incorporation.[7] Given that the majority of the Fortune 1000 U.S. stock exchange listed companies are incorporated in Delaware,[8] Delaware corporation law has a profound impact on the U.S. corporate governance landscape.[9]

Along with state law,[10] shareholder voting rights today are part of the federal corporate governance regimen, including the SEC shareholder proposal mandate, adopted by the Commission in 1942.[11] More recently, with the enactment

---

[4] American Law Institute (ALI), *Restatement of the Law of Corporate Governance: Analysis and Recommendations* § 3.02 (1994); Paul H. Edelman, Randall S. Thomas, and Robert B. Thompson, *Shareholder Voting in an Age of Intermediary Capitalism*, 87 S. Cal. L. Rev. 1359, 1367, 1371–72 (2014). The American Law Institute (ALI) Restatement (Third) of Agency states that shareholders may elect and remove directors, but the directors are "neither the shareholders' nor the corporation's agents . . . given the treatment of directors within contemporary corporation law in the United States." ALI, *Restatement (Third) of Agency* § 1.01 cmt. f(2) (2006). *See* James D. Cox and Thomas Lee Hazen, *The Law of Corporations* § 13.1 (3d ed. 2010); Robert B. Thompson, *Anti-Primacy: Sharing Power in American Corporations*, 71 Bus. Law. 381 (2016).

[5] *See, e.g.*, Model Bus. Corp. Act §§ 7.28(a) (2016) (election of directors), 8.08(a) (removal of directors), 10.03 (amendment of the articles of incorporation), 10.20(a) (amendment of bylaws), 11.04 (approval of merger or share exchange), 12.02 (approval of certain dispositions).

[6] *See, e.g.*, Model Bus. Corp. Act § 16.02 (inspection of books and records) (2016), §§ 7.40–7.48 (bringing of derivative action); *Seinfeld v. Verizon Commc'ns, Inc.*, 909 A.2d 117 (Del. 2006); *State, ex. rel. Pillsbury v. Honeywell, Inc.*, 191 N.W. 2d 406 (Minn. 1971). In *Security First Corp. v. U.S. Die Casting & Development Co.*, 687 A.2d 563, 571 (Del. 1997), the Delaware Supreme Court stated: "Stockholders have a right to at least a limited inquiry into books and records where they have established some credible basis to believe that there has been wrongdoing. . . ."

[7] *See* statutes cited *supra* note 5; Edelman et al., *supra* note 4, at 1367, 1371–72; Cox and Hazen, *supra* note 4, at § 13.1.

[8] *See* Douglas Branson, et al., *Business Enterprises—Legal Structures, Governance, and Policy* 201 (3d ed. 2016).

[9] *See* Marc I. Steinberg, *Developments in Business Law and Policy* 185–86 (2012); William Cary, *Federalism and Corporate Law: Reflections upon Delaware*, 83 Yale L.J. 663 (1974); Edelman, et al., *supra* note 4, at 1367, 1372–73; discussion Chapter 1 herein.

[10] *See, e.g., Blasius Indus., Inc. v. Atlas Corp.*, 564 A.2d 651, 659 (Del. Ch. 1988) (focusing on "the central importance of the franchise to the scheme of corporate governance").

[11] *See* Rule 14a-8, 17 C.F.R. § 240.14a-8 (2017); Securities Exchange Act Release No. 3347 (1942); Louis Loss and Joel Seligman, *Securities Regulation* 1939 (3d ed. 1990) (stating that the 1942 revision of the SEC's proxy rules included "a provision under which the registrant must include in its [proxy] material a 100-word statement in support of any proposal of a security holder that it opposes"); Patrick J. Ryan, *Rule 14a-8, Institutional Shareholder Proposals and Corporate Democracy*, 23 Ga. L. Rev. 97, 98 (1988) ("Since 1942, the Securities and Exchange Commission (SEC) has required corporate management to include shareholder proposals in its solicitation materials when management itself seeks shareholder voting proxies."). Shareholder proposals are

of the Dodd-Frank Wall Street Reform and Consumer Protection Act of 2010 ("Dodd-Frank" Act), advisory non-binding shareholder "voice" is mandated with respect to executive compensation, which has been coined as a "Say on Pay" vote.[12]

When assessing the degree of shareholder activism, institutional investors,[13] as compared to typical individual shareholders,[14] normally are more active proponents. From a historical perspective, from 1900 to 1945, institutional investors managed approximately five percent of all outstanding stock in the United States;[15] by contrast, in 2010, these investors beneficially owned 67 percent of all outstanding stock.[16] Institutional investors consist, for example, of hedge funds, mutual funds, pension funds, insurance companies, and universities.[17] Not surprisingly, the interests of these investors vary with significant frequency.[18] At times, a number of these investors may seek to influence corporate policies, being mindful of the fiduciary obligations they may owe under applicable law, such as ERISA or the Investment Advisers Act.[19] One manner in which this objective is sought to be achieved is by

---

precatory proposals put forth by shareholders. Generally, even if a shareholder proposal receives an overwhelming majority, it is merely advisory and thus not binding on the corporation. The subject board of directors, in exercising its business judgment, may conclude that the proposal is not in the best interests of the corporation.

[12] *See* Dodd-Frank Wall Street Reform and Consumer Protection Act, Pub. L. No. 111-203, § 951, 124 Stat. 1375, 1899 (2010) (adding new Section 14A to the Securities Exchange Act of 1934); Edelman, et al., *supra* note 4, at 1368. For further discussion, *see* Chapter 5 herein.

[13] Joann S. Lublin, *Investors Gain More Clout Over Boards*, Wall St. J., Jan. 11, 2016, at B1. *See* Marshall E. Blume and Donald B. Keim, Working Paper, *Institutional Investors and Stock Market Liquidity: Trends and Relationships*, The Wharton School, University of Pennsylvania (Aug. 21, 2012), *available at* http://finance.wharton.upenn.edu/~keim/research/ChangingInstitutionPreferences_21Aug2012.pdf; Matteo Tonello and Stephan Rabimov, The Conference Board, *2010 Institutional Investment Report: Trends in Asset Allocation and Portfolio Composition* (November 2010) [hereinafter "Conference Board Report"]; Sarah Cliff, *CEO View: Defending a Good Company from Bad Investors*, 95 Harv. Bus. Rev. No. 3 at 60, 61 (May–June 2017); George S. Geis, *Ex-Ante Corporate Governance*, 41 J. Corp. L. 609, 614–16 (2016).

[14] *See* Robert D. Rosenbaum, *Foundation of Sand: The Weak Premises Underlying the Current Push for Proxy Rule Changes*, 17 J. Corp. L. 163 (1991).

[15] *See* Blume and Keim, *supra* note 13, at 4.

[16] *Id.*; Conference Board Report, *supra* note 13.

[17] For example, the University of California was a lead plaintiff in the *Enron* litigation. *See In re Enron Corp. Sec., Derivative & ERISA Litig.*, Civil Action No. H-01-3624 (S.D. Tex. 2002).

[18] Many hedge funds are more aggressive, preferring companies with levels of debt that offer the prospect of greater returns; many mutual funds, on the other hand, are more risk-adverse. *See generally* John C. Coffee, Jr. and Darius Palia, *The Wolf at the Door: The Impact of Hedge Fund Activism on Corporate Governance*, 41 J. Corp. L. 545, 549 (2016) (exploring the debate "in which one side views hedge funds as the natural leaders of shareholders and the other side as short-term predators, intent on a quick raid to boost the stock price and then exit before the long-term costs are felt").

[19] While shareholders seek to influence management, their influence ordinarily is merely advisory and not binding on management. Note that the statutory fiduciary duty to vote in the beneficial shareholders' best

invoking the SEC's shareholder proposal rule—Rule 14a-8[20] promulgated under Section 14(a) of the Securities Exchange Act.

This book addresses the myriad of federal statutory, judicial, and regulatory actions through the decades that impact corporate governance. Many of these developments are analyzed in a collective manner in a select chapter, such as Chapter 5 herein, which focuses on SEC mandates emanating from the enactment of the Sarbanes-Oxley and the Dodd-Frank Acts. Because of the historical importance and meaningful impact of the SEC's shareholder proposal rule with respect to the federalization of corporate governance, this subject merits attention in a separate chapter.

II. Rule 14a-8—General Framework

Generally, there exist two avenues by which a shareholder may obtain support from fellow shareholders in relation to a shareholder proposal. First, such shareholder can "pay to issue a separate proxy statement, which must satisfy all of the disclosure requirements applicable to management's proxy statement."[21] Obviously, this approach entails considerable financial expense to the proponent-shareholder, hence making this alternative ordinarily an unattractive avenue. The second and more common route is for a shareholder to seek to have the company include its proposal and supporting statement in such company's proxy materials under SEC Rule 14a–8. Although this approach is financially more advantageous for the shareholder-proponent, as the subject company incurs the applicable costs, there are several categories of proposals that may be excluded by the company in its proxy materials.[22] Although Rule 14a-8 requires, as a general proposition, that a proposal submitted by an eligible shareholder is to be included in the subject company's proxy materials, the proposal in fact will be excluded if such shareholder fails to adhere to the procedural requirements or the content of the proposal falls within a substantive

---

interests has helped to create a market for proxy advisory firms. *See generally* Final Rule: Proxy Voting by Investment Advisers, Investment Advisers Act Release No. IA-2106 (2003) [hereinafter "Investment Advisers Act Release"], *available at* http://www.sec.gov/rules/final/ia-2106.htm; Edelman, et al., *supra* note 4, at 1367, 1395.

[20] 17 C.F.R. § 240.14a-8 (2017). For an insightful analysis of Rule 14a-8, *see* Alan R. Palmiter, *The Shareholder Proposal Rule: A Failed Experiment in Merit Regulation*, 45 Ala. L. Rev. 879 (1994). *See generally* Marc Folladori and Ryan Valenza, *Developments in Shareholder Proposals*, 45 Rev. Sec. & Comm. Reg. 33 (2012).

[21] *Trinity Wall St. v. Wal-Mart Stores, Inc.*, 792 F.3d 323, 335–36 (3d Cir. 2015), *cert. denied*, 136 S. Ct. 499 (2015).

[22] Rule 14a-8(i), 17 C.F.R. § 240.14a-8(i) (2017). *See* SEC Division of Corporation Finance, Staff Legal Bulletin No. 14I (2017).

ground for exclusion.[23] In practical effect, the shareholder proposal must be a precatory resolution—not a directive that the company implement the proposal upon receiving shareholder approval.[24]

---

[23] The chart below is from Shareholder Proposals, SEC Division of Corporation Finance, Staff Legal Bulletin No. 14 (2001) [hereinafter "SEC Bulletin No. 14"]. As set forth in the Bulletin, the substantive bases for exclusion of shareholder proposals under Rule 14a-8 are as follows:

Substantive Basis	Description
Rule 14a-8(i)(1)	The proposal is not a proper subject for action by shareholders under the laws of the jurisdiction of the company's organization.
Rule 14a-8(i)(2)	The proposal would, if implemented, cause the company to violate any state, federal or foreign law to which it is subject.
Rule 14a-8(i)(3)	The proposal or supporting statement is contrary to any of the Commission's proxy rules, including Rule 14a-9, which prohibits materially false or misleading statements in proxy soliciting materials.
Rule 14a-8(i)(4)	The proposal relates to the redress of a personal claim or grievance against the company or any other person, or is designed to result in a benefit to the shareholder, or to further a personal interest, which is not shared by the other shareholders at large.
Rule 14a-8(i)(5)	The proposal relates to operations that account for less than 5% of the company's total assets at the end of its most recent fiscal year, and for less than 5% of its net earnings and gross sales for its most recent fiscal year, and is not otherwise significantly related to the company's business.
Rule 14a-8(i)(6)	The company would lack the power or authority to implement the proposal.
Rule 14a-8(i)(7)	The proposal deals with a matter relating to the company's ordinary business operations.
Rule 14a-8(i)(8)	The proposal relates to an election for membership on the company's board of directors or analogous governing body.
Rule 14a-8(i)(9)	The proposal directly conflicts with one of the company's own proposals to be submitted to shareholders at the same meeting.
Rule 14a-8(i)(10)	The company has already substantially implemented the proposal.
Rule 14a-8(i)(11)	The proposal substantially duplicates another proposal previously submitted to the company by another shareholder that will be included in the company's proxy materials for the same meeting.
Rule 14a-8(i)(12)	The proposal deals with substantially the same subject matter as another proposal or proposals that previously has or have been included in the company's proxy materials within a specified time frame and did not receive a specified percentage of the vote. . . .
Rule 14a-8(i)(13)	The proposal relates to specific amounts of cash or stock dividends.

[24] Rule 14a-8(i)(1), 17 C.F.R. § 240.14a-8(i)(1) (2017). *See* Geis, *supra* note 13, at 614 (stating that "a corporation must include a shareholder proposal in its proxy materials unless the proposal suffers from a procedural defect or falls within one of thirteen grounds for exclusion"); sources cited *supra* note 11. This provision authorizes the subject company to exclude the proposal if it is improper under state law. The Note to this provision sets forth the following:

> Depending on the subject matter, some proposals are not considered proper under state law if they would be binding on the company if approved by shareholders. In our experience, most proposals that are cast as

Importantly, there are specified eligibility and procedural requirements that a shareholder must satisfy in order to submit a proposal pursuant to Rule 14a-8. For example, Rule 14a-8(b) sets forth that such shareholder: must have held the subject securities for at least one year at the time that the proposal is submitted, and continue to hold such securities through the date of such shareholder meeting; must beneficially own either $2,000 in market value *or* 1 percent of the corporation's securities that are entitled to vote on the proposal;[25] be limited to submitting one proposal per meeting and such proposal cannot exceed 500 words;[26] and be required to submit its proposal at least 120 calendar days before the release date set forth in the prior year's proxy statement.[27] If the company wishes to exclude the proposal from its proxy materials, such company must submit a no-action request to the SEC setting forth its reason(s) for seeking to exclude the proposal (and, at the same time, provide the shareholder-proponent with a copy of its submission to the Commission).[28]

---

recommendations or requests that the board of directors take specified action are proper under state law. Accordingly, we will assume that a proposal drafted as a recommendation or suggestion is proper unless the company demonstrates otherwise.

[25] Rule 14a-8(b), 17 C.F.R. § 240.14a-8(b) (2017). In 2017, the U.S. House of Representatives passed the Financial Choice Act of 2017, H.R. 10. Section 844 of the bill, if enacted, likely would adversely impact the ability of smaller shareholders to initiate shareholder proposals. Summarized in a succinct manner, the bill:

- Raises the ownership threshold to 1% of a company's outstanding shares (from the current lesser of $2,000 or 1%) and raises the holding period threshold to three years (from the current 1 year);
- Raises the percentage of the shareholder vote a proposal must win to be eligible for resubmission; [and]
- Eliminates proposals by a non-shareholder acting on behalf of a shareholder.

Dechert LLP, William G. Lawlor, et al., *Shareholder Proposal Reform under the Financial Choice Act of 2017: A Welcome Development for Companies or a Trojan Horse?*, at 1 (May 9, 2017). If enacted, unless institutional or larger individual shareholders become more active in this setting, the bill likely will curtail the number of shareholder proposals being initiated, especially for corporations that have large market capitalizations. *See* N. Peter Rasmussen, *Financial Regulation Bill Could Threaten Shareholder Proposal Process*, Bloomberg BNA (April 16, 2017).

[26] Rule 14a-8(c)–(d), 17 C.F.R. § 240.14a-8(c)–(d) (2017). The 500-word limit includes any accompanying supporting statement. *See* Shareholder Proposals, SEC Bulletin No. 14, *supra* note 23.

[27] Rule 14a-8(e)(2), 17 C.F.R. § 240.14a-8(e)(2) (2017) (providing that "[t]he proposal must be received at the company's executive offices not less than 120 calendar days before the date of the company's proxy statement released to shareholders in connection with the previous year's annual meeting"). The release date is disclosed in the previous year's annual meeting proxy statement. SEC Bulletin No. 14, *supra* note 23.

[28] Rule 14a-8(j), 17 C.F.R. § 240.14a-8(j) (2017); SEC Bulletin No. 14, *supra* note 23. The subject company must make its submission to the Commission at least 80 days before it files its proxy statement and form with the Commission, unless such company is able to demonstrate "good cause" for missing such submission deadline.

Set forth succinctly, the SEC no-action process may be described in the following manner:

> Under this process, counsel informs the SEC staff (not the Commission itself) of his or her client's contemplated conduct.... The staff generally responds by either issuing a no-action letter or by refusing to issue such a letter. At times, the staff's response communicates solely an enforcement posture—namely, whether the staff would recommend to the Commission that an enforcement action be initiated if the contemplated

Thereupon, such shareholder may (but is not required to) submit a reply to the SEC addressing the company's no-action letter request (and must provide the company a copy of its reply).[29] The SEC's Division of Corporation Finance will then either refrain from agreeing with the subject company's position or issue a no-action letter concurring with the company's position that the shareholder proposal may be properly excluded from its proxy materials.[30] Although the Commission is entitled to review a no-action letter issued by the Division of Corporation Finance, it does so only on relatively rare occasions.[31] An aggrieved shareholder is not entitled to seek judicial review of an SEC no-action letter; [32] nonetheless, such shareholder has a private right of action against the subject company for excluding the proposal.[33]

III. Issues Voted Upon in Shareholder Proposals

A. UTILIZING RULE 14a-8 FOR SOCIAL ISSUES

As an integral component of the corporate governance framework, concerned shareholders seek to invoke Rule 14a-8 with the objective of bringing social issues

---

> conduct were undertaken in the manner set forth in the written request. In other staff responses, in addition to the enforcement position taken, the staff may articulate interpretations of applicable SEC rules and regulations as they pertain to the proposed conduct. In either situation, the staff's views are not those of the Commission and are not binding in any manner. Notwithstanding the informal status of SEC no-action letters, they unquestionably have great significance and are relied upon by participants and their attorneys.

Marc I. Steinberg, *Understanding Securities Law* 60 (6th ed. 2014). *See* Thomas Lemke, *The SEC No-Action Letter Process*, 42 Bus. Law. 1019 (1987); Donna Nagy, *Judicial Reliance on Regulatory Interpretation in SEC No-Action Letters: Current Problems and a Proposed Framework*, 83 Cornell L. Rev. 921, 924 (1998).

29 Rule 14(a)-8(k), 17 C.F.R. § 240.14a-8(k) (2017).

30 *Id.*; SEC Bulletin No. 14, *supra* note 23; Nagy, *supra* note 28, at 939 ("Although Rule 14a-8 merely prescribes notification and filing requirements, virtually all companies that decide to omit a shareholder proposal seek a no-action letter in support of their decision."). *See* Geis, *supra* note 13, at 614. With respect to SEC no-action letters, *see generally* sources cited *supra* note 28.

31 *See* 17 C.F.R. § 202.1(d) (2017); Thomas Lee Hazen, *Treatise on the Law of Securities Regulation* § 10.8[1][A][2] (6th ed. 2009) (stating that Commission review of a staff no-action letter in the shareholder proposal context is "rare" and should be limited to "matters of substantial importance and where the issues are novel or highly complex").

32 *See, e.g., Amalgamated Clothing & Textile Workers Union v. SEC*, 15 F.3d 254 (2d Cir. 1994) (holding that judicial review of SEC staff no-action letter is not available, as a no-action letter does not constitute a "final order"); *Board of Trade v. SEC*, 883 F.2d 525 (7th Cir. 1989) (SEC staff no-action letter is tentative, not final order, and therefore not subject to judicial review); *Kixmiller v. SEC*, 492 F.2d 641 (D.C. Cir. 1974) (holding that judicial review is available for orders issued by the Commission, but not for staff no-action letters as they are not "final orders").

33 *See, e.g., Roosevelt v. E.I. DuPont de Nemours & Co.*, 958 F.2d 416 (D.C. Cir. 1992). *See generally* Marc I. Steinberg, *Securities Regulation: Liabilities and Remedies* § 9.03[6] (2017). As the court stated in *Roosevelt:* "Consistent with congressional intent and Supreme Court case law, we hold, a private right of action is properly implied from Section 14(a) of the Securities Exchange Act of 1934 to enforce a company's obligation to include shareholder proposals in annual meeting proxy materials." 958 F.2d at 417 (opinion by Judge Ruth B. Ginsburg).

to the attention of fellow shareholders and the subject company's board of directors. Compared with current practice, from a historical perspective, the shareholder proposal rule excluded proposals that sought "to obtain the consensus of other stockholders with respect to matters which are of a general political, social or economic nature."[34] In 1951, a federal district court upheld this exclusion. In that case, a plaintiff-shareholder petitioned the court to enjoin Greyhound Corporation from transmitting its proxy materials unless his proposal recommending "that Management Consider the Advisability of Abolishing the Segregated Seating System in the South" be included in the corporation's proxy statement.[35]

In October 1950, Mr. Peck, a Greyhound shareholder, requested that the corporation include his proposal in its proxy materials for the 1951 annual stockholders' meeting. In February 1951, Greyhound sought a no-action letter from the SEC on the basis that the proposal was not a proper subject matter for shareholder vote under the shareholder proposal rule. The company relied on a Commission release that stated: "It was not the intent of Rule X-14A-7 [now Rule 14a-8] to permit stockholders to obtain the consensus of other stockholders with respect to matters which are of a general political, social or economic nature. Other forums exist for the presentation of such views."[36] Agreeing with the company, the SEC's Division of Corporation Finance issued a no-action letter. In its ruling, the court deferred to the Division of Corporation Finance's position that the shareholder proposal was properly excluded from the company's proxy materials.[37]

In 1970, the United States Court of Appeals (in *Medical Committee for Human Rights v. SEC*) insinuated that these exclusions were inconsistent with the legislative

---

[34] Securities Exchange Act Release No. 3638 (1945). *See* Securities Exchange Act Release No. 4775 (1952).

[35] *Peck v. Greyhound Corp.*, 97 F. Supp. 679 (S.D.N.Y. 1951).

[36] Securities Exchange Act Release No. 3638 (1945). *See* Jay W. Eisenhofer and Michael J. Barry, *Shareholder Activism Handbook* 3–14 (2005); Marilyn B. Cane, *The Revised SEC Shareholder Proxy Proposal System: Attitudes, Results and Perspectives*, 11 J. Corp. L. 57, 76 (1985); Ryan, *supra* note 11, at 119.

[37] *Greyhound Corp.*, 97 F. Supp. 680–81. The court also noted that the plaintiff should have first appealed the decision of the Division of Corporation Finance to the Commission for administrative review prior to filing for an injunction. *Id.* Elaborating, the court reasoned:

> Rules and regulations adopted by administrative agencies pursuant to Congressional authorization are best interpreted, in the first instance, by the agency which has been entrusted with the power and authority to write them. Here, the Commission has interpreted and construed its own rule contrary to that which plaintiff contends is the proper interpretation. This court cannot hold, on the proof before it, unaided as it is by the vast experience of daily contact with the practical workings of this rule (which the Commission has had), that the interpretation should be set aside; this is especially so in the absence of any record of administrative review. The court is also unable to conclude that the denial of this temporary injunction will work irreparable harm and damage to plaintiff. The burden of establishing this is upon plaintiff, and that he has failed to do.

Id. at 681.

rationale underlying Section 14(a).[38] In that case, the Medical Committee for Human Rights submitted a shareholder proposal that it sought to include in the proxy materials for the 1968 annual meeting of Dow Chemical Co. The shareholder proposal requested that the corporation discontinue its manufacturing of napalm unless it could provide assurances that the product would not be used to inflict human injury.[39] Thereafter, Medical Committee for Human Rights amended its proposal to provide "that the company shall not make napalm."[40] Seeking to exclude the shareholder proposal from its proxy materials, the company requested a no-action letter from the SEC staff. After consideration, the SEC's Division of Corporation Finance issued the no-action letter.[41]

Medical Committee for Human Rights thereupon instituted suit. In response, Dow asserted that the shareholder proposal was excludable pursuant to the social and political exclusions. The corporation also pointed out that napalm sales generated minimal profit and that it manufactured and marketed napalm as part of its patriotic duty in support of the Vietnam War.[42] Thus, the proposal, according to Dow, also was excludable as it interfered with "ordinary business operations" and did not "significantly relate" to Dow's business.[43] The appellate court disagreed, holding that the proposal was not excludable. The court reasoned that Dow manufactured napalm in spite of its ordinary business and also apparently due to personal politics. Therefore, the company's determination to exclude the proposal was misplaced.[44]

---

[38] *Med. Comm. for Human Rights v. SEC*, 432 F.2d 659, 676, 680 (D.C. Cir. 1970), *vacated as moot*, 404 U.S. 403 (1972). *See* Eisenhofer and Barry, *supra* note 36, at § 3.03[b]; Cane, *supra* note 36, at 77; Ryan, *supra* note 11, at 111–20. As stated by the court:

> It is obvious to the point of banality to restate the proposition that Congress intended by its enactment of section 14 of the Securities Exchange Act of 1934 to give true vitality to the concept of corporate democracy. The depth of this commitment is reflected in the strong language employed in the legislative history: ". . . Fair corporate suffrage is an important right that should attach to every equity security bought on a public exchange. Management of properties owned by the investing public should not be permitted to perpetuate themselves by the misuse of corporate proxies."

Id. at 676, *quoting*, H.R. Rep. No. 1383, 73d Cong., 2d Sess. 5, 13 (1934). *See also SEC v. Transamerica Corp.*, 163 F.2d 511, 517–18 (3d Cir. 1947).

[39] 432 F.2d at 680. *See* Eisenhofer and Barry, *supra* note 36, at § 3.03[b]; Cane, *supra* note 36, at 77; Ryan, *supra* note 11, at 111–20.

[40] 432 F.2d at 663; Letter from Quentin D. Young, General Counsel, Dow Chemical Company, Feb. 3, 1969, *found in* Record 16a; 432 F.2d at 680; Eisenhofer and Barry, *supra* note 36, at § 3.03[b]; Cane, *supra* note 36, at 77; Ryan, *supra* note 11, at 111–120.

[41] 432 F.2d at 663. At that time, the SEC rules permitted exclusion of shareholder proposals that were "primarily for the purpose of promoting general economic, political, racial, religious, social or similar causes" (Rule 14a-8(c)(2)) or requested management to "take action with respect to a matter relating to the conduct of ordinary business operations of the [company]" (Rule 14a-8(c)(2) (among other exclusions)).

[42] 432 F.2d at 681–82.

[43] *Id.* at 679.

[44] *Id.* at 679–81.

Invoking corporate governance principles, the court of appeals reasoned that company management cannot utilize the proxy rules to unduly shield its decisions from shareholder input. The court determined that shareholder proposals are not necessarily excludable when they question the "political and moral predilections" of corporate fiduciaries and address corporate social responsibility. The appellate court asserted:

> No reason has been advanced in the present proceedings which leads to the conclusion that management may properly place obstacles in the path of shareholders who wish to present to their co-owners, in accord with applicable state law, the question of whether they wish to have their assets used in a manner which they believe to be more socially responsible but possibly less profitable than that which is dictated by present company policy.[45]

The appellate court's decision, together with congressional concerns regarding the Rule's social policy exclusion,[46] prompted the SEC to soften its position with respect

---

[45] *Id.* at 681. Elaborating, the court asserted:

> The proper political and social role of modern corporations is, of course, a matter of philosophical argument extending far beyond the scope of our present concern; the substantive wisdom or propriety of particular corporate political decisions is also completely irrelevant to the resolution of the present controversy. What *is* of immediate concern, however, is the question of whether the corporate proxy rules can be employed as a shield to isolate such managerial decisions from shareholder control. . . . We think that there is a clear and compelling distinction between management's legitimate need for freedom to apply its expertise in matters of day-to-day business judgment, and management's patently illegitimate claim of power to treat modern corporations with their vast resources as personal satrapies implementing personal political or moral predilections. It could scarcely be argued that management is more qualified or more entitled to make these kinds of decisions than the shareholders who are the true beneficial owners of the corporation; and it seems equally implausible that an application of the proxy rules which permitted such a result could be harmonized with the philosophy of corporate democracy which Congress embodied in section 14(a) of the Securities Exchange Act of 1934.

Id. (emphasis in original).

[46] In June 1970, Senator Edmund S. Muskie introduced the Corporate Participation Bill seeking to provide shareholders with greater access to pursue shareholder proposals impacting corporate general welfare. More particularly, the bill proposed that Section 14(a) of the Securities Exchange Act be amended to require a company to include a shareholder proposal that may involve "economic, political, racial, religious, or similar issues" in the proxy materials provided that such matter is within the control of the subject company. This bill signaled that some congressional members believed that shareholders should be able to raise matters of corporate social responsibility with respect to the companies in which they invest. Further, it conveyed that some congressional members feared that the SEC was permitting the erosion of shareholder rights and misconstruing the intent underlying the shareholder proposal rule. *See* S. 4003, 91st Cong., 2d Sess. (June 23, 1970), in 116 Cong. Rec. 20929 (1970); 116 Cong. Rec. 20928 (1970) (remarks of Senator Muskie). In introducing the bill, Senator Muskie stated:

> This [narrow] interpretation [of Rule 14a-8] by the SEC is contrary to the purpose of section 14(a) which was to promote shareholder suffrage by giving shareholders the right to vote on any issue of major

to social policy exclusions.[47] This change of position was seen in Campaign GM. In 1970, Campaign to Make General Motors Responsible, more commonly known as Campaign GM, submitted nine shareholder proposals to be included in the proxy materials for the annual meeting of General Motors.[48] The proposals concerned environmental responsibility and employee safety, amongst other issues. Ultimately, two of the shareholder proposals were included in GM's proxy materials.[49] The two proposals advocated that GM: (1) add three directors to its board of directors to represent the public viewpoint, and (2) create a corporate social responsibility shareholder committee that would submit a report to shareholders during the next annual meeting regarding GM's conduct with respect to corporate social responsibilities, including diversity issues and recommendations for improving its lack of diversity.[50] The proposals obtained less than three percent of shareholder votes, despite their publicity and advocacy from university students.[51] Although Campaign GM was unsuccessful in garnering extensive shareholder support, it generated meaningful dialogue. Notably, GM did create a public policy committee in 1970.[52]

> corporate policy regardless of whether or not it might have some relevance to broader questions of social policy. It may well be that a majority of shareholders will vote against proposals for major company actions which have some relevance to improving our environment or bettering race relations. But at least they should have the chance to vote.
>
> Accordingly, the bill which I am introducing would amend section 14(a) of the 1934 act to provide that, as long as the proposed action is one within the control of the corporation, the SEC may not permit corporate management to refuse to include that proposal in its proxy materials simply because the proposal may in some way also relate to an economic, political, racial, religious or social cause. Passage of this bill will assure that the original purpose of section 14(a)—to promote shareholder suffrage—is not eroded.

Id. at 20929.

[47] *See* Jill E. Fisch, *From Legitimacy to Logic: Reconstructing Proxy Regulation*, 46 Vand. L. Rev. 1129, 1154 (1993); Donald E. Schwartz, *Proxy Power and Social Goals—How Campaign GM Succeeded*, 45 St. John's L. Rev. 764 (1971).

[48] *See* Donald E. Schwartz, *The Public-Interest Proxy Contest—Reflections on Campaign GM*, 69 Mich. L. Rev. 419 (1971).

[49] *See* Fisch, *supra* note 47, at 1154; Schwartz, *supra* note 48, at 451–54; Schwartz, *supra* note 47, at 764–71.

[50] The shareholder proposal envisioned that the three additional directors would conduct an internal corporate social responsibility (CSR) audit of GM and would report to the board about GM's weaknesses in CSR with appropriate recommendations to address these perceived weaknesses. The directors initially sought were: "Dr. Rene Dubos, a professor of biology at Rockefeller University and a leading ecologist, Miss Betty Furness, adviser to President Johnson on consumer affairs, and Reverend Channing Phillips, a community leader in Washington, D.C. and the first black man nominated for President at a national party convention." Schwartz, *supra* note 47, at 764–65; Proxy Statement of Campaign GM (Mar. 25, 1970).

[51] *See* Wall St. J., May 25, 1970, at 4; N.Y. Times, May 23, 1970, at 15; Schwartz, *supra* note 47, at 765.

[52] Campaign GM found the members of the GM public policy committee to be unsatisfactory as the members were more concerned with science than ecology; however, it was precluded from bringing a subsequent shareholder proposal in 1971 pursuant to Rule 14a-8(c)(4), 17 C.F.R. § 240.14a-8(c)(4) (2017), which allows companies to exclude proposals that further personal grievances or special interests. Companies, such as First

Faced with the social and political climate of the 1960s and 1970s, the SEC revised Rule 14a-8, allowing shareholders to submit public policy proposals if any such proposal was "significantly related" to the subject company's business or a matter in which the subject company could control. Subsequently, the SEC restricted this broad approach.[53] As currently amended, pursuant to Rule 14a-8, a shareholder proposal may be excluded by the subject company if such "proposal relates to operations which account for less than 5 percent of the company's total assets at the end of its most recent fiscal year, and for less than 5 percent of its net earnings and gross sales for its most recent fiscal year, and is not otherwise significantly related to the company's business."[54]

During the 1970s, the SEC's more favorable approach with respect to Rule 14a-8 had a profound impact on the number of shareholder proposals included in proxy materials. For example, shareholder proposals touching on public policy issues in the 1976 proxy season increased by 537 percent from the 1972 proxy season.[55] Shortly thereafter, the SEC, in response to the appellate court's decision in *Medical Committee* (which questioned the validity of the Rule excluding shareholder proposals concerning corporate social responsibility in light of Congress's intention to provide shareholders a voice within the corporation), removed the social cause exclusion.[56] Rule 14a-8, as then revised, thereby authorized the inclusion of shareholder proposals addressing corporate social responsibility that were significantly related to such company's business.[57]

With the removal of the social cause exclusion, activists purchased securities with the objective of effecting change within the subject corporation. In the 1970s and

---

Pennsylvania Banking and Trust Company, the largest bank in Philadelphia in the 1970s, considered adding additional members to its board to create more diversity by including women, minorities, and members from lower socioeconomic backgrounds. Schwartz, *supra* note 47, at 768; Wall St. J., Aug. 5, 1970, at 14.

[53] *See* Securities Exchange Act Release No. 9784 (1972); Christine L. Ayotte, *Reevaluating the Shareholder Proposal Rule in the Wake of Cracker Barrel and the Era of Institutional Investors*, 48 Cath. U. L. Rev. 511, 524–25 (1999). *See generally Med. Comm. for Human Rights v. SEC*, 432 F.2d 659, 682 (D.C. Cir. 1970), *vacated as moot*, 404 U.S. 403 (1972).

[54] Rule 14a-8(h)(5), 17 C.F.R. § 240.14a-8(h)(5) (2017). *See* Ayotte, *supra* note 53, at 524–25; Michael J. Connell, *Shareholder Proposals, in Preparation of Annual Disclosure Documents 1997*, at 397, 407 (PLI Corp. L. & Practice Course Handbook Series No. B-970 1997); Thomas A. DeCapo, Note, *Challenging Objectionable Animal Treatment with the Shareholder Proxy Proposal Rule*, 1988 U. Ill. L. Rev. 119, 140 (1988).

[55] *See* Ayotte, *supra* note 53, at 526; Susan W. Liebeler, *A Proposal to Rescind the Shareholder Proposal Rule*, 18 Ga. L. Rev. 425, 431 (1984).

[56] Adoption of Amendments Relating to Proposals by Security Holders, Securities Exchange Act Release No. 12999, 41 Fed. Reg. 52,994, 52,998 (Nov. 22, 1976).

[57] *See* Myron P. Curzan and Mark L. Pelesh, *Revitalizing Corporate Democracy: Control of Investment Managers' Voting on Social Responsibility Proxy Issues*, 93 Harv. L. Rev. 670, 677 (1980); Fisch, *supra* note 47, at 1154–55.

1980s, social activist shareholders turned their focus to South Africa. Reverend Leon H. Sullivan, a director of General Motors and civil rights activist, embraced a set of principles to promote equal treatment of Blacks in South Africa during the apartheid.[58] The Sullivan Principles, inter alia, sought to effectuate desegregation in the workplace, pay equality for all workers, and equal advancement opportunities at work.[59] In the American Society of Corporate Secretaries Report on shareholder proposals for 1983–1984, there were 28 proposals in relation to South Africa, 8 of which proposed that the subject company's board of directors consider adopting the Sullivan Principles.[60] Significantly, the SEC staff declined to issue no-action letters with respect to shareholder proposals relating to South Africa.[61] The *New York Times* reported that in 1983, 120 of 350 American companies with South African operations agreed to honor the Sullivan Principles.[62] The Sullivan Principles thus provided shareholders with a standard by which to assess their company's embracement of these objectives.[63] Notably, the highest percentage of votes garnered in relation to the South African issue was 24.4 percent of Tinoca, Inc. shares voting in favor of the Sullivan Principles.[64]

One of the more influential institutional investors advocating for divestment in South Africa was New York's Common Retirement Fund. Ned Regan, the then Comptroller of New York state and the trustee of the state's Common Retirement Fund—rather than utilizing the Wall Street Rule[65]—submitted shareholder

---

[58] *See* Cane, *supra* note 36, at 78.

[59] The Sullivan Principles influenced corporations with South African operations. Those corporations that committed to the Sullivan Principles were also required to report on their progress toward the Principles. As of 1982, 29 of the 145 corporations that committed to the Sullivan Principles had opted out of the Principles. *See* Cane, *supra* note 36, at 78; Tamar Lewin, *Rev. Sullivan Steps Up His Anti-Apartheid Fight*, N.Y. Times, Nov. 6, 1983, § 3, at 12.

[60] American Society of Corporate Secretaries, Inc., Report on Shareholder Proposals 29–30 (1984). *See* discussion in Cane, *supra* note 36, at 78 n.177.

[61] *See* discussion in Eisenhofer and Barry, *supra* note 36, at § 3-14; *See, e.g., Texaco, Inc.*, 1985 No-Action LEXIS 1885 (Jan. 7, 1985) (shareholder proposal that requested report to shareholders on company's activities in South Africa and its withdrawal from South Africa, among other proposals, not excludable).

[62] *See* Cane, *supra* note 36, at 78; Robert Simon, *At a Crossroad in South Africa*, N.Y. Times, Nov. 6, 1983, at 1.

[63] *See* Cane, *supra* note 36, at 78; Simon, *supra* note 62.

[64] Virginia J. Harnisch, *Rule 14a-8 After Reagan: Does It Protect Social Responsibility Shareholder Proposals?*, 6 J.L. & Pol. 415, 441 (1990) (citing *Shareholder Proposals On Governance, Social Responsibility Gain Support, Study Indicates*, Daily Report on Executives (BNA) No. 122, at A-4 (June 26, 1987)).

[65] The Wall Street Rule posits that disgruntled shareholders may sell their holdings in the subject company in an actively traded securities market. *See Blasius Indus., Inc. v. Atlas Corp.*, 564 A.2d 651, 659 (Del. Ch. 1988) (stating that stockholders "may sell their stock (which, if done in sufficient numbers, may so affect security prices as to create an incentive for altered managerial performance), or they may vote to replace incumbent board members").

proposals to more than 100 companies in the pension fund's stock portfolio, requesting those companies to divest from South Africa.[66] More than half of these companies divested from their South African operations before shareholders voted on the proposals.[67] Mr. Regan's effort is viewed as the most successful shareholder campaign regarding divestment from South Africa. Shareholders thus emerged victorious in having their proposals on this subject included in the respective companies' proxy materials.[68]

Most recently, the United States Court of Appeals for the Third Circuit decided *Trinity Wall Street v. Wal-Mart Stores*.[69] Trinity is one of the wealthiest religious organizations in the United States, with asset holdings valued over $800 million and having approximately $3 billion in real estate.[70] Purchasing stock in many companies, Trinity has raised timely social issues, including that enterprises which sell firearms limit access to rifles equipped with high-capacity magazines (the type of assault weapons that have been used in committing mass murders).[71] Consistent therewith, Trinity submitted a shareholder proposal to Wal-Mart to be included in Wal-Mart's proxy materials. The shareholder proposal recommended a more uniform approach regarding Wal-Mart's policies

---

[66] *See* Vineeta Anand, *The Names That Made Corporate Governance: Key Players Saw Shift from Faceoff to Cooperation*, Pensions & Investments, Feb. 23, 1998; Eisenhofer and Barry, *supra* note 36, at § 3-15.

[67] *See* Anand, *supra* note 66; Eisenhofer and Barry, *supra* note 36, at § 3-15.

[68] *See* Tom Precious, *McCall Likely to Support "Socially Responsible" Firms*, Albany Times Union, May 25, 1993 (quoting Carolyn Mathiasen from the social issues branch of the Investor Responsibility Research Center); Eisenhofer and Barry, *supra* note 36, at § 3-15.

Another very significant shareholder proposal rule situation involved Cracker Barrel. In response to that company's position that it would not retain employees who were homosexual, the New York City Employees Retirement Systems (NYCERS) submitted a shareholder proposal requesting the company to institute nondiscriminatory policies, including based on sexual orientation. Issuing a no-action letter, the SEC staff agreed that Cracker Barrel was entitled to exclude the shareholder proposal from its proxy materials due to the fact that the shareholder proposal involved the company's "day-to-day" business and thus was within the "ordinary business" exception. *See Cracker Barrel Old Country Store Inc.*, SEC No-Action Letter, 1992 SEC No-Act LEXIS 984, at 4 (Oct. 13, 1992). Subsequently, the U.S. Court of Appeals for the Second Circuit upheld this no-action position. *See NYCERS v. SEC*, 45 F.3d 7 (2d Cir. 1995). Thereafter, in 1998, the SEC reversed its position—abandoning the bright-line analysis adopted in the *Cracker Barrel* no-action letter and adopting a case-by-case approach when addressing employment-related shareholder proposals. *See* Securities Exchange Act Release No. 40018 (1998); Shireen B. Rahnema, *The SEC's Reversal of Cracker Barrel: A Return to Uncertainty*, 7 U. Miami Bus. L. Rev. 273, 273–79 (1999).

[69] *Trinity Wall St. v. Wal-Mart Stores, Inc.*, 792 F.3d 323 (3d Cir. 2015), *cert. denied*, 136 S. Ct. 499 (2015). The district court decision is reported at 75 F. Supp. 3d 617 (D. Del. 2014). Note that there was a concurrence in the Third Circuit's decision. *See infra* notes 108–113 and accompanying text.

[70] 792 F.2d at 328.

[71] *Id.* at 327–29.

with respect to perceived dangerous and immoral products that it sells. In pertinent part, the proposal provided:

> *Resolved*:
>
> Stockholders request that the Board amend the Compensation, Nominating and Governance Committee charter . . . as follows:
>
> . . . Providing oversight concerning [and the public reporting of] the formulation and implementation of . . . policies and standards that determine whether or not the Company should sell a product that:
>
> 1) especially endangers public safety and well-being;
> 2) has the substantial potential to impair the reputation of the Company; and/or
> 3) would reasonably be considered by many offensive to the family and community values integral to the Company's promotion of its brand.[72]

The narrative portion of the proposal made clear that it sought to cover the company's sale of certain firearms:

> [O]versight and reporting is intended to cover policies and standards that would be applicable to determining whether or not the company should sell guns equipped with magazines holding more than ten rounds of ammunition ("high capacity magazines") and to balancing the benefits of selling such guns against the risks that these sales pose to the public and to the Company's reputation and brand value.[73]

The supporting statement for the proposal asserted:

> The company respects family and community interests by choosing not to sell certain products such as music that depicts violence or sex and high capacity magazines separately from a gun, but lacks policies and standards to ensure transparent and consistent merchandizing decisions across product categories. This results in the company's sale of products, such as guns equipped with high capacity magazines, that facilitate mass killings, even as it prohibits its sales of passive products such as music that merely depict such violent rampages. . . .[74]

---

[72] *Id.* at 329–30; 75 F. Supp. 3d at 621–22.

[73] 792 F.3d at 330.

[74] *Id.*

Wal-Mart sought a no-action letter from the SEC to exclude Trinity's proposal from its proxy materials, on the grounds that it meddled in the company's ordinary business operations.[75] Trinity contended that the proposal was not excludable as it sought to address corporate governance at the Board level in an effort to instill consistency in Wal-Mart's merchandizing policies—namely, those policies focusing on public safety and welfare.[76] After consideration, the SEC's Division of Corporation Finance issued a no-action letter siding with Wal-Mart that the proposal was excludable under Rule 14a–8(i)(7) as it related to ordinary business operations: "Proposals concerning the sale of particular products and services are generally excludable under rule 14a-8(i)(7)."[77]

Responding to the no-action letter, Trinity filed a declaratory judgment action,[78] 17 days prior to the proxy materials being due at the printer.[79] Reasoning that the proposal dealt "with guns on the shelves and not guns in society," the federal district court held that the proposal was excludable under Rule 14a-8(i)(7) as it related to

[75] *Id.* at 330–31 (seeking to exclude the proposal pursuant to Rule 14a-8(i)(7) that authorizes such exclusion "[i]f the proposal deals with a matter relating to the company's ordinary business operations").

[76] *Id.* at 330–32. Trinity also set forth additional reasons why its proposal was not excludable. *See id.* at 331, stating that the shareholder proposal:

> concerns the Company's standards for avoiding community harm while fostering public safety and corporate ethics and does not relate exclusively to any individual product; and . . . raises substantial issues of public policy, namely a concern for the safety and welfare of the communities served by the Company's stores.

Id.

[77] *Wal-Mart Stores, Inc.*, SEC No–Action Letter, 2014 WL 409085, at 1 (Mar. 20, 2014) [hereinafter "SEC, Wal-Mart No-Action letter"]. In pertinent part, the no-action letter of the Office of Chief Counsel, Division of Corporation Finance, provided:

> The proposal requests that the board amend the compensation, nominating and governance committee charter to provide for oversight concerning the formulation and implementation of policies and standards that determine whether or not the company should sell a product that especially endangers public safety and well-being, has the substantial potential to impair the reputation of the company and/or would reasonably be considered by many offensive to the family and community values integral to the company's promotion of its brand.
>
> There appears to be some basis for your view that Walmart may exclude the proposal under rule 14a-8(i)(7), as relating to Walmart's ordinary business operations. In this regard, we note that the proposal relates to the products and services offered for sale by the company. Proposals concerning the sale of particular products and services are generally excludable under rule 14a-8(i)(7). Accordingly, we will not recommend enforcement action to the Commission if Walmart omits the proposal from its proxy materials in reliance on rule 14a-8(i)(7).

[78] *See* 792 F.3d at 327; 75 F. Supp. 3d at 622; *see also* discussion *supra* notes 30–33 and accompanying text.

[79] *See Trinity*, 792 F.3d at 331.

an "ordinary business matter."[80] The ruling thus permitted Wal-Mart to exclude the shareholder proposal from its forthcoming shareholder meeting.

Nonetheless, pursuant to the district court's ruling, Wal-Mart had not at that time prevailed on the merits.[81] Wal-Mart thereafter sought to dismiss Trinity's amended complaint.[82] The district court disagreed with Wal-Mart that the exclusion of the shareholder proposal from its 2014 proxy materials was moot.[83]

Subsequently, the district court ruled that the proposal was *not* excludable pursuant to Rule 14a-8(i)(7),[84] reasoning that the proposal was directed at the board of Wal-Mart to "oversee the development and effectuation of a Wal-Mart policy."[85] The court recognized that the day-to-day management of implementing such policy was outside the scope of the shareholder proposal.[86] In the event that the proposal may impact the core of Wal-Mart's business, it "nonetheless focuses on sufficiently significant social policy issues [that] transcend the day-to-day business matters" of the company, making the proposal "appropriate for a shareholder vote."[87] The district court also ruled that the proposal was not excludable under Rule 14a-8(i)(3) for being "so inherently vague or indefinite that neither the stockholders voting on the proposal, nor the company in implementing the proposal (if adopted), would be able to determine with any reasonable certainty exactly what actions or measures the proposal requires."[88] The court reasoned that the "[p]roposal properly leaves the details of any policy formulation and implementation to the discretion of the Committee, showing once more that [it] does not dictate any particular outcome or micro-manage Wal-Mart's day-to-day business."[89] Given that the shareholder proposal did not recommend that the Wal-Mart board of directors act in a particular manner by setting forth what the company can and cannot sell, the proposal was

[80] Pursuant to Rule 14a-8(i)(7), shareholder proposals that relate to the subject company's "ordinary business operations" are excludable. The district court held that the proposal dealt with Wal-Mart's ordinary business, as the shareholder proposal concerned whether the company should "sell guns equipped with magazines holding more than 10 rounds of ammunitions, high capacity magazines." *See Trinity*, 792 F.3d at 332, *quoting*, 2014 WL 6790928, at *3 (D. Del. 2014).

[81] *Trinity*, 792 F.3d at 332.

[82] *Id. See Trinity Wall Street v. Wal-Mart Stores, Inc.*, 75 F. Supp. 3d 617 (D. Del. 2014).

[83] 75 F. Supp. 3d at 624–28. The court nonetheless did agree that the alleged "*reasonably anticipated* 2015 violation of Section 14(a) and Rule 14a–8 [was] not ripe for adjudication." 75 F. Supp. 3d at 624, 628 (emphasis supplied).

[84] 792 F.3d at 332; 75 F. Supp. 3d at 629–35.

[85] 792 F.3d at 333; *see* 75 F. Supp. 3d at 633.

[86] 792 F.3d at 333; 75 F. Supp. 3d at 629–32.

[87] 792 F.3d at 333; 75 F. Supp. 3d at 629.

[88] 792 F.3d at 333, *quoting*, 75 F. Supp. 3d at 633.

[89] *Trinity*, 792 F.3d at 334, *quoting*, 75 F. Supp. 3d at 631.

found not to deal with the "ordinary business" of Wal-Mart.[90] Wal-Mart appealed to the Court of Appeals.[91]

Disagreeing with the district court, the U.S. Court of Appeals for the Third Circuit held that the shareholder proposal, purportedly characterized as a corporate governance issue, was excludable under Rule 14a-8(i)(7) as the essence of the proposal impacted the core operational business of Wal-Mart. As the appellate court reasoned, "[s]tripped to its essence, Trinity's proposal—although styled as promoting improved governance—goes to the heart of Wal-Mart's business: what it sells on its shelves."[92] Or, as the appellate court stated in a similar fashion: "A retailer's approach to its product offerings is the bread and butter of its business."[93] The court further held: "A proposal need only *relate* to a company's ordinary business to be excludable."[94] Hence, the appellate court rejected Trinity's argument that its

---

[90] Ordinary business includes the daily management of the subject company. It is not feasible for shareholders to manage the business, unless the subject company is a closely-held enterprise. *See generally supra* notes 1–4 and accompanying text. Summarizing the district court's decision in pertinent part, the Third Circuit stated that the district court

> concluded that, although the proposal "could (and almost certainly would) shape what products are sold by Wal-Mart," it is "best viewed as dealing with matters that are *not* related to Wal-Mart's ordinary business operations." Thus Rule 14(a)-8 could not block its inclusion in Wal-Mart's proxy materials. The Court fastened its holding to the view that the proposal wasn't a directive to management but to the Board to "oversee the development and effectuation of a Wal-Mart policy." In this way, "[a]ny direct impact of adoption of Trinity's proposal would be felt at the Board level, it would then be for [it] to determine what, if any, policy should be formulated and implemented." Stated differently, the day-to-day responsibility for implementing whatever policies the Board develops was outside the scope of the proposal.
>
> In the alternative, the Court held that even if the proposal does tread on the core of Wal-Mart's business—the products it sells—it "nonetheless focuses on sufficiently significant social policy issues" that "transcend the day-to-day business matters" of the company, making the proposal "appropriate for a shareholder vote." Among the policy issues the District Court noted are "the social and community effects of sales of high capacity firearms at the world's largest retailer and the impact this could have on Wal-Mart's reputation, particularly if such a product sold at Wal-Mart is misused and people are injured or killed as a result."
>
> The Court also found helpful how "Trinity carefully drafted its proposal . . . to not dictate what products should be sold or how the policies regarding sales of certain types of products should be formulated or implemented." It stressed the difference between Trinity's proposal and the generally excludable proposals that ask a company to report on its "policies and reporting obligations regarding possible toxic and hazardous products offered for sale." . . .

792 F.3d at 332–33 (citations and brackets omitted) (emphasis in original).

[91] *Trinity*, 792 F.3d 333 (3d Cir. 2015).

[92] *Id.* at 328.

[93] *Id.* at 344.

[94] *Id.* (emphasis in original). *See AT&T Inc.*, SEC No-Action Letter, 2016 WL 7370135 (SEC Dec. 28, 2016) (SEC staff issuing no-action letter for company's exclusion of shareholder proposal focusing on blocking robocalls under ordinary business operations exclusion).

proposal raised significant social policy issues, thereby transcending the ordinary business of Wal-Mart and thus making the proposal an appropriate matter to be voted on by shareholders under Rule 14a-8.[95]

In analyzing whether the proposal contained a social policy that transcended the "ordinary business operations" exclusion, the appellate court expressed its frustration:

> Although a core business of courts is to interpret statutes and rules, our job is made difficult where agencies, after notice and comment, have hard-to-define exclusions to their rules and exceptions to those exclusions. For those who labor with the ordinary business exclusion and a social-policy exception that requires not only significance but "transcendence," we empathize. Despite the substantial uptick in proposals attempting to raise social policy issues that bat down the business operations bar, the SEC's last word on the subject came in the 1990s, and we have no hint that any change from it or Congress is forthcoming ... We thus suggest that [the SEC] consider revising its regulation ... and issue fresh interpretive guidance.[96]

The appellate court commented that the SEC apparently embraces a "we-know-it-when-we-see-it" approach in determining whether a proposal contains a significant social policy.[97] While the court recognized that the proposal raised a sufficiently significant policy, it held that the subject matter must also "transcend" the ordinary business of the company.[98] According to the court, this inquiry focuses on whether the policy issue is "divorced from how a company approaches the nitty-gritty of its core business."[99] It reasoned that for major retailers of myriad products, such as Wal-Mart, "a policy issue is rarely transcendent if it treads on the meat of management's responsibility: crafting a product mix that satisfies consumer demand."[100] Thus, "[f]or a policy issue here to transcend Wal-Mart's business operations, it must target something more than the choosing of one among tens of thousands of products it

---

[95] *Trinity*, 792 F.2d at 344–51.

[96] *Id.* at 351.

[97] *Id.* at 346, *citing* Alan R. Palmiter, *The Shareholder Proposal Rule: A Failed Experiment in Merit Regulation*, 45 Ala. L. Rev. 879, 910 (1994).

[98] 792 F.3d at 346–47.

[99] *Id.* at 347, *citing* SEC Staff Legal Bulletin, No. 14E, 2009 WL 4363205, at *3 (Oct. 27, 2009) (stating that CEO succession-planning "raises a significant policy issue regarding the governance of the corporation that transcends the day-to-day business matter of managing the workforce").

[100] 792 F.3d at 347

sells."[101] Because Trinity's proposal did not meet this standard, the court held that it was properly excludable under Rule 14a-8(i)(7).[102]

Thereafter, the SEC Division of Corporation Finance addressed the appellate court's application of the "social policy" test in *Trinity*, among other issues.[103] The staff agreed with the outcome of the case—that the Trinity proposal was properly excludable under Rule 14a-8(i)(7).[104] However, the staff disagreed with the majority's two-part test that "a shareholder must do more than focus its proposal on a significant policy issue; the subject matter of its proposal must 'transcend' the company's ordinary business."[105] The majority in *Trinity* held that, in order for a significant policy issue to transcend the subject company's ordinary business, it must be "divorced from how a company approaches the nitty-gritty of its core business."[106] The staff believed that this approach did not comport with the objectives of the shareholder proposal rule as well as the Commission's prior statements.[107]

Instead, the staff concluded that the concurring opinion in *Trinity* properly aligns with the Commission's view as to whether a "significant" policy issue is not excludable under the "ordinary business" exception.[108] As the concurring judge stated, "whether a proposal focuses on an issue of social policy that is sufficiently significant is not separate and distinct from whether the proposal transcends a company's ordinary business. Rather, a proposal is sufficiently significant 'because' it transcends day-to-day business matters."[109] The staff further approved of the concurring judge's assertion

---

[101] *Id.* at 351.

[102] *Id. See* Stephen M. Bainbridge, *Revitalizing SEC Rule 14a-8's Ordinary Business Exclusion: Preventing Shareholder Micromanagement by Proposal*, 85 Fordham L. Rev. 705 (2016).

[103] Division of Corporation Finance Securities and Exchange Commission, Shareholder Proposals, Staff Legal Bulletin No. 14H (CF) (Oct. 22, 2015) [hereinafter "SEC Bulletin No. 14H (CF)"]. *See* Statement from Chair White Directing Staff to Review Commission Rule for Excluding Conflicting Proxy Proposals (Jan. 16, 2015), *available at* http://www.sec.gov/news/statement/statement-on-conflicting-proxy-proposals.html.

[104] SEC Bulletin No. 14H (CF), *supra* note 103.

[105] *Trinity*, 792 F.3d at 346–47; SEC Bulletin No. 14H (CF), *supra* note 103.

[106] *Trinity*, 792 F.3d at 346–47; SEC Bulletin No. 14H (CF), *supra* note 103.

[107] *Trinity*, 792 F.3d at 353 (Shwartz, J., concurring); SEC Bulletin No. 14H (CF), *supra* note 103.

[108] *Trinity*, 792 F.3d at 353 (Shwartz, J., concurring); SEC Bulletin No. 14H (CF), *supra* note 103.

[109] *Trinity*, 792 F.3d at 353 ("Thus, the SEC treats the significance and transcendence concept as interrelated, rather than independent.") (Shwartz, J., concurring); SEC Bulletin No. 14H (CF), *supra* note 103. Critical of the majority's approach, the concurrence reasoned in *Trinity*:

> The Majority's test, insofar as it practically gives companies carte blanche to exclude any proposal raising social policy issues that are directly related to core business operations, undermines the principle of fair corporate suffrage animating Rule 14a-8: shareholders' "ability to exercise their right—some would say their duty—to control the important decisions which affect them in their capacity as . . . owners of [a] corporation." Section 14(a) of the Exchange Act ensures that "[a] corporation is run for the benefit of its stockholders and not for that of its managers," and "Congress intended by its enactment of [§] 14 . . . to give true vitality to the concept of corporate democracy. . . . Permitting shareholders to vote

that, historically, the Commission "treats the significance and transcendence concepts as interrelated, rather than independent."[110] Hence, "proposals [that] transcend the day-to-day business matters and raise policy issues so significant . . . would be appropriate for a shareholder vote."[111] Therefore, a shareholder proposal is capable of transcending the subject company's ordinary business operations "even if the significant policy issue relates to the 'nitty-gritty of its core business.'"[112] Hence, according to the SEC staff, a sufficiently focused shareholder proposal that is directed at a significant policy issue that "transcends" a subject corporation's ordinary business operations is not excludable under Rule 14a-8(i)(7).[113]

> on important social issues, including those that may be closely related to a company's ordinary business, is consistent with these principles, and I would not interpret the ordinary business exclusion to prohibit it."

791 F.3d at 353–54 (concurrence) (citations omitted).

[110] *Trinity*, 792 F.3d at 353 (Shwartz, J., concurring); SEC Bulletin No. 14H (CF), *supra* note 103.

[111] Securities Exchange Act Release No. 40018 (1998); SEC Bulletin No. 14H (CF), *supra* note 103.

[112] SEC Bulletin No. 14H (CF), *supra* note 103. In an article critical of the SEC and judicial interpretation of Rule 14a-8(i)(7), Professor Stephen Bainbridge asserted:

> In theory, Rule 14a-8 contains limits on shareholder micromanagement. . . . Rule 14a-8(i)(7) is intended to permit exclusion of a proposal that seeks to micro-manage the company by probing too deeply into matters of a complex nature upon which shareholders, as a group, would not be in a position to make an informed judgment. Unfortunately, court decisions have largely eviscerated the ordinary business operations exclusion. . . .

Bainbridge, *supra* note 102, at 705 (quotation marks omitted).

[113] SEC Bulletin No. 14H (CF), *supra* note 103, *relying on*, Securities Exchange Act Release No. 40018 (1998). The SEC staff made clear that it would continue to interpret the significant policy exception under Rule 14a-8(i)(7) consistent with the Commission's approach as set forth by the concurring opinion in *Trinity*. Expressly rejecting application of the *Trinity* majority opinion rationale to its analysis, the SEC staff stated:

> Although we had previously concluded that the significant policy exception does not apply to the proposal that was submitted to Wal-Mart, we are concerned that the new analytical approach introduced by the Third Circuit goes beyond the Commission's prior statements and may lead to the unwarranted exclusion of shareholder proposals. Whereas the majority opinion viewed a proposal's focus as separate and distinct from whether a proposal transcends a company's ordinary business, the Commission has not made a similar distinction. Instead, as the concurring judge explained, the Commission has stated that proposals focusing on a significant policy issue are not excludable under the ordinary business exception "because the proposals would transcend the day-to-day business matters and raise policy issues so significant that it would be appropriate for a shareholder vote." Thus, a proposal may transcend a company's ordinary business operations even if the significant policy issue relates to the "nitty-gritty of its core business." Therefore, proposals that focus on a significant policy issue transcend a company's ordinary business operations and are not excludable under Rule 14a-8(i)(7). The Division intends to continue to apply Rule 14a-8(i)(7) as articulated by the Commission and consistent with the Division's prior application of the exclusion, as endorsed by the concurring judge, when considering no-action requests that raise Rule 14a-8(i)(7) as a basis for exclusion.

SEC Bulletin No. 14H (CF), *supra* note 103.

B. UTILIZING RULE 14a-8 FOR BOARD DECLASSIFICATION PROPOSALS

Pursuant to established corporate governance principles and governing law, shareholders are empowered to elect directors to serve on the subject company's board of directors.[114] In an effort to minimize perceived undue minority shareholder influence, boards of directors initiated measures to institute staggered boards, whereby only a specified number of directors annually were up for election (such as three directors per year elected for a nine-director board).[115] Indeed, during the past four decades, classified boards have been utilized as a corporate defense mechanism to fend off (prospective) hostile takeovers.[116] If a board is classified and directors can be removed only for cause, a shareholder seeking control of the board of directors must launch two successful proxy campaigns to accomplish this objective.[117]

As evidenced by the Shareholder Rights Project at Harvard Law School,[118] there has been a successful campaign to induce many corporations to declassify boards, thereby requiring an annual election of all directors in one proxy season.[119] A key rationale underlying this campaign is that shareholders on an annual basis are entitled to determine the composition of the subject corporation's board of directors.[120] Seeking to effectuate this objective, the Shareholder Rights Project generated support for the submission of Rule 14a-8 board declassification proposals.[121] This effort

---

[114] *See supra* notes 5–7 and accompanying text.

[115] *See* Model Bus. Corp. Act § 8.06 (2016).

[116] *See* Response Symposium: *Classification Cancels Corporate Accountability*, 55 Stan. L. Rev. 839–917 (2002); Lucian Arye Bebchuk, Jesse M. Fried, and David I. Walker, *Managerial Power and Rent Extraction in the Design of Executive Compensation*, 69 U. Chi. L. Rev. 751, 785 (2002).

[117] *See* Bebchuk, et al., *supra* note 116, at 785; Bebchuk, et al., *The Powerful Antitakeover Force of Staggered Boards: Theory, Evidence and Policy*, 54 Stan. L. Rev. 887 (2002).

[118] *See* Shareholder Rights Project, www.srp.law.harvard.edu/companies-entering-into-agreements.shtml (2014):

> The Shareholder Rights Project (SRP) was established by the Harvard Law School Program on Institutional Investors to contribute to education, discourse, and research related to efforts by institutional investors to improve corporate governance arrangements at publicly traded firms. During the previous three academic years (2011–2012 through 2013–2014), the SRP operated a clinic that assisted institutional investors (several public pension funds and a foundation) in moving S&P 500 and Fortune 500 companies towards annual elections. This work contributed to board declassification at about 100 S&P 500 and Fortune 500 companies. . . .

[119] Empirical Study, Comment, Jason M. Loring and C. Keith Taylor, *Shareholder Activism: Directorial Responses to Investors' Attempts to Change the Corporate Governance Landscape*, 41 Wake Forest L. Rev. 321, 326 (2006).

[120] *Id. See* Patrick S. McGurn, *Classification Cancels Corporate Accountability*, 55 Stan. L. Rev. 839 (2002).

[121] Edelman, et al., *supra* note 4, at 1369; Lucian Bebchuk, Scott Hirst, and June Rhee, *Toward Board Declassification in 100 S&P 500 and Fortune 500 Companies: The SRP's Report for the 2012 and 2013 Proxy Seasons*, Harv. L. Sch. Forum on Corp. Governance and Fin. Reg. (Mar. 5, 2016, 3:48 PM), http://blogs.law.harvard.edu/corpgov/2014/02/25/toward-board-declassification-in-100-sp-500-and-fortune-500-companies-the-srps-report-for-the-2012-and-2013-proxy-seasons/.

largely has been successful.[122] Accordingly, a company that receives a board declassification shareholder proposal must include the proposal in its proxy materials pursuant to Rule 14a-8. As a general proposition, with frequency, shareholders have approved these precatory proposals to amend the corporation's articles of incorporation to declassify the board. The consequence of this effective campaign is that approximately only ten percent of S&P 500 corporations continue to have classified boards.[123]

C. UTILIZING RULE 14a-8 FOR SAY-ON-PAY

The proxy season of 2006 marked the first Say-on-Pay shareholder proposals submitted under Rule 14a-8.[124] By 2009, Say-on-Pay proposals dominated the number of shareholder proposals and frequently captured the majority of shareholder support.[125] As a governmental response to the global financial crisis of 2008, Congress enacted the Emergency Economic Stabilization Act of 2008 that established the Troubled Asset Relief Program (TARP), which generally authorized expenditures to financial institutions in need.[126] TARP required recipient institutions to hold shareholder Say-on-Pay votes commencing in 2009.[127] In 2010, Say-on-Pay votes were extended to all publicly-held companies under Section 951 of the Dodd-Frank Act,

---

[122] *See* sources cited *supra* notes 118, 121.

[123] *Id. See* Geis, *supra* note 13, at 615–16:

> These [board declassification] proposals could not be excluded under SEC proxy rules, so most firms were forced into a position where they would either need to appease the shareholders or include the proposal in their proxy materials. Many firms opted for the former—agreeing to sponsor a charter amendment (already approved by the board) for shareholder ratification during the next election cycle. [For boards that chose the second approach,] many of these [shareholder] proposals received majority approval, which put enough pressure on some boards to support a change [to declassify].

[124] *See* Challie Dunn and Carol Bowie, RiskMetrics Grp., Evaluating U.S. Company Management Say on Pay Proposals: Four Steps for Investors, Shareholder Forum, 4 (Mar. 16, 2009), http://www.shareholderforum.com/sop/Library/20090316_RiskMetrics.pdf.; Randall S. Thomas, et al., *Dodd-Frank's Say on Pay: Will It Lead to a Greater Role for Shareholders in Corporate Governance?*, 97 Cornell L. Rev. 1213, 1217 (2012).

[125] *See* Gary Larkin, *The Conference Bd., Say on Pay Takes Early Lead in Proxy Season Shareholder Proposal Race*, Governance Ctr. Blog (Mar. 12, 2010), http://tcbblogs.org/governance/2010/03/12/say-on-pay-takes-early-lead-in-proxy-season-shareholder-proposal-race (reported that there were 255 Say-on-Pay shareholder proposals, which received over 59 percent shareholder support in the 2009 proxy season); Thomas, et al., *supra* note 124, at 1216–17.

[126] The Emergency Economic Stabilization Act of 2008 (Division A of Pub. L. 110–343, 122 Stat. 3765, enacted October 3, 2008).

[127] American Recovery and Reinvestment Act of 2009, Pub. L. No. 111-5, § 111(e), 123 Stat. 115, 519; Thomas, et al., *supra* note 124, at 1218.

which added Section 14A to the Securities Exchange Act.[128] Pursuant to Section 14A, publicly-held companies are required:

> [T]o conduct a separate shareholder *advisory* vote to approve the compensation of executives, as disclosed pursuant to Item 402 of Regulation S-K or any successor to Item 402. Section 14A also requires companies to conduct a separate shareholder *advisory* vote to determine how often an issuer will conduct a shareholder *advisory* vote on executive compensation. In addition, Section 14A requires companies soliciting votes to approve merger or acquisition transactions to provide disclosure of certain "golden parachute" compensation arrangements and, in certain circumstances, to conduct a separate shareholder *advisory* vote to approve the golden parachute compensation arrangements.[129]

Section 14A thus mandates that shareholders have an advisory vote on approving or disapproving executive compensation and on the frequency of Say-on-Pay votes (as well as on golden parachute payments to executives in acquisitions or mergers). Any such vote, however, does not override compensation determinations made by the board of directors.[130] Nor does the statute impose additional fiduciary duties on directors.[131] Notably, shareholder Say-on-Pay proposals are not excludable under Rule 14a-8 from the company's proxy materials even if management is including its Say-on-Pay proposal in the proxy materials.[132] The company must disclose the results

---

[128] *See* discussion in Chapter 5 herein.

[129] Shareholder Approval of Executive Compensation and Golden Parachute Compensation, Securities Exchange Act Release No. 63768, 2011 WL 231597 (2011) [hereinafter "SEC Release 63768"] (emphasis supplied). The Say-on-Pay vote extends only to the subject corporation's CEO and its four other executive officers identified in such corporation's proxy compensation table. *See* 17 C.F.R. § 240.14a-21(a) (2017); Thomas, et al., *supra* note 124, at 1225.

[130] Dodd-Frank Wall Street Reform and Consumer Protection Act, Pub. L. No. 111-203, § 951, 124 Stat. 1375, 1899 (2010) (codified at 15 U.S.C. § 78n-1(a), (b), (c)(1)-(c)(3) (Supp. IV 2010)).

[131] *Id.* at §78n-1(c)(1)–(c)(3).

[132] *Id.* at §78n-1(c)(4). Note that pursuant to the SEC release, any such shareholder proposal is not excludable as it does not directly conflict with management's proposal. A management Say-on-Pay proposal and shareholder Say-on-Pay proposal both seek to address compensation, but with varying terms. *See* SEC Bulletin No. 14H (CF), *supra* note 103:

> After reviewing the history of Rule 14a-8(i)(9) and based on our understanding of the rule's intended purpose, we believe that any assessment of whether a proposal is excludable under this basis should focus on whether there is a direct conflict between the management and shareholder proposals. For this purpose, we believe that a direct conflict would exist if a reasonable shareholder could not logically vote in favor of both proposals, *i.e.*, a vote for one proposal is tantamount to a vote against the other proposal. While this articulation may be a higher burden for some companies seeking to exclude a proposal to meet than had been the case under our previous formulation, we believe it is most consistent with the

of the Say-on-Pay vote in its Form 8-K filed with the SEC within four business days after such shareholders' meeting.[133] Moreover, in the "Compensation Discussion and Analysis" (CD&A) portion of the subject company's proxy statement, disclosure must be set forth whether such company took into account the outcome of the shareholder Say-on-Pay vote in determining "compensation policies and decisions and, if so, how that consideration has affected its compensation policies and decisions."[134]

In 2011, then SEC Commissioner Luis Aguilar opined that, since the adoption of the advisory Say-on-Pay vote mandate, publicly-held companies have enhanced their performance-based compensation plans.[135] To some degree, this mechanism has ameliorated shareholder concerns regarding allegedly excessive perks and severance packages.[136] Indeed, in a number of cases, management has revised compensation packages in response to shareholder input, including Say-on-Pay votes.[137] With some success, the Say-on-Pay vote facilitates dialogue between management and institutional shareholders on matters of executive compensation.[138]

Perhaps surprisingly, the Say-on-Pay vote has not resulted in an avalanche of derivative suits, likely due to the advisory nature of the shareholder vote and the language of Section 14A, which clarifies that no additional fiduciary duties arise from shareholder advisory votes on executive compensation packages.[139] Initially, when instituting derivative actions in this setting, shareholders enjoyed brief and fleeting success. For example, in *NECA-IBEW Pension Fund ex. rel. Cincinnati Bell, Inc. v. Cox*, shareholders managed to fend off a motion to dismiss.[140] In 2010, the

history of the rule and more appropriately focuses on whether a reasonable shareholder could vote favorably on both proposals or whether they are, in essence, mutually exclusive proposals.

In considering no-action requests under Rule 14a-8(i)(9) going forward, we will focus on whether a reasonable shareholder could logically vote for both proposals. . . .

We will not, however, view a shareholder proposal as directly conflicting with a management proposal if a reasonable shareholder, although possibly preferring one proposal over the other, could logically vote for both. . . .

[133] *See* SEC Form 8-K, Item 5.07; SEC Release 63768, *supra* note 129; Thomas, et al., *supra* note 124, at 1225.

[134] Note that the mandated disclosure is limited to the most recent Say-on-Pay vote. SEC Release 63768, *supra* note 129, at *11–13; Thomas, et al., *supra* note 124, at 1225–26.

[135] *See* Luis A. Aguilar, Comm'r, SEC, *An Inflection Point: The SEC and the Current Financial Reform Landscape* (June 10, 2011).

[136] *See* Thomas, et al., *supra* note 124, at 1256–57.

[137] *See* Louis Truong, *Say-on-Pay with Bite: Shareholder Derivative Suits on Executive Compensation*, 65 Hastings L.J. 1191, 1203–04 (2014).

[138] *See* Thomas, et al., *supra* note 124, at 1256–57; Truong, *supra* note 137, at 1203.

[139] Dodd-Frank Wall Street Reform and Consumer Protection Act, Pub. L. No. 111-203, § 951, 124 Stat. 1375, 1899 (2010) (codified at 15 U.S.C. § 78n-1(c)(1)-(c)(3) (Supp. IV 2010)).

[140] 2011 WL 4383368 (S.D. Ohio 2011).

It should be noted that it often is problematic for a derivative suit to survive a motion to dismiss. A derivative suit is brought by shareholders on behalf of the company, in the name of the company, and any monetary

Cincinnati Bell board of directors approved generous compensation packages for its top executives despite the company's disappointing financial performance.[141] Under the stewardship of its top executives, Cincinnati Bell's net income declined by $61.3 million, earnings per share dropped from $0.37 to $0.09, and the share price decreased from $3.45 to $2.80.[142] In Cincinnati Bell's 2011 proxy materials, the directors sought non-binding shareholder approval for the compensation package. Although approximately two-thirds of the shares voted against the proposed package, the directors implemented the compensation package.[143] In the derivative suit, plaintiffs alleged that the defendant directors breached their duty of loyalty by approving the compensation package in light of the company's poor performance.[144] The federal district court denied the company's motion to dismiss, reasoning that:

> Given that the director defendants devised the challenged compensation, approved the compensation, recommended shareholder approval of the compensation, and suffered a negative shareholder vote on the compensation, plaintiff has demonstrated sufficient facts to show that there is reason to doubt these same directors could exercise their independent business judgment over whether to bring suit against themselves for breach of fiduciary duty in awarding the challenged compensation.[145]

The *Cincinnati Bell* decision evidently represents a minority view. To the contrary, several other courts have held that an unsuccessful Say-on-Pay vote, by itself, does not rebut the presumption of the business judgment rule.[146] As stated by one court,

---

award (other than attorneys' fees and expenses) goes to the company. Prior to instituting a derivative suit, a shareholder ordinarily must provide the company with a demand that it intends to bring a derivative suit if the company: (1) does not address the issue complained about in the demand, or, (2) if the company fails to bring the suit on its own accord. Thereafter, shareholders generally must plead with particularity facts that sufficiently establish that the board's decision to seek the dismissal of the suit is not entitled to deference under the business judgment rule. *See Aronson v. Lewis*, 473 A.2d 805, 814 (Del. 1984); Marc I. Steinberg, *The Use of Special Litigation Committees to Terminate Shareholder Derivative Suits*, 35 U. Miami L. Rev. 1 (1980); Randall S. Thomas and Kenneth J. Martin, *Litigating Challenges to Executive Pay: An Exercise in Futility?*, 79 Wash. U. L.Q. 569, 587 (2001); Truong, *supra* note 137, at 1210.

[141] The CEO's and CFO's compensation packages increased from approximately $4.985 million and $1.15 million in 2009 to $8.52 million and $2.074 million in 2010, respectively. Cincinnati Bell Inc. Executive Pay Under Investor Investigation, *available at* http://shareholdersfoundation.com/caseinvestigation/cincinnati-bell-inc-executive-pay-under-investor-investigation (February 29, 2016).

[142] *See Cincinnati Bell*, 2011 WL 4383368, at 1; Truong, *supra* note 137, at 1212.

[143] *See Cincinnati Bell*, 2011 WL 4383368, at 1; Truong, *supra* note 137, at 1212.

[144] *See Cincinnati Bell*, 2011 WL 4383368, at 1.

[145] *Id.*

[146] *See, e.g., Robinson Family Trust v. Greig*, 2013 WL 1943330, at 5 (N.D. Ohio 2013); *Laborers' Local v. Intersil*, 868 F. Supp. 2d 838, 849 (N.D. Cal. 2012); *Swanson v. Weil*, 2012 WL 4442795, at *10 (D. Colo. 2012);

"the Board's failure to change course in light of the [negative] say-on-pay vote does not give rise to a substantial likelihood of personal liability, nor demonstrate that the Board would have been unable objectively to evaluate a demand to bring suit."[147] Consequently, shareholder derivative actions challenging management compensation after the receipt of a negative advisory Say-on-Pay vote ordinarily fail.[148]

D. UTILIZING RULE 14a-8 FOR GOLDEN PARACHUTES

Generous severance benefits, also known as "golden parachutes," are granted to executives when the subject company undergoes an acquisition, merger, consolidation, or other disposition that results in a change of control of the subject company.[149] The rationale underlying golden parachutes for executives is twofold: first, such severance agreements attract highly qualified executives to companies that at some point in the future may be the target of a takeover; and, second, these agreements facilitate executive objectivity in change-of-control decision-making situations.[150]

Prior to the enactment of the Dodd-Frank Act, companies were not required to submit for shareholder vote golden parachute agreements triggered on a potential or actual change in control. Today, the Securities Exchange Act requires that adequate disclosure be made to shareholders with respect to compensation agreements between members of management and the subject company that are directly related to the acquisition, merger, consolidation, or proposed sale or other disposition of all or substantially all of such company's assets.[151] In addition, unless the agreements were subject to the periodic Say-on-Pay shareholder vote, there must be a separate

---

Gordon v. Goodyear, 2012 WL 2885695, at *10 (N.D. Ill. 2012); *Iron Workers Local No. 25 Pension Fund ex rel. Monolithic Power Sys., Inc. v. Bogart*, 2012 WL 2160436, at *4 (N.D. Cal. 2012); *Plumbers Local No. 137 Pension Fund v. Davis*, 2012 WL 104776, at *8 (D. Or. 2012); *Charter Twp. of Clinton Police & Fire Ret. Sys. v. Martin*, 162 Cal. Rptr. 3d 300, 313–14 (Cal. Ct. App. 2013); *Weinberg ex rel. BioMed Realty Trust, Inc. v. Gold*, 838 F. Supp. 2d 355, 361 (D. Md. 2012) (finding that an unsuccessful Say-on-Pay vote is one factor in determining demand on futility, but is not a conclusive factor); *Brehm v. Eisner*, 746 A.2d 244, 263 (Del. 2000) ("It is the essence of business judgment for a board to determine if a particular individual warrant[s] large amounts of money, whether in the form of current salary or severance provisions.") (quoting *Grimes v. Donald*, 673 A.2d 1207, 1217 (Del. 1996)). *See generally* Truong, *supra* note 137, at 1213.

[147] *Raul v. Rynd*, 929 F. Supp. 2d 333, 346 (D. Del. 2013). *See* Truong, *supra* note 137, at 1213.

[148] *See, e.g.*, *Laborers' Local*, 868 F. Supp. 2d at 849; *Swanson*, 2012 WL 4442795, at 10; *Gordon*, 2012 WL 2885695, at 10; *Bogart*, 2012 WL 2160436, at 4; *Davis*, 2012 WL 104776, at 8; *Martin*, 162 Cal. Rptr. 3d at 313–14; *Gold*, 838 F. Supp. 2d at 361; *Brehm*, 746 A.2d at 263; Truong, *supra* note 137, at 1213.

[149] *See, e.g.*, Bart Schwartz, Amy Goodman, and Sean Feller, *Corporate Governance: Law and Practice* § 16.01 (2015). *See generally Heckmann v. Ahmanson*, 168 Cal. App. 3d 119, 214 Cal. Rptr. 177 (1986); Note, *Golden Parachutes: Executive Employment Contracts*, 40 Wash. & Lee L. Rev. 1117 (1983); Note, *Golden Parachutes and the Business Judgment Rule: Toward a Proper Standard of Review*, 94 Yale L.J. 909 (1985).

[150] *See* Schwartz, et al., *supra* note 149, at § 16.01.

[151] *See* Exchange Act Section 14A(b)(1).

shareholder advisory vote concerning these compensation agreements.[152] Like Say-on-Pay votes, the shareholders' vote on "golden parachute" agreements is not binding and does not give rise to additional fiduciary duties.[153]

E. RULE 14a-11—PROXY ACCESS

Typically, with the significant influence (if not determination) of the nominating committee,[154] the board of directors of a nationally traded publicly-held company nominates director candidates.[155] Thereafter, the subject company timely notifies shareholders of the name and background of each director candidate by mailing or otherwise transmitting proxy statements and ballots to shareholders before the shareholder meeting. Then, the shareholders are permitted to vote for the proposed directors. However, unlike a democratic political election where voters typically choose from two or more candidates, shareholders in a non-contested election may choose either to exercise their voting rights for the only slate of candidates nominated, to abstain, or to withhold support.[156] Because in a non-contested election directors run unopposed and in many publicly-held companies still are elected by plurality[157] (absent a provision in the articles of incorporation otherwise[158]), the board's slate of nominees is elected. Traditionally, other than mounting a proxy contest or tender offer,[159] shareholders have minimal input in the director election

---

[152] *See* Exchange Act Section 14A(b)(2).

[153] Exchange Act Section 14A(c)(2). The provision states that no additional fiduciary duties are to be imposed upon the board of directors due to this advisory vote. *Id. See* discussion in Chapter 5 herein.

[154] Nominating committees are discussed in Chapters 5, 6 herein.

[155] *See, e.g.*, Securities Exchange Act Release No. 79164 (2016); NYSE, Inc., Listed Company Manual § 303A.04 (2017); Lawrence A. Hamermesh, *Director Nominations*, 39 Del. J. Corp. L. 117 (2014); discussion in Chapters 5, 6 herein.

[156] *See* Douglas Branson, et al., *Business Enterprises—Legal Structures, Governance, and Policy* 394–95 (3d ed. 2016).

[157] *See, e.g.*, Model Business Corporation Act § 7.28(a) (2016).

[158] *Id.* Today, due to institutional shareholder activism, including by means of the Rule 14a-8 shareholder proposal route, approximately "90% of S&P 500 companies have adopted either majority or plurality plus voting [but] only about 60% of midcap and 38% of small cap companies have adopted either. . . ." Nicholas L. Simon and Reid S. Hooper, *Renewed Shareholder Push for Majority Voting in Director Elections May Affect More Small and Middle Market Banks*, Nat. L. Rev. (Covington & Burling LLP Nov. 4, 2016). *See* Council of Institutional Investors, *Majority Voting for Directors*, Jan. 5, 2017 (urging companies to adopt majority vote requirement in shareholder election of directors), *available at* www.cil.org/majority_voting_directors; Mary Siegel, *The Holes in Majority Voting*, 2011 Colum. Bus. L. Rev. 364 (2011).

[159] *See, e.g.*, *Tender Offers—Developments and Commentaries* (M. Steinberg ed. 1985). In 2016, the SEC proposed that universal proxies be required in contested elections of directors. The Commission stated:

> We are proposing amendments to the federal proxy rules to require the use of universal proxies in all non-exempt solicitations in connection with contested elections of directors other than those involving

process. This process has been an effective way for incumbent directors to maintain control of the subject company.

Should a shareholder wish to suggest a director candidate to the board of directors, the shareholder could propose this candidate to the board of directors or nominating committee of the subject company. If the subject individual were to receive the board's or nominating committee's support, then such individual would be included in the subject company's proxy statement.[160] However, if the shareholder fails to garner approval from the nominating committee or the board of directors, but still wishes to nominate that director candidate, then such shareholder must bear the costs of composing, printing, and transmitting its ballots and proxy materials to shareholders.[161] And, of course, if a dissident shareholder seeks to oust the incumbent members of the board and replace them with its nominees, a proxy contest was and remains the likely alternative.[162]

In the last few years, a number of states have amended their corporation laws in order to facilitate shareholder access to the company's proxy statement to nominate directors. Notably, in 2009, Delaware added Section 112 to the Delaware General Corporation Law, which permits a Delaware corporation to adopt bylaws that grant eligible shareholders access to the company's proxy statement to nominate directors.[163] Similar amendments have been made to the Model Business Corporation Act (MBCA).[164] The MBCA amendments authorize a corporation to amend its

---

> registered investment companies and business development companies. Our proposal would require the use of universal proxies that include the names of both registrant and dissident nominees and thus allow shareholders to vote by proxy in a manner that more closely resembles how they can vote in person at a shareholder meeting. We further propose amendments to the form of proxy and proxy statement disclosure requirements to specify clearly the applicable voting options and voting standards in all director elections.

Universal Proxy Proposal, Securities Exchange Act Release No. 79164 (2016). This proposal is unlikely to be adopted in view of the election of President Donald Trump and the new composition of SEC Commissioners.

[160] *See* Courtney Johnson, *SEC Rule 14a-8(i)(9) & The Whole Foods Proxy Saga*, 34 Rev. Banking & Fin. L. 458, 459 (2015); Robert Murphy, et al., *Proxy Access on the Horizon*, LEXOLOGY (Jan. 29, 2015), http://www.lexology.com/library/detail.aspx?g=2227f750-c854-4d24-ab73-eba6bf742a21, *archived at* http://perma.cc/U9DJ-XNL9.

[161] *See* Johnson, *supra* note 160, at 459; Kaja Whitehouse, *Shareholders Threaten Boards Over "Proxy Access,"* USA Today (Jan. 27, 2015, 12:43 PM), http://www.usatoday.com/story/money/business/2015/01/27/proxyaccess-investors-businessroundtable-wholefoods/22234271; *Administrative Law—Corporate Governance Regulation—D.C. Circuit Finds SEC Proxy Access Rule Arbitrary and Capricious for Inadequate Economic Analysis—Business Roundtable v. SEC*, 647 F.3d 1144 (D.C. Cir. 2011), 125 Harv. L. Rev. 1088 (2012) [hereinafter "Harvard Note"].

[162] *See, e.g.*, Marc I. Steinberg, *Fiduciary Duties and Disclosure Obligations in Proxy and Tender Contests for Corporate Control*, 30 Emory L.J. 169 (1981).

[163] Delaware General Corporation Law § 112 (2011); John F. Olson and Ashley Wright, *Corporate Governance: Law and Practice* § 8.03 (2015).

[164] Note that approximately 30 states have adopted the MBCA. Olson and Wright, *supra* note 163, at § 8.03; Model Business Corporation Act §§ 2.06, 10.20 (2016).

bylaws to permit shareholder proxy access to nominate directors. The Act also permits the nominating shareholders to be reimbursed for reasonable expenses that are incurred.[165]

Section 971 of the Dodd-Frank Act authorizes the SEC to promulgate appropriate rules granting shareholder access to the corporate proxy statement and ballot for the purpose of nominating director candidates for the board of directors.[166] Acting pursuant to this perceived authority, the SEC adopted Rule 14a-11 to "facilitate the effective exercise of shareholders' traditional state law rights to nominate and elect directors to company boards of directors."[167] Rule 14a-11 allowed eligible shareholders access to the corporate proxy statement in order to nominate directors. The Rule was aimed at shareholders who possessed a "significant, long-term stake,"[168] making the Rule unavailable to those shareholders who sought a change in control.[169] Accordingly, the Rule "generally entitled the [company's] largest shareholder (or largest group of shareholders), who own at least three percent of the shares entitled to be voted and who held such shares for at least three years, to nominate the greater of one director-candidate or up to 25 percent of the total number of directors who serve on such company's board of directors."[170] The Rule also precluded a state from opting-out or significantly modifying the Rule, unless the state subsequently enacted legislation prohibiting shareholders from nominating candidates for the board of directors.[171]

Subsequently, Rule 14a-11 was invalidated by the U.S. Court of Appeals for the D.C. Circuit in *Business Roundtable v. SEC*.[172] The Business Roundtable, an

---

[165] Olson and Wright, *supra* note 163, at § 8.03; Model Business Corporation Act §§ 2.06, 10.20 (2016).

[166] *See* Section 971 of the Dodd-Frank Act, 124 Stat. at 1915 (codified at 15 U.S.C. § 78n(a) (2006 & Supp. IV 2011)).

[167] SEC's Adopting Release, Facilitating Shareholder Director Nominations, Securities Exchange Act Release No. 62764 (2010), 75 Fed. Reg. 56668 (Sept. 16, 2010) [hereinafter "Adopting Release"]; Christopher Takeshi Napier, Comment, *Resurrecting Rule 14a-11: A Renewed Call for Federal Proxy Access Reform, Justifications and Suggested Revisions*, 67 Rutgers L. Rev. 843, 861 (2015).

[168] This objective is facilitated by requiring that the nominating shareholder possesses a minimum of 3 percent of the voting power of the subject company's securities that are entitled to be voted on during the meeting. The nominating shareholder(s) are permitted to aggregate their shares in order to meet the requisites. In this regard, the nominating shareholder(s) must hold investment and voting power, which has been held continuously at least three years from the date that the nominating shareholder(s) notified the subject company that it intends to exercise its proxy access rights pursuant to Rule 14a-11. *See* Adopting Release, *supra* note 167.

[169] Adopting Release, *supra* note 167; Napier, *supra* note 167, at 862.

[170] Marc I. Steinberg, *Understanding Securities Law* 190 (6th ed. 2014). *See* Adopting Release, *supra* note 167, 75 Fed. Reg. at 56669; Napier, *supra* note 167, at 862. Note that, pursuant to Rule 14a-11, if more than one shareholder (or group of shareholders) met the eligibility criteria, then only the shareholder (or group of shareholders) having the largest ownership percentage was entitled to invoke the proxy access regimen. Bylaws adopted by corporations granting proxy access have similar limitations.

[171] Adopting Release, *supra* note 167, 75 Fed. Reg. at 56668; Napier, *supra* note 167, at 862.

[172] 647 F.3d 1144 (D.C. Cir. 2011).

association of chief executive officers of prominent U.S. companies, challenged Rule 14a-11 based "on a fundamentally flawed assessment of the rule's costs, benefits, and effects on efficiency, competition, and capital formation."[173] The plaintiffs also contended that the Rule's application was arbitrary and capricious for investment companies.[174] Holding that Rule 14a-11 was invalid, the appellate court asserted that the SEC "failed once again . . . adequately to assess the economic effects of a new rule."[175]

The court penned a scathing decision holding that the Rule was arbitrary and capricious under the Administrative Procedure Act.[176] The court held that the SEC did not adequately analyze the economic consequences of the Rule.[177] It found that "the Commission inconsistently and opportunistically framed the costs and benefits of the rule, failed adequately to quantify the certain costs or to explain why those costs could not be quantified, neglected to support its predictive judgments, contradicted itself, and failed to respond to substantial problems raised by commenters."[178] The SEC declined to appeal the decision.[179]

Although the court of appeals ruled against the SEC in *Business Roundtable*, the strong presence of institutional shareholder persuasion prompted several companies in their 2013 annual meeting proxy materials to submit company-sponsored proxy access proposals for shareholder approval.[180] Companies, such as Hewlett-Packard Co.[181]

---

[173] Opening Brief of Petitioners Business Roundtable and Chamber of Commerce of the United States of America at 31, *Business Roundtable*, 647 F.3d 1144; Harvard Note, *supra* note 161.

[174] Plaintiffs also argued that the Rule violated the First Amendment protections of corporate speech; however, the court did not rule on the First Amendment corporate speech issue. Opening Brief, *supra* note 173, at 31, 53–59; *Business Roundtable*, 647 F.3d at 1156.

[175] *Business Roundtable*, 647 F.3d at 1148.

[176] *Id.*

[177] *Id.*

[178] *Id.* at 1148–49.

[179] *See* Olson and Reilly, *supra* note 163, at § 2.01.

[180] *See* Gibson, Dunn & Crutcher LLP, *Shareholder Proposal Developments During the 2013 Proxy Season* (July 9, 2013), *available at* http://www.gibsondunn.com/publications/Documents/Shareholder-Proposal-Developments-2013-Proxy-Season.pdf; Olson and Reilly, *supra* note 163. *See also* Council of Institutional Investors, Proxy Access: Best Practices (Aug. 2015), *available at* www.cii.org/files/publications/MISC/08_05_15BestPractices-ProxyAccess.pdf (setting forth best practices for shareholder proxy access and stating: "Companies should provide access to management proxy materials for a long-term investor or a group of long-term investors [who have owned the stock for a minimum of two years and who own in aggregate at least three percent of a company's voting stock] to nominate less than a majority of the directors.") *See* Glen Schleyer, *2016 Shareholder Activism Review and Analysis*, 50 Rev. Sec. & Comm. Reg. 25 (2017). *See generally* Jayne W. Barnard, *Shareholder Access to the Proxy Revisited*, 40 Cath. U. L. Rev. 37 (1990); Bernard S. Sharfman, *Why Proxy Access Is Harmful to Corporate Governance*, 37 J. Corp. L. 387 (2012); John Mark Zeberkiewicz and Joseph L. Christensen, *The Delaware and SEC Proxy Access Regimes*, 42 Rev. Sec. & Comm. Reg. 233 (2009).

[181] Hewlett-Packard submitted the proposal in order for a 2012 proxy access shareholder proposal to be withdrawn. Shareholders approved the 2013 proxy access proposal by 68 percent. Gibson, Dunn & Crutcher LLP, *supra* note 180; Olson and Reilly, *supra* note 163.

and Chesapeake Energy Corporation,[182] proposed to amend their respective corporation's bylaws to permit proxy access to those shareholders who held three percent ownership for three years.[183] The ensuing proxy seasons confirmed an increased trend of proposals opting for shareholders who own three percent of the subject company's stock for three years to have proxy access to nominate up to 20 percent of the board of directors. Indeed, a significant percentage of such shareholder proposals received approval, generating significant momentum for shareholder proxy access with respect to director-nominees.[184]

Prior to the adoption of Rule 14a-11 and the emergence of vigorous institutional shareholder activism in this setting, corporations typically sought to block shareholder proxy access proposals. Indeed, within the past few years, irrespective of the keen presence of this corporate governance issue, corporations nonetheless sought to exclude these proposals by requesting a no-action letter from the SEC staff under Rule 14a-8(i)(9). This provision allows for exclusion of a "shareholder proposal that 'directly conflicts' with a management proposal."[185] The SEC applied this exclusion as reflected in its December 1, 2014, no-action letter granted to Whole Foods. Whole Foods sought to exclude a shareholder proxy access proposal, which provided that shareholders having three percent or more ownership for three years be permitted to "nominate up to two directors on the company's proxy."[186] Whole Foods asserted that the shareholder proposal conflicted with its own proxy access proposal that permitted shareholders who held nine percent ownership for five years to nominate a specified number of director candidates on the Whole Foods' proxy statement and ballot.[187]

---

[182] Chesapeake Energy submitted its 2013 proxy access proposal after a 2012 proxy access shareholder proposal received majority support at the 2012 annual meeting. Chesapeake Energy's 2013 proxy access proposal was not approved as it did not obtain the required supermajority vote. Gibson, Dunn & Crutcher LLP, *supra* note 180; Olson and Reilly, *supra* note 163.

[183] *See* Gibson, Dunn & Crutcher LLP, *supra* note 180; Olson and Reilly, *supra* note 163.

[184] *See* Janet T. Geldzahler and Bernd P. Delahaye, *Preparing for Proxy Access 2016*, November 20, 2015, Law 360, http://www.law360.com/articles/728348/preparing-for-proxy-access-2016; Virginia Harper Ho, *Risk-Related Activism: The Business Case for Monitoring Nonfinancial Risk*, 41 J. Corp. L. 647, 659 (2016). *See also Avon Near Deal with Activist Investors*, Wall St. J., Mar. 28, 2016, at B1 (stating that Avon plans to announce that it has agreed that certain activist investors may approve a new independent director to serve on the company's board of directors).

[185] Johnson, *supra* note 160, at 459; Scott Lesmes, et al., *SEC Suspends Review of Conflicting Shareholder Proposal No-Action Requests*, LEXOLOGY (Jan. 28, 2015), http://www.lexology.com/library/detail.aspx?g=1302dd52-6aa7-4c62-aa6b-b85bfe247c8d, *archived at* http://perma.cc/64A4-HDLW.

[186] Andrew Brady, et al., *SEC Staff Will No Longer Issue No-Action Letters on Conflicting Shareholder Proposals During the 2015 Proxy Season*, JDSUPRA (Jan. 29, 2015), http://www.jdsupra.com/legalnews/sec-staff-will-no-longer-issue-no-action-23445/, *archived at* http://perma.cc/B4WQ-7LX6.

[187] This was later amended to five percent ownership rather than nine percent. Brady, *supra* note 186.

The SEC staff stated the shareholder proposal was excludable under Rule 14a-8(i)(9) as it overlapped with Whole Foods' proxy access proposal.[188]

Not surprisingly, the SEC received numerous complaints with respect to the Whole Foods no-action letter.[189] In January 2015, SEC Chairperson Mary Jo White directed the staff to review Rule 14a-8(i)(9) "[d]ue to questions that have arisen about the proper scope and application of [the Rule]."[190] The Division of Corporation Finance thereupon responded that it "would not express any views under rule 14a-8(i)(9) for the current proxy season."[191] The Division also rescinded its no-action position pertaining to Whole Foods's exclusion of the subject shareholder's proxy access proposal.[192]

In October 2015, the staff announced that the SEC will no longer issue no-action letters with respect to a company's requested exclusion of a shareholder's proxy access proposal on the ground that the company has a similar measure in its proxy materials.[193] The staff observed that shareholders could affirmatively vote for both proposals without the two proposals causing a substantial conflict. Effectively, both such proposals would permit shareholders to nominate directors, although the criteria for nominating such directors may well differ.[194] The impact of the SEC's position

---

[188] *Id.*

[189] Kat Greene, *SEC Changes Course on Whole Foods Shareholder Proposal*, LAW 360 (Jan. 16, 2015, 9:55 PM), http://www.law360.com/articles/612823/sec-changes-course-on-whole-foods-shareholder-proposal.

[190] *Id.*

[191] David R. Fredrickson, Chief Counsel, Sec. & Exch. Comm'n, to James McRitchie (Jan. 16, 2015), *available at* http://www.sec.gov/divisions/corpfin/cf-noaction/14a-8/2015/jamesmcritchiecheveddenrecon011615-14a8.pdf, *archived at* http://perma.cc/X64R-L42F. [hereinafter "SEC - Whole Foods shareholder proposal"]; Press Release, Mary Jo White, Chairperson, Sec. & Exch. Comm'n, Statement from Chair White Directing Staff to Review Commission Rule for Excluding Conflicting Proxy Proposals (Jan. 16, 2015), *available at* http://www.sec.gov/news/statement/statement-on-conflicting-proxy-proposals.html#.VLogmIqYmyg, *archived at* http://perma.cc/QVJ6-PR28 [hereinafter "SEC Public Statement 2015"].

[192] SEC—Whole Foods shareholder proposal, *supra* note 191; SEC Public Statement 2015, *supra* note 191.

[193] SEC Bulletin No. 14H (CF), *supra* note 103.

[194] *Id. See AES Corp.*, SEC No-Action Letter, 2016 WL 7048900 (Dec. 20, 2016) (SEC staff declining to issue a no-action letter with respect to shareholder proposal seeking to recommend modification of company's proxy access bylaw); *Apple Inc.*, SEC No-Action Letter, 2016 WL 5930444 (Oct. 27, 2016) (declining Apple's request for no-action letter to exclude shareholder proxy access bylaw proposal); *Microsoft Corp.*, SEC No-Action Letter, 2016 WL 4010127 (Sept. 27, 2016) (declining to issue no-action letter with respect to shareholder proxy access bylaw proposal). Note that other corporate governance matters also are pursued by seeking to invoke the SEC's shareholder proposal rule. For example, in 2016, the SEC staff declined to issue a no-action letter to General Electric with respect to performance-based pay. The shareholder proposal recommended that the company's board of directors implement a policy that a portion of future stock option grants awarded to corporate senior executives be performance-based. *General Electric Co.*, SEC No-Action Letter, 2015 WL 9002923 (Feb. 23, 2016). For another example, *see Apple Inc.*, SEC No-Action Letter 2016 WL 5930446 (Oct. 26, 2016) (declining Apple's request for no-action letter to exclude shareholder proposal seeking to reform Apple's executive compensation policies and practices).

is that shareholder proposals for proxy access continue to be made and are receiving substantial support with regularity.[195]

IV. Conclusion

The SEC shareholder proposal rule has played a positive influence in the corporate governance process. Although shareholder proposals as well as Say-on-Pay votes are advisory, they provide key examples of the federalization of corporate governance. Notably, the SEC shareholder proposal rule represents an early "intrusion" by the Commission—dating from 1942—with respect to federalizing an area traditionally within the exclusive purview of state company law. Today, the Rule is well entrenched as an accepted facilitator of shareholder activism and of dialogue between management and institutional shareholders. Unfortunately, application of the Rule in numerous contextual settings remains murky, thereby causing uncertainty and an onslaught of litigation. To the extent practicable, the SEC should engage in further clarification of Rule 14a-8 in a manner that is consistent with promoting shareholder participation in a cost-effective and law-compliant manner. The shareholder proposal rule thus should be recognized as a vintage asset—a Rule that has symbolized for 75 years that vibrant federal corporate governance at times is an appropriate vehicle for ameliorating state law shortcomings.[196]

---

[195] *See* Ho, *supra* note 184, at 650:

> In 2014, New York City's public pension funds kicked off a "Boardroom Accountability" campaign targeting 75 major public companies and seeking shareholder approval for proxy access—corporate bylaw changes that would open certain board seats to candidates nominated directly by shareholders. In 2015, over 70% of these proposals were approved by at least a majority vote, creating new momentum for proxy access among leading firms. . . .

[196] *See generally* Marc I. Steinberg, *Corporate Internal Affairs—A Corporate and Securities Law Perspective* (1983); Marc I. Steinberg, *Developments in Business Law and Policy* (2012); Marc I. Steinberg, *Securities Regulation* (7th ed. 2017).

5

THE SOX AND DODD-FRANK ACTS—MODERN FEDERAL CORPORATE GOVERNANCE INITIATIVES

I. The Sarbanes-Oxley and Dodd-Frank Acts—Entrenchment of Federal Corporate Governance

In response to several corporate scandals, such as the Enron and WorldCom debacles that implicated fraudulent accounting practices and executive self-dealing, the Sarbanes-Oxley Act of 2002 (SOX) implemented substantive corporate governance mandates that were adopted as federal law.[1] Focused on restoring financial disclosure

[1] 15 U.S.C. § 7201 et seq. (2002). *See* Robert Charles Clark, *Corporate Governance Changes in the Wake of the Sarbanes-Oxley Act: A Morality Tale for Policymakers Too*, 22 Ga. St. U. L. Rev 251 (2005) (providing a "synthetic overview" of the numerous reforms that have taken shape in relation to the Sarbanes-Oxley Act). *See generally* John T. Bostleman, Robert E. Buckholz, Jr., and Marc R. Trevino, *Public Company Deskbook: Sarbanes-Oxley and Federal Governance Requirements* (2d ed. 2011); James Hamilton and Ted Trautmann, *Sarbanes-Oxley Act of 2002—Law and Explanation* (2002); CCH Attorney-Editor Staff, *Dodd-Frank Wall Street Reform and Consumer Protection Act—Law, Explanation and Analysis* (2010); Symposium, 3 J. Bus. & Tech. L. Rev. No. 2 (2008); Symposium, 39 Loy. U. Chicago L. Rev. No. 3 (2008); Symposium, 105 Mich. L. Rev. No. 8 (2007); Kit Addleman, *The Impact of Dodd-Frank on Public Companies*, 38 Sec. Reg. L.J. 181 (2010); Robert H. Ahdieh, *From "Federalization" to "Mixed Governance" in Corporate Law: A Defense of Sarbanes-Oxley*, 53 Buffalo L. Rev. 721 (2005); Roberta S. Karmel, *Realizing the Dream of William O. Douglas—The Securities and Exchange Commission Takes Charge of Corporate Governance*, 30 Del. J. Corp. L. 79 (2005); Charles W. Murdock, *The Dodd-Frank Wall Street Reform and Consumer Protection Act: What Caused the Financial Crisis and Will Dodd-Frank Prevent Future Crises?*, 64 SMU L. Rev. 1243 (2011); Frank Partnoy, *A Revisionist View of Enron and the*

transparency and revitalizing investor confidence in the financial markets' integrity, these mandates far exceed the corporate governance framework that federal securities regulation envisioned before the debacles.[2]

A few years thereafter, the 2008 financial crisis (or what is now widely known as the "Great Recession"[3]) precipitated the enactment of the Dodd-Frank Wall Street Reform and Consumer Protection Act of 2010 ("Dodd-Frank Act").[4] As one of its principal objectives, the Dodd-Frank Act aims at forestalling another financial crisis through enhanced corporate governance regulation and placing meaningful restraints on undue risk-taking conduct.[5] Considered, either singularly or together, the SOX and Dodd-Frank Acts constitute a major expansion of the federal securities laws into the corporate governance arena previously dominated by state law.[6]

The following discussion focuses on several key provisions of the SOX and the Dodd-Frank Acts, as well as SEC rules and regulations promulgated thereunder. Among these provisions are: (1) CEO and CFO certifications, (2) audit committees, (3) executive clawback provisions, (4) director independence, (5) nominating and corporate governance committees, (6) codes of ethics, (7) corporate governance disclosures, (8) say-on-pay and golden parachute provisions, (9) loans to insiders, (10) officer and director bars and penalties, (11) equitable relief, (12) insider trading during "blackout" periods, (13) compensation committees, (14) bifurcation of the CEO and board of directors' chair roles, (15) pay versus performance, and (16) internal

---

Sudden Death of "May," 48 Vill. L. Rev. 1245 (2003); Roberta Romano, *The Sarbanes-Oxley Act and the Making of Quack Corporate Governance*, 114 Yale L.J. 1521 (2005).

[2] Marc I. Steinberg, *Sarbanes-Oxley, A Note from the Editor-in-Chief*, 30 Sec. Reg. L.J. 358 (2002) ("The Sarbanes-Oxley Act federalizes state corporation law in several ways, going far beyond the disclosure framework that serves as the keystone to federal regulation.").

[3] *See* Matt Egan, *2008: Worse than the Great Depression?*, CNN MONEY (Aug. 27, 2014, 5:34 PM), http://money.cnn.com/2014/08/27/news/economy/ben-bernanke-great-depression.

[4] Dodd-Frank Wall Street Reform and Consumer Protection Act, Pub. L. No. 111-203, 124 Stat. 1376 (2010).

[5] Terrance Gallogly, *Enforcing the Clawback Provision: Preventing the Evasion of Liability under Section 954 of the Dodd-Frank Act*, 42 Seton Hall L. Rev. 1229, 1237 (2012) (stating that the Dodd-Frank Act "is aimed at preventing another financial crisis by regulating the behaviors, instruments, and practices that are seen as having facilitated the collapse") (citing Binyamin Appelbaum and David M. Herszenhorn, *Financial Overhaul Signals Shift on Deregulation*, N.Y. Times (July 15, 2010), http://www.nytimes.com/2010/07/16/business/16regulate.html?adxnnl=1&ref=financial_regulatory_reform&adxnnlx=1284934684-Ea8YFikIeLLsoO5a4h+3Cw). *See also* Ralph T. Wutscher and David L. Beam, *The Dodd-Frank Act's New Federalism*, 66 Bus. Law 519 (2011) (describing provisions of the Dodd-Frank Act that amend the National Bank Act and the Home Owners' Loan Act in order "to 'clarify' the circumstances under which these two laws will preempt state laws, and for which types of institutions and their subsidiaries").

[6] *See generally* Marc I. Steinberg, *Securities Regulation* 320–38 (7th ed. 2017); sources cited *supra* note 1; Steinberg, *supra* note 2, at 358–59.

pay equity disclosure.[7] With respect to several of these provisions, the analysis contained in Chapter 6 of this book also is pertinent.

II. Key Provisions of the SOX and Dodd-Frank Acts

The following discussion highlights key corporate governance provisions of the SOX and Dodd-Frank Acts. Any doubt that federal law statutorily regulates meaningful aspects of corporate governance is now foreclosed.

A. CEO AND CFO CERTIFICATIONS

Section 302 of SOX institutes a certification responsibility for chief executive officers (CEOs) and chief financial officers (CFOs) of publicly-held companies when their subject companies file quarterly and annual reports (e.g., Forms 10-K and 10-Q) with the SEC under either Section 13(a) or 15(d) of the Securities Exchange Act.[8] These certifications are designed to help effectuate transparency as well as law compliance. Stated succinctly, Section 302 requires that CEOs and CFOs certify in periodic reports that are filed with the SEC that: the financial statements and other disclosures contained in any such report are accurate, and the financial statements and other financial information contained therein fairly and accurately present the company's operations and financial condition.[9]

Specifically, Section 302 of SOX requires that the CEO and CFO, who sign and certify the subject company's annual Form 10-K report or quarterly Form 10-Q report, must state the following in each such report (for the respective reporting period):

- The officer has actually reviewed the report;
- Based on the officer's knowledge, the report does not contain any untrue statement of a material fact or omit to state a material fact necessary to make the statements made, in light of the circumstances under which such statements were made, not misleading;
- Based on the officer's knowledge, the financial statements, and other financial information included in the report, fairly present in all material respects

[7] *See* Steinberg, *supra* note 6, at 320–38.

[8] Pub. L. No. 107-204, SOX § 302, 15 U.S.C. § 7241 (2012).

[9] *Id. See* Lisa M. Fairfax, *Form Over Substance? Officer Certification and the Promise of Enhanced Personal Accountability Under the Sarbanes-Oxley Act*, 55 Rutgers L. Rev. 1 (2002).

the financial condition and results of operations of the issuer as of, and for, the periods presented in the report;

- The officer is responsible for establishing and maintaining "disclosure controls and procedures" and "internal control over financial reporting" for the issuing company and has:
    - Designed such disclosure controls and procedures to ensure that material information relating to the company and its consolidated subsidiaries is made known to such officer by others within those entities, particularly during the period in which the periodic reports are being prepared;
    - Designed internal control over financial reporting to provide reasonable assurance regarding the reliability of financial reporting and the preparation of financial statements for external purposes in accordance with generally accepted accounting principles (GAAP);
    - Evaluated the effectiveness of the issuing company's disclosure controls and procedures as of the end of the period covered by the report within 90 days prior to the report and has presented his/her conclusions about the effectiveness of the disclosure controls and procedures in the report; and
    - Disclosed in the report any change in the issuing company's internal control over financial reporting that occurred during the issuing company's most recent fiscal quarter that has materially affected, or is reasonably likely to materially affect, the issuer's internal control over financial reporting.
- The officer has identified and disclosed, based on the officer's most recent evaluation of internal controls regarding financial reporting, to the issuing company's auditors and audit committee:
    - All significant deficiencies and material weaknesses in the design or operation of internal controls of financial reporting which could adversely affect the company's ability to record, process, summarize, and report financial information; and
    - Any fraud, whether or not material, that involves management or other employees who have a significant role in the issuer's internal controls of financial reporting.[10]

The certification requirements seek to induce subject CEOs and CFOs to more vigilantly engage in the accuracy and completeness of the disclosure process. The certification mandate enhances transparency by requiring the signing officers to

[10] SOX § 302; Rules 13a-14(a), 15d-14(a). *See* Securities Act Release No. 8124 (2002); *SEC v. Jensen*, 835 F.3d 1100 (9th Cir. 2016).

affirm that the financial statements together with the disclosures contained in the subject SEC report, taken as a whole, are accurate and fairly represent, in all material respects, the company's operations and financial condition. If enforced in an appropriate manner, the certification requirement incentivizes CEOs and CFOs to become more actively involved in the thoroughness and accuracy of their respective company's disclosure regimen.[11]

B. AUDIT COMMITTEES

Section 301 of SOX requires the SEC to adopt a final rule[12] that directs all national securities exchanges to establish audit committee requirements for listed companies within each respective exchange's listing standards.[13] Implementing SOX's audit committee mandates, the SEC promulgated Rule 10A-3.[14] Discussion of stock exchange rules with respect to audit committees is contained in Chapter 6 herein.

SOX also requires a second certification under § 906 that adds § 1350 (18 U.S.C. § 1350) to the criminal statutes. The § 906 certification, containing significant criminal sanctions for knowingly false certification, applies to each Exchange Act report containing financial statements. Pursuant to the § 306 certification, the CEO and CFO each must state that, "based on my knowledge, the periodic report containing the financial statements fully complies with the [Exchange Act periodic reporting] requirements and that information contained in the [subject] periodic report fairly presents, in all material respects, the financial condition and results of operations of the issuer." 18 U.S.C. §1350 (2012). *See generally* Joris Hogan, *The Enron Legacy: Corporate Governance Requirements for a New Era*, 31 Sec. Reg. L.J. 142, 143–44 (2003), *interpreting*, 18 U.S.C. § 1350.

[11] Interestingly, the need for this certification requirement may be questioned in view that, since 1980, the SEC required that a majority of the subject company's directors sign the Form 10-K. *See* Securities Act Release No. 6231 (1980) ("With the expanded signature requirement, the Commission anticipates that directors will be encouraged to devote the needed attention in reviewing the Form 10-K and to seek the involvement of other professionals to the degree necessary to give them sufficient comfort. In the Commission's view, this added measure of discipline is vital to the disclosure objectives of the federal securities laws. . . ."). It may be posited that, if this requirement has been adequately enforced by the SEC, the certification requirement would have been unnecessary. *See* Marc I. Steinberg, *Understanding Securities Law* 240–41 (6th ed. 2014).

Note also that SOX and SEC rules prohibit any person from engaging in any conduct that seeks to influence, coerce, or mislead an accountant who is auditing the subject company's financial statements. The mental culpability for engaging in such violation evidently is negligence. *See* SOX § 303; Securities Exchange Act Rule 13b2-2(b); Securities Exchange Act Release No. 47890 (2003).

[12] Standards Relating to Listed Company Audit Committees, Securities Act Release No. 8220 (2003).

[13] *See* Terence Sheppey and Ross McGill, *Sarbanes-Oxley: Building Working Strategies for Compliance* 40 (2007) ("The audit committee of the public company is a key entity in the process of making financial reporting open and transparent. This section ensures that this committee will be 'independent' and drawn from, and responsible to, the board of directors. It makes clear that the issuer should properly fund the operation of the audit committee, and goes on to list the responsibilities of the audit committee in relation to auditing under the terms of the Act.").

[14] 17 C.F.R. § 240.10A-3 (2017). *See* Rule 10A-3(a)(1) (stating that "[t]he rules of each national securities exchange registered pursuant to section 6 of the [Securities Exchange] Act must, in accordance with the provisions of this rule, prohibit the initial or continued listing of any security of an issuer that is not in compliance with the requirements of . . . this rule").

Viewed generally, audit committees undertake the responsibility of overseeing the subject company's procedures for reporting its financial data, as well as monitoring corporate internal controls.[15] Section 3(a)(58) of the Securities Exchange Act (as added by Section 205 of SOX) defines an audit committee as: "A committee (or equivalent body) established by and amongst the board of directors of an issuer for the purpose of overseeing the accounting and financial reporting processes of the issuer and audits of the financial statements of the issuer."[16]

As discussed in Chapter 6, a key component of Rule 10A-3 is that the members of the issuer's audit committee be independent. The independence requirement mandates that no audit committee member may: (1) accept from the company any compensation or fees other than for serving as a director (or as a board committee member),[17] or (2) be a person affiliated with the issuer or any subsidiary of such issuer (including being in a control relationship with the issuer).[18] Unlike the independence standards set out in the NYSE and nasdaq listing standards,[19] "independence" under Rule 10A-3 looks to existing relationships—not having a "look back" test.[20]

Further, Rule 10A-3 requires that the audit committee undertake specified responsibilities, including, for example: (1) appointing, setting the compensation for, retaining, and overseeing the company's outside auditors;[21] (2) addressing disagreements that may arise regarding financial reporting matters between management and the outside auditor;[22] (3) implementing procedures for the receipt, retention, and handling of complaints submitted by employees concerning questionable accounting and/or auditing matters;[23] (4) engaging, when appropriate, independent counsel and other advisers that are deemed necessary to carry out the

[15] *See* Securities Act Release No. 8220 (2003).

[16] 15 U.S.C. § 78c(a)(58) (2012) (also providing that "[i]f no such committee exists with respect to an issuer, the entire board of directors of the issuer").

[17] 17 C.F.R. § 240.10A-3 (2017) (provided also that, "unless the rules of the national securities exchange or national securities association provide otherwise, compensatory fees do not include the receipt of fixed amounts of compensation under a retirement plan (including deferred compensation) for prior service with the listed issuer (provided that such compensation is not contingent in any way on continued service).").

[18] 15 U.S.C. § 78j-1(m)(3) (2012). Note that Rule 10A-3(e)(1)(ii)(A) provides a safe harbor from "control" status for any person who: (1) is not a beneficial owner of more than ten percent of a class of voting equity securities of such issuer, and (2) does not serve as an executive officer.

[19] *See* discussion in Chapter 6 herein.

[20] 1 Robert E. Buckholz Jr., Marc R. Trevino and Glen T. Schleyer, *Public Company Deskbook: Complying with Federal Governance & Disclosure Requirements* § 3:1, at 3B-15 (3d ed. 2014); Chapter 6 herein.

[21] *See* discussion in Chapter 6 herein.

[22] *Id.*

[23] 17 C.F.R. § 240.10A-3(b)(2) (2017). *See* 1 Buckholz, et al., *supra* note 20, § 3:1; discussion in Chapter 6 herein.

audit committee's duties;[24] and (5) insisting that the company sufficiently fund payment for such advisers.[25] When engaging an outside auditor, the audit committee is responsible for approving the terms and fees of such engagement.[26] In order for the audit committee to effectively undertake its functions, the outside auditor is tasked with reporting directly to that committee.[27]

As mentioned, Rule 10A-3 requires the audit committee to establish procedures for: the receipt, retention, and handling of complaints by employees of the company concerning accounting and/or auditing matters; and the confidential, anonymous submission by such issuer's employees of concerns relating to accounting or auditing matters.[28] While the SEC required that these procedures be established, the Commission declined to set forth specific procedures that must be implemented. Instead, the subject company's audit committee is charged with establishing compliant procedures that are consistent with such listed company's individual culture and other relevant circumstances.[29]

---

[24] "The adopting release notes that the assistance of independent advisors may be necessary to identify potential conflicts of interest, assess the company's disclosure and other compliance obligations, and independently investigate questions that may arise regarding financial reporting and compliance with the securities laws. The adopting release clarifies, however, that the requirement would not preclude access to or advice from the issuer's internal counsel or regular outside counsel and should not be construed to require an audit committee to retain independent counsel." 1 Buckholz, et al., *supra* note 20, § 3:1, at 3A-39 (citing Standards Relating to Listed Company Audit Committees, Securities Exchange Act Release No. 47654 (Apr. 9, 2003)). *See* Chapter 6 herein.

[25] 17 C.F.R. § 240.10A-3(b)(2) (2017). *See* Chapter 6 herein.

[26] 1 Buckholz, et al., *supra* note 20, § 3:1. *See* Chapter 6 herein.

[27] 1 Buckholz, et al., *supra* note 20, § 3:1. *See* Chapter 6 herein. *See generally* Gregory S. Rowland, *Earnings Management, the SEC, and Corporate Governance: Director Liability Arising from the Audit Committee Report*, 102 Colum. L. Rev. 168 (2002).

[28] Rule 10A-3(b)(3); 1 Buckholz, et al., *supra* note 20, § 3:1.

[29] *See* Standards Relating to Listed Company Audit Committees, Securities Exchange Act No. 47654 (Apr. 9, 2003), 68 Fed. Reg. 18,788 (Apr. 16, 2003), *available at* https://www.sec.gov/rules/final/33-8220.htm#audit.

Two other SOX-related developments are worthy of discussion at this point. First, SOX mandates that the subject company's management create, maintain, and evaluate the effectiveness of the company's internal controls. Moreover, with specified exceptions, SOX also requires that the company's independent auditor report on the adequacy of such company's internal controls. *See* SOX § 404. In Securities Act Release No. 8238 (2002), the Commission stated:

> As directed by Section 404 of the Sarbanes-Oxley Act of 2002, we are adopting rules requiring companies subject to the reporting requirements of the Securities Exchange Act of 1934, other than registered investment companies, to include in their annual reports a report of management on the company's internal control over financial reporting. The internal control report must include: a statement of management's responsibility for establishing and maintaining adequate internal control over financial reporting for the company; management's assessment of the effectiveness of the company's internal control over financial reporting as of the end of the company's most recent fiscal year; a statement identifying the framework used by management to evaluate the effectiveness of the company's internal control over financial reporting; and a statement that the registered public accounting firm that audited the

Pursuant to SOX and SEC rule-making thereunder,[30] a subject issuer must disclose in its annual report whether a financial expert (as determined by its board of directors) serves on such issuer's audit committee and if so, the disclosure must include the identity of such expert and whether such person is independent as defined by applicable stock exchange rules.[31] The rationale underlying the designation of an audit committee's financial expert is to instill a greater degree of comfort with respect to the integrity of the company's internal financial controls and representation of such company's financial condition.[32] To qualify as a financial expert, a person must: (1) understand Generally Accepted Accounting Principles (GAAP); (2) be able "to assess the general application of such principles in connection with the accounting for estimates, accruals, and reserves"; (3) have sufficient "experience in preparing, auditing, analyzing or evaluating financial statements. . . ."; (4) understand "internal control over financial reporting"; and (5) understand "audit committee functions."[33] The ultimate determination of whether a person meets these criteria to be designated as the audit committee's financial expert rests with the board of directors.[34] Significantly, the rule provides a safe harbor that clarifies that a director who serves as the audit committee's financial expert is not considered to be an

---

company's financial statements included in the annual report has issued an attestation report on management's assessment of the company's internal control over financial reporting. . . .

Note that small issuers and emerging growth companies are exempt from the auditor's (however, not management's) internal control report. *See* SOX § 404(b).

Second, SOX mandates that an Exchange Act reporting company disclose in its financial statements any off-balance-sheet transaction, obligation, or arrangement having a material effect on such company's financial condition. In addition, SOX "requires the SEC to promulgate rules providing that subject companies must present pro forma financial information in an SEC filing or other public disclosure (such as a press release) in a non-misleading manner and must reconcile such pro forma financial information with the subject company's financial condition and results of operation under GAAP." Marc I. Steinberg, *Securities Regulation* 327 (7th ed. 2017). The SEC has issued such implementing rules, including Regulation G, under this directive. *See* SOX § 401, *amending*, § 13(i)-(j) of the Securities Exchange Act; Securities Act Release No. 8176 (2003).

[30] *See* Item 407(d)(5) of Regulation S-K, 17 C.F.R. § 229.407(d)(5) (2017).

[31] Disclosure Required by Sections 406 and 407 of the Sarbanes-Oxley Act of 2002, Securities Act Release No. 8177 (2003). Note that under the SEC rules, the term "financial expert" is now termed "audit committee financial expert." Item 407(d)(5) of Regulation S-K. If the subject company does not have a financial expert on its audit committee, such company must provide its reasons for declining to have one. *Id.*

[32] *See* Securities Act Release No. 8177 (2003) ("The new disclosure items are intended to enhance investor confidence in the fairness and integrity of the securities markets by increasing transparency as to whether a company has an audit committee financial expert on its audit committee and whether a company has adopted a code of ethics that applies to its principal executive officer and senior financial officers. We believe that these rules will help investors to understand and assess certain aspects of a company's corporate governance.").

[33] 17 C.F.R. § 229.407(d)(5) (2017).

[34] *Id.* (requiring the registrant to "[d]isclose that [its] board of directors has determined that the registrant either: (1) has at least one audit committee financial expert serving on its audit committee; or (2) does not have an audit committee financial expert serving on its audit committee").

"expert" for purposes of Section 11 of the Securities Act[35] and thereby is not subject to heightened due diligence as compared to other members of the audit committee in regard to any portion of the registration statement.[36]

In addition to establishing requirements for auditing committees, SOX also establishes requirements of auditing *firms*. SOX's Section 201 amended Section 10A of the Securities Exchange Act to ban, with certain exceptions, auditing firms from rendering such non-audit[37] services as: (1) bookkeeping and other accounting-related services; (2) design and implementation of financial information systems; (3) appraisal and valuation services, including the rendering of opinion letters; (4) actuarial services; (5) internal audit outsourcing services; (6) management functions or human resources; (7) any broker or dealer, investment adviser, or investment banking services; (8) legal services and expert services unrelated to the audit; and

---

[35] 15 U.S.C. § 77k (2012). Section 11 provides for a private right of action on behalf of purchasers against specified persons based on a material misstatement or half-truth contained in the registration statement. Except for the issuer, defendants have due diligence defenses. As stated by this author:

> To prevail on a Section 11 claim, a plaintiff need only prove: (1) a requisite jurisdictional nexus; (2) that he/she acquired a security pursuant to a registration statement; (3) that at the time the registration statement became effective, it contained a materially misleading statement or half-truth; and (4) that the claim was brought within the applicable statute of limitations. These minimal pleading requirements, combined with the virtually absolute strict liability against the issuer and imposition of a stringent due diligence defense upon other subject defendants, make Section 11 an attractive weapon for aggrieved investors.

Marc I. Steinberg and Brent A. Kirby, *The Assault on Section 11 of the Securities Act: A Study in Judicial Activism*, 63 Rutgers L. Rev. 1, 10 (2010).

[36] 17 C.F.R. § 229.407(d)(5)(iv) (2017). With respect to the due diligence defense for an "expert" under § 11, such person must show that, after reasonable investigation, he or she did not reasonably believe and in fact did not believe that the part of the registration statement that he or she "expertised" contained any material misrepresentation or omission that was required to be stated therein. Note that this standard is the same as for nonexperts with respect to the non-expertised part of the registration statement. With respect to the expertised portion of the registration statement, such nonexpert has no duty to investigate but must prove that he or she reasonably believed that the expertised portion of the registration statement was accurate. Nonetheless, status as an audit committee member, even if one is not designated as an expert under § 11, may heighten such person's due diligence obligations. Due to the director's position as an audit committee member and thereby having this significant relationship with the subject issuer, that person's due diligence obligations may be enhanced if a material disclosure deficiency is contained in the registration statement with respect to the financial statements and other financially-related matters that are considered within the purview of the audit committee. *See In re WorldCom, Inc. Sec. Litig.*, 346 F. Supp. 2d 628 (S.D.N.Y. 2004); *Feit v. Leasco Data Processing Equip. Corp.*, 332 F. Supp. 544 (E.D.N.Y. 1971); *Escott v. BarChris Constr. Corp.*, 283 F. Supp. 643 (S.D.N.Y. 1968); SEC Rule 176, 17 C.F.R. § 229.176 (2017); Securities Act Release No. 6335 (1981); Rowland, *supra* note 27, at 188–92.

[37] Non-audit services include services that a registered public accounting firm renders to the subject enterprise apart from auditing or evaluating such enterprise's financial statements. *See* 15 U.S.C. § 7201(8) (2012). *See also* Section 10A(h), 15 U.S.C. § 78j-1(h) (2012) (with respect to other non-audit services, not described in the statute, the subject accounting firm may undertake "only if the activity is approved in advance by the audit committee of the issuer, in accordance with [the statute]").

(9) such services as the Public Company Accounting Oversight Board (PCAOB)[38] deems impermissible.[39] The audit committee has the authority to engage independent advisers, including retention of its own legal counsel, with the subject issuer obligated to provide appropriate funding as the audit committee so determines for payment of such services.[40]

C. EXECUTIVE CLAWBACK PROVISIONS

Section 304 of SOX[41] and Section 954 of the Dodd-Frank Act[42] govern executive "clawback" actions.[43] The general thrust of both provisions is similar, with the provisions seeking to deter undue executive officer risk-taking and improper conduct.[44]

---

[38] The Public Company Accounting Oversight Board (PCAOB) was established pursuant to the Sarbanes-Oxley Act. *See* 15 U.S.C. § 7211 *et seq.* (2012). The PCAOB was established by SOX (*see* § 101) and its constitutionality generally was upheld by the U.S. Supreme Court in *Free Enterprise Fund v. PCAOB*, 561 U.S. 477 (2010). The PCAOB is a nonprofit corporation organized under the laws of the District of Columbia; it is not an agency of the federal government. From a general perspective:

> The Board's fundamental purpose is to oversee the auditing of public companies in order to help ensure accurate and independent financial reporting by public companies subject to the federal securities laws. The Board has sweeping powers to establish quality control, ethical, and auditing standards for accounting firms. The PCAOB also has the power and authority to inspect, investigate, and bring disciplinary proceedings against public auditing firms.

Steinberg, *supra* note 11, at 181.

[39] Section 10A(g) of the Securities Exchange Act; 15 U.S.C. § 78j-1(g) (2012). Note that § 10A(b) provides the PCAOB with the authority to exempt any person from the prohibition of § 10A(g).

[40] Section 10A(m)(5) of the Securities Exchange Act, 15 U.S.C. § 78j-1(m)(5) (2012). *See also* 1 Buckholz, et al., *supra* note 20, § 3:1, at 3A-49; discussion Chapter 6 herein.

[41] 15 U.S.C. § 7243 (2012).

[42] Dodd-Frank Act § 954.

[43] Significantly, only the SEC may bring a cause of action against an issuer under Section 304 of SOX because courts have found that the statute fails to provide a private right of action. *See, e.g., In re Digimarc Corp. Derivative Litig.*, 549 F. 3d 1223, 1238 (9th Cir. 2008) (holding that there "is no private right of action under section 304 of the Sarbanes-Oxley Act"). *See also* Gallogly, *supra* note 5, at 1243–44 (discussing the Ninth Circuit's conclusion that there is no explicit language or language denoting intent within Section 304 of Sarbanes-Oxley in order to imply a private right of action). Thus far, the most cited case involving SEC enforcement under Section 304 is *SEC v. Jenkins*. In *Jenkins*, a U.S. district court held that the SEC could bring an enforcement action against executives who were not alleged to have engaged in misconduct, because to trigger an issuer's liability under Section 304, it is sufficient for the issuer to engage in misconduct. *SEC v. Jenkins*, 718 F. Supp. 2d 1070, 1074–75 (D. Ariz. 2010). In a subsequent decision, *SEC v. Jensen*, 835 F.3d 1104 (9th Cir. 2016), the Ninth Circuit agreed with *Jenkins*. *See also SEC v. Jasper*, 678 F.3d 1116 (9th Cir. 2012) (affirming order of clawback pursuant to SOX § 304).

[44] Gallogly, *supra* note 5, at 1242 (noting that "[t]he general aim of both [Section 304 of the Sarbanes-Oxley Act and Section 954 of the Dodd-Frank Act] is similar—they both attempt to discourage certain types of behavior by executive officers"; and further noting that Section 954 seeks to "discourage excessive risk-taking by executive officers, while Section 304 is intended to improve corporate management to discourage fraudulent or wrongful conduct by executive officers").

Both clawback provisions mandate that CEOs and CFOs reimburse the subject issuer for incentive-based compensation when such issuer is required to prepare an accounting restatement based on its failure to materially comply with the financial reporting obligations of the securities laws.[45]

1. Sarbanes-Oxley § 304

SOX Section 304 establishes the requirement that subject CEOs and CFOs must reimburse incentive-based compensation to the company if there is a financial restatement due to misconduct. Accordingly, in circumstances where misconduct relating to financial reporting calls for a subject issuer to produce an "accounting restatement due to the material noncompliance of [such] issuer," the CEO and CFO of such issuer must reimburse the issuer for any bonus or other incentive or equity-based compensation that they have received. As interpreted thus far, misconduct by the CEO or CFO need not be proven as a condition for compulsory reimbursement.[46]

2. Dodd-Frank § 954

Section 954 of the Dodd-Frank Act (which added Section 10D to the Securities Exchange Act) requires that, as a condition of being listed, each listed company must adopt and implement its own internal "clawback" policy on incentive-based compensation. This statute expands on the compensation "clawback" concept contained in Section 304 of SOX. Importantly, however, the statute is not self-executing: It is dependent upon the SEC promulgating a rule that directs the national securities exchanges to prohibit the listing of a subject company's security based on such company's noncompliance with Section 10D. To date, the SEC has not adopted an implementing rule.

From a general standpoint, Section 954 of the Dodd-Frank Act (i.e., Section 10D of the Securities Exchange Act) is broader than its SOX counterpart in several ways:

- Pursuant to Section 304, the accounting restatement triggering the clawback (due to material noncompliance with any financial reporting requirement of

[45] *Id.* at 1241–42. The clawback provision under the Dodd-Frank Act extends beyond the subject company's CEO and CFO to encompass other current and former executive officers. *See infra* note 49 and accompanying text.

[46] *See, e.g., SEC v. Jensen*, 835 F.3d 1100, 1104 (9th Cir. 2016) ("The disgorgement remedy authorized under SOX 304 applies regardless whether a restatement was caused by the personal misconduct of an issuer's CEO and CFO or by other issuer misconduct.").

the federal securities laws) must have been caused by misconduct; Section 954 contains no such limitation.[47]

- Second, whereas Section 954 extends liability exposure to "any current or former executive officer,"[48] Section 304 of SOX limits such exposure to the subject company's CEO and CFO.[49]
- Third, whereas Section 954 authorizes the recoupment of executive compensation received in the three years prior to the issuer's filing of the restatement,[50] Section 304 is more limited, providing for recovery of executive compensation for "the 12-month period following the first public issuance or filing with the Commission (whichever occurs first) of the financial document."[51]

On the other hand, Section 304 of SOX is broader than Section 954 of the Dodd-Frank Act in mandating executive reimbursement of all types of compensation, encompassing incentive- and equity-based payments as well as stock profits.[52] Section 954 only permits the recovery of incentive-based compensation "in excess of what would have been paid to the executive officer under the accounting restatement."[53] In 2015, the SEC proposed (but has not adopted to date) Rule 10D-1 to implement Section 954.[54]

---

47 While "material noncompliance of the issuer with any financial reporting requirement" will trigger Dodd-Frank Section 954 (Securities Exchange Act of 1934 § 10D(b)(2)), Section 304 of SOX specifies that "the material noncompliance of the issuer [occur], as a result of misconduct, with any financial reporting requirement." 15 U.S.C. § 7243(a) (2012). *See* Jeffrey M. Benton, *Executive Clawback Actions*, 59 The Advoc. (Texas) 15, 17 (2012).

48 Section 10D(b)(2) of the Securities Exchange Act, 15 U.S.C. § 78jD(b)(2) (2012).

49 15 U.S.C. § 7243(a) (2012).

50 Securities Exchange Act of 1934 § 10D(b)(2).

51 15 U.S.C. § 7243(a)(1) (2012).

52 15 U.S.C. § 7243 (2012).

53 Securities Exchange Act § 10D(b)(2). *See* Benton, *supra* note 47, at 17.

54 In 2015, the SEC issued a release proposing a new Rule 10D-1 under the Securities Exchange Act that would require national securities exchanges to implement listing standards directing listed issuers to institute executive clawback provisions. Listing Standards for Recovery of Erroneously Awarded Compensation, Securities Exchange Act Release No. 75342 (July 1, 2015). In the accompanying press release, the SEC stated:

> The Securities and Exchange Commission today proposed rules directing national securities exchanges and associations to establish listing standards requiring companies to adopt policies that require executive officers to pay back incentive-based compensation that they were awarded erroneously. With this proposal, the Commission has completed proposals on all executive compensation rules required by the Dodd-Frank Wall Street Reform and Consumer Protection Act.
>
> Under the proposed new Rule 10D-1, listed companies would be required to develop and enforce recovery policies that, in the event of an accounting restatement, "claw-back" from current and former

D. EQUITABLE RELIEF

As discussed later in this chapter, Section 305 of SOX authorizes the SEC to seek "any equitable relief that may be appropriate or necessary" for the benefit of the investing public.[55] In application, this language expressly authorizes the SEC to seek additional equitable relief in its enforcement actions. Although the Commission prior to SOX procured a wide range of equitable remedies,[56] dispute existed regarding the scope of this authority.[57] The enactment of this statute clarifies that the SEC is empowered to procure far-reaching equitable relief.[58] Hence, if appropriate, such equitable relief as appointment of a receiver, retention of consultants or independent monitors, and implementation of corrective measures may be ordered.[59]

> executive officers incentive-based compensation they would not have received based on the restatement. Recovery would be required without regard to fault. The proposed rules would also require disclosure of listed companies' recovery policies, and their actions under those policies.
>
> ....
>
> Under the proposed rules, the listing standards would apply to incentive-based compensation that is tied to accounting-related metrics, stock price or total shareholder return. Recovery would apply to excess incentive-based compensation received by executive officers in the three fiscal years preceding the date a listed company is required to prepare an accounting restatement.

SEC Press Release 2015-136 (July 1, 2015). Note that several companies voluntarily have implemented clawback policies. *See* American Accounting Association, *Executive Pay Clawbacks* (Jan. 30, 2015). *See generally*, Benton, *supra* note 47; J. Royce Fichtner, et al., *The Unfulfilled Promise of Sarbanes-Oxley Section 304: A Call for Pervasive Enforcement*, 14 DePaul Bus. & Com. L.J. 49 (2015); Gallogly, *supra* note 5; John Patrick Kelsh, *Section 304 of the Sarbanes-Oxley Act of 2002: The Case for a Personal Culpability Requirement*, 59 Bus. Law. 1005 (2004); Isaac U. Kimes, *Unfettered Clawbacks—Why Section 304 of the Sarbanes-Oxley Act Requires a Personal Misconduct Standard*, 42 U. Mem. L. Rev. 797 (2012); Rachel E. Schwartz, *The Clawback Provision of Sarbanes-Oxley: An Underutilized Incentive to Keep the Corporate House Clean*, 64 Bus. Law. 1 (2008); Michael Spafford, et al., *An Executive's Guide to Defeating the SOX 304 Clawback*, 49 Sec. Reg. & L. Rep. (BNA) 634, 665 (2017).

[55] 15 U.S.C. § 7243 (2012). *See infra* notes 164–171 and accompanying text.

[56] For example, in *SEC v. Wencke*, 622 F.2d 1363, 1369 (9th Cir. 1980), the appellate court stated:

> The federal courts have inherent equitable authority to issue a variety of "ancillary relief" measures in actions brought by the SEC to enforce the federal securities laws.... The power of a district court to impose a receivership or grant other forms of ancillary relief... derives from inherent power of a court of equity to fashion effective relief.

For several examples where the SEC procured equitable relief, *see* Marc I. Steinberg and Ralph C. Ferrara, *Securities Practice: Federal and State Enforcement* §§ 5:8-5:9 (2d ed. 2001 & 2017–2018 supp.). *See also* James Ferrand, *Ancillary Remedies in SEC Civil Enforcement Suits*, 89 Harv. L. Rev. 1779 (1976); Arthur Mathews, *Recent Trends in SEC Requests for Ancillary Relief in SEC Civil Injunctive Actions*, 31 Bus. Law. 1323 (1976).

[57] *See* George Dent, *Ancillary Relief in Federal Securities Law: A Study in Federal Remedies*, 67 Minn. L. Rev. 865 (1983).

[58] *See* § 21(d) of the Securities Exchange Act ("In any action or proceeding brought by the Commission under any provision of the securities laws, the Commission may seek, and any Federal Court may grant, any equitable relief that may be appropriate or necessary for the benefit of investors.").

[59] *See, e.g., SEC v. Contorinis*, 743 F.3d 296 (2d Cir. 2014) (disgorgement ordered); *SEC v. Enter. Trust Co.*, 559 F.3d 649 (7th Cir. 2009) (appointment of receiver); *SEC v. Avon Prods., Inc.*, 46 Sec. Reg. & L. Rep. (BNA)

E. OFFICER AND DIRECTOR BARS

In addition, SOX authorizes the SEC to bar an individual from serving as an officer or director of any publicly-held company who is deemed "unfit" and who engages in fraudulent conduct under the federal securities laws.[60] A court may grant such relief on a permanent or temporary basis and either conditionally or unconditionally.[61] The Sarbanes-Oxley Act strengthened the SEC's power by expanding the scope of the officer-and-director bar by lowering the standard and by making it an available sanction in administrative proceedings. In this respect, Section 305 of SOX expands the scope of the officer-and-director bar by altering the standard from "substantial unfitness" to "unfitness."[62] Furthermore, Section 1105 of SOX grants the Commission authority to seek officer-and-director bars in its administrative proceedings against those who have violated such antifraud provisions as Section 10(b) of the Securities Exchange Act and Section 17(a)(1) of the Securities Act.[63] Thus, an officer's or director's violation of these antifraud provisions in such a manner that evinces "unfitness" to serve as an officer or director of a publicly-held enterprise triggers the bar sanction.[64]

F. INSIDER TRADING DURING BLACKOUT PERIODS

Section 306 of SOX focuses on insider trades during pension fund blackout periods. Under this statute, "executive officers and directors are prohibited from trading any equity security of the issuer, acquired through the scope of employment, during a blackout period, when at least half of the issuer's individual account plan participants are not permitted to trade in the equity security for more than three

872 (S.D.N.Y. 2014) (appointment of monitor); *SEC v. Royal Dutch Petroleum Co.*, 36 Sec. Reg. & L. Rep. (BNA) 1585 (S.D. Tex. 2004) (implementation of internal compliance program); cases cited in Steinberg and Ferrara, *supra* note 56, at § 5:9. *See generally* Jayne Barnard, *Corporate Therapeutics at the Securities and Exchange Commission*, 2008 Colum. Bus. L. Rev. 793 (2008); James Doty and Brad Bennett, *Independent Consultants in SEC Enforcement Actions*, 43 Rev. Sec. & Comm. Reg. 259 (2010); Helene Glotzer, *Recent Trends in SEC Enforcement Remedies*, 37 Rev. Sec. & Comm. Reg. 185 (2004); Daniel Morrissey, *SEC Injunctions*, 68 Tenn. L. Rev. 427 (2001).

60 15 U.S.C. § 7243(a)(1), (b)(5) (2012). *See also* Remedies Act of 1990, Pub. L. No. 101-429, §§ 101, 201, 104 Stat. 931, 932, 935 (1990) ("substantial unfitness").

61 Steinberg, *supra* note 6, at 1082.

62 SOX § 305, *amending*, §§ 8A, 20(e) of the Securities Act, §§ 21(d)(2), 21C of the Securities Exchange Act.

63 *See, e.g., In re Hackney*, Securities Exchange Act Release No. 76879 (2016).

64 15 U.S.C. §§ 77t(e), 78u(d)(2) (2012). *See generally* Steinberg and Ferrara, *supra* note 56, at § 6:18; Jayne Barnard, *SEC Debarment of Officers and Directors after Sarbanes-Oxley*, 59 Bus. Law. 391 (2004); Stephen Crimmins, *Where Are We Going with SEC Officer and Director Bars?*, 38 Sec. Reg. & L. Rep. (BNA) 717 (2006).

consecutive business days."[65] To clarify the statute's application and enhance its effectiveness, the SEC promulgated rules governing this prohibition—Regulation Blackout Trading Restriction (BTR).[66] In the event of violation of the statute or Regulation BTR, SEC enforcement action may ensue as well as a suit brought by or on behalf of the subject company seeking disgorgement of all profits improperly made by the defendant fiduciary.[67]

G. DIRECTOR INDEPENDENCE

While SOX and the Dodd-Frank Act, in practical effect, mandate the presence of independent directors and specify their responsibilities in certain contexts,[68] neither Act defines the characteristics of an "independent director" at a general level. For audit committee independence, Section 301 of SOX generally defines an "independent director" as one who may not accept remuneration (other than fees as a director) and is not an affiliated person of the subject listed company or any subsidiary thereof.[69] Likewise, Section 952 of the Dodd-Frank Act directs the SEC to direct the national stock exchanges to mandate that a listed company's compensation committee be comprised solely of "independent" directors—with the term "independence" defined pursuant to standards established by the exchanges in compliance with SEC rules.[70]

---

[65] Steinberg, *supra* note 11, at 327, *citing*, SOX § 306, 15 U.S.C. § 7244 (2012). *See* Report of the Committee on Banking, Housing, and Urban Affairs, U.S. Senate S. Rep. No. 107-205 (July 3, 2002):

> In some cases, officers and directors have profited by selling off large portions of company stock during a time when employees were prevented from selling company stock in their Section 401(k) retirement plans. To address this problem, the bill prohibits key individuals from engaging in transactions involving any equity security of the issuer during a "blackout" period . . . [T]his section applies to directors and executive officers in order to ensure that the prohibition is limited to individuals in policy-making positions.

[66] 17 C.F.R. §§ 245.100-104 (2017). *See* Securities Exchange Act Release No. 47225 (Jan. 23, 2003). With certain exceptions, plan participants and beneficiaries are entitled to receive a minimum of 30 days' advance notice with respect to a blackout period. *See* SOX § 306(b), 15 U.S.C. § 7244(b) (2012). Pursuant to Regulation BTR, during a blackout period, a subject company's executive officer or director may not trade equity securities that such person acquired in connection with his or her service to the company.

[67] *See* § 306(a)(2), 15 U.S.C. § 7244(a)(2) (2012); Rule 103 of Regulation BTR. For further discussion, *see* Marc I. Steinberg and William K.S. Wang, *Insider Trading* §§ 12:1-12:5 (Oxford University Press 3d ed. 2010).

[68] The Acts generally do so by means of, in practicality, requiring that a majority of the subject company's board of directors must be independent directors as a condition of such company listing its securities on a national securities exchange. *See* discussion in Chapter 6 herein.

[69] *See* discussion *supra* notes 17–20 and accompanying text; Chapter 6 herein.

[70] *See* NYSE Stock Exchange Listed Company Manual § 303A.02; Nasdaq, Inc. Stock Market Rule § 5605(a)(2). The discussion in Chapter 6 herein addresses the definition of director "independence" under applicable national securities exchange rules.

By promulgating Item 407 of Regulation S-K, the SEC requires meaningful disclosure with respect to director independence.[71] All U.S. issuers that are subject to the SEC proxy rules must provide the disclosure called for by Item 407 in their proxy statements relating to the election of directors.[72] Among the mandated disclosures regarding director independence are: (1) an explanation of the subject company's definition of independence that it employs in ascertaining independence criteria in compliance with the relevant stock exchange listing standards;[73] (2) disclosure of the members of the nominating, audit, or compensation committee who are not independent pursuant to the applicable committee's independence standards; [74] and (3) if the company uses its own definition for determining director independence, making such definition accessible either on such company's website or in its proxy statement at least once during three fiscal years.[75]

As addressed in Chapter 6, director independence for listed companies is based on the applicable national securities exchange listing standards.[76] The listing standards, such as those adopted by the NYSE, require that a majority of the directors serving on a listed company's board of directors be independent.[77] For example, as elaborated upon in Chapter 6, stated succinctly, in order for a director to be deemed independent, the NYSE listing standards mandate that an issuer's board of directors "affirmatively" establish that such director has no "material relationship" with the listed issuer.[78] Only independent directors, pursuant to NYSE rules, may serve on a listed company's audit, compensation, and nominating committees.[79] Further, independent directors "must meet at regularly scheduled executive sessions without management."[80]

---

[71] 17 C.F.R. § 229.407(a) (2017).

[72] *Id.*

[73] *Id.* § 229.407(a)(1)(i).

[74] *Id.* § 229.407(a).

[75] *Id.* § 229.407(a)(2).

[76] Generally, a national securities exchange is registered in accordance with Section 6(a) of the Securities Exchange Act. *See generally* 15 U.S.C. § 78f(a) (2012); *see also*, NASD and NYSE Rulemaking: Relating to Corporate Governance, Securities Exchange Act Release No. 48745 (2003).

[77] *See, e.g.*, NYSE Listed Company Manual § 303A.01, *available at* http://nysemanual.nyse.com/LCMTools/PlatformViewer.asp?selectnode=chp_1_4&manual=%2F1cm%2Fsections%F1cm-sections%2F; *see also* Self-Regulatory Organizations; New York Stock Exchange LLC; Order Approving a Proposed Rule Change as Modified by Amendment No. 1 to Amend Certain Corporate Governance Requirements, Securities Exchange Act Release No. 61067, File No. SR-NYSE-2009-89 (Nov. 25, 2009), *available at* https://www.sec.gov/rules/sro/nyse/2009/34-61067.pdf; *Initial Listing Guide*, Nasdaq (Jan. 2017), *available at* https://listingcenter.nasdaq.com/assets/initialguide.pdf.

[78] NYSE Listed Company Manual § 303A.02; discussion Chapter 6 herein. If the issuer is not listed on a national securities exchange, the director independence definition from a suitable national securities exchange or inter-dealer quotation system is to be used. *See* Item 407(a)(1)(ii) of Regulation S-K, 17 C.F.R. § 229.407(a)(1)(ii).

[79] NYSE Listed Company Manual § 303A.04-07.

[80] *Id.* § 303A.03. *See* Robert V. Hale II, *The Uncertain Efficacy of Executive Sessions under the NYSE's Revised Listing Standards*, 61 Bus. Law. 1413 (2006) ("explor[ing] key issues relating to the use of non-management

Further, a subject company, consistent with applicable SRO listing standards,[81] must disclose whether its audit, nominating, and compensation committees have a charter. If so, then the company must disclose whether such charter may be accessed by means of its website.[82] If such charter is not accessible through the company's website, the company generally must provide such charter as an appendix to its proxy statement once every three fiscal years.[83] Finally, if the subject registrant "does not have a separately designated audit, nominating or compensation committee or committee performing similar functions, the registrant must provide the disclosure of directors that are not independent with respect to all members of the board of directors. . . ."[84]

H. LEADERSHIP STRUCTURE

As discussed as well later in this chapter, with the addition of Section 14B of the Securities Exchange Act pursuant to the Dodd-Frank Act, a subject company must disclose in its proxy statement why such company has selected "(1) the same person to serve as chairman of the board of directors and chief executive officer . . . or (2) different individuals to serve as chairman of the board of directors and chief executive officer. . . ." [85] In regard thereto, Item 407 of SEC Regulation S-K mandates disclosure focusing on the board of director's leadership structure and its role with respect to risk management. Specifically, Item 407 requires the subject company to state whether such company has separate individuals or the same person in the positions of CEO and chairman of the board. If the same individual serves as CEO and board chairman, disclosure must be made whether a lead independent director has been designated "and what specific role [such] lead director plays in the leadership of the board." [86] The disclosure also should explain why the company has determined that "its leadership structure is appropriate given [its] specific

---

executive sessions under Section 303A.03 of the NYSE's revised listing standards, including the authority of the SEC to enforce such a requirement, the status of board actions taken at such meetings, and whether such sessions may result in altering the principal roles of the board and management").

[81] While the charter requirements of the NYSE and Nasdaq are different, both exchanges must incorporate the specific responsibilities mandated by statute. *See* NYSE Listed Company Manual § 303A.06; Nasdaq Stock Market Rules § 5605; discussion Chapter 6 herein.

[82] 17 C.F.R. § 229.407(c)(2)(i), (d)(1), (e)(2) (2017).

[83] *Id.* § 229.407(a)(2).

[84] *Id.* § 229.407(a).

[85] Section 14B of the Securities Exchange Act, 15 U.S.C. § 78n-2 (2012). *See* discussion *infra* notes 132–137 and accompanying text.

[86] Item 407(h) of Regulation S-K, 17 C.F.R. § 229.407(h) (2017).

characteristics or circumstances [and] the board's role in the risk oversight" of such company.[87]

I. INDEPENDENT COMPENSATION COMMITTEES

Section 952 of the Dodd-Frank Act, in practical effect, requires that the compensation committee of any nationally listed company be comprised solely of independent directors. Pursuant to this statute, which added Section 10C to the Securities Exchange Act, as directed by the SEC and as implemented by the respective exchanges, no company may list its equity securities on a national securities exchange unless such company has an independent compensation committee.[88] The Dodd-Frank Act does not define "independence" for compensation committee purposes, but rather leaves that determination to the exchanges.[89] This provision of the Dodd-Frank Act is similar to Section 301 of SOX; however, Section 952 is applicable to compensation committees whereas Section 301 is applicable to audit committees;[90] moreover, Section 301 by its terms (and as implemented by Rule 10A-3) sets forth more strict criteria for director audit committee independence.[91]

Generally, members of a subject company's compensation committee must meet two requirements: (1) be a member of the company's board of directors, and (2) be independent.[92] The statute and SEC rule give latitude to the exchanges in

---

[87] *Id.* As another example, the issuer must disclose what procedures, if any, shareholders need to follow to communicate with the board. If the board has no such procedures, the issuer must explain why it has none. *Id.* § 229.407(f).

[88] Securities Exchange Act § 10C(a)(1)(2); *see also* Exchange Act Rule 10C-1; Dodd-Frank Act § 952. Section 10C(1) of the Securities Exchange Act provides:

> (1) Listing standards.—
> The Commission shall, by rule, direct the national securities exchanges and national securities associations to prohibit the listing of any equity security of an issuer, other than an issuer that is a controlled company, limited partnership, company in bankruptcy proceedings, open-ended management investment company that is registered under the Investment Company Act of 1940, or a foreign private issuer that provides annual disclosures to shareholders of the reasons that the foreign private issuer does not have an independent compensation committee, that does not comply with the requirements of this subsection.

[89] In defining independence, the exchanges must consider "relevant factors," including: "the source of [the director's] compensation . . . including any consulting, advisory or other compensatory fee paid by the issuer," or an affiliate of such issuer to the director. *See* § 10C(a)(3), as added by the Dodd-Frank Act.

[90] *See* discussion in Chapter 6 herein.

[91] For example, a director serving on a subject company's audit committee can receive no fees or other financial benefit other than compensation as a director or board committee member. *See supra* notes 15–18 and accompanying text; Chapter 6 herein.

[92] Section 10C of the Securities Exchange Act, 15 U.S.C. § 78j-3 (2012); Rule 10C-1(b)(1), 17 C.F.R. § 240.10C-1(b)(1) (2017).

establishing the criteria for determining independence.[93] The Commission, however, specified the following factors, in addition to other relevant factors, that the exchanges must consider in determining director compensation committee "independence": "(A) The source of compensation of a member of the board of directors of an issuer, including any consulting, advisory or other compensatory fee paid by the issuer to such member of the board of directors; and (B) Whether a member of the board of directors of an issuer is affiliated with the issuer, a subsidiary of the issuer or an affiliate of a subsidiary of the issuer."[94] The stock exchange rules focusing on compensation committees are discussed in Chapter 6 herein.[95]

Pursuant to SEC rule, a compensation committee may, in its sole discretion, obtain the advice of compensation consultants, as well as other advisers, so long as such committee considers specified independence standards.[96] In this regard, the compensation committee "shall be directly responsible for the appointment, compensation and oversight of the work of any compensation adviser retained by the compensation committee, and each listed issuer must provide for appropriate funding for payment of reasonable compensation, as determined by the compensation committee, to any compensation adviser retained by the compensation committee."[97]

The compensation committee is not required to procure the advice of "independent" consultants or advisers. Nonetheless, as discussed in Chapter 6, the committee must consider the factors identified by the Commission and as buttressed by the relevant exchange.[98] The SEC directed that a compensation committee of a listed issuer consider the following factors (as well as other factors specified by the relevant exchange) in determining whether to retain a compensation consultant or other adviser: "[1] the provision of other services to the issuer by the person that employs the compensation consultant, legal counsel or other adviser; [2] the amount of fees received from the issuer by the person that employs the compensation consultant, legal counsel, or other adviser, as a percentage of the total revenue of the person that

[93] *See* discussion Chapter 6 herein.

[94] 17 C.F.R. § 240.10C-1(3)(A)-(B) (2017). The exchanges may exempt "a particular relationship" from the independence-determining requirements mentioned above as "appropriate" considering the respective issuer's size and other pertinent factors. *Id.* § 240.10C(a)(4).

[95] The Dodd-Frank Act excludes several categories of issuers from the compensation committee independence requirement. *See* § 10(C)(1) of the Exchange Act, *supra* note 88.

[96] *See* § 10C(b)-(e) of the Securities Exchange Act, 15 U.S.C. § 78j-3(b)-(e) (2012); Rule 10C-1(b), 17 C.F.R. § 240.10C-1(b) (2017); Listing Standards for Compensation Committees, Securities Exchange Act Release No. 67220 (July 27, 2012), *available at* https://www.sec.gov/rules/final/2012/33-9330.pdf.

[97] Securities Exchange Act Release No. 67220, *supra* note 96. The compensation committee is held responsible for those advisers and/or consultants that it retains.

[98] *Id.* ("The statute does not require a compensation adviser to be independent, only that the compensation committee of a listed issuer consider the enumerated independence factors before selecting a compensation adviser.").

employs the [adviser]; [3] the policies and procedures of the person that employs the compensation consultant, legal counsel, or other adviser that are designed to prevent conflicts of interest; [4] any business or personal relationship of the compensation consultant, legal counsel, or other adviser with a member of the compensation committee; [5] any stock of the issuer owned by the compensation consultant, legal counsel, or other adviser; and [6] any business or personal relationship of the compensation consultant, legal counsel, other adviser or the person employing the adviser with an executive officer of the issuer."[99] Hence, under the applicable rules, a compensation committee may retain non-independent consultants, but must assess the above criteria in its decision-making.[100]

J. NOMINATING COMMITTEES

In 2006, the SEC amended Item 407 of Regulation S-K.[101] The amendments focused on disclosure with respect to nominating committees.[102] First, defining the scope of the term "Nominating Committee," the Instruction to Item 407(c)(2) explains that this term "refers not only to nominating committees and committees performing similar functions, but also to groups of directors fulfilling the role of a nominating committee, including the entire board of directors."[103] Second, pursuant to Item 407(c)(2), a subject company must provide information in its proxy statement regarding its director nomination process, including as to the following topics: (1) whether the nominating committee has adopted a charter and, if so, disclosure in regard thereto; (2) consideration by the nominating committee of director-candidates recommended by shareholders; (3) in the view of the nominating committee, candidates' qualifications that must be met; (4) the process employed by the nominating committee to identify and evaluate director-candidates; (5) source(s) of recommendation with respect to director-candidates; (6) existence of a diversity policy; (7) fees paid to a third-party to identify or evaluate potential director-nominees; and (8) candidates recommended by a shareholder who has beneficially owned more than five percent of the company's voting common stock for a minimum of one year.[104]

---

[99] Rule 10C-1(b)(4), 17 C.F.R. § 240.10C-1(b)(4) (2017).

[100] For further discussion on compensation committees, *see* Chapter 6 herein.

[101] Executive Compensation and Related Person Disclosure, Securities Exchange Act Release No. 54302A (2006). *See* 1 Buckholz, et al., *supra* note 20, § 1:2, at 1D-23.

[102] 17 C.F.R. § 229.407(c) (2017).

[103] *Id.* Instruction to Item 407(c)(2).

[104] *Id.* 407(c). *See* 1 Buckholz, et al., *supra* note 20, § 1:2, at 1D-7. It bears mentioning that, in line with SOX's corporate governance enhancements, the NYSE and NASD amended its listing standards regarding nominating

As to shareholder nominations, the subject company must describe whether its nominating committee has adopted a policy that enables shareholders to recommend director-candidates. If such a policy exists, then the company must disclose the policy's "material elements." Further, the company must set forth the procedures by which shareholders may submit director-candidate recommendations. If, however, the nominating committee declines to have such a policy, the company must state that fact and "the basis for the view . . . that it is appropriate . . . not to have such a policy."[105]

Relatedly, the Dodd-Frank Act sought to expand the ability of certain large shareholders to impact the director nomination process through the "proxy access" mechanism.[106] Stated generally, the "proxy access" procedure, as enacted, empowers the SEC to adopt rules enabling certain larger shareholders to require a subject issuer to designate in its proxy statement a specified number of director-nominee candidates for election to the board of directors.[107] Pursuant to this statutory grant, the SEC adopted Rule 14a-11.[108] That rule, however, was invalidated by the U.S. Court of

---

committees. *See* NASD and NYSE Rulemaking: Relating to Corporate Governance, Securities Exchange Act Release No. 48745 (2003). *See* discussion Chapter 6 herein.

[105] *Id.* Item 407(c)(ii)-(iv). In 2003, the NYSE, as part of its adoption of heightened corporate governance listing standards, adopted Rule 303A.04, which requires each listed company to establish a nominating/corporate governance committee (the Nasdaq rules have a similar requirement in regard to nominating committees). Rule 303A.04 further requires that this committee be composed solely of independent directors, and that it maintain a written charter that addresses:

i. the committee's purpose and responsibilities—which, at minimum, must be to: identify individuals qualified to become board members, consistent with criteria approved by the board, and to select, or to recommend that the board select, the director nominees for the next annual meeting of shareholders; develop and recommend to the board a set of corporate governance guidelines applicable to the corporation; and oversee the evaluation of the board and management; and
ii. an annual performance evaluation of the committee.

NYSE Listed Company Manual § 303A.04. *See* Self-Regulatory Organizations; New York Stock Exchange, Inc. and National Association of Securities Dealers, Inc.; Order Approving Proposed Rule Changes (SR-NYSE-2002-33 and SR-NASD-2002-141) and Amendments No. 1 thereto; Order Approving Proposed Rule Changes (SR-NASD-2002-77, SR-NASD-2002-80, SR-NASD-2002-138; and SR-NASD-2002-139) and Amendments No. 1 to SR-NASD-2002-80 and SR-NASD-2002-139; and Notice of Filing and Order Granting Accelerated Approval of Amendments Nos. 2 and 3 to SR-NYSE-2002-33, Amendments Nos. 2, 3, 4, and 5 to SR-NASD-2002-141, Amendment Nos. 2 and 3 to SR-NASD-2002-80, Amendment Nos. 1, 2, and 3 to SR-NASD-2002-138, and Amendment No. 2 to SR-NASD-2002-139, Relating to Corporate Governance, Rel. No. 34-48745 (Nov. 4, 2003), 68 Fed. Reg. 64, 154 (Nov. 12, 2003), *available at* www.sec.gov/rules/sro/34-48745.htm; discussion Chapter 6 herein.

[106] 15 U.S.C. § 78n(a) (2012).

[107] 15 § 78n(a)(2)(b) (2012).

[108] Securities Exchange Act Rule 14a-11, 17 C.F.R. § 240.140a-11, adopted pursuant to § 971 of the Dodd-Frank Act.

Appeals for the District of Columbia Circuit in *Business Roundtable v. SEC.*[109] Rule 14a-11 and its subsequent nullification are discussed elsewhere in this book.[110]

As to candidates' qualifications for service, such issuer must disclose "any specific minimum director qualifications that the nominating committee believes must be met by a nominating committee-recommended nominee. . . ."[111] Further, Item 401(e) of Regulation S-K mandates that the issuer describe each director-nominee's business experience during the past five years—"briefly discuss[ing] the specific experience, qualifications, attributes or skills that led to the conclusion that the person should serve as a director for the registrant at the time that the disclosure is made, in light of the registrant's business and structure."[112]

The company must set forth the committee's identification and evaluation process. Also, regarding the selection of director-nominees, if a shareholder recommends a director-candidate pursuant to the subject company's policy, then disclosure must be made whether any differences exist with respect to how the committee evaluates the candidate under such circumstances.[113]

As to the source of a recommendation for a director-nominee (other than nominees who are incumbent directors or executive officers), when such nominee is set forth in the company's proxy card, disclosure must be provided whether a "security holder, non-management director, chief executive officer, other executive officer, third-party search firm, or other specified source" recommended the nominee.[114]

As to shareholders' recommendations of candidates, when a shareholder or group of shareholders owning for at least one year more than five percent of the company's common stock timely recommends a candidate, the company must disclose

---

[109] 647 F.3d 1147 (D.C. Cir. 2011).

[110] *See* Chapters 4 and 6 herein. In adopting Rule 14a-11, the Commission sought to afford large shareholders an avenue for nominating and electing directors without initiating a proxy contest. The SEC considered the traditional way of director nomination by the mounting of a shareholder proxy contest in this context to be an insufficient means. Accordingly, the Commission adopted Rule 14a-11. Securities Exchange Act Release No. 62764 (2010). To avail itself of the rule, a shareholder—either by itself or as part of a group of shareholders—must have: (a) held no less than 3% of the voting authority of the reporting issuer's securities entitled to be voted for no less than three years before such shareholder or group of shareholders could seek to invoke the rule and (b) continued to hold such securities through the date of the annual meeting. In the event that more than one shareholder or one group of shareholders met this eligibility threshold, the largest holder would be entitled to engage in this nomination process. *See generally* Thomas Stratman and J.W. Verret, *Does Shareholder Proxy Access Damage Share Value in Publicly Traded Companies?*, 64 Stan. L. Rev. 1431 (2012).

[111] 17 C.F.R. § 229.407(c)(2)(v) (2017).

[112] 17 C.F.R. § 229.401(e)(1) (2017). Note that, depending on the circumstances, the disclosures required may exceed the past five years. *See, e.g., Kelsey v. Allin*, 2016 WL 825236 (N.D. Ill. 2016) (holding actionable a company's alleged omission to disclose that its chief executive officer had a previous relationship with criminally convicted stock promoters eight years earlier).

[113] 17 C.F.R. § 229.407(c)(2)(vi) (2017).

[114] *Id.* § 229.407(c)(2)(vii).

the identity of the candidate, the shareholder or group of shareholders who recommended such candidate, and whether the committee chose to nominate the candidate.[115] Significantly, however, no such disclosure is required unless written consent is provided by both the shareholder (or group of shareholders) and the director-candidate recommended.[116]

Concerning diversity, a subject company must disclose whether its board of directors (or nominating committee) considers diversity in selecting director-nominees. If a director-nominee diversity policy exists, then disclosure must be made how the policy is implemented and its effectiveness assessed.[117] Generally, companies have broad discretion with respect to the parameters of "diversity."[118]

K. "FEDERALIZING" CORPORATE CODES OF ETHICS

Section 406 of SOX directs the SEC to promulgate rules requiring that a subject publicly-held company disclose whether it has adopted a code of ethics for its senior financial officers (and, if not, set forth the reasons why the company has not adopted such a code of ethics).[119] Neither SOX nor the SEC rules expressly require public companies to maintain a code of ethics. Nonetheless, as discussed in Chapter 6, the federal codification of corporate codes of ethics and SEC rules thereunder induced the national stock exchanges to require a listed company to adopt a code of ethics encompassing its directors, officers, and employees.[120]

The adoption and implementation of a reasonably effective code of ethics is generally designed to promote law compliance and sound ethical practices that are applicable to the subject company's business. As set forth by SOX, a "code of ethics" refers to such "written standards that are reasonably designed to deter wrongdoing and

---

[115] *Id.* § 229.407(c)(2)(ix).

[116] *Id.*

[117] *Id.* § 229.407(c)(2)(vi).

[118] Securities Exchange Act Release No. 61175 (2009).

[119] *See* Sarbanes-Oxley Act of 2002, Pub. L. No. 107-204 (July 30, 2002) § 406; Item 406 of Regulation S-K, 17 C.F.R. § 229.406 (2017). *See generally* Z. Jill Barclift, *Codes of Ethics and State Fiduciary Duties: Where Is the Line?*, 1 J. Bus. Entrepreneurship & L. 237 (2008); Kimberly D. Krawiec, *Cosmetic Compliance and the Failure of Negotiated Governance*, 81 Wash. U. L.Q. 487 (2003); Donald C. Langavoort, *Placebo Statutes? Sarbanes-Oxley and Ethics Code Disclosures*, 96 Va. L. Rev. in Brief 9 (2010); William S. Laufer, *Corporate Liability, Risk Shifting, and the Paradox of Compliance*, 54 Vand. L. Rev. 1343 (1999); Joshua A. Newberg, *Corporate Codes of Ethics, Mandatory Disclosure, and the Market for Ethical Conduct*, 29 Vt. L. Rev. 253 (2005); Mary Ellen Oliverio, *The Implementation of a Code of Ethics: The Early Efforts of One Entrepreneur*, 8 J. Bus. Ethics 367 (1989); Usha Rodriguez and Mike Stegemoller, *Placebo Ethics*, 96 Va. L. Rev. 1 (2010); John C. Ruhnka and Heidi Boerstler, *Governmental Incentives for Corporate Self-Regulation*, 17 J. Bus. Ethics 309 (1998); discussion in Chapter 6 herein.

[120] *See* discussion Chapter 6 herein. *See generally* Harvey L. Pitt and Karl A. Groskaufmanis, *Minimizing Corporate Civil and Criminal Liability: A Second Look at Corporate Codes of Conduct*, 78 Geo. L.J. 1559 (1990).

to promote: [h]onest and ethical conduct; . . . ethical handling of actual or apparent conflicts of interest between personal and professional relationships; . . . accurate, timely, and understandable disclosure in [SEC] reports and documents . . . and [in the company's] other public communications; [law] [c]ompliance; . . . prompt internal [and appropriate] reporting of violations of the code . . . ; and [a]ccountability for adherence to the code."[121]

Item 406 of SEC Regulation S-K implements this statutory framework by setting forth that the subject company must disclose whether it has adopted a code of ethics for its principal executive officer, principal financial officer, and principal accounting officer or controller, as well as individuals who perform similar functions. Pursuant to SOX and SEC regulation, a code of ethics means:

> [W]ritten standards that are reasonably designed to deter wrongdoing and to promote:
>
> (1) Honest and ethical conduct, including the ethical handling of actual or apparent conflicts of interest between personal and professional relationships;
> (2) Full, fair, accurate, timely, and understandable disclosure in reports and documents that a registrant files with, or submits to, the Commission and in other public communications made by the registrant;
> (3) Compliance with applicable governmental laws, rules and regulations;
> (4) The prompt internal reporting of violations of the code to an appropriate person or persons identified in the code; and
> (5) Accountability for adherence to the code.[122]

In adopting this requirement, the SEC expanded the SOX disclosure directive to encompass whether the subject company has adopted a code of ethics that includes its principal executive officer. If the subject company has not adopted a code of ethics, it must "explain" why it has declined to implement this measure.[123] As discussed in Chapter 6, the NYSE and Nasdaq each has adopted a code of conduct for listed companies that covers directors, officers, and employees.

---

[121] Sarbanes-Oxley Act § 406(c).

[122] 17 C.F.R. § 229.406(b) (2017). *See also* Disclosure Required by Sections 406 and 407 of the Sarbanes-Oxley Act of 2002, Securities Act Release No. 8177 (2003).

[123] Sarbanes-Oxley Act § 406(a). *See also* 1 Buckholz, et al., *supra* note 20, § 1:3, at 1G-3. *Cement & Concrete Workers District Council Pension Fund v. Hewlett Packard Co.*, 2013 WL 4082011 (N.D. Cal. 2013) (ruling CEO's violation of subject company's code of ethics and subsequent firing did not render the company's code of ethics materially misleading).

As set forth above, a code of ethics must provide a system of accountability to help effectuate compliance with the code's directives. In this regard, the code of ethics must identify the "appropriate person or persons" to whom violations of the code of ethics should be reported. To comply with the code's directives, a subject company should implement effective internal mechanisms with respect to the prompt reporting of violations of the code as well as providing sound accountability for adherence.[124]

Instructions to Item 406 of Regulation S-K provide that a company may opt to adopt a code of ethics "for different types of officers."[125] Note that, if a company implements a code of ethics, the company must provide public access to such code. One such method is by posting the text of the company's code of ethics on its website and setting forth in its annual SEC report the website address where such code has been posted.[126] Alternatively, the company may elect to file a copy of the code as an exhibit to its annual report with the Commission.[127] Any amendment to or waiver from a subject company's code of ethics must be publicly disclosed.[128]

While SOX Section 406 declines to mandate that subject companies adopt a code of ethics, this statute and SEC rules thereunder represent another example of federal action impacting corporate governance. Prompted by Congress and the SEC, the New York Stock Exchange[129] and the Nasdaq Stock Market[130] both promulgated rules that require subject companies to adopt codes of ethics as a condition of listing. To help effectuate the subject code's effective implementation, the

---

[124] 17 C.F.R. § 229.406(b)(4)-(5) (2017).

[125] 17 C.F.R. § 229.406 (2017), Instructions to Item 406. *See also* 1 Buckholz, et al., *supra* note 20, § 1:3, at 1G-5.

[126] 17 C.F.R. § 229.406(c)(2) (2017). With respect to the NYSE and Nasdaq rules, *see* NYSE Listed Company Manual § 303A.10 (Nov. 25, 2009), *available at* http://nysemanual.nyse.com/lcm/Help/mapContent.asp?sec=lcm-sections&title=sx-ruling-nyse-policymanual_303A.10&id=chp_1_4_3_11. For the Nasdaq's code of ethics rules, *see* § 5610 (Mar. 12, 2009), *available at* http://nasdaq.cchwallstreet.com/nasdaq/main/nasdaq-equityrules/chp_1_1/chp_1_1_4/chp_1_1_4_3/chp_1_1_4_3_8/default.asp. For further discussion on stock exchange rules in this context, *see* Chapter 6 herein.

[127] 17 C.F.R. § 229.406(c)(1) (2017). A third manner in which a company may provide public access to its code of ethics is to "[u]ndertake in its annual report filed with the Commission to provide to any person without charge, upon request, a copy of such code of ethics and explain the manner in which such request may be made." *Id.* § 406(c)(3).

[128] *Id.* § 229.406(d). *See* Form 8-K, Item 10.

[129] "Listed companies must adopt and disclose a code of business conduct and ethics for directors, officers, and employees, and promptly disclose any waivers of the code for directors and executive officers." NYSE Listed Company Manual § 303A.10. The commentary to the rule lists several significant topics to be included in each company's code of conduct and ethics. *See* NYSE Listed Company Manual § 303A.10 comment. *See* Chapter 6 herein.

[130] Nasdaq Rule 4350(a) provides that "[e]ach issuer shall adopt a code of conduct applicable to all directors, officers and employees, which shall be publicly available. A code of conduct satisfying this rule must comply with the definition of a 'code of ethics' set out in Section 406(c) of the Sarbanes-Oxley Act of 2002 . . . " Nasdaq Stock Market Rules § 4350(a). *See* Chapter 6 herein.

stock exchange rules require listed companies to promulgate compliance procedures and standards.[131]

L. BIFURCATION DISCLOSURE: CEO AND BOARD OF DIRECTORS' CHAIR ROLES

The bifurcation of the CEO position from that of the chair of the board of directors is widely viewed as a salutary corporate governance measure. The rationale is that this practice promotes enhanced impartial oversight of managerial performance and facilitates transparency of the board's decision-making process.[132] Additionally, disclosure of the board leadership structure alerts investors to the structure adopted by the subject company.[133] As discussed earlier in this chapter, Section 972 of the Dodd-Frank Act (codified in Section 14B of the Securities Exchange Act) mandates that subject issuers disclose in their proxy statements whether and why they opt to (or elect not to) bifurcate the two roles.[134] Regulation S-K, Item 407 implements this directive by requiring such disclosure.[135] If the roles are unified, then the subject company must explain if there is a lead independent director on its board of directors and "what specific role [such] lead independent director plays in the leadership of the board."[136]

Significantly, the statute and SEC regulation focus on disclosure of the board's leadership structure, declining to prescribe a mandated CEO/Board Chair framework. Accordingly, companies may opt for the same individual to serve as the CEO and the chair of the board of directors or elect to bifurcate these positions.

---

[131] *See* Securities Exchange Act Release No. 48125, 2003 WL 21523894 (July 2, 2003), which states:

> By expressly setting out the conduct in this manner, Nasdaq intends to provide further assurance to investors, regulators and itself that each of its issuers has in place a system to focus attention throughout the company on the obligation of ethical conduct, encourage reporting of potential violations, and deal fairly and promptly with questionable behavior. A code of conduct provides objective standards for compliance, increasing transparency and accountability in this key area.

See also Retail Wholesale & Dep't Store Union Local 338 Retirement Fund v. Hewlett-Packard Co., 845 F.3d 1208 (9th Cir. 2017) (holding that CEO's alleged violation of company's corporate code of ethics did not give rise to a duty to disclose and that subject information was not material).

Hence, the requirement "is intended to demonstrate to investors that the board and management of Nasdaq issuers have carefully considered the requirements of ethical dealing and have put in place a system to ensure that they become aware of and take prompt action against any questionable behavior." *Id. See* discussion Chapter 6 herein.

[132] *Dodd-Frank Wall Street Reform and Consumer Protection Act: Law, Explanation, and Analysis*, ¶ 4335 (CCH Attorney-Editor Publ. 2010).

[133] *See* Proxy Disclosure and Solicitation Enhancements, Securities Exchange Act Release No. 60280 (2009).

[134] Section 14B of the Securities Exchange Act, 15 U.S.C. § 78n-2 (2012); discussion *supra* notes 85–87 and accompanying text.

[135] 17 C.F.R. § 229.407(h) (2017).

[136] *Id. See also* Paul Rose, *Regulating Risk by "Strengthening Corporate Governance,"* 17 Conn. Ins. L.J. 1, 10 (2010).

Irrespective of the approach adopted, a subject company is to "indicate why [it] has determined that its leadership structure is appropriate given the [company's] specific characteristics or circumstances. . . ."[137]

M. SAY-ON-PAY AND GOLDEN PARACHUTES—ADVISORY VOTES

1. "Say on Pay"

As more extensively addressed in Chapter 4, Section 951 of the Dodd-Frank Act amended the Securities Exchange Act by adding Section 14A, requiring a subject company to conduct a separate shareholder advisory vote to approve the compensation of its executives (as disclosed under Item 402 of Regulation S-K or any successor thereto). Pursuant to the statute, such company's shareholders are entitled to cast an advisory non-binding vote on executive officers' compensation, known as the "say-on-pay provision," as well as with respect to "golden parachutes."[138] The "say on pay" provision, although not setting any parameters with respect to executive remuneration, guarantees that shareholders have a "voice" regarding executive pay practices. Hence, while the "say-on-pay" provision does not bind the company (or its board of directors) in determining the amount of executive officer compensation, it nevertheless instills a certain measure of shareholder activism, thereby enabling the company to ascertain the views of its shareholders with respect to the propriety of its executive remuneration practices.[139] Accordingly, the "say-on-pay" provision

---

[137] *See* Proxy Disclosure and Solicitation Enhancements, Securities Exchange Act Release No. 60280 (2009).

[138] Dodd-Frank Act § 951, *amending*, Securities Exchange Act § 14A, 15 U.S.C. § 78n-1 (2012). The shareholder vote is not binding on the company and does not impose any additional fiduciary duty on directors. Similarly, the advisory vote does not restrict shareholders' ability to make proposals for inclusion in the proxy materials related to executive compensation. *See* Securities Exchange Act § 14A(c). Note that an emerging growth company may elect to opt out of these advisory votes. *See* § 14A(d)(2).

[139] *See* Shareholder Approval of Executive Compensation and Golden Parachute Compensation, Securities Exchange Act Release No. 63768 (2011); Dodd-Frank Law, Explanation, and Analysis, *supra* note 132, at 421. *See also* the testimony of Ann Yerger, representing the Council of Institutional Investors, who explained the purpose of this provision:

> [A]n annual, advisory shareowner vote on executive compensation would efficiently and effectively provide boards with useful information about whether investors view the company's compensation practices to be in shareowners' best interests. Nonbinding shareowner votes on pay would serve as a direct referendum on the decisions of the compensation committee and would offer a more targeted way to signal shareowner discontent than withholding votes from committee members. They might also induce compensation committees to be more careful about doling out rich rewards, to avoid the embarrassment of shareowner rejection at the ballot box. In addition, compensation committees looking to actively rein in executive compensation could use the results of advisory shareowner votes to stand up to excessively demanding officers or compensation consultants.

S. Rep. No. 111-176, p. 134. Nonetheless, "[t]he median [annual] pay for CEOs at the biggest U.S. companies was $11.7 million in 2016 . . . a post-recession record. . . ." Wall St. J., June 1, 2017, at A1.

sets forth that, at least once every three years, a separate resolution for shareholder approval of executive compensation must be undertaken.[140] Additionally, the "say-on-pay" provision requires a subject company to hold a separate shareholder advisory vote to decide how frequently the company will conduct an advisory shareholder vote on executive compensation—namely, whether such vote is to occur annually, biannually, or triannually.[141]

2. "Golden Parachutes"

With respect to "golden parachutes," the subject company's shareholders are entitled either to have a separate non-binding vote on executive golden parachute compensation or an advisory vote on this matter when they cast their "say-on-pay" vote.[142] Pursuant to SEC rule-making regarding disclosure of these arrangements as well as shareholder advisory approval in regard thereto, the Commission stated:

> ... [C]ompanies are required to provide additional disclosure regarding compensation arrangements with executive officers in connection with merger transactions, known as "golden parachute" arrangements. Disclosure is required of all agreements and understandings that the acquiring and target companies have with the named executive officers of both companies. The rule requires this disclosure in both narrative and tabular formats.

---

[140] Securities Exchange Act § 14A(a)(1). *See* Item 402 of Regulation S-K, 17 C.F.R. § 229.402 (2017).

[141] Securities Exchange Act § 14A(a)(2). *See* Rule 14a-21, 17 C.F.R. § 240.14a-21 (2017). For further discussion, *see* Chapter 4 herein. *See generally More Companies Back Annual Shareholder Say on CEO Pay*, 49 Sec. Reg. & L. Rep. (BNA) 730 (2017) (stating most U.S. publicly-held companies "give investors an annual 'say-on-pay' in the form of an advisory vote on pay packages"); *So Far in Proxy Season, 32 Companies from Russell 3000 Fail Say-on-Pay Votes*, 47 Sec. Reg. & L. Rep. (BNA) 1227 (2015) (stating that 32 corporations in the Russell 3000 Index as of June 10, 2015, "failed their say-on-pay votes" for that year); Emily Chasen, *Companies Say 'No Way' to 'Say on Pay'*, Wall St. J. Aug. 26, 2014, at B1 (stating that two dozen companies, including Oracle Corp., "keep giving top officers sky-high pay packages and luxury perks despite shareholder ire"); Suzanne Kapner, et al., *Citigroup Investors Reject Pay Plan*, Wall St. J. April 18, 2012, at A1 (stating that Citigroup shareholders "handed the bank a scathing rebuke, rejecting a board-approved compensation package for its senior executives"); Minor Myers, *The Perils of Shareholder Voting on Executive Compensation*, 36 Del. J. Corp. L. 417, 418 (2011) (proposing that the Dodd-Frank Act be amended to permit subject companies "to opt-out of the say-on-pay regime by shareholder vote"). *See also* David J. Berger, et al., *Tenure Voting and the U.S. Public Company*, 72 Bus. Law. 295 (2017) (exploring the tenure voting model whereby this structure "awards long-term stockholders more votes per share than short-term stockholders"); Mary J. Mullany, *Shareholder Approval of Equity Plans—Current Considerations*, 49 Rev. Sec. & Comm. Reg. 93 (2016) (addressing "current considerations for procuring shareholder approval of equity plans, including the new Institutional Shareholder Services Scorecard evaluation system and the rise of litigation relating to equity plan disclosures and non-employee director compensation").

[142] Securities Exchange Act § 14A(b)(2). "Golden parachutes generally are generous severance benefits that high level executives receive upon a 'change in control' of the company." Steinberg, *supra* note 11, at 189.

The "golden parachute" disclosure also is required in connection with other transactions, including going-private transactions and third-party tender offers, so that the information is available for shareholders no matter the structure of the transaction.

The rules require companies to provide a separate shareholder advisory vote to approve certain "golden parachute" compensation arrangements in connection with a merger, acquisition, consolidation, proposed sale or other disposition of all or substantially all assets. Companies are required to comply with the golden parachute compensation shareholder advisory vote and disclosure requirements in proxy statements and other schedules and forms . . . filed [with the SEC].[143]

N. INTERNAL PAY EQUITY DISCLOSURE

Section 953(b)(1) of the Dodd-Frank Act directed the SEC to amend Regulation S-K, Item 402 to mandate that a subject issuer disclose in its annual report and proxy statement the following: (1) the median of the yearly total compensation of all its employees, except the chief executive officer; (2) the CEO's annual total compensation; and (3) the ratio of these two amounts. [144] In 2015, the SEC added Regulation S-K Item 402(u), requiring such disclosures.[145] With the Commission adopting the regulation by a narrow (3 to 2) vote, then SEC Chair Mary Jo White commented: "To say that the views on the pay ratio disclosure requirement are divided is an obvious understatement. Since it was mandated by Congress, the pay ratio rule has been controversial, spurring a contentious and, at times, heated dialogue."[146] Proponents of the pay ratio rule assert that the disclosures are significant for investors as they enhance transparency with respect to executive compensation.

---

[143] SEC Adopts Rules for Say-on-Pay and Golden Parachute Compensation as Required under Dodd-Frank Act, SEC Press Release No. 2011-25 (Jan. 25, 2011). *See* Shareholder Approval of Executive Compensation and Golden Parachute Compensation, Securities Exchange Act Release No. 63768 (2011). Hence, the solicitation of the shareholder vote on the golden parachute compensation must disclose "in a clear and simple form in accordance with [SEC] regulations" any agreement or understanding concerning compensation between the subject issuer and any named executive. *See* § 14A(b)(1) of the Securities Exchange Act.

[144] Dodd-Frank Act § 953(b)(1)(A)-(C).

[145] 17 C.F.R. § 229.402(u) (2017). *See* Securities Exchange Act Release No. 75610 (2015). In addition, enhanced requirements have been added to Regulation S-K, Item 402 in regard to an issuer's disclosure of stock and option awards to subject executives. *See generally* Proxy Disclosure and Solicitation Enhancements, Securities Exchange Act Release No. 60280 (2009).

[146] *SEC Adopts CEO Pay Ratio Rule, Adds Flexibility for Company Calculations*, 47 Sec. Reg. & L. Rep. (BNA) 1557 (2015). The Commission received more than 287,400 comment letters addressing the rule proposal. *See* Jayne E. Juvan, *SEC Rule Requires Disclosure of CEO Pay to Median Pay of Employees*, 47 Sec. Reg. & Rep. (BNA) 1756 (2015).

Also, such disclosure, according to proponents, may deter excessive remuneration practices that adversely impact employee morale and that also may have contributed to the 2008 financial crisis.[147] To the contrary, critics assert that compliance with the rule will impose undue costs and burdens on the affected company, subjecting such company to adverse publicity (such as negative press coverage) and failing to provide meaningful information to shareholders.[148] With the pay ratio rule's adoption by the SEC, companies need to be proactive in dealing with the fallout that may ensue from damaging media coverage and other adverse developments.[149] Nonetheless, vigorous debate continues with respect to this rule, signifying that the controversy is still unresolved—and with the prevailing policies of Congress and the Trump Administration—perhaps resulting in the SEC's repeal of the rule, or congressional legislation mandating this course of action.[150]

O. PAY VERSUS PERFORMANCE DISCLOSURE

Another provision that pertains to executive compensation is the "pay versus performance" disclosure that is to be set forth in a subject company's annual proxy statement.[151] Under Section 953 of the Dodd-Frank Act, the SEC is directed to prescribe a rule that requires a subject company[152] to disclose the correlation, or lack thereof, between such company's financial performance and the actual executive compensation paid.[153] The disclosure under this provision is to include "information that shows the relationship between executive compensation actually paid and

[147] *See* Juvan, *supra* note 146, at 1756.

[148] *Id.* at 1756–57. *See* Victor M. Resenzweig, *SEC Adopts Final Rule on Pay Ratio Disclosure*, 43 Sec. Reg. L.J. 397 (2015) ("Although the final Rule gives companies flexibility in allowing companies to identify its median employee, the company must disclose the methodology, assumptions and estimates that it uses to ascertain such median employee.").

[149] *See* Juvan, *supra* note 146, at 1757. Of course, negative public reaction may arise from the overall compensation disclosure that must be provided in accordance with Regulation S-K, Item 402 as well as the shareholder advisory say-on-pay vote. *See generally CEOs Earn 347 Times What U.S. Workers Make, Tracker Shows*, 49 Sec. Reg. & L. Rep. (BNA) 773 (2017) (based on a tracker from a federation of labor unions).

[150] *See* H.R. 414, 114th Cong. (2015), S. 1722, 114th Cong. (2015) (both bills aimed at repealing the SEC's pay ratio rule); *SEC Changes Threaten Local Taxes Targeting High CEO Pay*, 49 Sec. Reg. & L. Rep. (BNA) 457 (2017) (stating that the new composition of SEC Commissioners "is likely to alter or kill its pay-ratio rule"); Alla Zayenchik, *SEC Reconsiders CEO-to-Worker Pay Ratio Rule*, The Advocate for Institutional Shareholders at 12 (Summer 2017), *available at* www.blbglaw.com ("On February 6, 2017, Acting SEC Chairman Michael S. Piwowar announced that the Commission is reconsidering the implementation of the CEO-to-Worker Pay Ratio Rule.").

[151] Dodd-Frank Act § 953, *adding*, Securities Exchange Act § 14(i), 15 U.S.C. § 78n(i) (2012).

[152] Emerging growth companies, for example, may be excluded from the provision. *See* the Jumpstart Our Business Startups Act ("JOBS Act") § 102(a)(2), Pub. L. No. 112-106, 126 Stat. 306 (2012).

[153] 15 U.S.C. § 78n(i) (2012). *See* Pay versus Performance, Securities Exchange Act Release No. 74835 (2015) (proposing amendments to Regulation S-K, Item 402).

the [company's] financial performance, taking into account the change in the value of the shares of stock, . . . dividends . . . and any distributions."[154] The rationale is that shareholders should be apprised when executive compensation is significantly increasing while financial performance is falling.[155] Such disclosures, proponents assert, should help enable shareholders to compare the level of executive compensation with the company's overall performance. Nonetheless, to date, the SEC has proposed but not adopted a rule implementing this statute.

P. LOANS TO INSIDERS

In a clear "intrusion" on traditional state corporate governance matters, Section 402 of SOX bars a publicly-held issuer from making loans to its directors as well as executive officers.[156] Prior to SOX, publicly-held companies routinely extended attractive loans to corporate insiders under permissive state law standards.[157] Insider loans gained the spotlight of Congressional attention once it became widely known that several companies extended such loans contrary to shareholders' and employees' best interests.[158] In response thereto, SOX generally prohibits a publicly-held company from making loans to its directors and executive officers.

To a limited degree, Section 402 excludes certain loans from its ban. For example, the statute provides exceptions, if specified conditions are met, with respect to "any home improvement and manufactured home loans," "consumer credit" loans, extensions of credit by registered broker-dealers to their employees "to buy, trade, or carry securities," or "any loan made or maintained by an insured depository institution . . . if the loan is subject to [applicable] insider lending restrictions . . . of the Federal Reserve Act."[159] To be excluded from the Section 402 loan prohibition, home improvement loans, consumer credit loans, and extensions of credit by a

---

[154] Securities Exchange Act § 14(i), as added by the Dodd-Frank Act. *See* Theo Francis and Joann S. Lublin, *Should Bar Be Lifted on CEO Bonuses?*, Wall St. J., June 2, 2017, at B3 (stating that some investors are expressing concern that performance goals are set too low by boards, thereby enabling executive bonuses based on these goals to be triggered without excellent performance as compared to the market).

[155] S. Rep. No. 111-176, p. 135. *See Dodd-Frank Law, Explanation, and Analysis, supra* note 132, at 425.

[156] SOX § 402, *adding*, § 13(k) of the Securities Exchange Act, 15 U.S.C. § 78m(k) (2012).

[157] *See, e.g., Lewis v. Aronson*, 473 A.2d 475 A.2d 805, 817 (Del. 1984) (in response to assertion that extending interest-free loan by board of directors to company executive was a breach of fiduciary duty, stating "the mere existence of such loans, given the broad corporate powers conferred by Delaware law, does not even state a claim").

[158] *See* Roberta Romano, *The Sarbanes-Oxley Act and the Making of Quack Corporate Governance*, 114 Yale L.J. 1521, 1538 (2005). *See id.* at 1539 (asserting "[b]ecause executive loans in many cases appear to serve their purpose of increasing managerial stock ownership, thereby aligning managers' and shareholders' interests, the blanket prohibition of executive loans in SOX is self-evidently a public policy error").

[159] 15 U.S.C. § 78m(k)(2) (2012).

broker or dealer must: (1) be made in the "ordinary course" of the enterprise's consumer credit business, (2) be "of a type that is generally made available [by such enterprise] to the public," and (3) be made by such enterprise on the same market terms as "those offered . . . to the general public for such extensions of credit."[160] Examples of transactions that are viewed as still permissible under SOX include: (1) indemnification advances by a corporation to its directors and executive officers pursuant to such corporation's certification of incorporation or bylaws, or pursuant to employment agreements;[161] (2) "*bona fide* business-related advances, such as travel advances or company credit cards used primarily for business purposes of the issuer, made or used in the ordinary course of business and repaid promptly in accordance with reasonable business practices";[162] (3) personal use of a company automobile, regardless of whether reimbursement must be made; (4) certain forms of "split-dollar" life insurance; (5) loans from 401(k) plans; and (6) cashless option exercises.[163]

Q. EQUITABLE RELIEF AND MONEY PENALTIES

As discussed earlier in this chapter,[164] the SEC may seek expansive equitable relief as well as money penalties. For instance, disgorgement is an example of a sanction that the SEC has invoked for several decades to prevent unjust enrichment and to deter wrongdoing by compelling such defendants to relinquish ill-gotten gains.[165] From a general perspective, disgorgement has received

[160] *Id.* § 78m(k)(2)(A)–(C).

[161] Buckholz, et al., *supra* note 20, § 5:5, at 5N-14 ("Indemnification advances should not be seen to violate section 402. At the time the commitment to make the advance is made (generally at the outset of employment), and presumably even when the advance occurs, the director or officer's obligation to repay is truly contingent and that contingency makes the likelihood that repayment will be required reasonably uncertain. . . .").

[162] *Id.* at 5N-16.

[163] *See id.* at 5N-17, 5N-18 (discussing how some forms of split-dollar life insurance, such as "equity" or "loan regime" arrangements, are prohibited under § 402, whereas others, such as "non-equity" or "economic benefit," should not be in conflict with § 402). *See also* James Hamilton and Ted Trautmann, *Sarbanes-Oxley Act of 2002—Law and Explanation* 64 (2002).

[164] *See supra* notes 55–59 and accompanying text.

[165] Securities Act, § 22(a); 15 U.S.C. § 77v(a) (2012); Securities Exchange Act § 27, 15 U.S.C. § 78aa (2012). *See, e.g., SEC v. Manor Nursing Ctrs., Inc.*, 458 F.2d 1082, 1102 (2d Cir. 1972); *SEC v. Texas Gulf Sulphur Co.*, 446 F.2d 1301, 1307 (2d Cir. 1971); *see also* Elaine Buckberg and Frederick C. Dunbar, *Disgorgement: Punitive Demands and Remedial Offers*, 63 Bus. Law 347, 349–50 (2008). In 2017, the Supreme Court held that disgorgement is punitive within the meaning of 28 U.S.C. § 2462 and, accordingly, a five-year statute of limitations applies. *See Kokesh v. Securities and Exchange Commission*, 137 S. Ct. 1635 (2017). In an accompanying footnote, the Supreme Court stated:

> Nothing in this opinion should be interpreted as an opinion on whether courts possess authority to order disgorgement in SEC enforcement proceedings or on whether courts have properly applied

judicial approbation in SEC enforcement proceedings for several decades in cases, involving, for example, insider trading, financial fraud, and broker-dealer misconduct.[166] With respect to clawbacks, the Dodd-Frank Act specifically authorizes the disgorgement remedy against executive officers whereas only CEOs and CFOs are subject to this remedy under SOX.[167]

In addition, the SEC may seek (and the subject court may order) monetary penalties against any person for violating the federal securities laws if it is determined that the penalty is in the public interest.[168] Generally, the amount of the penalty levied is directly proportionate to the violation's severity as well as the degree of harm inflicted.[169] With respect to monetary penalties, a five-year statute of limitations applies.[170] Notably, where disgorgement or a money penalty is ordered, the

> disgorgement principles in this context. The sole question presented in this case is whether disgorgement, as applied in SEC enforcement actions, is subject to § 2462's limitations period.

Id. at 1642 n.3. Judicial interpretation of the above language may well result in differing approaches being adopted by the federal district and appellate courts.

166 *See* cases cited in Steinberg and Ferrara, *supra* note 56, at § 5:9 (and 2017–2018 supp.). At times, disgorgement has been ordered even though the court denied the Commission's request for an injunction. *See, e.g., SEC v. Commonwealth Chem. Sec., Inc.*, 574 F.2d 90 (2d Cir. 1978). As stated by one federal court: "To prevent unjust enrichment and to deter others from violating the securities laws, the Court has broad equity powers to order defendants to disgorge all illicit gains and impose prejudgment interest on those gains." *SEC v. Poirier*, 140 F. Supp. 2d 1033, 1047 (D. Ariz. 2001); discussion *supra* notes 55–59 and accompanying text.

167 *See* discussion *supra* notes 41–54 and accompanying text.

168 Section 21(d)(3), 15 U.S.C. § 78u(d)(3) (2012).

169 Monetary penalties are divided into three tiers, with each successive tier triggering greater penalties due to the nature of the violation and injury caused. *See* 15 U.S.C. § 78u-2(b) (2012). *See* Steinberg and Ferrara, *supra* note 56 at §§ 5:8, 6:8-6:11 (discussing monetary penalties as authorized by congressional legislation, SEC enforcement actions in regard thereto, and court decisions construing these penalty provisions). With respect to the imposition of monetary civil penalties based on violations of the federal securities laws, the amount levied is to be decided in view of the facts and circumstances. The penalty for a subject violation is subject to a three-tier maximum amount for such violation. The tiers may be summarized as follows:

> The penalties are subject to three-tier maximums for each "violation." First, [with respect to so-called technical violations,] the maximum is the greater of $5,000 for a natural person or $50,000 for a corporation or other entity, or the "gross amount of pecuniary gain to such defendant" resulting from the violation. Second, if the violation included "fraud, deceit, manipulation, or deliberate disregard of a regulatory requirement," the maximums are $50,000 and $250,000, respectively, or the gross pecuniary gain. Third, if the violation in addition resulted in or created, directly or indirectly, "substantial losses" or "a significant risk of substantial losses to others," the maximums are $100,000 [for a natural person] and $500,000 [for a corporation or other entity], or the gross pecuniary gain.

To Our Clients: Memorandum from Wachtell, Lipton, Rosen & Katz, *SEC Enforcement Powers and Remedies Are Greatly Expanded* (1990). *See generally* Arthur Laby and W. Hardy Callcott, *Patterns of SEC Enforcement under the 1990 Remedies Act: Civil Money Penalties*, 58 Albany L. Rev. 5 (1994); Seth McNew, *Money Penalties against Publicly-Held Companies: A Proposal for Restraint*, 37 Sec. Reg. L.J. 48 (2008).

170 *See e.g.*, 28 U.S.C. § 2462 (2012). *See also Gabelli v. SEC*, 568 U.S. 442 (2013).

SEC may establish a "Fair Fund" payable to aggrieved investors in order to help offset their financial losses due to the defendants' misconduct.[171]

III. Conclusion

With the election of George W. Bush as President, it was assumed that further deregulation of the securities markets would ensue. Rather, in the wake of massive financial scandals, Congress enacted the Sarbanes-Oxley Act of 2002—the most pro-regulatory securities legislation since the Securities Exchange Act of 1934. Undoubtedly, SOX contained meaningful disclosure provisions, such as the embracement of a continual disclosure regime.[172] In addition, the oversight of the accounting profession was greatly enhanced by the creation of the PCAOB.[173] Nonetheless, the Act's main focus was to federalize state corporation law in several aspects—thereby going far beyond the disclosure framework that serves as the foundation of federal regulation.[174]

Eight years later, in reaction to the financial crisis, Congress enacted the Dodd-Frank Act of 2010, which impacted further the federalization of state company law and policy. Director independence—both on board committees and the board itself—today is an accepted practice for publicly-held companies. Indeed, these Acts and their impact on the SEC tell a large part—but not all—of the story. Due to mandates set forth in SOX and the Dodd-Frank Act, stock exchange regulation today plays a key role in the enhancement of corporate governance standards. This important aspect—stock exchange regulation—is addressed in the next chapter of this book.

---

[171] Sarbanes-Oxley Act § 308. *See Official Committee of Unsecured Creditors of WorldCom, Inc. v. SEC*, 467 F.3d 73 (2d Cir. 2006) (affirming "Fair Fund" of $750 million to be distributed to aggrieved WorldCom investors); Steinberg, *supra* note 11, at 187.

[172] *See* § 409 of the Sarbanes-Oxley Act, 15 U.S.C. § 78m(l) (2012) (requiring publicly-held companies to "disclose to the public on a rapid and current basis such additional information concerning material changes in the financial condition or operations of the issuer, in plain English, ... as the Commission determines, by rule...."); Securities Exchange Act Release No. 49424 (2004) (expansion of SEC Form 8-K to comply with this SOX mandate).

[173] The PCAOB is not a federal government agency; rather, it is a nonprofit corporation that "has sweeping powers to establish quality control, ethical, and accounting standards for accounting firms [and] also has the power and authority to inspect, investigate, and bring disciplinary proceedings against public auditing firms." M. Steinberg, *supra* note 6, at 291. The constitutionality of the PCAOB generally was upheld by the U.S. Supreme Court in *Free Enter. Bd. v. PCAOB*, 561 U.S. 477 (2010).

[174] Steinberg, *supra* note 2, at 358–59 (also stating that "[h]opefully, the enactment of the Sarbanes-Oxley Act as well as vigorous implementation and enforcement of its provisions will help restore investor confidence in the integrity of our financial markets").

6

THE IMPACT OF STOCK EXCHANGE RULES ON THE FEDERALIZATION OF CORPORATE GOVERNANCE

I. Introduction

Assessment of the federalization of corporate governance focuses on the enactment of federal legislation, bills introduced in Congress, decisions by the federal courts, and actions undertaken by the Securities and Exchange Commission (SEC). This book covers in depth these subjects. Also of importance are the corporate governance rules promulgated by the national stock exchanges. Responding to federal legislative and SEC directives and, at times, acting on their own initiative, the stock exchanges have promulgated meaningful rules that comprise a significant component of this landscape. Accordingly, this chapter addresses key measures undertaken by the stock exchanges that impact the federalization of corporate governance.

II. Overview of Stock Exchange Regulation Impacting Corporate Governance

The New York Stock and Exchange Board (Board) was formed in 1817 and in 1863 became the New York Stock Exchange (NYSE or Exchange).[1] Adopting a small set

[1] Stuart Banner, *The Origin of the New York Stock Exchange, 1791–1860*, 27 J. Legal Stud. 113, 114, 115 (1998). As stated by the author:

> A small number of early nineteenth-century New York stockbrokers built, from scratch, an organization that by the end of the century would be one of the most powerful nongovernmental bodies in the world.

of rules to regulate trading and membership, the Board continued a trend toward the self-regulation of stock exchanges and brokers.[2] During the nineteenth century, each company listed on the NYSE signed an individual listing agreement because the NYSE lacked a uniform set of listing standards.[3]

Initially, the NYSE's primary governance focus was on financial disclosure. Subsequently, this focus expanded to encompass additional corporate governance measures. For example, by 1900, NYSE listing agreements required subject companies to provide annual reports to stockholders.[4] In 1909, the Exchange required listed companies to hold an annual stockholder meeting.[5] These actions were followed by additional NYSE corporate governance listing rules in the first four decades of the twentieth century. Examples include: requiring notification to the NYSE of changes in shareholder rights (1914), providing of a semiannual balance sheet and income statement (1917), requiring quarterly earnings reports (1923), and promulgating a corporate publicity policy (1928).[6]

> The origin and the early growth of the New York Stock and Exchange Board can be attributed in large part to the brokers' success in regulating themselves, a success that enabled them to create wealth and to capture wealth from nonmenbers. . . .

Id. at 113. *See generally* Comment, *Stock Exchange Listing Agreement as a Vehicle for Corporate Governance*, 129 U. Pa. L. Rev. 1427 (1981).

[2] Banner, *supra* note 1, at 114–15. (stating that the earliest indication of self-regulation by U.S. brokers dates back to September 1791).

[3] Special Study Group of the Committee on Federal Regulation of Securities, Section of Business Law, American Bar Association, *Special Study on Market Structure, Listing Standards and Corporate Governance*, 57 Bus. Law. 1487, 1497–98 (2002) (pointing out that enforcement of listing standards at this time was simply a matter of contract law).

[4] *Id.* at 1498.

[5] *Id.*

[6] *Id.* at 1498–99. Some of these listing rules have survived. *See, e.g.,* NYSE Listed Company Manual (hereinafter NYSE Manual) § 204.23 (requiring a minimum of 20 days notice to NYSE when a listed company proposes changing rights or privileges of listed securities). Others have been modified or deleted. *See, e.g.,* Securities Exchange Act Release No. 54344, 2006 WL 3472381 (Aug. 21, 2006) (allowing a listed company to post its annual finance report (e.g., Form 10-K) "on or by a link through its corporate Web site" instead of distributing the report directly to shareholders). *See* NYSE Manual § 203.01. Note that the one-share, one-vote listing standard also has been diluted as companies listing their stock on the NYSE pursuant to an initial public offering (IPO) now may have disparate voting rights for their common stock (e.g., Google), or, indeed, no-voting rights for a class of common stock (e.g., Snap). *See* Weil, Kaitlin Descovich, et al., *Governance & Securities Alert—Voting Rights Gone in a Snap—Unequal Voting Rights Back in the Spotlight* (Apr. 3, 2017).

Although by the early 1900s stock exchanges had been operating in the United States for approximately a century, some sources have posited that the lack of a systematic disclosure system for adequately informing stockholders was due to the fact that bonds were the most issued securities until 1928. *See* A.C. Pritchard, *Markets as Monitors: A Proposal to Replace Class Actions with Exchanges as Securities Fraud Enforcers*, 85 Va. L. Rev. 925, 1009 (1999). Due to its perceived sense of safety, bond trading generally did not require the amount of information that stock trading did. *Id.* at 1009 n.360. Therefore, far-reaching disclosure standards were viewed as unnecessary.

It would not be until the mid-1980s that Nasdaq (formed in 1971) would create similar rules, such as providing annual and periodic reports to stockholders, appointment of independent directors, establishment of an independent audit committee, and enhanced shareholder participation in specified corporate transactions.[7] By that time, the NYSE listing rules had expanded to include similar requirements. For example, in 1977, the SEC approved the NYSE rule requiring a listed company to have an audit committee composed entirely of independent directors.[8]

In 1934, the SEC stepped into the fray by means of Section 19 of the Securities Exchange Act.[9] Section 19(b)(1) requires self-regulatory organizations (SROs) to submit proposed rule changes to the Commission for its approval.[10] Section 19(b) describes the approval process at length, and subsection (c) details the SEC's power to amend SRO rules.[11] Although the statutory language sets forth the applicable procedures, relatively sparse attention is paid to the standards the SEC must or should use in deciding whether to approve an SRO rule. Section 19(c) can be read to provide three general bases for regulation: "(1) assurance of fair administration of self-regulatory organizations, (2) conformity to the requirements of the [Securities] Exchange Act, and (3) promulgation of rules otherwise in furtherance of the Act's

---

[7] Special Study Group, *supra* note 3, at 1502. For another excellent history of corporate governance listing standards, *see* Douglas C. Michael, *Untenable Status of Corporate Governance Listing Standards under the Securities Exchange Act*, 47 Bus. Law. 1461, 1465–76 (1992) (also addressing the corporate governance listing standards of the American Stock Exchange (Amex)):

> Most of the Amex's listing standards were first set in the early 1960s, during a comprehensive reform of the Amex.... The first "meaningful" quantitative listing requirements imposing minimum public shareholdings and stock prices came into effect in 1962, and a stricter voting rights policy was announced the following year. At about the same time, listing standards requiring proxy solicitation and shareholder approval of certain stock issuances first appeared....

Id. at 1473, *citing*, Report of Special Study of Securities Markets of the Securities and Exchange Commission, H.R. Doc. No. 95, 88th Cong., 1st Sess. (1963).

[8] *See In the Matter of New York Stock Exchange, Inc.*, Securities Exchange Act Release No. 13346, 1977 WL 173602 (Mar. 9, 1977). This independent audit committee listing standard was not adopted pursuant to the NYSE's own initiative but rather pursuant to the SEC's "suggestion." *See* Homer Kripke, *The SEC, Corporate Governance and the Real Issues*, 36 Bus. Law. 178, 190 (1980); Michael, *supra* note 7, at 1471–72.

[9] *See* 15 U.S.C. § 78s (2012).

[10] Securities Exchange Act of 1934, § 19(b)(1), *codified*, 15 U.S.C. § 78s(b)(1) (2012).

[11] *See id.* at § 78s(b)(1) ("Each self-regulatory organization shall file with the Commission, in accordance with such rules as the Commission may prescribe, copies of any proposed rule or any proposed change in addition to, or deletion from the rules of such self-regulatory organization...."); *id.* at § 78s(c) ("The Commission, by rule, may abrogate, add to, and delete from ... the rules of a self-regulatory organization ... as the Commission deems necessary or appropriate to insure the fair administration of the self-regulatory organization...."). Irrespective of this language, Professor (and former SEC Commissioner) Roberta Karmel opined that "until 1975, exchange listing standards were clearly the subject of private or contract law between an exchange and listed companies." Roberta Karmel, *Qualitative Standards for "Qualified Securities": SEC Regulation of Voting Rights*, 36 Cath. U. L. Rev. 809, 828 (1987).

purpose."[12] As a generality, most of the Exchange Act's rules in this context are procedural, disclosure-based, or focused on fraud,[13] leaving the adoption of corporate governance listing standards normally to be crafted by the exchanges themselves.[14] This regimen aligns with the Exchange Act's treatment of SROs: allowing them to maneuver while retaining SEC oversight—a system meant to enhance effective corporate governance while alleviating the Commission's ongoing burden.[15]

Notwithstanding the powers originally granted in 1934 to the SEC with respect to SROs, it may be asserted that, generally, the Commission did not play a meaningful role with respect to corporate governance SRO listing standards until 1975. That year Congress passed the Securities Reform Act (the 1975 Amendments),[16] seeking to require more effective government oversight of the national exchanges' self-regulation.[17] As the U.S. Court of Appeals for the Second Circuit put it: "The legislative history of the 1975 Amendments indicates that their purpose was to make the hybrid scheme of self-regulation and government regulation work better. . . ."[18] The 1975 Amendments thus facilitated the emergence of the modern era of stock exchange oversight. Indeed, the 1975 Amendments empowered the SEC to censure national exchanges.[19] These Amendments did not displace the existing Section 19 framework; rather, they amplified the SEC's ability to enforce Section 19. It is

---

[12] Thomas Lee Hazen, 5 *Treatise on the Law of Securities Regulation* § 14.1[4] (2015) (quotation marks omitted).

[13] Exceptions to this, such as amendments of the Exchange Act by the Sarbanes-Oxley Act of 2002, Pub. L. 107–204, 116 Stat. 745 (2002), and the Dodd–Frank Wall Street Reform and Consumer Protection Act, Pub. L. 111-203, 124 Stat. 1376 (2010), are addressed more comprehensively in Chapter 5.

[14] James D. Cox and Thomas Lee Hazen, 2 *Treatise on the Law of Corporations* § 9:3 (3d ed. 2015) ("One looks to the listing requirements of the NYSE and Nasdaq, as well as prevailing practices, to find specific requirements to inform us regarding the composition of the board as well as the procedures to be followed for the board to carry out its statutory and fiduciary responsibilities.").

[15] Larry Soderquist and Theresa Gabaldon, *Securities Law (Concepts and Insights)* 186 (2014) (quoting William O. Douglas as describing the SEC's role as keeping "the shotgun, so to speak, behind the door, loaded, well oiled, cleaned, ready for use but with the hope it [will] never have to be used"). Professor Onnig H. Dombalagian suggests that SROs serve a "gatekeeping" function by adopting quantitative (enhancing liquidity) and qualitative (curtailing manipulative and deceptive conduct) listing standards, thereby aligning an SRO's commercial interests with the SEC's regulatory interests. Onnig H. Dombalagian, *Self and Self-Regulation: Resolving the SRO Identity Crisis*, 1 Brook. J. Corp. Fin. & Com. L. 317, 322–23 (2007).

[16] Securities Acts Amendments of 1975, Pub. L. 94-29, 89 Stat. 97 (1975).

[17] *See* Roberta S. Karmel, *Should Securities Industry Self-Regulatory Organizations Be Considered Government Agencies?*, 14 Stan. J.L. Bus. & Fin. 151, 196 (2008) ("At what point did these powers become transmogrified into governmental powers? This was a gradual development, probably finally accomplished without much consideration by the 1975 Act Amendments to the Exchange Act."). *See also* Norman S. Poser and James A. Fanto, *Broker-Dealer Law and Regulation*, 2015 Supplement, 4-34 (4th ed. 2015).

[18] *Feins v. Am. Stock Exchange, Inc.*, 81 F.3d 1215, 1222 (2d Cir. 1996) (discussing the legislative history of the 1975 Amendments).

[19] *See* § 19(h) of the Securities Exchange Act, 15 U.S.C. § 78s(h) (2012). (The SEC may suspend or revoke an SRO's registration, censure such SRO, or levy other sanctions "if in its opinion such action is necessary or appropriate in the public interest, for the protection of investors, or otherwise in furtherance of this Chapter. . . .").

under this regime that the NYSE and Nasdaq formulated their rules in response to the Sarbanes-Oxley Act of 2002 (Sarbanes-Oxley or SOX)[20] and the Dodd-Frank Wall Street Reform and Consumer Protection Act of 2010 (Dodd-Frank).[21] Today, because of these developments, the exchanges and the Commission have significant impact on corporate governance, directives, and practices.

While the exchanges continue to impact the corporate governance of listed companies, the Commission itself attempted to federalize a one share, one vote rule. This resulted in a defeat for the Commission in *Business Roundtable v. SEC*.[22] In the late 1980s, Nasdaq had no listing rules concerning disparate voting rights.[23] Concerned that companies fearful of hostile takeovers would flock to Nasdaq, the NYSE requested SEC approval of a rule allowing under certain conditions the listing of classes of shares having disparate voting rights.[24] Declining to act on the Exchange's proposal, in 1988 the SEC adopted its own rule (Rule 19c-4) that, with certain exceptions, barred exchanges from listing companies that disparately affected per-share voting rights for shareholders—even if approved by shareholders.[25] In its opinion, the U.S. Court of Appeals for the District of Columbia detailed the SEC's stance at oral argument, which was that Section 19 granted the agency

---

[20] Pub. L. 107–204, 116 Stat. 745 (2002).

[21] Pub. L. 111-203, 124 Stat. 1376 (2010). Thus, for example, in 2016, the SEC observed:

> The development, implementation, and enforcement of standards governing the initial and continued listing of securities on an exchange are activities of critical importance to financial markets and the investing public. Listing requirements, among other things, serve as a means for an exchange to provide listed status only to companies that meet certain initial and continued quantitative and qualitative criteria that help to ensure that fair and orderly markets can be maintained once the company is listed. The corporate governance standards embodied in the listing standards of national securities exchanges, in particular, play an important role in assuring that exchange-listed companies observe good governance practices, including that listed companies provide adequate disclosure to allow investors to make informed investment and voting decisions. The Commission has long encouraged exchanges to adopt and strengthen their corporate governance listing standards in order to, among other things, provide greater transparency into the governance processes of listed issuers and enhance investor confidence in the securities markets.

Securities Exchange Act Release No. 78223 (2016).

[22] 905 F.2d 406 (D.C. Cir. 1990) (invalidating SEC Rule 19c-4).

[23] Joel Seligman, *Equal Protection in Shareholder Voting Rights: The One Common Share, One Vote Controversy*, 54 Geo. Wash. L. Rev. 687, 700 (1986) (also pointing out that the Amex also did not have a one share, one vote policy).

[24] *Id.* at 692–93. *See* Securities Exchange Act Release Nos. 23724, 23803 (1986).

[25] *Bus. Roundtable v. SEC*, 905 F.2d 406, 407 (D.C. Cir. 1990). Disparate voting rights plans take many forms, but a simple version is called dual class recapitalization. The company creates a new class of stock that retains all the properties of the original class but with a greater number of votes per share. Transfer restrictions will over time funnel the high-vote shares to long-term investors, namely management. With greater voting control, executives and management are better able to forestall and prevent hostile takeovers. For an excellent discussion of disparate voting rights plans and Rule 19c-4, *see* Stephen M. Bainbridge, *The Short Life and Resurrection of SEC Rule 19c-4*, 69 Wash. U.L.Q. 565 (1991). *See also* discussion *supra* note 6.

"immensely broad" power to do what it thought necessary to "protect investors and the public interest."[26] Rejecting the Commission's position, the appellate court reasoned that the SEC's one share, one vote rule was not consistent with the objectives of the Exchange Act: "If [the one share, one vote rule] were validated on such broad grounds, the Commission would be able to establish a federal corporate law by using access to national capital markets as its enforcement mechanism."[27] Declining to unduly interfere with state corporate governance standards, the court concluded that the SEC lacked authority to amend SRO rules to create a federal corporate governance one share, one vote stock listing mandate.[28]

Drawing such lines around the SEC's power to federalize corporate law seemed more straightforward in 1990. Now, after the enactment of the Sarbanes-Oxley and Dodd-Frank Acts, such lines are harder to decipher. Both Acts expand the powers of the national stock exchanges to set the ground rules for listed companies' corporate governance practices and policies. As addressed in this chapter, national stock exchanges have multifaceted corporate governance rules. This chapter will discuss several of these rules, including those focused on: independent directors; audit, compensation, and nominating committees; and codes of ethics. While the SEC is not itself creating these new stock exchange standards, it is "encouraging" the exchanges to propose these standards and then subsequently approving them for

---

[26] *Bus. Roundtable*, 905 F.2d at 412.

[27] *Id.*

[28] *Id.* at 413 ("We read the Act as reflecting a clear congressional determination not to make any such broad delegation of power to the Commission."). Holding that the SEC exceeded its authority in promulgating Rule 19c-4, the appellate court further reasoned:

> In fact the Commission's apparent perception of its § 19 powers has been immensely broad, unbounded even by any pretense of a connection to § 14. In reviewing the previous SRO rule changes on issues of independent directors and independent audit committees, it grounded its review in a supposed mandate to "protect investors and the public interest." . . . The Commission made no attempt to limit the concept by reference to the concrete purposes of any section. Rather, it reasoned that the rule changes protected investors by "creat[ing] uniformity that helps to assure investors that all the companies traded in those markets have the fundamental safeguards they have come to expect of major companies." . . . If Rule 19c-4 were validated on such broad grounds, the Commission would be able to establish a federal corporate law by using access to national capital markets as its enforcement mechanism. This would resolve a longstanding controversy over the wisdom of such a move in the face of disclaimers from Congress and with no substantive restraints on the power. It would, moreover, overturn or at least impinge severely on the tradition of state regulation of corporate law. As the Supreme Court has said, "[c]orporations are creatures of state law, and investors commit their funds to corporate directors on the understanding that, except where federal law *expressly* requires certain responsibilities of directors with respect to stockholders, state law will govern the internal affairs of the corporation."

Id. at 412, *quoting Santa Fe Ind., Inc. v. Green*, 430 U.S. 462, 497 (1977) (emphasis in original). *See generally* Robert B. Thompson, *Collaborative Corporate Governance: Listing Standards, State Law, and Federal Regulation*, 38 Wake Forest L. Rev. 961 (2003).

implementation. With this regimen now in place, corporate governance today is increasingly within the purview of federal law.

III. Focus on Independent Directors

Boards of directors in publicly held companies have an essential role as the monitor of corporate affairs and policies. Oversight of corporate management is a core board function. Key functions of a publicly-traded company's board of directors encompass "strategic planning, selection (and termination) of executive officers, risk identification, oversight and compensation of senior management, succession planning, communications with shareholders, overseeing the implementation of reasonably extensive financial controls, and adoption and application of law compliance programs."[29] As stated by the Business Roundtable, a publicly-held company's board of directors should:

1. Select, regularly evaluate and, if necessary, replace the chief executive officer. Determine management compensation. Review succession planning.
2. Review and, where appropriate, approve the financial objectives, major strategies, and plans of the corporation.
3. Provide advice and counsel to top management.
4. Select and recommend to shareholders for election an appropriate slate of candidates for the board of directors; evaluate board process and performance.
5. Review the adequacy of systems to comply with all applicable laws/regulations.[30]

Nevertheless, when the board's composition consists of corporate officers and others who are aligned with or beholden to corporate management, the monitored are engaging in the monitoring—thereby compromising the board's oversight function. This arrangement significantly heightens the risk of fiduciary misconduct and lack of objectivity. Seeking to avoid this eventuality, the focus today is on the role of independent directors in the corporate governance framework.[31]

[29] Marc I. Steinberg, *Developments in Business Law and Policy* 145 (2012).

[30] The Business Roundtable, *Corporate Governance and American Competitiveness*, 46 Bus. Law. 241, 246 (1990).

[31] Steinberg, *supra* note 29, at 147.

Under state law, director independence has been linked to the business judgment rule. The Supreme Court of Delaware described director independence as "inher[ing] in the conception and rationale of the business judgment rule."[32] The court reasoned:

> The presumption of propriety that flows from an exercise of business judgment is based in part on this unyielding precept. Independence means that a director's decision is based on the corporate merits of the subject before the board rather than extraneous considerations or influences. While directors may confer, debate, and resolve their differences through compromise, or by reasonable reliance upon the expertise of their colleagues and other qualified persons, the end result, nonetheless, must be that each director has brought his or her own informed business judgment to bear with specificity upon the corporate merits of the issues without regard for or succumbing to influences which convert an otherwise valid business decision into a faithless act. Thus, it is not enough to charge that a director was nominated by or elected at the behest of those controlling the outcome of a corporate election. That is the usual way a person becomes a corporate director. It is the care, attention and sense of individual responsibility to the performance of one's duties, not the method of election, that generally touches on independence.[33]

In several contexts, state courts have addressed the importance of director independence. For example, these situations arise in: related party transactions (including parent-subsidiary cash-out mergers),[34] special litigation committees (SLCs) in the

---

[32] *Aronson v. Lewis*, 473 A.2d 805, 816 (Del. 1984). *See Brehm v. Eisner*, 746 A.2d 244 (Del. 2000).

[33] *Aronson* 473 A.2d at 816. *See In re Oracle Corp. Derivative Litig.*, 824 A.2d 917, 938 (Del. Ch. 2003) ("At bottom, the question of independence turns on whether a director is, for any substantial reason, incapable of making a decision with only the best interests of the corporation in mind"). *See generally* Jeffrey N. Gordon, *The Rise of Independent Directors in the United States, 1950–2005: Of Shareholder Value and Stock Prices*, 59 Stan. L. Rev. 1465 (2007); discussion Chapter 1 herein.

[34] *Kahn v. M & F Worldwide Corp.*, 88 A.3d 635 (Del. 2014) (applying business judgment rule in parent-subsidiary cash-out merger setting if special committee is independent and fulfills its obligations and if merger is approved by an informed vote of the majority of the minority shares, provided no coercion is present); *Weinberger v. UOP, Inc.*, 457 A.2d 701 (Del. 1983) (setting forth standard of entire fairness in parent-subsidiary cash-out merger context); *Boylan v. Boston Sand & Gravel Co.*, No. CIV.A. 02-2296BLS2, 2007 WL 836753, at *11 (Mass. Super. Ct. Mar. 16, 2007) ("An independent and unbiased [board] committee can weigh and balance the diverse factors in a given case and make a business judgment as to the proper course of action.") (quoting *Houle v. Low*, 556 N.E.2d 51, 57 (Mass. 1990)). *See generally* Marc I. Steinberg and Evelyn N. Lindahl, *The New Law of Squeeze-Out Mergers*, 62 Wash. U. L.Q. 351 (1984).

derivative suit setting,[35] and the process by which a target corporation seeks to fend off a hostile takeover bid.[36]

With respect to the stock exchanges, the subject of director independence was not taken up until 1956 when the NYSE recommended that a listed company's board of directors should have two outside directors.[37] The first listing requirement invoking independence was not until 1977, when the NYSE (at the behest of the SEC) made it mandatory for a listed company to maintain an audit committee comprised solely of independent directors.[38] At that time, audit committees were already widely implemented. In 1973, roughly 80 percent of NYSE listed companies had audit committees.[39] Nonetheless, the independence requirement was significant. Pointing to "recent revelations of questionable and illegal corporate payments," the SEC approved the NYSE's audit committee rule, reasoning:

> The NYSE's revision of its listing policies appears to be an appropriate way to implement, at this time, an independent audit committee requirement. Exchange rules are, among other things, required to be designed to remove impediments to and perfect the mechanism of a free and open market, to prevent fraudulent and manipulative acts and practices and, in general, to protect investors and the public interest. In many cases of questionable corporate payments, there were elaborate efforts by corporate executives, including some directors, to conceal their activities from auditors, as well as from other company officials and members of the board, thereby undermining purposes of the Act with which exchanges (and other securities markets) are directly concerned. While independent audit committees will not eliminate all instances of abuse, their establishment can be an important step in a broader effort to remedy the problems of corporate accountability and disclosure that have been uncovered.[40]

---

[35] *See Zapata Corp. v. Maldonado*, 430 A.2d 779, 789 (Del. 1981) (stating a "corporation's best interests [are] expressed by an independent investigating committee"). *See generally* Marc I. Steinberg, *The Use of Special Litigation Committees to Terminate Shareholder Derivative Actions*, 35 U. Miami L. Rev. 1 (1980).

[36] *Unocal Corp. v. Mesa Petroleum Co.*, 493 A.2d 946, 955 (Del. 1985) (stating that proof of good faith and reasonable investigation "is materially enhanced, as here, by the approval of a board comprised of a majority of outside independent directors"). *See generally Tender Offers—Developments and Commentaries* (Marc I. Steinberg, editor 1985); discussion Chapter 1 herein.

[37] *See* Wachtell, Lipton, Rosen & Katz, *The Future of Corporate Governance and the Board of Directors*, Nov. 17, 2010, *available at* http://www.wlrk.com/webdocs/wlrknew/WLRKMemos/WLRK/WLRK.18080.10.pdf.

[38] *See* New York Stock Exchange, Inc., Order Approving Proposed Rule Change, Securities Exchange Act Release No. 13346, 1977 WL 173602 (Mar. 16, 1977).

[39] *Id.* at *1 n.9 (additionally, 13 percent of NYSE companies had plans to form audit committees).

[40] *Id.* at *1 n.2. *See also* Report of the Securities and Exchange Commission on Questionable and Illegal Corporate Payments and Practices, submitted to the Senate Committee on Banking, Housing and Urban Affairs (May

Today, the NYSE test for director independence is multifaceted. First, "[i]n order to tighten the definition" of independence, the listing rules require that a director's independence be "affirmatively determine[d]" by the subject company's board of directors, meaning the director in question has no "material relationship with the listed company."[41] For compensation committee members, the description of independence is taken from the Dodd-Frank Act, consisting of two facts: source of compensation and affiliation.[42] Because many directors work amidst a complicated

---

12, 1976), *available at* http://3197d6d14b5f19f2f440-5e13d29c4c016cf96cbbfd197c579b45.r81.cf1.rackcdn.com/collection/papers/1970/1976_0512_SECQuestionable.pdf (detailing the problem of illegal payments, examples of Commission enforcement, and legislative proposals).

Interestingly, a stock exchange rule that predates what may be viewed as significant corporate governance regulation is the NYSE's 20 percent (20%) rule. Adopted in 1955, this rule generally requires shareholder approval of an issuance of common stock that increases the number of outstanding shares by 20 percent or more. *See* NYSE Stock Exchange Listed Company Manual (hereinafter NYSE Manual) § 312.03(b); Joel Seligman, *Stock Exchange Rules Affecting Takeovers and Control Transactions*, in *Knights, Raiders, and Targets: The Impact of the Hostile Takeover* 482 (John C. Coffee, Jr., et al. eds. 1988). At times, this mandate results in more corporate governance matters being subject to shareholder approval. One such example involves triangular mergers whereby, but for the NYSE rules, a globally-traded company could issue more than 20 percent of its common stock without its shareholders having a vote with respect to such issuance. This situation arose, for example, in the Time-Warner acquisition. *See Paramount Commc'ns, Inc. v. Time, Inc.*, 571 A.2d 1140, 1146 (Del. 1990). With respect thereto, this author reflected:

> The [Delaware Supreme Court in *Time*] states that . . . the Time Board did not deprive the corporation's shareholders of any right that they had under Delaware law. Approval of the initially-planned merger by Time shareholders was mandated by the New York Stock Exchange, not Delaware law. . . . Nonetheless, it is a poignant commentary on corporate governance that, in carrying out such a transaction, a board of directors can cause a subsidiary to be formed, have the partner to the transaction merged into the subsidiary, and thereby deny the corporation's shareholders their right to vote on such a fundamental issue directly impacting upon their economic interest. But for the rules of the New York Stock Exchange, if the merger had proceeded, former Warner shareholder would have owned sixty-two percent of Time-Warner without Time shareholders having a voice in the transaction.

Marc I. Steinberg, *Nightmare on Main Street: The Paramount Picture Horror Show*, 16 Del. J. Corp. L. 1, 14 (1991).

[41] NYSE Manual, § 303A.02(a)(i).

[42] *Compare id.* at § 303A.02(a)(ii) *with* 15 USC § 78j-3(a)(3) (2012). This two-part test for compensation committee independence was adopted by the SEC in 2012 in response to the Dodd-Frank Act. *See* Listing Standards for Compensation Committees, Securities Exchange Act Release No. 67220, 2012 WL 2339280 (June 20, 2012) (adopting Rule 10C-1). The SEC approved the NYSE's amendments in compliance with Rule 10C-1 in 2013. *See* Order Granting Accelerated Approval for Proposed Rule Change, Securities Exchange Act Release No. 68639, 2013 WL 166322 (Jan. 11, 2013) (adding two-factor independence test to § 303A.02(a)(ii)). *See* discussion *infra* notes 61–62, 119–158 and accompanying text; Chapter 5 herein.

With certain exceptions, a listed company must comply with the compensation committee independence directives of the Dodd-Frank Act, and as implemented by the subject national securities exchange, as a condition of having its securities listed on such exchange. As set forth by the statute:

> The Commission shall, by rule, direct the national securities exchanges and national securities associations to prohibit the listing of any equity security of an issuer, other than an issuer that is a controlled company,

web of business and personal relationships, the Commentary included in Section 303A.02 of the NYSE Manual prescribes that "it is best that boards making 'independence' determinations broadly consider all relevant facts and circumstances," thereby encompassing an already sweeping inquiry into director relationships.[43]

Additionally, the NYSE rules enumerate five situations where a director is *not* independent. These rules apply to the director as well as to such director's "immediate family members."[44] The rules are multifaceted—concise summaries are listed below:

(1) Being an employee or executive officer of the listed company within the last three years;
(2) Having been directly compensated (other than receipt of director and committee fees or payment of deferred compensation based on prior service) more than $120,000 by the listed company within any twelve-month period during the last three years;
(3) Being a current employee or partner of the listed company's internal or external auditor;
(4) Being or having been an executive officer within the past three years of another company where any of the listed company's current executive officers "serves or served" on such other company's compensation committee;
(5) Being a current employee of an enterprise that within any of the past three fiscal years "has made payments to, or received payments from, the listed company for property or services," provided such amount "exceeds the greater of $1 million, or 2% of such other [enterprise's] consolidated gross revenues."[45]

---

limited partnership, company in bankruptcy proceedings, open-ended management investment company that is registered under the Investment Company Act of 1940, or a foreign private issuer that provides annual disclosures to shareholders of the reasons that the foreign private issuer does not have an independent compensation committee, that does not comply with the requirements of this subsection.

15 U.S.C. § 78j-3(a)(1) (2012). *See* Securities Exchange Act Release No. 67220, 2012 WL 2339280, at *1 (June 20, 2012) ("In accordance with the statute, new Rule 10C-1 directs the national securities exchanges to establish listing standards that, among other things, require each member of a listed issuer's compensation committee to be a member of the board of directors and to be 'independent,' as defined in the listing standards of the national securities exchanges adopted in accordance with the final rule.").

[43] NYSE Manual, § 303A.02(a), Commentary.

[44] The Commentary to Section 303A.02 defines "immediate family member" to include a spouse, parent, child, sibling, parent-in-law, child-in-law, sibling-in-law, or anyone else "(other than a domestic employee)" who shares such director's home. *Id.* at § 303A.02(b), Commentary.

[45] *Id.* at § 303A.02(b). Significantly, the NYSE requires "the non-management directors of each listed company [to] meet at regularly scheduled executive sessions without management." *Id.* at § 303A.03. For an article focusing on this subject, *see* Robert V. Hale II, *The Uncertain Efficacy of Executive Sessions under the NYSE's Revised Listing Standards*, 61 Bus. Law. 1413 (2006).

Nasdaq, in a similar fashion, defines an "independent director" to mean: "a person other than an Executive Officer or employee of the Company or any other individual having a relationship which, in the opinion of the Company's board of directors, would interfere with the exercise of independent judgment in carrying out the responsibilities of a director." [46] Like the NYSE listing rules, Nasdaq categorizes several persons as being *not* independent.[47] Such persons include: a director "who is, or at any time during the past three years was, employed by the Company"; with certain exceptions, a director or Family Member of such director who received compensation exceeding $120,000 during any twelve-consecutive month period within the preceding three years; a director who is a Family Member of an individual who currently is or was an executive officer of the Company within the past three years; with certain exceptions, a director or whose Family Member was a partner, controlling shareholder, or executive officer of "any organization to which the Company made, or from which the Company received, payments for property or services in the current or any of the past three fiscal years that exceed 5% of the recipient's consolidated gross revenues for that year, or $200,000, whichever is more . . ."; and a director or Family Member who currently is or has been within any of the preceding three years "a partner or employee of the Company's outside auditor. . . ."[48] Moreover, Nasdaq includes an independence disqualifier for investment companies. Under that provision, the board of directors looks to the definition of "interested person" in Section 2(a)(19) of the Investment Company Act of 1940. That statute assesses whether an individual is an "interested person" through similar factors as Nasdaq's tests for independence, taking into account such factors as the presence of control as well as business, family, and professional relationships.[49]

[46] Nasdaq, Inc. Stock Market Rule § 5605(a)(2). For purposes of this Rule, "'Family Member' means a person's spouse, parents, children and siblings, whether by blood, marriage or adoption, or anyone residing in such person's home."

[47] *Id.*

[48] *Id.* The Nasdaq rules recognize that audit committee members must adhere to additional, more stringent requirements. *Id.* §§5605(a)(2)(B); 5605(c)(2).

[49] *See id.* § 5605(a)(2), 15 U.S.C. § 80a-2(a)(19) (2012). Interestingly, an aspect illustrating the federalization of corporate governance is seen by the presence and obligations of independent directors in the investment company setting. As set forth in SEC Interpretation: Matter Concerning Independent Directors of Investment Companies, Release No. IC-24083 (1999):

> The critical role of independent directors of investment companies is necessitated, in part, by the unique structure of investment companies. Unlike a typical corporation, a fund generally has no employees of its own. Its officers are usually employed and compensated by the fund's investment adviser, which is a separately owned and operated entity. The fund relies on its investment adviser and other affiliates—who are usually the very companies that sponsored the fund's organization—for basic services, including investment advice, administration, and distribution.

The exchange rules described above were created during the approximate same time period as the enactment of the SOX and Dodd-Frank Acts. On the eve of SOX's enactment, the NYSE Corporate Accountability and Listing Standards Committee issued a Report focusing on the importance of independent directors.[50] Seeking to enhance the board of directors' oversight function,[51] the Committee set forth a range of recommendations. For instance, the Report recommended requiring all NYSE listed companies to have a majority of independent directors, as well as tightening the definition of "independence."[52] Furthermore, independent directors were recommended to comprise entirely the nominating/corporate governance, compensation, and audit committees.[53] Many of these recommendations subsequently were adopted in the NYSE listing requirements.

SOX did not create a general definition of "independence" but rather provided such a definition specifically for audit committees.[54] All members of an audit committee must be independent. Instead of a prescribed list of elements, SOX provides two specified disqualifications: an independent director on an audit committee may not—outside of his or her capacity as a director or committee member—either: (1) accept

---

Due to this unique structure, conflicts of interest can arise between a fund and the fund's investment adviser because the interests of the fund do not always parallel the interests of the adviser. An investment adviser's interest in maximizing its own profits for the benefit of its owners may conflict with its paramount duty to act solely in the best interests of the fund and its shareholders.

In an effort to control conflicts of interest between funds and their investment advisers, Congress required that at least 40% of a fund's board be composed of independent directors. Congress intended to place independent directors in the role of "independent watchdogs," who would furnish an independent check upon the management of funds and provide a means for the representation of shareholder interests in fund affairs.

Independent directors play a critical role in policing the potential conflicts of interest between a fund and its investment adviser. The Act requires that a majority of a fund's independent directors: approve the fund's contracts with its investment adviser and principal underwriter; select the independent public accountant of the fund; and select and nominate individuals to fill independent director vacancies resulting from the assignment of an advisory contract. In addition, rules promulgated under the Act require independent directors to: approve distribution fees paid under rule 12b-1 under the Act; approve and oversee affiliated securities transactions; set the amount of the fund's fidelity bond; and determine if participation in joint insurance contracts is in the best interest of the fund. Each of these duties and responsibilities is vital to the proper functioning of fund operations and, ultimately, the protection of fund shareholders.

[50] *See* Report of the New York Stock Exchange Corporate Accountability and Listing Standards Committee (June 6, 2002), *available at* http://www.iasplus.com/en/binary/resource/nysegovf.pdf (last accessed January 23, 2016) (hereinafter "Corporate Accountability Report").

[51] *Id.* at 1 ("Our system depends upon the competence and integrity of corporate directors, as it is their responsibility to diligently oversee management while adhering to unimpeachable ethical standards.").

[52] *See id.* at 6–7. Note that the recommendations have a five-year "look-back" period whereas the NYSE and Nasdaq listing rules "look-back" three years. *See supra* notes 44–49 and accompanying text.

[53] *See id.* at 9–11.

[54] *See* SOX § 301 (codified at 15 U.S.C. 78j-1(m) (2012)). Note that disclosure as to director independence is required pursuant to Item 407 of Regulation S-K. *See* discussion in Chapter 5 herein.

any compensatory fee from the issuer, or (2) be an "affiliated person" of the subject issuer.[55]

The NYSE submitted proposed rules to the SEC in 2002.[56] In those proposed rules, the NYSE required the establishment of an audit committee, nominating committee, and a compensation committee—all three committees composed entirely of independent directors.[57] Subsequently, the NYSE refined its proposal and Nasdaq proposed similar listing requirements, including mandating that a majority of board directors of listed companies be "independent" and that the audit committee be comprised entirely of independent directors.[58] The proposals defined "independent" in the same manner that the current listing rules do—both describing contexts in which a director *is not* independent.[59] The SEC approved all of these proposals in 2003.[60]

Section 952 of the Dodd-Frank Act of 2010 provides a somewhat different definition in the context of compensation committee independence.[61] Unlike the two-part disqualification definition of SOX with respect to audit committee independence, the Dodd-Frank Act instructs the national exchanges and securities associations to consider "relevant factors" as well as two specific factors:

> (A) *the source of compensation* of a member of the board of directors of an issuer, including any consulting, advisory, or other compensatory fee paid by the issuer to such member of the board of directors; and
> (B) whether a member of the board of directors of an issuer is *affiliated with the issuer*, a subsidiary of the issuer, or an affiliate of a subsidiary of the issuer.[62]

Hence, the Dodd-Frank Act sought to discern director compensation committee independence through consideration of such factors as compensation and affiliation.

[55] SOX § 301(m)(3). Being "affiliated" means that a person directly or indirectly controls or is controlled by the subject issuer. *See* 17 C.F.R. 240.10A-3(e)(1)(i) (2017). The regulations specify several positions as being "affiliates": executive officers, directors who are also employees, general partners, and managing members. *Id.* at (e)(1)(iii). Disclosure as to audit committee composition, functions, and responsibilities is required pursuant to Item 407(d) of Regulation S-K. *See* discussion in Chapter 5 herein.

[56] *See* Securities Exchange Act Release No. 47672, 2003 WL 1870339 (Apr. 11, 2003).

[57] *See* The Exchange, NYSE, August 2002, vol. 9 num. 8, at 2; *In re New York Stock Exchange, Inc.*, Securities Exchange Act Release 47672, 2003 WL 1870339 (Apr. 11, 2003).

[58] *In the Matter of Self-Regulatory Organizations,* Securities Exchange Act Release No. 48745, 2003 WL 22509738 (Nov. 4, 2003).

[59] *See id.* at *4–*5 (NYSE), *11–*13 (Nasdaq).

[60] *See id.* at *3.

[61] *See* Dodd-Frank § 952(a)(3) (codified at 15 U.S.C. § 78j-3(a)(3) (2012)).

[62] *Id.* (emphasis added).

Accordingly, in this context, the focus is on compensation (where does the director's remuneration come from?) and control (how much power does the director have with respect to company policies, practices, and decisions?).

Thus, federal statutory standards as well as the NYSE and Nasdaq rules contain definitions of independence that are more precise than state law. By contrast, Delaware common law has enunciated a general definition of independence: "that a director's decision is based on the corporate merits of the subject before the board rather than extraneous considerations or influences."[63] This definition falls well short of the multi-factor and multi-tier definitions adopted by federal law and the stock exchanges.

Even states using enumerated factors to determine director independence do not reach the particularity of federal law and the exchange rules.[64] For instance, a Massachusetts statute covering dismissal of derivative proceedings lists three factors as conditions that will *not* by themselves preclude the subject director's independence: (1) nomination or election by a named defendant in the derivative action, (2) being named as a defendant in a derivative action, or (3) approving the action being challenged in the derivative action.[65] The same independence factors are codified, for example, in Wisconsin, Arizona, Nebraska, North Carolina, and Hawaii.[66]

IV. Recognition of Audit Committees Comprised of Independent Directors

Four decades ago, the SEC stressed the importance of vigilant directors, stating: "The Commission believes that development of stronger committee systems will enable boards of directors to better serve corporations in an oversight capacity."[67] Moreover, for over a century in this country, the appointment of independent auditors has been espoused.[68]

---

[63] *Aronson v. Lewis*, 473 A.2d 805, 816 (Del. 1984). *See Brehm v. Eisner*, 746 A.2d 244 (Del. 2000); *Teamsters Union 25 Health Servs. & Ins. Plan v. Baiera*, 2015 WL 4192107, at *11 (Del. Ch. 2015).

[64] The narrowness of the exchanges' rules has not always been greeted favorably. *See In re Oracle Derivative Litig.*, 824 A.2d 917, 941 n.62 (Del. Ch. 2003) ("The recent reforms enacted by Congress and by the stock exchanges reflect a narrower conception of who they believe can be an independent director. These definitions, however, are blanket labels that do not take into account the decision at issue.").

[65] *See* Mass. Gen. Laws Ann. ch. 156D, § 7.44(c) (2015).

[66] *See, e.g.*, Ariz. Rev. Stat. Ann. § 10-3634(C) (2005); Haw. Rev. Stat. Ann. § 414-175 (2010); Neb. Rev. Stat. § 21-2074(3) (2006); N.C. Gen. Stat. Ann. § 55-7-44 (1995); Wis. Stat. Ann. § 180.0744(3) (1991).

[67] Shareholder Communications, Shareholder Participation in the Corporate Electoral Process & Corporate Governance Generally, Securities Exchange Act Release No. 14970, 1978 WL 196325 (July 18, 1978).

[68] *See* Standing Audit Committees Composed of Outside Directors, Securities Accounting Series Release No. AS-123, 1972 WL 125505, at *1 (Mar. 23, 1972) ("As far back as 1917, it was urged that auditors in the United States should be appointed or selected by the stockholders in accordance with the practice in Great Britain and in Canada, and that State laws or company bylaws should contain a provision for an independent report on

The SEC first suggested the establishment of a corporate audit committee in 1940. In a report focusing on troublesome financial disclosures, the SEC discussed the appointment of Price, Waterhouse & Co. as auditor, noting that the company president and comptroller chose the auditor.[69] With rare exceptions, board members played no part.[70] Although this was consistent with generally accepted practices of the time, the SEC felt it did not create enough auditing independence to protect investors.[71] Therefore, the Commission suggested the "[e]stablishment of a committee to be selected by nonofficer members of the board of directors which shall make all company or management nominations of auditors and shall be charged with the duty of arranging the details of the engagement."[72]

During the post-Watergate 1970s, attention was focused on publicly-held companies maintaining reasonably accurate books and records and internal account controls. This emphasis was generated by the payment of foreign bribes and use of political slush funds. Part of deterring corporate fraud was the implementation of enhanced auditing procedures,[73] including audit committees comprised entirely of independent directors.[74] Accordingly, the SEC urged all publicly-held companies to establish "audit committees composed of outside directors."[75]

---

the affairs of the company by an auditor appointed by the stockholders.") (quotation marks omitted); Lester A. Pratt, *Directors Responsibilities in Safeguarding Bank Operations*, 70 Banking L.J. 661, 665 (1953) ("The independent accounting firm should always be engaged by, and considered directly responsible to, the board of directors or a special audit committee of the board."); *SEC v. Transamerica Corp.*, 163 F.2d 511, 517 (3d Cir. 1947) (opining that "the employment of independent auditors to be selected by the stockholders beyond any question is a proper subject for action by the stockholders").

[69] *In the Matter of McKesson & Robbins, Inc.*, Securities Exchange Act Release No. 2707, 1940 WL 977, at *4 (Dec. 5, 1940).

[70] *Id.* ("The testimony of the directors is that with rare exceptions members of the board had no part in arranging for the audit and did not know the content either of the letters of engagement or of the long form report addressed to [the company president] in which the character of the work was set forth.").

[71] *Id.*

[72] *Id.* The SEC went on to advise auditors that they "must now recognize fully [their] responsibility to public investors." *Id.*

[73] *See* Robert B. Thompson, *Collaborative Corporate Governance: Listing Standards, State Law, and Federal Regulation*, 38 Wake Forest L. Rev. 961, 978 (2003) ("In the wake of the post-Watergate revelations of improper corporate payments, the SEC urged revision of listing requirements.... As a result, the NYSE modified its listing standards in 1977 to require an audit committee made up of independent members.").

[74] *See* R.K. Mautz and F.L. Neumann, *Corporate Audit Committees* 1 (University of Illinois, 1970) ("Interest in corporate audit committees appears particularly appropriate at this time.... The corporate audit committee concept has been suggested as offering significant assistance to a number of groups in meeting their business responsibilities.").

[75] Standing Audit Committees Composed of Outside Directors, Securities Accounting Release No. AS-123, 1972 WL 125505, at *1–2 (Mar. 23, 1972).

Rather than engaging in the controversial task of implementing an audit committee rule itself, the Commission "persuaded" the NYSE to undertake this task.[76] In 1977, the NYSE proposed a listing rule requiring audit committees to be comprised solely of independent directors.[77] At the time, the position that audit committees should be comprised solely of independent directors found strong support in the wake of "revelations of questionable and illegal corporate payments."[78] In order to bring about such change, the SEC leaned on the NYSE and other SROs, invoking the rationale that stock exchange listing rules were "designed to remove impediments to and perfect the mechanism of the free and open market, to prevent fraudulent and manipulative acts and practices and, in general, to protect investors and the public interest."[79] With independent directors, audit committees would serve as a needed resource to reduce the risk of financial fraud.

Nonetheless, it should be noted that audit committees were not a rarity during that era. As the SEC itself pointed out in discussing the 1977 proposed NYSE rule, 80 percent of NYSE listed companies by 1973 had audit committees (not necessarily comprised exclusively of independent directors), and another 13 percent had plans to form such committees.[80] This fact does not detract from the formalization of independent audit committees as a component of federal regulation, but rather puts it in context: As a necessary condition for a publicly-held company to have its stock listed on the NYSE, such company must have an audit committee comprised entirely of independent directors. By analogy, nominating committees comprised of independent directors were seldom utilized until the SEC and stock exchanges decades later pushed for their implementation, seeking to limit the influence of CEOs and other executive officers in this process.[81]

---

[76] *In the Matter of New York Stock Exchange, Inc.*, Securities Exchange Act Release No. 13346, 1977 WL 173602, *1 (Mar. 9, 1977) (stating that "the Commission has urged strengthening the independence and vitality of corporate boards of directors and has suggested that, at least initially, those principles could be implemented by amending the listing requirements of the NYSE and other self-regulatory organizations, rather than by direct Commission action").

[77] *See* Notice of Filing of Proposed Rule Change by New York Stock Exchange, Inc., Securities Exchange Act Release No. 13245, 1977 WL 174220 (Feb. 4, 1977).

[78] *In the Matter of New York Stock Exchange, Inc.*, Securities Exchange Act Release No. 13346, 1977 WL 173602, *1 (Mar. 9, 1977). The SEC also expressed support for congressional action to show "national commitment to ending the types of corporate misconduct uncovered, and ending defiance of the recordkeeping systems on which disclosure under the securities laws is premised." *Id.* at *1 n.10.

[79] *Id.* at *2. "The NYSE ... is in a position to respond to practical considerations of corporate procedures and compliance as well as considerations of the public interest." *Id.*

[80] *Id.* at *1 n.9.

[81] *See infra* notes 164–170 and accompanying text (explaining how federal regulation took control in changing attitudes toward boardroom composition and the nomination process); discussion Chapters 5, 6 herein.

Nasdaq was slower in requiring audit committees. It was not until 1985 that Nasdaq proposed a requirement that a company whose securities are listed on the Nasdaq National Market System have an audit committee.[82] Two years later, the SEC approved the measure.[83] Subsequently, spurred to action by the reports and committee findings discussed below, in 1999, the SEC approved the Nasdaq proposal to require that audit committees be comprised entirely of *independent* directors for all listed companies.[84] It has been suggested that the SEC allowed this delay because Nasdaq issuers tended to be smaller and less able to afford costly corporate governance changes.[85]

Pressure for the SEC and the exchanges to act on audit committees grew again through the 1980s and 1990s. In response to debacles of the 1980s—such as the savings and loan crisis[86]—former SEC Commissioner James Treadway was appointed Chair of the National Commission on Fraudulent Financial Reporting.[87] In 1987, the Commission issued its Report recommending greater audit committee oversight.[88] Specifically, the Report endorsed, among other suggestions, that audit committees review management's evaluation of the independence of outside auditors and that the committee's obligations be set forth in a written charter.[89] In 1994, the American Institute of Certified Public Accountants (AICPA) released a Report embracing strengthened communication between a subject company's board of

---

[82] *See* Proposed Rule Change by National Association of Securities Dealers, Inc. Relating to Corporate Governance Rules for Issuers for Nasdaq National Market System Securities, Securities Exchange Act Release No. 22506, 1985 WL 547883 (Oct. 4, 1985).

[83] *See* Designation of National Market System Securities, Securities Exchange Act Release No. 24635, 1987 WL 847520 (June 23, 1987).

[84] *See* Order Approving Proposed Rule Change by the National Association of Securities Dealers, Inc., Securities Exchange Act Release No. 42231, 1999 WL 1206631 (Dec. 14, 1999) ("In response to the Blue Ribbon Committee's recommendations, Nasdaq proposes to amend its listing standards regarding audit committee requirements.").

[85] *See* John C. Coffee, Jr., *Regulating the Market for Corporate Control: A Critical Assessment of the Tender Offer's Role in Corporate Governance*, 84 Colum. L. Rev. 1145, 1260 (1984) ("Thus, when the SEC pushed the major exchanges to require independent audit committees as a condition of eligibility for listing, it declined to do the same with respect to NASDAQ's listing criteria, largely on the grounds that a mandatory requirement of independent directors might prove too expensive for smaller issuers.").

[86] The savings and loan crisis was the nationwide failure of many savings and loan associations (financial institutions that primarily accepted savings deposits and extended home mortgage loans), as well as regular banks, due to a purported combination of unduly relaxed regulatory supervision and high interest rates. *See generally* Note, B. Seth Bailey, *Chopping at the Roots: A Proposal to Change the Focus of Criminal Laws Dealing with Savings and Loan Fraud*, 24 Am. J. Crim. L. 401 (1997).

[87] National Commission on Fraudulent Financial Reporting, Report of the National Commission on Fraudulent Financial Reporting (Oct. 1987), *available at* http://www.coso.org/publications/ncffr.pdf.

[88] *Id.* at 12 ("To be effective, audit committees should exercise vigilant and informed oversight of the financial reporting process, including the company's internal controls.").

[89] *Id.*

directors, its audit committee, and the outside auditor.[90] In its Report, the AICPA emphasized "the important role of audit committees."[91]

A few years later, SEC Chairman Arthur Levitt suggested that a "blue ribbon" committee be created to assess audit committee effectiveness.[92] The NYSE and National Association of Securities Dealers (NASD) subsequently formed the Blue Ribbon Committee on Improving the Effectiveness of Corporate Audit Committees.[93] The Committee's report, issued in 1999, included, among other items, "five guiding principles" for audit committees: (1) the audit committee's "key role in monitoring the other components of the audit process"; (2) "independent communication and information flow between the audit committee and the internal auditor"; (3) "independent communication and information flow between the audit committee and the outside auditors"; (4) "candid discussions with management, the internal auditor, and outside auditors regarding issues implicating judgment and impacting quality"; and (5) "diligent and knowledgeable committee membership."[94]

The SEC largely adopted the findings and recommendations of the Committee in 1999, including independent auditor review of Form 10-Q filings, and disclosures as to: whether the subject board of directors has promulgated a written charter with respect to the audit committee, and whether audit committee members are independent (as defined in the pertinent exchange's listing standards).[95] As recognized in that SEC Release, "[a]udit committees play a critical role in the financial reporting system."[96] Significant changes in the securities markets, including technological changes and market pressure to meet earnings forecasts, signified that the corporate financial reporting process needed to "remain disciplined and credible."[97]

The growth of audit committee functions peaked in 2002 with the passage of SOX. For the first time, a federal law systematically organized the structure and

---

[90] Advisory Panel on Auditor Independence, Strengthening the Professionalism of the Independent Auditor, at 15 (Public Oversight Board of the SEC Practice Section, ALCPA 1994), *available at* http://www.publicoversightboard.org/Strengthening_the_Professionalism.pdf.

[91] *Id.* at 14.

[92] Jody K. Upham, *Audit Committees: The Policemen of Corporate Responsibility*, 39 Tex. J. Bus. L. 537, 540 (2004); *see* Arthur Levitt, The "Numbers Game," Remarks at the New York University Center for Law and Business (Sept. 28, 1998), *available at* http://www.sec.gov/news/speech/speecharchive/1998/spch220.txt.

[93] Report and Recommendations of the Blue Ribbon Committee on Improving the Effectiveness of Corporate Audit Committees, 54 Bus. Law. 1067 (1999); *see* Upham, *supra* note 92, at 541.

[94] Blue Ribbon Committee, *supra* note 93, at 1089-94.

[95] *See* Audit Committee Disclosure, Securities Exchange Act Release No. 42266, 1999 WL 1244029, at *1–*3 (Dec. 22, 1999) (stating that "the new rules and amendments are based in large measure on recommendations made by the Blue Ribbon Committee").

[96] *Id.* at *2.

[97] *Id.*

performance criteria of audit committees.[98] Section 301 of SOX instructed the SEC to direct all national exchanges to cease listing any security not in compliance with the audit committee mandates of that statute.[99] As set forth in the statute: (1) an audit committee is "directly responsible" to appoint, compensate, and oversee the company's outside auditor;[100] (2) each audit committee member must be an independent director, meaning that he or she neither accepts compensation (other than fees as a director or board committee member) from the issuer nor is an affiliated person of the issuer (or any subsidiary of such issuer);[101] (3) an audit committee is to establish procedures with respect to "the receipt, retention, and treatment of complaints" concerning accounting and auditing matters;[102] (4) an audit committee has authority to engage independent legal counsel as well as other advisers to carry out such committee's duties;[103] and (5) the subject company is to provide appropriate funding for the retention of separate legal counsel and other advisers.[104] In essence, SOX provides for a stronger and more solidified oversight and outreach role for independent audit committees.

Implementing this legislative directive, the SEC in 2003 proposed new standards[105] and adopted a final rule only a few months later.[106] A swift response from

---

[98] *See* Stephanie Tsacoumis, Stephanie R. Bess, and Bryan A. Sappington, *The Sarbanes-Oxley Act: Rewriting Audit Committee Governance*, 3 B.L.I. 212, 225 (2003).

[99] *See* SOX § 301(1)(A) (codified at 15 U.S.C. 78j-1(m)(1)(A)) (2012).

[100] *See id.* at 15 U.S.C. 78j-1(m)(2) (2012).

[101] *Id.* at (m)(3).

[102] *Id.* at (m)(4).

[103] *Id.* at (m)(5).

[104] *Id.* at (m)(6). *See* Robert E. Buckholz Jr., Marc R. Trevino, and Glen T. Schleyer, *Public Company Deskbook: Complying with Federal Governance & Disclosure Requirements* § 3:1 (3d ed. 2014); Terence Sheppey and Ross McGill, *Sarbanes-Oxley: Building Working Strategies for Compliance* 40 (2017); discussion in Chapter 5 herein.

[105] *See* Standards Relating to Listed Company Audit Committees, Securities Exchange Act Release No. 47137, 2003 WL 60824 (Jan. 8, 2003).

[106] *See* Standards Relating to Listed Company Audit Committees, Securities Exchange Act Release No. 47654, 2003 WL 1833875 (Apr. 9, 2003). The SEC Release stated:

> As directed by the Sarbanes-Oxley Act of 2002, we are adopting a new rule to direct the national securities exchanges and national securities associations to prohibit the listing of any security of an issuer that is not in compliance with the audit committee requirements mandated by the Sarbanes-Oxley Act of 2002. These requirements relate to: the independence of audit committee members; the audit committee's responsibility to select and oversee the issuer's independent accountant; procedures for handling complaints regarding the issuer's accounting practices; the authority of the audit committee to engage advisors; and funding for the independent auditor and any outside advisors engaged by the audit committee. The rule implements the requirements of Section 10A(m)(1) of the Securities Exchange Act of 1934, as added by Section 301 of the Sarbanes-Oxley Act of 2002. . . .

2003 WL 1833875, at *1.

the exchanges followed.[107] The SEC's final rule is Securities Exchange Act Rule 10A-3. Utilizing much of the language from SOX, Rule 10A-3 also adds additional criteria in defining independence. For example, Rule 10A-3 breaks down independence between investment and non-investment company registrants.[108] In addition, Rule 10A-3 includes certain exemptions for foreign private issuers.[109] As discussed below, both NYSE and Nasdaq listing rules refer back to Rule 10A-3 as a foundation for defining an audit committee's duties and responsibilities.

NYSE's listing standards contain two sections for audit committees—both added in response to SOX. The first, Section 303A.06, simply references SEC Rule 10A-3.[110] SEC Rule 10A-3 reiterates and expands upon the audit committee functions set forth in Section 301 of SOX.[111] The second, Section 303A.07 (entitled "Audit Committee Additional Requirements"), delineates specific responsibilities of an audit committee that must be addressed in its written charter, including:

> [T]he committee's purpose . . . ; an annual performance evaluation of the audit committee; . . . the duties and responsibilities of the audit committee; . . . as well as to: at least annually, obtain and review a report by the independent auditor describing [among other matters] the firm's internal quality-control procedures . . . ; meet to review and discuss the listed company's annual audited financial statements and quarterly financial statements with management and the internal auditor . . . ; discuss the listed company's press releases, as well as financial information and earnings guidance provided to analysts and rating agencies; . . . discuss policies with respect to risk assessment and risk management; . . . meet separately, periodically, with management, with internal auditors and with independent auditors; review with the independent auditor any audit problems or difficulties and management's response; set clear hiring

---

[107] *See* Self-Regulatory Organizations: Notice of Filing of Proposed Rule Change and Amendment No.1 thereto by the New York Stock Exchange, Inc. Relating to Corporate Governance, Securities Exchange Act Release No. 47672, 2003 WL 1870339 (Apr. 11, 2003); Self-Regulatory Organizations; Notice of Filing of Proposed Rule Change and Amendment No. 1 thereto by the National Association of Securities Dealers, Inc. Relating to Proposed Amendments to NASD Rules 4200 and 4350 Regarding Board Independence and Independent Committee, Securities Exchange Act Release No. 47516, 2003 WL 1248830 (Mar. 17, 2003).

[108] The standards are almost identical. However, for non-investment companies, independence bars "affiliated" persons, whereas in investment companies independence bars "interested" persons. *Compare* 17 C.F.R. 240.10A-3(b)(1)(ii) (2017) *with* 17 C.F.R. 240.10A-3(b)(1)(iii) (2017).

[109] *See, e.g., id.* at (b)(1)(iv)(D) (audit committee member of a foreign private issuer is exempt from independence standard if such person serves as a nonvoting observer).

[110] NYSE Manual § 303A.06 (providing that "Listed companies must have an audit committee that satisfies the requirements of Rule 10A-3 under the Exchange Act"). *See* 17 C.F.R. § 240.10A-3 (2017).

[111] 17 C.F.R. § 240.10A-3 (2017); discussion *supra* notes 106–109 and accompanying text; discussion in Chapter 5 herein.

policies for employees or former employees of the independent auditors; and . . . report regularly to the board of directors. . . .[112]

Accordingly, a NYSE-listed company must meet three basic requirements under Section 303A.07: its audit committee must have at least three independent members, that committee must have a written charter that addresses the functions set forth above, and the company "must have an internal audit function."[113] According to the NYSE Listing Manual, the audit committee's purpose encompasses "assist[ing]" board of director "oversight" with respect to: the integrity of the company's financial statements, legal and regulatory compliance, auditor qualifications and independence, and the undertaking of the company's internal audit function.[114]

Nasdaq has similar listing standards. It requires listed companies to have an audit committee comprised solely of independent directors. Committee members must meet the independence definitions in both the Nasdaq rules and SEC Rule 10A-3.[115] Moreover, the audit committee members must not have participated in preparing the financial statements during the prior three years for the company or any current subsidiary, and members must "be able to read and understand fundamental financial statements."[116] Each listed company must also have a written audit committee charter that encompasses such matters as the committee's responsibilities, its structure, relationship with outside auditors, and purpose.[117]

Because "[i]nvestor confidence is based on both reality and perception, . . . both will be enhanced with the improved controls on the audit committee."[118] Audit committees have been a long-standing staple of corporate board oversight. Now, with the enactment of the SOX and Dodd-Frank Acts, as well as the implementation of stock exchange rules, the composition and functions of audit committees are firmly entrenched for publicly-held companies.

---

112 *See* NYSE Manual § 303A.07.

113 *Id.* at § 303A.07(a)–(c). *See supra* note 112 and accompanying text. With respect to the internal audit function, § 303A.07(c) states in the Commentary: "Listed companies must maintain an internal audit function to provide management and the audit committee with ongoing assessments of the listed company's risk management processes and system of internal control. A listed company may choose to outsource this function to a third-party service provider other than its independent auditor."

114 *Id.* at § 303A.07(b)(i)(A).

115 Nasdaq, Inc., Stock Market Rules §§ 5605(a)(2), 5605(c)(2)(A).

116 *Id.* at § 5605(c)(2)(A) (including such listed company's balance sheet, cash flow statement, and income statement).

117 *Id.* at § 5605(c)(1) (requiring each listed company to certify that "it has adopted a formal written audit committee charter and that the audit committee will review and reassess the adequacy of the formal written charter on an annual basis"). *See also*, §5605(c)(3) (outlining specific responsibilities and authority of the audit committee).

118 Upham, *supra* note 92, at 559.

V. Establishment of Compensation Committees Composed of Independent Directors

In 1976, the SEC approved rule changes for the Midwest Stock Exchange allowing the establishment of a compensation committee for that exchange.[119] The new rule gave the compensation committee power to review overall compensation policy while the president of the exchange retained the power to set officer compensation.[120]

For several decades, the SEC has focused on executive compensation through disclosure requirements. For instance, in 1978, the SEC addressed modifications to the proxy disclosure requirements, including an item requiring companies to disclose whether they had compensation committees.[121] Compensation committees should be tasked with enhancing transparency and governance standards with respect to remuneration arrangements, adoption of compensation plans, and the grant of options or other benefits under said plans.[122] The Commission explained the disclosures by stating:

> [T]he Commission believes that disclosure concerning an issuer's compensation committee and its composition would permit investors to better assess the process by which management and director compensation is determined. Although the Commission is aware that compensation committees are less prevalent than audit committees, and that their roles are still evolving, it is the Commission's view, based on its administrative experience, that management compensation is a matter of significant concern to investors.[123]

The same focus on disclosure can be seen over a decade later in a 1992 rule on modifications to Item 402 of SEC Regulation S-K.[124] In that release, attention was directed at the Board Compensation Committee Report, which addressed the bases for executive compensation and its relation to corporate performance.[125] The SEC proposed

---

[119] Notice of Filing of Proposed Rule Change by the Midwest Stock Exchange, Securities Exchange Act Release No. 13039, 1976 WL 161784, at *1 (Dec. 3, 1976).

[120] *Id.*

[121] Shareholder Communications, Shareholder Participation in the Corporate Electoral Process & Corporate Governance Generally, Securities Exchange Act Release No. 14970, 1978 WL 196325, at *7 (July 18, 1978).

[122] 1978 WL 196325, at *7–8.

[123] *Id.* at *8.

[124] Executive Compensation Disclosure, Securities Exchange Act Release No. 31327, 1992 WL 301259 (Oct. 16, 1992).

[125] *Id.* at *21. Not surprisingly, "[w]hile shareholders expressed great enthusiasm for the report, the corporate community and practicing bar raised substantial concerns." *Id.*

that a subject company's compensation committee write such a report in order for shareholders to have a clearer understanding of executives' compensation packages as well as a sounder basis for assessing if executives are adequately representing shareholder interests.[126] As in 1978, the SEC's concern was to enhance shareholder understanding of executive remuneration as well as to subtly promote improved corporate governance: "The Commission continues to believe that disclosure of the Compensation Committee's policies will enhance shareholders' ability to assess how well directors are representing their interests, and thus is an appropriate and necessary improvement to the disclosure concerning executive compensation. . . ."[127]

The financial debacles at the beginning of this century altered the discussion on executive compensation from one of disclosure to encompass that of enhanced oversight.[128] In 2002, both the NYSE and Nasdaq proposed sweeping amendments to their listing standards that subsequently were approved by the SEC in 2003.[129] Both exchanges proposed, and received approval for, the requirement of compensation committees for all listed companies.[130] The NYSE proposed that listed companies have a compensation committee comprised of all independent directors, with a written charter required.[131] Nasdaq's proposal was somewhat more deferential. It allowed CEO compensation to be determined or recommended by either a compensation committee or a majority of independent directors.[132] Moreover, as with the nominating committee, Nasdaq proposed to allow one non-independent director to be added to a compensation committee of at least three members under "exceptional and limited circumstances."[133]

---

[126] Executive Compensation Disclosure, Securities Exchange Act Release No. 30851, 1992 WL 151018, at *18 (June 23, 1992).

[127] Executive Compensation Disclosure, Securities Exchange Act Release No. 31327, 1992 WL 301259, at *21 (Oct. 16, 1992). Note at that time publicly-traded companies were not required to have such a committee. If a registrant elected not to have a compensation committee, then the 1992 Release gave this function to the entire board of directors.

[128] *See infra* notes 129–153 and accompanying text.

[129] *See* In Matter of New York Stock Exchange, Inc., Securities Exchange Act Release No. 48745, 2003 WL 22509738 (Nov. 4, 2003). The NYSE's proposals were amended three times between April and October 2003. *Id.* at *1. Nasdaq amended its proposals five times in the same period of time. *Id.* Moreover, these proposals covered more than simply compensation committees—director independence, nominations, auditing, and codes of ethics (among other things) were amended through these changes.

[130] *Id.* at *6, *13 (proposals from NYSE and Nasdaq, respectively).

[131] *Id.* at *6 (stating that the compensation committee's written charter would address, among other things, the committee's purpose and responsibilities and an annual performance evaluation of the compensation committee).

[132] *Id.* at *13.

[133] *Id.* In such circumstances, "the nature of the relationship and the reasons for the determination" were to be disclosed in the company's next annual meeting proxy statement.

Interestingly, NYSE's first proposal was stronger, giving the compensation committee the sole authority to determine CEO pay.[134] The Exchange later amended its proposal and deleted this provision, possibly in response to numerous public commenters who argued for greater involvement for all directors in making remuneration determinations.[135]

After amendments by the NYSE and Nasdaq responding to the Commission,[136] both the NYSE's and Nasdaq's listing rules were approved by the SEC. Regarding compensation committees, the SEC affirmed that "directors [who] are independent of management are more likely to evaluate the performance of the CEO and other officers impartially and to award compensation on an objective basis."[137]

Nonetheless, the presence of excessive executive compensation, as evidenced by the stock options backdating misconduct,[138] drew the attention of Congress. Consequently, the Dodd-Frank Act of 2010 (Section 952), adding Section 10C to the Securities Exchange Act, directs that the SEC, by rule, prohibit the national securities exchanges from listing any equity security of a subject issuer that fails to have an independent compensation committee that complies with the statutory mandates.[139] Pursuant to Section 10C and implementing SEC Rule 10C-1, each member of a subject company's compensation committee must be a director who is independent.[140] Independence is to be determined by assessing such factors as:

> [1] The source of compensation of a member of the board of directors of an issuer, including any consulting, advisory or other compensatory fee paid by the issuer to such member of the board of directors; and

---

[134] *Id.* at *6.

[135] *Id.* at *24.

[136] *See id.* at *38 ("[I]n response to these comments, NYSE revised its proposal to state that the committee's responsibility is to determine and approve the CEO's compensation level either as a committee or together with the other independent directors.... Nasdaq also amended its proposal to clarify that an issuer has the flexibility to empower a compensation committee either to take action itself or to recommend that the board take action.").

[137] *Id.* at *39. (The Commission determined the exchanges' proposals were "appropriate.")

[138] *See, e.g., Ryan v. Gifford*, 918 A.2d 341 (Del. Ch. 2007); Lucian A. Bebchuk, Yaniv Grinstein and Uris Peyer, *Lucky CEOs and Lucky Directors*, 65 J. Fin. 2363 (2010) (stating that "[t]he opportunistic timing of executives' option grants—via backdating... or otherwise—has attracted a great deal of attention [resulting in] [m]ore than 200 companies com[ing] under scrutiny, and dozens of executives and directors [being] forced to resign").

[139] 15 U.S.C. § 78j-3 (2012). Issuers that are exempted from this mandate include: "an issuer that is a controlled company; limited partnership; company in bankruptcy proceedings; [eligible] open-ended investment company; ... or a [specified] foreign private issuer." *Id.*

[140] *Id. See* 17 C.F.R. § 240.10C-1(b)(1)(i) (2017). *See* Listing Standards for Compensation Committees, Securities Exchange Act Release No. 67220 (June 12, 2012).

[2] Whether a member of the board of directors of an issuer is affiliated with the issuer, a subsidiary of the issuer or an affiliate of a subsidiary of the issuer.[141]

The statute and SEC rule also set forth applicable criteria that the compensation committee must consider when deciding whether to engage the advice of a compensation consultant (or other adviser).[142] Notably, legal counsel as well as other advisers also may be retained by the compensation committee.[143]

Implementing the directives set forth by Section 10C and SEC Rule 10C-1, the NYSE listing rules for compensation committees are similar to those for audit committees. Listed companies must have a compensation committee composed exclusively of independent directors.[144] The committee must have a written charter addressing such matters as: the committee's purpose, responsibilities, non-CEO executive officer compensation recommendations, and, with respect to the CEO, "evaluate [such] CEO's performance . . . and, either as a committee or together with the other independent directors, . . . determine and approve the CEO's compensation. . . ."[145] Compensation committees may retain outside compensation consultants as well as independent legal counsel and other advisers.[146] The committee must be responsible for overseeing any such compensation adviser or other adviser.[147] Additionally, when retaining a compensation consultant or other adviser, the committee must consider several enumerated factors, including: other services provided to and amount of fees received from the listed company by the consultant's employer, stock in the listed company owned by the consultant, and any relationships the consultant's employer or the consultant has with executive officers or members of the compensation committee of the listed company.[148]

---

[141] 15 U.S.C. § 78j-3(a)(3) (2012); 17 C.F.R. § 240.10C-1(b)(1)(ii) (2017).

[142] 15 U.S.C. § 78j-3(a)(3)(b)–(c) (2012); 17 C.F.R. § 240.10C-1(b)(2), (4) (2017).

[143] 15 U.S.C. § 78j-3(d) (2012); 17 C.F.R. § 240.10C-1(b)(2) (2017). Appropriate funding for such adviser(s) must be provided by the subject listed issuer. 15 U.S.C. § 78j-3(e) (2012); 17 C.F.R. § 240.10C-1(b)(3) (2017). In addition, Item 407(e) of Regulation S-K requires disclosure by a registrant with respect to such matters as the compensation committee's existence, composition, functions, conflicts, and its retention of compensation consultants or other advisors. *See* discussion Chapter 5 herein.

[144] NYSE Manual § 303A.05(a). Committee member independence is defined, as discussed above, in § 303A.02. The SEC approved the NYSE proposed rules in 2013. *See* Securities Exchange Act Release No. 68639 (Jan. 11, 2013).

[145] *Id.* at § 303A.05(b). The Commentary to this subsection provides in part that: "The compensation committee charter should also address the following items: committee member qualifications; committee member appointment and removal; committee structure and operations . . . ; and committee reporting to the board."

[146] *Id.* at § 303A.05(c)(i).

[147] *Id.* at § 303A.05(c)(ii). The listed company must provide the committee appropriate funding to pay for such outside consultants. *Id.* at § 303A.05(c)(iii).

[148] *Id.* at § 303A.05(c)(iv). Notably, the Commentary to this subsection states in part: "Nothing in this Section 303A.05(c) requires a compensation consultant, legal counsel, or other compensation adviser to be

Nasdaq's listing rules cover similar ground to the NYSE's standards, addressing the compensation committee's composition, functions, and responsibilities.[149] Under the Nasdaq rules, the subject company's CEO may not be present during compensation committee deliberations or voting determinations concerning his or her compensation.[150] The committee's responsibilities mirror those contained in the NYSE listing rules.[151] Pursuant to Nasdaq rule, the board of directors "must consider all factors specifically relevant to determining whether a director has a relationship to the Company which is material to that director's ability to be independent from management in connection with the duties of a compensation committee member. . . ."[152] Two factors are enumerated in the rule: the source of the member's compensation ("including any consulting, advisory or other compensation fee paid by the company to such director"), and whether the committee member is affiliated with the listed company or a subsidiary.[153]

---

independent, only that the compensation committee consider the enumerated independence factors before selecting or receiving advice from a compensation [or other] adviser. . . ." Discussion on Say-or-Pay is contained in Chapters 4 and 5 herein.

[149] *See* Nasdaq, Inc., Stock Market Rules § 5605(d)(1)–(3). The SEC approved Nasdaq's proposed rules in 2013. *See* Securities Exchange Act Release No. 68640 (Jan. 11, 2013).

[150] Nasdaq Stock Market Rules, at § 5605(d)(1)(C).

[151] *Id. See* NYSE Manual § 303A.05(c); 17 C.F.R. 240.10C-1 (2017) (regulations pursuant to Dodd-Frank Act describing compensation committee standards, from which the exchanges promulgated their rules for compensation committee responsibilities).

[152] Nasdaq Stock Market Rules, § 5605(d)(2)(A).

[153] *Id.* Under current Nasdaq rules, receipt of compensatory fees from the listed company or a subsidiary by the compensation committee member is not prohibited. *See* Nasdaq Stock Market Rule § 5605(d)(2)(A), IM-5605-6; Securities Exchange Act Release No. 71037 (Dec. 11, 2013) (SEC approval of Nasdaq proposed rule change). In this regard, Nasdaq Manual Rule IM-5605-6 ("Independent Director Oversight of Executive Compensation") states in part:

> Rule 5605(d)(2)(A) includes an additional independence test [beyond Rule 5605(a)(2)] for compensation committee members. When considering the sources of a director's compensation for this purpose, the board should consider whether the director receives compensation from any person or entity that would impair the director's ability to make independent judgments about the Company's executive compensation. Similarly, when considering any affiliate relationship a director has with the Company, a subsidiary of the Company, or an affiliate of a subsidiary of the Company, in determining independence for purposes of compensation committee service, the board should consider whether the affiliate relationship places the director under the direct or indirect control of the Company or its senior management, or creates a direct relationship between the director and members of senior management, in each case of a nature that would impair the director's ability to make independent judgments about the Company's executive compensation. . . .

Such receipt of fees by compensation committee members has generated criticism. *See* Theo Francis and Brody Mullins, *Lobbyists Test Post-Crisis Rules for Boards*, Wall St. J., Oct. 5, 2016, at A1.

In 2016, the SEC approved a proposed Nasdaq rule change "to require listed companies to publicly disclose compensation or other payments by third parties to board of director's members or nominees for directors." Securities Exchange Act Release No. 78223 (July 1, 2016). *See* Brian R. Rosenau, *Nasdaq Adopts Rule Requiring Disclosure of Golden-Leash Arrangements*, Bus. Law. Today, Sept. 2016, at 1 (discussing SEC approval

As the SEC and stock exchanges have taken a more active role with respect to executive compensation, the influence of state courts has not gone unnoticed. The marathon litigation surrounding then-president of Disney, Michael Ovitz, reinforced that, while Delaware courts were not willing to play an active role with respect to shareholder challenges to allegedly excessive executive compensation, their decisions retained "norm-generating value" in guiding future considerations of executive payments.[154] In the *Disney* derivative action, shareholders sued the board of directors for approving a compensation package that included, among other things, a no-fault termination payment to Disney's president Michael Ovitz that approximated $140 million.[155] Rejecting the claims, the Delaware Supreme Court found that the members of Disney's compensation committee comprised of independent directors did not breach their fiduciary duties in approving Ovitz's pay package.[156] The *Disney* decision signifies that Delaware courts, absent a strong reason otherwise, intend to " 'stay out of the business of [policing executive compensation decisions] in a meaningful way.' "[157] To its supporters, the Delaware Supreme Court's approach wisely focuses on upholding the propriety of "evolving board practices" with respect to executive compensation.[158]

---

of Nasdaq rule requiring disclosure by listed companies of golden-leash arrangements, which "generally are defined as agreements or arrangements made by activist shareholders to pay a director or director nominee in connection with his or her service on, or candidacy for, a company's board of directors, usually in connection with a proxy fight").

[154] Jill E. Fisch, *Leave It to Delaware: Why Congress Should Stay Out of Corporate Governance*, 37 Del. J. Corp. L. 731, 743–51 (2013). *See also* Jeffrey N. Gordon, *Executive Compensation: If There's a Problem, What's the Remedy? The Case for "Compensation Discussion and Analysis,"* 30 J. Corp. L. 675, 692 (2005) ("The *Disney* litigation [is] . . . an extended morality tale on the board's responsibility to monitor executive compensation.").

[155] *In re Walt Disney Co. Derivative Litig.*, 825 A.2d 275, 279 (Del. Ch. 2003), *aff'd*, 906 A.2d (Del. 2006).

[156] *See In re Walt Disney Co. Derivative Litig.*, 906 A.2d 27, 55–60 (Del. 2006).

[157] Fisch, *supra* note 154 at 747, *quoting*, Jennifer S. Martin, *The House of Mouse and Beyond: Assessing the SEC's Efforts to Regulate Executive Compensation*, 32 Del. J. Corp. L. 481, 489 (2007).

[158] Fisch, *supra* note 154, at 749. *See generally* James G. McMillan, III, *Private Planes, Investors and the NASDAQ Rules: Delaware Supreme Court Gives Guidance on Director Independence*, Bus. Law Today, Apr. 2007, at 1. Critical of the Delaware Supreme Court's decision in *Disney*, this author posited:

> With this current climate of corporate governance in mind, the wider implications of the *Disney* case became more apparent. This holding goes well beyond a mere reaffirmance of the business judgment rule. Rather, the *Disney* case raises serious questions about the efficacy of recent corporate governance reforms. The emphasis on director "independence" has been recognized by legislators, courts, regulators, the private sector, scholars, and observers alike. Reforms have accentuated the need for "independent" directors to serve on boards in order to improve corporate governance in the United States. Nonetheless, if such reforms are as important as they seem, then how can they be reconciled with the *Disney* case? If a CEO such as Michael Eisner can legitimately wield such unilateral power as was demonstrated in this case, the inquiry is raised whether the Delaware courts are willing to enunciate meaningful corporate governance standards in controversial cases.

Marc I. Steinberg and Matthew D. Bivona, *Disney Goes Goofy: Agency, Delegation, and Corporate Governance*, 60 Hastings L.J. 201, 229–30 (2008). *See* discussion in Chapter 1 herein.

VI. Emergence of Nominating/Corporate Governance Committees Comprised of Independent Directors

Boards of directors have had long-standing authority to nominate directors.[159] This practice fits within the framework of corporate law: by giving a board of directors managerial as well as oversight power, it follows that the board also should have the power to nominate candidates to shareholders for election to the board.[160] Board nominations of directors, it may be asserted, is a process that "facilitates the subsequent exercise of collective choice in the form of voting."[161] Although shareholders may be said to "own" a subject corporation, the board of directors ordinarily wields control over it.[162] Therefore, the nomination and ultimate election of directors is an essential corporate governance function.[163]

Historically, boards did not often utilize formal nominating committees. Until the late 1970s, formal nomination procedures were relatively rare because slating nominees was seen as a prerogative of the CEO.[164] A number of developments ensued to alter this practice. For example, the SEC issued a rule in 1978 that, among other things, required the disclosure of the makeup and procedures of a company's nominating committee. If there was not a nominating committee, the company had to explain why.[165] In the face of comments against these rules, the SEC responded

[159] Lawrence A. Hamermesh, *Director Nominations*, 39 Del. J. Corp. L. 117, 134 (2014) ("The power of the board of directors to nominate candidates for election to that body is implicit and reflected in, among many other places, SEC and stock exchange rules.").

[160] *Id. See* Stephen M. Bainbridge, *The New Corporate Governance in Theory and Practice* 155–56 (2008) (director primacy is inherent in the corporate management structure).

[161] *See* Hammermesh, *supra* note 159, at 131.

[162] Michael K. Molitor, *The Crucial Role of the Nominating Committee: Re-inventing Nominating Committees in the Aftermath of Shareholder Access to the Proxy*, 11 U.C. Davis Bus. L.J. 97, 99, 101 (2010) (stating that shareholders "have certain control and financial rights within the corporation, but not direct control over or even access to the firm's underlying assets") (quotation marks omitted).

[163] "The shareholder franchise is the ideological underpinning upon which the legitimacy of directorial power rests." *Blasius Indus., Inc. v. Atlas Corp.*, 564 A.2d 651, 659 (Del. Ch. 1988); discussion in Chapter 1 herein. Hence, the director nomination and election process is key for activist investors—shareholders who either purchase stock or coordinate with other significant shareholders to wield blocks of voting power in order to place themselves or their designees on the board of directors and thereby have greater influence or attain control of the company to better suit their vision of its operation. *See generally* PricewaterhouseCoopers LLP, *Shareholder Activism: Who, What, When, and How?* (Mar. 2015), *available at* http://www.pwc.com/us/en/corporate-governance/publications/assets/pwc-shareholder-activism-full-report.pdf.

[164] Michael E. Murphy, *The Nominating Process for Corporate Boards of Directors: A Decision-Making Analysis*, 5 Berkeley Bus. L.J. 131, 145 (2008) (stating that in 1971 only 8 percent of companies had nominating committees, which increased to 15 percent by 1977).

[165] Shareholder Communications, Shareholder Participation in the Corporate Electoral Process, Securities Exchange Act Release No 15384, 1978 WL 195744, at *22 (Dec. 6, 1978).

that, even though "the adoption of this disclosure requirement in some instances may indirectly stimulate the establishment of [a nominating committee], the Commission believes that disclosure ... serves a valid informational purpose."[166] Moreover, explained the Commission, such information "could improve the director selection process by increasing the range of candidates under consideration while intensifying the scrutiny given to their qualifications."[167]

Another impetus for change was the American Law Institute's (ALI) corporate governance project. In 1982, the ALI published a tentative draft of the *Principles of Corporate Governance and Structure: Restatement and Recommendations*, which proposed that nominating committees be composed solely of directors "who are not officers or employees of the corporation, including at least a majority of directors who have no significant relationships with the corporation's senior executives."[168] Noting the tendency of directors to feel especially loyal to the CEO who appointed them, the ALI drafters encouraged an "independent locus of responsibility" premised not exclusively on duty or efficiency, but also on director independence.[169] Other influential organizations adopted a similar posture. During the late 1970s, for example, the American Bar Association and the Business Roundtable advocated for a significant role for nominating committees.[170]

Nominating committees are now ubiquitous. Although only 8 percent of companies had them in 1971, that number rose to 32 percent by 1980, and then 99 percent of S&P 500 companies by 2006.[171] It may be posited that, while nominating committees were once dominated by company CEOs, the movement toward nominating committees being composed of independent directors (exemplified by the passage of SOX and subsequent exchange listing standards) has broadened the corporate power structure, at least in appearance, and, in several companies, in actuality.

---

[166] *Id.*

[167] *Id.* Note that today Item 407(c) of SEC Regulation S-K requires disclosure as to the existence, composition, and functions of a registrant's nominating committee. *See* Chapter 5 herein.

[168] *See* American Law Institute, *Principles of Corporate Governance and Structure: Restatement and Recommendations* (Tent. Draft No. 1, 1982). The ALI's work went through several drafts in the 1980s and early 1990s, and the ALI published the work in its final form in 1994. *See Corporate Governance: Analysis and Recommendations* (1994); Symposium, *ALI Corporate Governance Project*, 37 U. Miami L. Rev. No. 2 (1983); Jayne W. Barnard, *Shareholder Access to the Proxy Revisited*, 40 Cath. U.L. Rev. 37, 48 (1990).

[169] Barnard, *supra* note 168, at 48.

[170] The ABA said that "[t]he nominating committee is potentially the most significant channel for improved corporate governance ..." Comm. on Corp. Laws, A.B.A., *Corporate Director's Guidebook*, 32 Bus. Law. 5, 35 (1976). In a similar fashion, the Business Roundtable wrote in 1978 that "we believe that as a general rule, the board should establish a Nominating Committee ... composed in its majority of non-management directors." Statement of the Business Roundtable: *The Role and Composition of the Board of Directors of the Large Publicly Owned Corporation*, 33 Bus. Law. 2083, 2110 (1978).

[171] Molitor, *supra* note 162, at 108.

Notwithstanding the proliferation of nominating committees, in many corporations, CEOs play a zealous role in the director nomination process.[172] Nonetheless, during the past decade, institutional shareholders have become more active and integral with respect to the director nominating process.[173]

In adopting disclosure requirements for nominating committees in 2003, the SEC referenced the NYSE and Nasdaq listing standards and noted that they did not require nominating committees to consider shareholder nominees.[174] The Commission responded by adopting new proxy statement disclosures calling for explanation of the nominating committee processes, material changes to such processes, and how shareholders can communicate with the board.[175] Due to the perceived need for timely implementation of these changes, the SEC, rather than relying on the promulgation of stock exchange listing standards, elected to promulgate its own disclosure mandates.[176] In so doing, the SEC also required proxy statements to include detailed descriptions of the nominating committee and its processes.[177]

Interestingly, neither SOX nor the Dodd-Frank Act addresses nominating committees. The closest the Dodd-Frank Act comes is Section 971, which authorized the SEC to adopt proxy access rules empowering specified shareholders to include director nominees in the subject company's proxy materials. In adopting Rule 14a-11 in 2010 (which subsequently was declared invalid), the SEC discussed how the director electoral process is the "principal way" that shareholders hold boards accountable.[178] Part of the Commission's rationale was facilitating

---

[172] *See* Murphy, *supra* note 164, at 146–49 ("For all practical purposes, institutional investors and other shareholders continue to be excluded from the nominating process. Surveys reveal that representatives of institutional investors do not figure among the populations from which directors are drawn."). *See* ALI, Principles of Corporate Governance, *supra* note 168, at 122 (stating that "the chief executive officer can be expected to be highly active in recommending to and discussing candidates with the [nominating] committee and in recruiting candidates for the board").

[173] *See* Emily Glazer, *Wells Fargo Directors Face Shareholders' Ire*, Wall St. J., Apr. 26, 2017, at A1; Joann Lublin, *Investors Gain More Clout Over Boards*, Wall St. J., Jan. 11, 2016, at B1; discussion Chapters 4, 5 herein. *See also* David Benoit, *Activist Investors Step Up Efforts to Throw Out CEOs*, Wall St. J., May 17, 2017, at A1.

[174] Disclosure Regarding Nominating Committee Functions and Communications between Security Holders and Boards of Directors, Securities Exchange Act Release No. 48825, 2003 WL 22794459, at *10–11 (Nov. 24, 2003) ("[T]he disclosure requirements we are adopting today will operate in conjunction with the revised [NYSE and NASDAQ] listing standards regarding nominating committees.").

[175] *See id.* at *2–14.

[176] *Id.* at *11 (asserting that "we believe that the disclosure standards that we adopt today are a necessary complement to those listing standards and, accordingly, do not believe such a delay is necessary or appropriate").

[177] *Id.* at *2–3.

[178] Facilitating Shareholder Director Nominations, Securities Exchange Release No. 62764, 2010 WL 3343532, at *2 (Aug. 25, 2010) (adopting Rule 14a-11, *codified at*, 17 C.F.R. § 240.14a11) (2017). *See* Del. Code Ann. tit. 8, § 112 (2011). Rule 14a-11 was declared invalid in *Bus. Roundtable v. SEC*, 647 F.3d 1144 (D.C. Cir. 2011). *See infra* notes 181–183 and accompanying text; discussion Chapters 4, 5 herein.

uniformity—although Delaware allows the inclusion of shareholder nominees in proxy materials (if the subject company's bylaws so permit), many states do not.[179] The SEC reasoned: "We believe that having a uniform standard that applies to all companies subject to the rule will simplify use of the rule for shareholders; allowing different procedures and requirements to be adopted by each company could add significant complexity and cost for shareholders and undermine the purposes of our new rule."[180]

Nonetheless, Rule 14a-11 was invalidated. The U.S. Court of Appeals for the District of Columbia struck it down in 2011 due to the SEC's violation of the Administrative Procedure Act.[181] The appellate court reasoned that Rule 14a-11 had been promulgated without proper economic justification or consideration of efficiency, competition, and capital formation. In sum, the court found that the SEC's cost/benefit analysis was speculative and insufficient.[182] Nonetheless, due to enhanced institutional shareholder activism, many publicly-held corporations have amended their bylaws to permit eligible shareholders to nominate a specified number of directors, with such nominees included on the company's proxy card.[183]

With respect to the national securities exchanges, in 2003, both the NYSE and Nasdaq proposed amending their listing standards in relation to nominating committees.[184] The language in those proposals, almost unchanged, became NYSE § 303A.04 and Nasdaq § 5605(e) as the SEC expeditiously approved these proposals.[185]

The NYSE and Nasdaq listing standards for director nominations are similar in scope but differ somewhat from one another. The NYSE rules require directors to form a "nominating/corporate governance" committee comprised entirely

---

[179] Facilitating Shareholder Director Nominations, Securities Exchange Release No. 62764, at *4.

[180] *Id.* at *19.

[181] *See Bus. Roundtable*, 647 F.3d 1144. Under the Administrative Procedure Act, agency actions cannot be "arbitrary, capricious, an abuse of discretion, or otherwise not in accordance with law." 5 U.S.C. § 706(2)(A) (2012).

[182] *Bus. Roundtable*, 647 F.3d at 1148, 1150 ("We agree with the petitioners that the Commission's prediction [that] directors might choose not to oppose shareholder nominees had no basis beyond mere speculation."). For further discussion, *see* Chapters 4, 5 herein.

[183] *See* Weil, Gotshal & Manges LLP, Governance & Securities Alert (Nov. 11, 2016) ("Since January 1, 2015, 300 companies have adopted a proxy access bylaw following a shareholder proposal, negotiations with a proponent or proactively."); discussion Chapters 4, 5 herein.

[184] *See In re New York Stock Exchange, Inc.*, Securities Exchange Act Release No. 47672, 2003 WL 1870339 (Apr. 11, 2003); *In re Nat'l Ass'n of Securities Dealers, Inc.*, Securities Exchange Act Release No. 47516, 2003 WL 1248830 (Mar. 17, 2003).

[185] *See* Securities Exchange Act Release No. 48745, 2003 WL 22509738 (Nov. 4, 2003).

of independent directors.[186] The committee must adopt a written charter that addresses such committee's purpose and responsibilities as well as providing an annual performance evaluation of the committee.[187] The charter must be available on the company's website, and the company's annual proxy statement or annual report on Form 10-K must disclose how to access the charter online.[188] Nasdaq, on the other hand, does not mandate that a nomination committee be established. Rather, director nominees may be selected by either a vote of a majority of independent directors or by a committee comprised of only independent directors.[189] Nasdaq also does not require a charter—depending on the option selected, a listed company may either adopt a charter or board resolution to address the nomination process.[190]

Nasdaq also offers an exception to its own independence requirements. If the nomination committee has at least three members, then another director may be appointed to the committee—even though that person is not independent so long as he or she is not an executive officer or a relative of one—provided that the board of directors determines that such an appointment is "required by the best interests of the Company and its Shareholders."[191] Whatever circumstance leads to this eventuality must be "exceptional and limited."[192]

---

[186] NYSE, Inc., Listed Company Manual § 303A.04(a). While § 303A.04 does not specify how to determine independence for nominating committee members, it may well be that the test in § 303A.02 should apply.

Focusing on the corporate governance functions of the nominating/corporate governance committee, The Conference Board's Commission on Public Trust and Private Enterprise (2010) recommended:

> The Commission believes that it is important that each corporation establish a committee of independent directors to oversee corporate governance issues, including the statement of corporate governance principles and the performance evaluations of the board, its committees, and each director, as necessary. The Commission therefore endorses the principle that each listed company, other than controlled companies, have a nominating/corporate governance committee composed entirely of independent directors (or functional equivalent consisting solely of independent directors). . . .

[187] NYSE Manual § 303A.04(b). At a minimum, the nominating/corporate governance committee must be responsible for "identify[ing] individuals qualified to become board members, consistent with criteria approved by the board, and [selecting], or recommend[ing] that the board select, the director nominees for the next annual meeting of shareholders; develop[ing] and recommend[ing] to the board a set of corporate governance guidelines applicable to the corporation; and oversee[ing] the evaluation of the board and management." *Id.* Commentary.

[188] *Id.* at § 303A.04, Commentary.

[189] Nasdaq, Inc., Stock Market Rules § 5605(e)(1).

[190] *Id.* at § 5605(e)(2). *See id.* IM-5606-7 (stating that § 5605(e) is "intended to provide flexibility for a company to choose an appropriate board structure and reduce resource burdens, while ensuring that Independent Directors approve all nominations").

[191] *Id.* at § 5605(e)(3).

[192] *Id.* For further discussion, *see* Chapter 5 herein.

VII. The Emergence and Codification of Corporate Codes of Ethics

Corporate codes of conduct are not new. One commentator estimated that in 1998, four years before SOX was enacted, that over 80 percent of Fortune 1000 companies had formal written codes of conduct.[193] Nearly a century beforehand, in 1913, J.C. Penney had a corporate code of ethics.[194] However, the real boom of ethics codes did not transpire until the latter quarter of the twentieth century. In response to new laws and revelations of corporate fraud and corruption, companies implemented ethics codes to help effectuate law compliance and dissuade government scrutiny.[195] Nonetheless, some critics assert that these ethics codes are merely window dressing, ineffectual in actually enhancing employee behavior.[196]

In view of these developments, it is not surprising that SOX included provisions governing codes of ethics. At the turn of the twenty-first century, the dot-com bubble that had been growing for almost a decade burst in grand fashion, revealing financial debacles and massive fraud.[197] Now household names, the country watched Enron, WorldCom, Tyco, Adelphia, Global Crossings, and others implode.[198]

---

[193] *See* John C. Ruhnka and Heidi Boerstler, *Governmental Incentives for Corporate Self-Regulation*, 17 J. Bus. Ethics 309, 324 (1998) (stating also that "at least some of these codes contain[ed] explicit mechanisms for monitoring compliance, employee reporting of code violations, investigations and punishment of violations of such codes").

[194] Joshua A. Newberg, *Corporate Codes of Ethics, Mandatory Disclosure, and the Market for Ethical Conduct*, 29 Vt. L. Rev. 253, 255 n.8 (2005); Mary Ellen Oliverio, *The Implementation of a Code of Ethics: The Early Efforts of One Entrepreneur*, 8 J. Bus. Ethics 367, 368–69 (1989).

[195] *See* Newberg, *supra* note 194, at 255–56 (describing the growth of corporate codes of ethics in response to the Foreign Corrupt Practices Act of 1977, the 1987 publication of the Treadway Commission Report on financial reporting, and the 1991 publication of the U.S. Sentencing Guidelines for Organizations); *see also* Z. Jill Barclift, *Codes of Ethics and State Fiduciary Duties: Where Is the Line?*, 1 J. Bus. Entrepreneurship & L. 237, 241 (2008) (recounting the state of ethics codes pre-SOX).

[196] *See* Kimberly D. Krawiec, *Cosmetic Compliance and the Failure of Negotiated Governance*, 81 Wash. U. L.Q. 487, 511 (2003) (despite the ubiquity of ethics codes, "little evidence exists to support the theory that ethics codes modify employee behavior"); William S. Laufer, *Corporate Liability, Risk Shifting, and the Paradox of Compliance*, 54 Vand. L. Rev. 1343, 1406 (1999) (stating, with respect to corporate ethics code, "[t]he prospects of moral hazards are . . . confirmed after viewing the evidence that corporate deviance is often tolerated, if not tacitly encouraged, by an implicit agenda of top management").

[197] *See* William H. Donaldson, Testimony Concerning Implementation of the Sarbanes-Oxley Act of 2002, Senate Committee on Banking, Housing and Urban Affairs (Sept. 9, 2003), *available at* https://www.sec.gov/news/testimony/090903tswhd.htm.

[198] *Id.* In his testimony before the Senate Committee on Banking, Housing and Urban Affairs, SEC Chairman Donaldson stated:

> Starting in the second quarter of 2000, the bubble burst. Stock prices plummeted. Investors fled the markets. The IPO market disappeared. As happened after the crash of 1929, the falling market that began in 2000 led to other revelations. Starting with the unfolding of the Enron story in October 2001, it became apparent that the boom years had been accompanied by fraud, other misconduct and a serious erosion

Shortly thereafter, "[t]o address the widespread collapse of investor confidence and [in] recognition that something had gone seriously awry in segments of corporate America," SOX expeditiously was enacted.[199]

Among SOX's mandates, Section 406 directed the SEC to issue rules requiring a subject issuer to disclose whether it has adopted an ethical code for its senior financial officers and, if not, set forth the reasons why such company does not have such a code.[200] Another SOX provision required the SEC to adopt regulations to require a subject company promptly to disclose any change to its ethical code or waiver thereof.[201] The definition of a "code of ethics" under SOX is a written standard "reasonably necessary to promote" the following attributes:

(1) honest and ethical conduct, including the ethical handling of actual or apparent conflicts of interest between personal and professional relationships;
(2) full, fair, accurate, timely and understandable disclosure in the periodic reports required to be filed by the issuer; and
(3) compliance with applicable governmental rules and regulations.[202]

The SEC proposed rules in accordance with SOX[203] and adopted final rules in 2003.[204] In doing so, the Commission elaborated upon the somewhat amorphous canvas of SOX's statutory provisions. For example, Section 406 of SOX calls for disclosure by a subject company of its code of ethics, encompassing "senior financial

in business principles. The low points in this story are now household names—not just Enron, but also WorldCom, Tyco, Adelphia and others. There was other serious misconduct as well, including in the once-celebrated IPO market, which in too many cases lacked both fairness and integrity. The cost of this corner-cutting to investors has been enormous. . . .

. . . .

To address the widespread collapse of investor confidence and the recognition that something had gone seriously awry in segments of corporate America, Congress approved and the President signed into law the Sarbanes-Oxley Act. At the East Room signing ceremony, the President promised, "to use the full authority of the Government to expose corruption, punish wrongdoers, and defend the rights and interests of American workers and investors."

[199] *Id.*

[200] Sarbanes-Oxley Act, § 406(a) (codified at 15 U.S.C.A. § 7264(a) (2012)). *See* discussion in Chapter 5 herein.

[201] SOX at § 406(b). Such prompt disclosure is to be made by a Form 8-K filing. *Id.*

[202] *Id.* at § 406(c). *See* discussion in Chapter 5 herein.

[203] Proposed Rule: Disclosure Required by Sections 404, 406, 407 of the Sarbanes-Oxley Act of 2002, Securities Exchange Act Release No. 46701, 2002 WL 31370458 (Oct. 22, 2002) (among other items, proposing that subject companies be "required to disclose whether they have adopted a code of ethics that covers their principal executive officers and senior financial officers, or if they have not, an explanation of why they have not").

[204] Disclosure Required by Sections 406 and 407 of the Sarbanes-Oxley Act of 2002, Securities Exchange Act No. 47235, 2003 WL 164269 (Jan. 23, 2003).

officers"—applicable to such company's "principal financial officer and comptroller or principal accounting officer, or persons performing similar functions."[205] Implementing this mandate, the SEC adopted Item 406 of Regulation S-K, which applies not only to the positions set forth in SOX but extends as well to the company's "principal executive officer."[206] The definition of "code of ethics" was expounded, adding that such code also should seek to effectuate "[t]he prompt internal reporting . . . to an appropriate person" of code violations, as well as "[a]ccountability for adherence to the code."[207] Accordingly, the SEC took the following approach:

> We continue to believe that ethics codes do, and should, vary from company to company and that decisions as to the specific provisions of the code, compliance procedures and disciplinary measures for ethical breaches are best left to the company. Such an approach is consistent with our disclosure-based regulatory scheme. Therefore, the rules do not specify every detail that the company must address in its code of ethics, or prescribe any specific language that the code of ethics must include. They further do not specify the procedures that the company should develop, or the types of sanctions that the company should impose, to ensure compliance with its code of ethics. We strongly encourage companies to adopt codes that are broader and more comprehensive than necessary to meet the new disclosure requirements.[208]

---

[205] Sarbanes-Oxley Act, § 406(a).

[206] 17 C.F.R. § 229.406(a) (2017). *See* Disclosures Required by Section 406 and 407, Securities Exchange Act Release No. 47235, 2003 WL 164269 at *16 (Jan. 23, 2003) (stating that "we continue to think that it is appropriate and consistent with the purposes of the Sarbanes-Oxley Act to extend the scope of our rules under Section 406").

[207] 17 C.F.R. § 229.406(b)(4)–(5) (2017). Hence, as stated by the SEC in the adopting release:

> The final rule defines the term "code of ethics" as written standards that are reasonably designed to deter wrongdoing and to promote:
>
> - Honest and ethical conduct, including the ethical handling of actual or apparent conflicts of interest between personal and professional relationships;
> - Full, fair, accurate, timely, and understandable disclosure in reports and documents that a registrant files with, or submits to, the Commission and in other public communications made by the registrant;
> - Compliance with applicable governmental laws, rules and regulations;
> - The prompt internal reporting to an appropriate person or persons identified in the code of violations of the code; and
> - Accountability for adherence to the code.

2003 WL 164269, at *17. *See* discussion Chapter 5 herein.

[208] Securities Exchange Act Release No. 47235, 2003 WL 164269 at *17.

This federal codification of corporate codes of ethics and subsequent SEC regulation propelled the stock exchanges to undertake their own rule-making. Indeed, the brevity of SOX Section 406 may be viewed as impacting stock exchange regulation.[209] The NYSE requires listed companies to "adopt and disclose a code of business conduct and ethics for directors, officers and employees, and promptly disclose any waivers of the code for directors or executive officers."[210] Any waiver of said code for directors or executive officers may only be made by the board of directors or a committee of the board.[211] Furthermore, companies must promulgate compliance standards and procedures to help effectuate the subject code's effective operation.[212] And while the NYSE gives listed companies leeway to determine their own policies, the "most important topics" should be addressed, including: conflicts of interest, corporate opportunities, competing with the corporation, fair dealing, confidentiality, protection and appropriate use of listed company assets, adherence to applicable laws and regulations, and facilitating the reporting of illegal or unethical behavior.[213]

Interestingly, these NYSE provisions derived, at least in large part, from a NYSE Corporate Accountability and Listing Standards Committee Report from 2002[214] that included code of ethics recommendations. According to the Report, a business's code of conduct can "focus the board and management on areas of ethical risk, provide guidance to personnel to help them recognize and deal with ethical issues, provide mechanisms to report unethical conduct, and help to foster a culture of honesty and accountability."[215] Thus, the Committee recommended that NYSE listed companies be required to adopt and disclose a code of business conduct for officers, directors, and employees.[216] The Committee also recommended seven topics for codes of conduct to cover—all of which were adopted into NYSE Section 303A.10.[217]

While like the NYSE in requiring that a listed company adopt a code of conduct and similar in its application to directors, officers, and employees, the applicable

---

[209] *See* Donald C. Langevoort, *Placebo Statutes?: Sarbanes-Oxley and Ethics Code Disclosures*, 96 Va. L. Rev. In Brief 9, 10 (2010) (calling the text of Section 406 "frightfully ambiguous"). *See also* Usha Rodriguez and Mike Stegemoller, *Placebo Ethics*, 96 Va. L. Rev. 1 (2010).

[210] NYSE, Inc., Listed Company Manual § 303A.10. Both the NYSE and Nasdaq code of ethics requirements were approved by the SEC in November 2003. *See* Securities Exchange Act Release No. 48745, 2003 WL 22509738 (Nov. 4, 2003).

[211] NYSE, Inc., Listed Company Manual § 303A.10 Commentary.

[212] *Id.*

[213] *Id*

[214] *See* Corporate Accountability Report, *supra* note 50.

[215] *Id.* at 20.

[216] *Id.* (as well as requiring prompt disclosure of any waiver of such code of ethics for executive officers and directors).

[217] *See id.* at 21–22; NYSE, Inc., Listed Company Manual § 303A.10.

Nasdaq listing rule attaches its definition of a code of ethics to SOX itself and Item 406 of SEC Regulation S-K.[218] Moreover, an interpretive publication following the adoption of the Nasdaq rule stresses that "[e]thical behavior is required and expected of every corporate director, officer and employee. . . ."[219] The rationale underlying the requirement that a listed company implement and enforce a code of conduct is explained by Nasdaq as follows:

> As the Sarbanes-Oxley Act recognizes, investors are harmed when the real or perceived private interest of a director, officer or employee is in conflict with the interests of the Company, as when the individual receives improper personal benefits as a result of his or her position with the Company, or when the individual has other duties, responsibilities or obligations that run counter to his or her duty to the Company. Also, the disclosures a Company makes to the Commission are the essential source of information about the Company for regulators and investors—there can be no question about the duty to make them fairly, accurately and timely. Finally, illegal action must be dealt with swiftly and the violators reported to the appropriate authorities.[220]

VIII. Conclusion

Stock exchange rules are a fundamental component of the federalization of the corporate governance landscape. Although technically not government regulation, the directives issued by federal legislation and the SEC (and thereafter implemented by the securities exchanges) make clear that SRO rules play a central role in the enhancement of sound corporate governance practices and policies. Hence, it would be an oversight to address the federalization of corporate governance without examining the importance of stock exchange regulation. This chapter thus seeks to achieve this objective by focusing on key mandates set forth in stock exchange rules that directly impact the federalization of corporate governance.

---

[218] Nasdaq, Inc., Stock Market Rules § 5610 (2009); *See* Securities Exchange Act Release No. 48745 (Nov. 4, 2003) (approving Nasdaq ethics rule).

[219] Nasdaq, Inc., Stock Market Rules § 5610, IM-5610 (2009).

[220] *Id.* Note that, at the 2016 SEC Speakers Conference, the SEC's Investor Advocate warned that there has been a downward movement in the stock exchanges' listing standards since 2015 when the NYSE began its conversion to a for-profit business. *See* Jacquelyn Lamb, *SEC's Investor Advocate Warns of Downward Drift in Exchange Listing Rules*, Feb. 23, 2016, at http://jimhamilton.blogspot.com/2016/02/secs-investor-advocate-warns-of.html. For further discussion, *see* Chapter 5 herein.

7

UNRESOLVED BUSINESS: FEDERAL CORPORATE GOVERNANCE ENHANCEMENTS

I. Introduction

In the preceding chapters, the analysis has focused on the federalization of corporate governance from both a historical and contemporary perspective. A myriad of different subject matters have been explored—ranging from the federal incorporation fervor of proponents over a century ago to the mandates emanating from the enactment of the Sarbanes-Oxley and Dodd-Frank Acts.

While critics contend that this march toward federal corporate governance standards is ill-conceived,[1] another view is that glaring deficiencies remain in both applicable state company law and current federal regulation. The appropriate response to remediate these deficiencies is the application of federal standards in a measured and directed manner. Consistent therewith, this chapter focuses on several important matters that merit reconsideration.

---

[1] *See, e.g.*, Stephen M. Bainbridge, *Dodd-Frank: Quack Federal Corporate Governance Round II*, 95 Minn. L. Rev. 1779 (2011); Jill E. Fisch, *Leave It to Delaware: Why Congress Should Stay Out of Corporate Governance*, 37 Del. J. Corp. L. 731 (2013); Roberta Romano, *The Sarbanes-Oxley Act and the Making of Quack Corporate Governance*, 114 Yale L.J. 1521 (2005). *See generally* Roberta S. Karmel, *Is It Time for a Federal Corporation Law?*, 57 Brook. L. Rev. 55 (1991).

II. Undue Deference by Federal Courts to State Law

U.S. Supreme Court decisions have stressed the applicability of state law with respect to the internal affairs of corporations. As stated by the Court in a decision over 40 years ago: "Corporations are creatures of state law, and investors commit their funds to corporate directors on the understanding that, except where federal law *expressly* requires certain responsibilities of directors with respect to stockholders, state law will govern the internal affairs of the corporation."[2] This proposition has been expansively interpreted by the Supreme Court, extending even to shareholder derivative actions seeking redress under the *federal* securities laws. In *Kamen v. Kemper Financial Services, Inc.*,[3] the Court held that in shareholder derivative suits brought under the federal securities laws, the board of director demand futility exception is to be determined pursuant to the law of the applicable state of incorporation.[4] Following *Kamen*, this directive routinely is applied by the lower federal courts to claims based on the federal securities laws in shareholder derivative actions.[5]

As a matter of federal jurisprudence, this holding is troubling: the determination of whether relief is available under a federal statute in the derivative suit context frequently hinges upon the law of the subject corporation's state of incorporation.[6] Indeed, as discussed in Chapter 3 and later in this chapter, the Supreme Court at times has construed the parameters of a federal securities statute by applying state law principles. A key example is the federal law of insider trading under Section

---

[2] *Cort v. Ash*, 422 U.S. 66, 80 (1975), *quoted in*, *Santa Fe Indus., Inc. v. Green*, 430 U.S. 462, 479 (1977) (emphasis in *Santa Fe*).

[3] 500 U.S. 90 (1991).

[4] *Id.* at 108–09. *See id.* at 108 (stating that "where a gap in the federal securities laws must be bridged by a rule that bears on the allocation of governing powers within the corporation, federal courts should incorporate *state* law into federal common law unless the particular state law in question is inconsistent with the policies underlying the federal statute") (emphasis in original), *relying on*, *Burks v. Lasker*, 441 U.S. 471 (1979). Moreover, where the federal court lawsuit seeks relief based on state law, the federal district judge must determine demand futility pursuant to Rule 23.1 of the Federal Rules of Civil Procedure consistent with the applicable law in the subject state of incorporation. *Id.*; cases cited note 5 *infra*. *See generally* Theresa A. Gabaldon, *State Answers to Federal Questions: The Common Law of Federal Securities Regulation*, 20 J. Corp. L. 155 (1994).

[5] *See, e.g.*, *Cottrell v. Duke*, 829 F.3d 983, 990 n.5 (8th Cir. 2016) (applying the *Kamen* directive "even though some of the shareholders' claims are based on federal law"); *In re ZAGG Inc. Shareholder Derivative Action*, 826 F.3d 1222, 1228 (10th Cir. 2016) (applying *Kamen*); *Hillman v. Loga*, 697 F.3d 299, 302 (5th Cir. 2012) (applying *Kamen*).

[6] The demand futility requirements in a shareholder derivative action filed in a state, such as Delaware, the premier state of incorporation for publicly-traded companies (*see* discussion in Chapter 2 herein), have far-reaching impact on the likelihood of a plaintiff's success in the subject litigation. *See, e.g.*, *Levine v. Smith*, 591 A.2d 194 (Del. 1991); *Aronson v. Lewis*, 473 A.2d 805 (Del. 1984); *Zapata Corp. v. Maldonado*, 430 A.2d 779 (Del. 1981); discussion in Marc I. Steinberg, *Securities Regulation: Liabilities and Remedies* §§ 14.02–14.05 (2017).

10(b) of the Securities Exchange Act where the Court has held that state common law principles be applied to determine the scope of this prohibition.[7]

One may question whether this deference to state law to determine the application and scope of various provisions of the federal securities laws is warranted. As Chapters 3 and 4 of this book illustrate, for the last half of the twentieth century, significant matters within the ambit of the federal securities laws greatly impacted corporate governance. The Sarbanes-Oxley and Dodd-Frank Acts, enacted since the beginning of this century, entrench this federalization reality. Accordingly, the Supreme Court's reliance on state law standards to interpret federal law, given the federalization of corporate governance that has occurred, is misplaced.

III. Tender Offer Tactics—Federal Law Should Apply

The legality of defensive tactics undertaken by a target corporation to fend off a hostile bid today, for the most part, is determined pursuant to state law fiduciary standards.[8] While, as discussed in Chapter 3, federal law addresses the process by which tender offers are conducted[9] and, on occasion, prohibits a particular defensive maneuver,[10] defensive tactics implicate the duties of care and loyalty, thereby coming within the purview of the internal affairs doctrine.[11] Due to its status as

---

[7] *See, e.g.*, *United States v. O'Hagan*, 521 U.S. 642 (1997); *Dirks v. SEC*, 463 U.S. 646 (1983); *Chiarella v. United States*, 445 U.S. 222 (1980); discussion in Chapter 3 herein as well as later in this chapter.

[8] *See Schreiber v. Burlington N. Inc.*, 472 U.S. 1 (1985) (holding that § 14(e), the federal antifraud tender offer provision, does not encompass substantive fairness and is limited in scope to that of disclosure).

In this regard, enactment by several states of anti-takeover and stakeholder statutes also comprise an aspect of this framework. These state statutes frequently supplement takeover defenses implemented by a target company's board of directors. As discussed in Chapter 1 herein, a number of these statutes have passed constitutional scrutiny, thus surviving challenges to their validity. From a general perspective, although these statutes remain pertinent, determinations regarding the propriety of defensive tactics normally are made by the state courts applying state law fiduciary standards of care and loyalty. *See CTS Corp. v. Dynamics Corp. of Am.*, 481 U.S. 69 (1987); *Edgar v. MITE Corp.*, 457 U.S. 624 (1982); Symposium, *Delaware Antitakeover Statute*, 65 Bus. Law. No. 3 (2010); discussion in Chapter 1 herein.

[9] For example, as discussed in Chapter 3, federal statutes as well as SEC rules address such subjects as the time period that a tender offer must remain open, that all shareholders are entitled to pro rata treatment during the period in which the tender offer remains open, and that the best price paid to any shareholder must be paid to any other shareholder who tenders its shares.

[10] *See, e.g.*, SEC Rule 13e-4(f)(8), 14d-10, 17 C.F.R. §§ 240.13e-4(f)(8), 14d-10 (2017) (prohibiting exclusionary tender offers, thereby mandating that a subject tender offer must be made to all shareholders). The promulgation of these SEC rules, in practical effect, nullified the Delaware Supreme Court's decision in *Unocal Corp. v. Mesa Petroleum Co.*, 493 A.2d 949 (Del. 1985), which upheld the use of an exclusionary tender offer that precluded the hostile bidder from participating in such offer. *See* discussion in Chapter 3 herein.

[11] As discussed in Chapter 1, the internal affairs doctrine generally provides that the law where the subject corporation is incorporated governs the relations among such corporation, its officers and directors, and its shareholders. *See CTS Corp. v. Dynamics Corp. of Am.*, 481 U.S. 69, 91 (1987) (stating that it is "an accepted part of

the jurisdiction where most significant publicly-traded companies incorporate,[12] Delaware is the principal decision-maker with respect to the legality of defensive tactics. For example, the validity of a Delaware-incorporated company's adoption and implementation of a shareholder rights plan (i.e., "poison pill") that thereby renders that company significantly more difficult to acquire, is assessed under Delaware law.[13] The same holds true with respect to the adoption and execution by the target company's board of directors of a long-term business strategy that has the effect of defeating a prospective acquirer's takeover bid.[14] Likewise, lockups extended by a Delaware-incorporated company (including the grant of an option to purchase an attractive corporate asset) to a favored bidder is evaluated under principles of Delaware law.[15] The consequence is that the Delaware courts, applying Delaware statutory and case law, frequently determine whether tender offers involving tens of billions of dollars will be consummated.

Prior to the U.S. Supreme Court's 1985 decision in *Schreiber v. Burlington Northern, Inc.*,[16] a number of federal courts held that Section 14(e) of the Securities Exchange Act extended beyond requiring disclosure, to encompass certain substantive conduct. The rationale was that, even though fully disclosed, defensive measures that artificially inhibited the operation of a fair market with respect to the target company's stock, thereby preventing such company's stockholders from tendering

---

the business landscape in this country for States to create corporations, to prescribe their powers, and to define the rights that are acquired by purchasing their shares [; and that a] State has an interest in promoting stable relationships among parties involved in the corporations it charters. . . .").

[12] *See, e.g.*, William L. Cary, *Federalism and Corporate Law: Reflections Upon Delaware*, 83 Yale L.J. 663 (1974); Jill E. Fisch, *The Peculiar Role of the Delaware Courts in the Competition for Corporate Charters*, 68 U. Cin. L. Rev. 1061 (2000); Panel, Lawrence A. Hamermesh, *Sarbanes-Oxley Governance Issues—The Policy Foundations of Delaware Corporate Law*, 106 Colum. L. Rev. 1749 (2006); Mark J. Roe, *Delaware's Competition*, 117 Harv. L. Rev. 588 (2003); discussion in Chapters 1, 2, 3 herein.

[13] *See, e.g.*, *Versata Enters., Inc. v. Selectica, Inc.*, 5 A.3d 586 (Del. 2010); *Unitrin, Inc. v. Am. Gen. Corp.*, 651 A.2d 1361 (Del. 1995); *Unocal Corp. v. Mesa Petroleum Co.*, 493 A.2d 946 (Del. 1985). Generally, a shareholder rights plan, also called a poison pill, is "an antitakeover provision whereby certain securities (such as rights or warrants) of the target company, upon consummation of an enumerated transaction or event, are convertible into the common stock or other security of the target (or of the acquirer) or into cash." Marc I. Steinberg, *Understanding Securities Law* 494 (6th ed. 2014).

[14] *See, e.g.*, *Paramount Commc'ns, Inc. v. Time, Inc.*, 571 A.2d 1140 (Del. 1990). For an article critical of this decision, *see* Marc I. Steinberg, *Nightmare on Main Street: The Paramount Picture Horror Show*, 16 Del. J. Corp. L. 1 (1991).

[15] *See, e.g.*, *Omnicare, Inc. v. NCS Healthcare, Inc.*, 818 A.2d 914 (Del. 2000). Generally, a lockup is "an arrangement, made in connection with the contemplated acquisition of a publicly-held entity, that gives the prospective acquirer an advantage in acquiring the subject company over other potential acquirers." Steinberg, *supra* note 13, at 491. The Delaware courts have invalidated a number of these lockups. *See, e.g.*, *Paramount Commc'ns, Inc. v. QVC Network, Inc.*, 637 A.2d 34 (Del. 1994); *MacAndrews & Forbes Holdings v. Revlon, Inc.*, 506 A.2d 173 (Del. 1986); discussion in Chapter 1 herein.

[16] 472 U.S. 1 (1985).

their shares to a prospective acquirer, were "manipulative" within the ambit of Section 14(e).[17] Relying on that provision's statutory language, its legislative history, and policy reasons, the assertion was made that Section 14(e) had a dual purpose: "first, to provide shareholders the required information; and second, to prevent any conduct that unduly impedes the shareholders' exercise of the decision-making prerogative guaranteed to them by Congress."[18]

The reasoning underlying the above approach is that the disclosure mandate contained in Section 14(e) is of limited value to informed shareholder decision-making when the impact of certain defensive tactics is to prevent shareholders from, in practicality, making any meaningful decision. As stated by a former SEC Chairman, the statute's objective was "to provide the investor, the person who is required to make a decision, an opportunity to examine and to assess the relevant facts and to reach a decision without being pressured and without being subject to unwarranted techniques which are designed to prevent that from happening."[19] And, as stated by a federal district court judge, the statute was designed to protect "the rights of shareholders to transfer managerial power by tendering their shares, with proper information and without undue interference."[20]

This rationale was swiftly rebuked by the Supreme Court in *Schreiber*. Holding that Section 14(e) encompasses only the adequacy and accuracy of disclosure, the Court stated: "All three species of misconduct listed in section 14(e), i.e., fraudulent, deceptive or manipulative . . . are directed at failure to disclose."[21] The *Schreiber* decision thus signifies that the legitimacy of takeover tactics is largely within the province of state law.

---

[17] *See, e.g., Mobil Corp. v. Marathon Oil Co.*, 669 F.2d 366 (6th Cir. 1981); *Data Probe Acquisition Corp. v. Datatab, Inc.*, 568 F. Supp. 1538 (S.D.N.Y.), *rev'd*, 722 F.2d 1 (2d Cir. 1983).

[18] *Data Probe Acquisition*, 568 F. Supp. at 1545. *See* James Junewicz, *The Appropriate Limits of Section 14(e) of the Securities Exchange Act of 1934*, 62 Tex. L. Rev. 1171 (1984); Mark Loewenstein, *Section 14(e) of the Williams Act and the Rule 10b-5 Comparisons*, 71 Geo. L.J. 1311 (1983); Gary Lynch and Marc Steinberg, *The Legitimacy of Defensive Tactics in Tender Offers*, 64 Cornell L. Rev. 901 (1979); Elliott Weiss, *Defensive Responses to Tender Offers and the Williams Act Prohibition against Manipulation*, 35 Vand. L. Rev. 1087 (1982). Another argument posited was that target board of director conduct that prevented shareholders from tendering their stock constituted constructive fraud under Section 14(e). This argument was unlikely to succeed due to the Supreme Court's holding in *Santa Fe Indus., Inc. v. Green*, 430 U.S. 462 (1977), that breach of fiduciary duty, unaccompanied by deficiency in disclosure, is not "deceptive" within the scope of Section 10(b) and Rule 10b-5. *See* discussion in Chapters 1, 2, and 3 herein.

[19] Senate Committee on Banking and Currency, Full Disclosure of Corporate Equity Ownership and in Corporate Takeover Bids, S. Rep. No. 550, 90th Cong., 1st Sess., at 15 (1967) (statement of SEC Chairman Manuel F. Cohen).

[20] *Data Probe Acquisition*, 568 F. Supp. at 1545, *rev'd*, 722 F.2d 1 (2d Cir. 1983). *See Mobil Corp. v. Marathon Oil Co.*, 669 F.2d 366 (6th Cir. 1981); sources cited note 18 *supra*.

[21] 472 U.S. at 8.

Clearly, the Supreme Court has spoken on this subject—and has spoken without equivocation. But the more pressing question is whether Congress should enact federal legislation encompassing the use of defensive tactics in tender offers involving companies traded on a national securities exchange. This way, state courts would continue to adjudicate substantive tactics with respect to smaller companies whereas federal law would be the determiner with respect to national and global corporations. Congress has used this approach in its enactment of the Sarbanes-Oxley and Dodd-Frank Acts by requiring that companies whose securities are listed on a national securities exchange are subject to certain requirements—for example, that the composition of an exchange-listed company's audit and compensation committees be comprised entirely of independent directors.[22] As Professor Ted Fiflis astutely inquired shortly after the Supreme Court handed down its decision in *Schreiber*: "One may properly ask whether it is appropriate for Delaware, which conceivably may not be the abode of a single Unocal [or other global company] shareholder, to fix national policy in the international securities market, while Congress and the federal courts, Nero-like, abdicate a policymaking role."[23]

It indeed is striking that, by means of the Sarbanes-Oxley Act, Congress has prohibited publicly-held companies from ordinarily extending loans to their directors and executive officers.[24] Prior to enactment of this provision, assessment of the substantive propriety of such loans was solely within the province of state corporate law.[25] Displeased with the laxity the state courts showed in upholding these loans, Congress determined to remedy this perceived void in meaningful review by legislating a general prohibition of such loans.[26]

---

[22] *See* discussion in Chapters 5 and 6 herein.

[23] Ted Fiflis, *Of Lollipops and Law—A Proposal for a National Policy concerning Tender Offer Defenses*, 19 U.C. Davis L. Rev. 303, 306 (1986).

[24] Sarbanes-Oxley Act § 402, *amending*, § 13(k) of the Securities Exchange Act, 15 U.S.C. § 78m(k) (2012). As discussed in Chapter 5 herein, certain categories of loans are allowed if any such loan is made in the company's ordinary course of business and is provided to the director or officer on the same basis as loans extended to the general public.

[25] *See, e.g., Aronson v. Lewis*, 473 A.2d 805, 817 (Del. 1984) (stating, with respect to interest-free loan provided to company's largest shareholder who had a 47 percent stock interest, "the mere existence of such loans, given the broad corporate powers conferred by Delaware law, does not even state a claim").

[26] Sarbanes-Oxley Act § 402, *amending*, § 13(k) of the Securities Exchange Act, 15 U.S.C. § 78m(k) (2012). Interestingly, § 402 of S. 2673 called for the timely disclosure, rather than prohibition, of such loans. *See* S. Rep. No. 107-205, at 54 (2002). As explained by Professor Harold S. Bloomenthal: Section 402 "as amended on the floor of the Senate and adopted by the Act deleted the disclosure requirement and in lieu thereof provides that it is unlawful for a public company to directly or indirectly 'extend, maintain, or arrange' or 'renew' a personal loan to any director or officer (or equivalent) of the company." Harold S. Bloomenthal, *Sarbanes-Oxley Act in Perspective* 88 (2002). *See* discussion *supra* notes 24–25 and accompanying text; Chapter 5 herein.

Yet, Congress has declined to legislate a national policy focusing on defensive maneuvers utilized in tender offers having national and global ramifications. It makes little sense that Delaware, a state with beautiful beaches and a population of fewer than one million individuals,[27] is the key determiner of whether these types of major acquisitions come to fruition. Irrespective of the approach ultimately adopted by Congress,[28] the use of defensive tactics and other maneuvers (either offensively or defensively) that significantly impact the conducting of tender offers as well as other types of acquisitions (such as mergers) for companies whose securities are nationally traded should be a matter of federal law. The time is far past due for Congress to remedy this oversight and enact federal legislation, thereby recognizing that this dilemma is one of national and global magnitude.[29]

---

[27] *See Delaware Population to Approach 1 Million in 2020*, delawareonline (July 5, 2016), *available at* http://www.delawareonline.com/story/news/2016/07/05/delaware-population-approach-1-million-2020/86708466/.

[28] Several different approaches have been advanced with respect to the use of defensive tactics in tender offers, including, for example: (1) the business judgment rule should be applied to the legitimacy of defensive tactics (*see* Martin Lipton, *Takeover Bids in the Target's Boardroom*, 35 Bus. Law. 101 (1979)); (2) deference should be given to defensive tactics approved by the independent directors of the target corporation (*see* former SEC Chairman Harold M. Williams, *The Role of Directors in Takeover Offers*, 13 Rev. Sec. Reg. 963 (1980)); (3) "tender offers should be submitted to an independent person or institution, selected by the SEC, for evaluation as to (a) whether the offer is fair to the shareholders of both the offeror and target company, and (b) whether, in economic terms, the public interest is protected" (former U.S. Supreme Court Justice Arthur J. Goldberg, *Regulation of Hostile Tender Offers: A Dissenting View and Recommended Reforms*, 43 Md. L. Rev. 225 (1984)); (4) mandating a "freeze" period whereby a hostile tender offer would be open for a significant period, such as six months, during which any structural change (such as granting an option to sell a valuable asset) would be permissible only if shareholder approval were obtained (*see* Louis Lowenstein, *Pruning Deadwood in Hostile Takeovers: A Proposal for Legislation*, 83 Colum. L. Rev. 249 (1983)); (5) requiring that the target corporation's management and board of directors remain totally passive (*see* Frank Easterbrook and Daniel Fischel, *The Proper Role of Target Management in Responding to a Tender Offer*, 94 Harv. L. Rev. 1161 (1981)); (6) providing target shareholders with an unimpeded entitlement to tender their shares to the bidder, with the proviso that the target's board of directors may take appropriate measures to fend off the hostile bid if it proves that the bidder posed a clear threat to the corporation's business (*see* Marc I. Steinberg, *Tender Offer Regulation: The Need for Reform*, 23 Wake Forest L. Rev. 1 (1988)); and (7) upon receipt of a bona fide tender offer, the target company must put itself up for "auction" in an effort to procure more favorable bids from other potential offerors (*see generally* Lucian Bebchuk, *The Case for Facilitating Competing Tender Offers*, 95 Harv. L. Rev. 1028 (1982)).

[29] Thirty years ago, then SEC Chairman David S. Ruder reflected:

> Limitations on the free transferability of securities of corporations which are owned by shareholders nationwide diminish the efficiency, depth, and liquidity of the nation's securities markets. Accordingly, I believe that federal law should control in that area by preempting state statutes that unduly interfere with the free transferability of securities. I believe that corporations whose activities and ownership are national in scope should not be given protection against takeovers by the states where their primary production facilities are located. Just as I believe it to be imprudent for Congress to regulate internal corporate affairs through tender offer regulation, I believe it is imprudent for states to use their authority over matters of internal governance as a means of regulating the interstate market for corporate control.

Remarks of SEC Chairman David S. Ruder, *Federal Preemption of State Anti-Takeover Legislation*, Before the 26th Annual Corporate Counsel Institute (Chicago, Oct. 7, 1987), *reported in* Fed. Sec. L. Rep. (CCH) No.

IV. The Need for a Federal Statute on Insider Trading

As addressed in Chapter 3, the regulation of insider trading today generally is a matter of federal securities law. The states play only a minimal role in this context. Outside of Section 16 of the Securities Exchange Act and statutes that focus on particular topics,[30] the federal insider trading prohibition is judge-made law.[31] This situation has proven unfortunate. U.S. law on this subject, all too frequently, is ambiguous and subjects like persons to disparate treatment.[32] This poorly constructed framework is evidenced by scores of other countries that have rejected the U.S. regimen.[33] The appropriate solution to this dilemma is the enactment of comprehensive federal legislation on insider trading.[34]

1256, at 8–9 (1987). *See generally* James J. Park, *Reassessing the Distinction Between Corporate and Securities Law* 64 UCLA L. Rev. 116, 179 (2017) (opining that "[a] system where Delaware makes most corporate law would . . . offer more diversity than if corporate law is defined by federal statute [and that] preemption of state law through uniform policies would result in the risk that the law systematically favors one set of owners at the expense of others").

[30] Although Congress has declined to provide a comprehensive approach to the law of insider trading, it has enacted legislation focusing on particular subjects. Examples include: Section 20A of the Securities Exchange Act, 15 U.S.C. § 78tA (2012) (providing an express right of action for "contemporaneous traders" who traded the same class of security on the other side of the allegedly illegal transaction); Section 20(d) of the Securities Exchange Act, 15 U.S.C. § 78t(d) (2012) (providing that whenever conduct would violate the insider trading prohibitions with respect to purchasing, selling, or communicating regarding a subject security, "such conduct in connection with a purchase or sale of a put, call, straddle, option, privilege or security-based swap with respect to such security or with respect to a group or index of securities including such security, shall also violate and result in comparable liability to any purchaser or seller of that security under such provision, rule or regulation"); Section 21A of the Securities Exchange Act, 15 U.S.C. § 78uA (2012) (providing for the levying of up to a treble money penalty for engaging in illegal insider trading); Section 306 of the Sarbanes-Oxley Act, 15 U.S.C. § 7244 (2012) (under specified circumstances, prohibiting any director or executive officer of a publicly-held company from engaging in any trade of an equity security of such company, acquired by means of employment with that company, during a "blackout" period); The Stop Trading on Congressional Knowledge (STOCK) Act, Pub. L. No. 112-105 (2012), *modified*, S. 716 (2013) (generally applying insider trading prohibitions to U.S. Senators, members of the U.S. House of Representatives, employees of Congress, and judicial and executive branch officials as well as their staffs). Note that Section 16 of the Securities Exchange Act, 15 U.S.C. § 78p (2012), is addressed in Chapter 3 herein.

[31] *See, e.g., United States v. Salman*, 137 S. Ct. 420 (2016); *O'Hagan v. United States*, 521 U.S. 642 (1997); *Dirks v. SEC*, 463 U.S. 646 (1983); *Chiarella v. United States*, 445 U.S. 222 (1980); discussion in Chapter 3 herein.

[32] *Compare* § 10(b) of the Securities Exchange Act, 15 U.S.C. § 78j(b) (2012), *with* SEC Rule 14e-3, 17 C.F.R. § 240.14e-3 (2017); discussion *infra* notes 39–43 and accompanying text.

[33] *See* discussion *infra* notes 50–56 and accompanying text.

[34] Efforts have been made to codify the substantive law of insider trading. *See, e.g.*, The Insider Trading Proscriptions Act, S. 1380, 100th Cong., 1st Sess. (1987); The American Law Institute, *Federal Securities Code* §§ 1602, 1603, 1724 (1980). *See generally* Marc I. Steinberg and William K.S. Wang, *Insider Trading* 703–11 (3d ed. Oxford University Press 2010); Harvey Pitt and Karen Shapiro, *The Revised Insider Trading Proscriptions Act of 1988: A Legislative Remedy for a Problem That Persists*, 26 Am. Crim. L. Rev. 7 (1988); Note, *The Codification of Rule 10b-5 Private Actions in the Proposed Federal Securities* Code, 33 U. Miami L. Rev. 1615, 1623–29 (1979).

Today, because of U.S. Supreme Court decisions,[35] principles focusing on fiduciary relationship, misappropriation, and financial benefit play a key role in determining the legality of securities trades undertaken. The objective that all parties to a securities transaction have roughly equal access to material nonpublic information no longer is a viable tenet under Section 10(b) insider trading law.[36] Although the federal securities acts were intended to provide greater protection than state law,[37] the Supreme Court's undue reliance on state law principles focusing on fiduciary duty when interpreting the contours of the federal law of insider trading impedes that congressional objective.[38]

As explored in Chapter 3, the SEC, faced with restrictive Supreme Court and lower court decisions, has expanded the reach of the insider trading prohibitions pursuant to its rule-making authority. Examples include the promulgation of Rules 10b5-1, 10b5-2, and 14e-3 as well as Regulation FD—all of which are addressed in Chapter 3. Rule 14e-3 provides one striking illustration implicating different treatment in the tender offer setting. Generally, Rule 14e-3 prohibits insider trading and tipping in connection with a tender offer based on a parity of information approach: with certain exceptions, Rule 14e-3 prohibits the trading or tipping of material nonpublic information in connection with a tender offer when a person knows or has reason to know that such information was derived, directly or indirectly, from the bidder, the target company, or any intermediary who acts on behalf of either the offeror or target enterprise.[39] Because Rule 14e-3 applies solely in the tender offer context whereas Section 10(b) and SEC rules thereunder extend to any situation where there is deceptive insider trading or tipping, disparate treatment arises in similar situations. For example, a tippee, who inadvertently is the recipient of material nonpublic information from a known insider, can legally trade if the subject transaction is structured as a merger but would violate Rule 14e-3 if structured

---

[35] *See* cases cited note 31 *supra*; discussion in Chapter 3 herein.

[36] *See, e.g., SEC v. Texas Gulf Sulphur*, 401 F.2d 833 (2d Cir. 1968); *In re Cady, Roberts & Co.*, 40 S.E.C. 907 (1961); discussion in Chapter 3 herein.

[37] As Justice Blackmun opined in *Chiarella v. United States*:

> By its narrow construction of § 10(b) and Rule 10b-5, the Court places the federal securities laws in the rearguard of this movement, a position opposite to the expectations of Congress at the time the securities laws were enacted.... I cannot agree that the statute and Rule are so limited. The Court has observed that the securities laws were not intended to replicate the law of fiduciary relations. Rather, their purpose is to ensure the fair and honest functioning of impersonal national securities markets where common-law protections have proved inadequate. As Congress itself has recognized, it is integral to this purpose to assure that dealing in securities is fair and without undue preferences or advantages among investors.

445 U.S. 222, 248 (1980) (Blackmun, J., dissenting). *See also* Alison G. Anderson, *Fraud, Fiduciaries, and Insider Trading*, 10 Hofstra L. Rev. 241 (1982).

[38] *See* Marc I. Steinberg, *Insider Trading Regulation—A Comparative Analysis*, 37 Int'l. Law. 153, 158 (2003).

[39] Rule 14e-3, 17 C.F.R. § 240.14e-3 (2017); discussion in Chapter 3 herein.

as a tender offer.[40] Because the insider did not tip for personal gain or to convey a gift to the tippee, no liability would be incurred under Section 10(b).[41] However, if the "deal" goes forward as a tender offer, the tippee would know that the material nonpublic information was received from a corporate insider, thereby bringing such information within the ambit of Rule 14e-3.[42] The result is that one's fate of going to prison or legally becoming a multimillionaire hinges on the structure of the contemplated acquisition—a determination that is made by the subject dealmakers ordinarily without reference to the application of whether specific federal securities law insider trading proscriptions apply.[43]

Frustrated with these types of results, the SEC has sought to expand the scope of the insider trading prohibition through rule-making. For example, when displeased with the Second Circuit's decision in *Chestman* that no misappropriation occurred (hence, no violation of Section 10(b)) due to the court's view that marriage is not a relationship of trust and confidence,[44] the Commission promulgated Rule 10b5-2, which, in practical effect, vitiated that decision.[45] Likewise, when concerned with the practice of selective disclosure by company insiders to financial analysts in order to curry their favor,[46] the Commission, viewing its task under *Dirks*' personal benefit test as being too arduous,[47] adopted Regulation FD.[48] In this manner, the SEC, not

---

[40] *See, e.g., SEC v. Switzer*, 590 F. Supp. 756 (W.D. Okla. 1984) (because a cash-out merger was involved, Coach Switzer's trading and tipping of material inside information inadvertently conveyed to him by the chief executive officer held not a violation of § 10(b) and Rule 10b-5).

[41] *See United States v. Salman*, 137 S. Ct. 420 (2016); *Dirks v. SEC*, 463 U.S. 646 (1983); discussion in Chapter 3 herein.

[42] *See O'Hagan v. United States*, 521 U.S. 642 (1997); discussion in Chapter 3 herein.

[43] *See* Steinberg, *supra* note 38, at 159.

[44] *United States v. Chestman*, 947 F.2d 551, 571 (2d Cir. 1991) (en banc), (stating that "Keith's status as Susan's husband could not itself establish fiduciary status" and that no relationship of trust and confidence existed between the husband and wife as "[s]uperiority and reliance did not mark this relationship. . . ."), *discussed in* Chapter 3 herein.

[45] *See* Rule 10b5-2(b)(3), 17 C.F.R. § 240.10b5-2(b)(3) (2017). This provision sets forth that a relationship of trust and confidence exists when "a person receives or obtains [material] nonpublic information from certain enumerated family members: spouses, parents, children, and siblings [and provides] an affirmative defense [when] the person receiving or obtaining the information demonstrate[s] that under the facts and circumstances of the family relationship, no duty of trust and confidence existed." Securities Exchange Act Release No. 43154, [2002 Transfer Binder] Fed. Sec. L. Rep. (CCH) ¶ 86,319, at 83,686-87 (2000); discussion in Chapter 3 herein.

[46] *See, e.g.*, Fred Barbash, *Companies, Analysts a Little Too Cozy*, Wash. Post, Oct. 31, 1999, at H1 (reporting that analysts were basing their recommendations to an increasing degree on information procured by means of selective disclosure made by corporate insiders rather than by undertaking independent research).

[47] Apparently the only enforcement action the Commission instituted under Section 10(b) with respect to selective disclosure was *SEC v. Stevens*, Securities Litigation Release No. 12813, 1991 SEC LEXIS 451 (1991) (settlement whereby subject corporation's CEO allegedly received a "direct, tangible benefit to his status as a corporate manager" through his selective disclosure of material nonpublic information to analysts).

[48] *See* Securities Exchange Act Release No. 43154 (2000); discussion in Chapter 3 herein.

invoking the insider trading laws, sought to remedy the perceived unfairness of such selective disclosure.[49]

Given the ambiguity and disparity in the U.S. insider trading framework, it is clear why other countries have declined to adopt this approach. Rather, countries with developed markets have adopted either the "access" or "parity" of information approach.[50] Premising insider trading liability based on a fiduciary relationship or a relationship of trust and confidence (as embraced by the U.S. Supreme Court) has been rejected by these countries.[51] For example, the European Union recently issued a Directive expressly adopting the parity of information approach.[52] Australia also embraces this parity doctrine.[53] By comparison, China, Japan, and Ontario (Canada) adhere to an approach resembling that of the "access" rationale.[54] These

---

[49] *See* discussion in Chapter 3 herein.

[50] These approaches are discussed in Chapter 3 herein.

[51] *See* Steinberg, *supra* note 38, at 165 (stating that "many countries opt for an insider trading prohibition based on the 'access' doctrine, generally proscrib[ing] insider trading by those who have unequal access to the material confidential information [while] fewer jurisdictions elect a more expansive approach based on the parity of information principle"). Note that the European Union's adoption of the parity of information approach signifies that this approach now is more favored in many countries. *See infra* note 52 and accompanying text.

[52] Directive 2014/57/EU of the European Parliament and of the Council (16 April 2014). As the Directive is binding on all Member States and is implemented by each Member State as part of that nation's securities laws, this chapter will not address the insider trading framework of specific countries within the European Union. *See* Donald C. Langevoort, *Insider Trading: Regulation, Enforcement & Prevention* § 14:4 (2016) ("Since the common market unification date in June 1992, each of the EEC (now EU) member states have had to have a regulatory system in place that prohibits insider trading in conformity with certain minimum standards."); Marc I. Steinberg, *International Securities Law—A Contemporary and Comparative Analysis* 7 (1999) (pointing out that the EU Directives set forth requirements that must be complied with by Member States). In this regard, Article 3 of the most recent insider trading Directive (2014/57/EU), in part, provides:

> 2. For the purposes of this Directive, insider dealing arises where a person possesses inside information and uses that information by acquiring or disposing of, for its own account or for the account of a third party, directly or indirectly, financial instruments to which that information relates.
> 3. This Article applies to any person who possesses inside information as a result of:
>   (a) being a member of the administrative, management or supervisory bodies of the issuer or emission allowance market participant;
>   (b) having a holding in the capital of the issuer or emission allowance market participant;
>   (c) having access to the information through the exercise of an employment, profession or duties; or
>   (d) being involved in criminal activities.
>
> This Article also applies to any person who has obtained inside information under circumstances other than those referred to in the first subparagraph where that person knows that it is inside information.

[53] *See* Corporations Law § 1002G (Australia); Langevoort, *supra* note 52, at § 14:11 (describing "possession" standard of Australian statute).

[54] *See* Ontario Securities Act, ch. S-5, § 76(5) (1990) (note that securities legislation in Canada is enacted by the individual provinces and territories); Langevoort, *supra* note 52, at §§ 14:10, 14:12, 14:13; Steinberg, *supra* note 38, at 163.

statutes extend to tippers and tippees without application of a "personal benefit" test as required under the U.S. Supreme Court's decision in *Dirks*.[55] Although a statute normally is only as rigorous as its effective enforcement,[56] the insider trading laws outside of the United States generally are more even-handed and clear in their application. It is time for Congress to follow the path traversed by other developed securities markets and enact an insider trading law premised on either the parity of information or equal access to information approach.

V. The Sentinel's Lax Surveillance—The SEC and Missed Opportunities

The Securities and Exchange Commission has been lauded as one of the premier regulatory agencies.[57] Nonetheless, more recently, the Commission has been criticized for its failure to detect major financial scandals, including the Madoff fraud.[58] The discussion in this chapter is directed at the SEC's undue reluctance to invoke its

---

[55] *See* discussion in Langevoort, *supra* note 52, at §§ 14:4–14:14; Steinberg, *supra* note 38, at 162–66.

[56] In many countries, insider trading prosecutions are rare. *See, e.g.*, James H. Thompson, *A Global Comparison of Insider Trading Regulations*, 3 Int'l J. Acc. & Fin. Rep. § 4:2 (2013) (stating that there had been 12 publicly reported insider trading cases in China and that "from 2001 to 2005 the United States brought 271 enforcement actions while China only brought three"). On this point, this author has opined:

> U.S. regulation of insider trading is far from perfect. Without sufficient justification, ambiguity, complexity, and disparate treatment of similarly situated market participants, at times, prevail. Perhaps cognizant of these shortcomings, nations with developed securities markets have declined to follow U.S. standards in the insider trading context. The approaches endorsed by these other countries seek to set forth clear statutory direction in regard to the insider trading prohibition. Focusing on the statutes, these nations may have largely achieved their objectives. However, because of insufficient funding, resources, personnel and surveillance, inadequate enforcement has generally been prevalent in markets abroad. Laws ordinarily are as potent as their effective implementation. The deterrent effect of rigorous statutes lessens drastically as the likelihood of successful usage decreases. Hence, statutes designed to promote market integrity and investor protection have relatively minor impact if widespread noncompliance persists. The lack of successful enforcement accordingly may induce disobedience by market participants.

Steinberg, *supra* note 38, at 171.

[57] *See* Joel Seligman, *The Transformation of Wall Street—A History of the Securities and Exchange Commission and Modern Corporate Finance* (1982); Judith Miller, *S.E.C.: Watchdog 1929 Lacked*, N.Y. Times, Oct. 31, 1979; David Ratner, *The SEC: Portrait of the Agency as a Thirty-Seven Year Old*, 45 St. John's L. Rev. 583 (1971). *See generally* Symposium, *The SEC at 75*, 78 U. Cin. L. Rev. No. 1 (2009).

[58] *See* Eamonn Fingleton, *Madoff and the SEC: The Story You Don't Know*, Forbes, June 4, 2013 (stating that "the SEC emerges from the [Madoff] affair not so much as incompetent, as many have charitably assumed, but corrupt"); Matt Taibbi, *Why Didn't the SEC Catch Madoff? It Might Have Been Policy Not To*, Rolling Stone, May 31, 2013 (stating that "aggressively clueless comes pretty close to summing up the atmosphere that seems to be ruling" the SEC). *See generally* Diana Henriques, *The Wizard of Lies* (2011). The SEC also has been criticized for its allegedly overzealous regulatory approach. *See, e.g.*, Roberta Karmel, *Regulation By Prosecution—The Securities and Exchange Commission versus Corporate America* (1982); Homer Kripke, *The SEC in Search of a Purpose* (1979); Jonathan Macey, *Administrative Agency Obsolescence and Interest Group Formation: A Case*

authority as granted by express federal legislation. This failure has impaired investor protection and impeded the implementation of enhanced corporate governance standards.

Three examples are provided to illustrate these missed opportunities: first, the SEC's inadequate implementation of a "current" disclosure regime as directed by Congress under the Sarbanes-Oxley Act, second, the Commission's refusal to effectively utilize its Standards of Professional Conduct for Attorneys, and third, the SEC's failure to exercise its statutory authority to pursue corporate insiders under the control person provision of the Securities Exchange Act. Each of these examples focuses on the Commission's failure to implement appropriate measures that likely would have redounded to improve corporate governance norms.

A. THE "CURRENT" DISCLOSURE REGIME

Prior to the enactment of the Sarbanes-Oxley Act of 2002, the federal securities laws and SEC rules generally did not require a subject corporation to disclose material nonpublic information during the period between the filing of its periodic reports with the Commission. Some exceptions did exist. For example, at that time, SEC Form 8-K mandated disclosure of a small number of specified events.[59] Other instances included when a subject company was obligated to correct or update its previous disclosures[60] and when rumors prevalent in the securities marketplace were attributable to such company.[61] Except for these situations, a "black hole" existed in the U.S. continuous disclosure framework,[62] thereby enabling companies to avoid disclosing adverse financial information (also called "bad news") during the interval between the filing of SEC periodic reports. This approach was contrary to that adopted in other developed securities markets outside of the United States, where,

---

Study of the SEC at Sixty, 15 Cardozo L. Rev. 909 (1984); Nicholas Wolfson, *A Critique of the Securities and Exchange Commission*, 30 Emory L.J. 119 (1981).

[59] At that time, the Form 8-K mandated disclosure of the following events: changes in the control of the company, the company's acquisition or disposition of its assets (as specified in Form 8-K), bankruptcy or receivership, changes in the company's certifying accountant, and resignation of any of the company's directors. In addition, at its election, the company could disclose additional information that it deemed "of importance" to its shareholders. *See* 17 C.F.R. § 249.308 (2000).

[60] *See, e.g.*, *Backman v. Polaroid Corp.*, 910 F.2d 10, 17 (1st Cir. 1990) (en banc).

[61] *See, e.g.*, *State Teachers Retirement Bd. v. Fluor Corp.*, 654 F.2d 843, 850 (2d Cir. 1981) ("A company has no duty to correct or verify rumors in the marketplace unless those rumors can be attributed to the company.").

[62] *See* Marc I. Steinberg, *Insider Trading, Selective Disclosure, and Prompt Disclosure: A Comparative Analysis*, 22 U. Pa. J. Int'l Econ. L. 635, 657 (2001).

absent the presence of a sufficient business reason, material nonpublic information is required to be disclosed promptly to the affected securities markets.[63]

Recognizing this gap in the disclosure regimen, Congress directed the SEC in the Sarbanes-Oxley Act to promulgate rules that require a publicly-held issuer to disclose "on a rapid and current basis such additional information concerning material changes in the financial condition or operations of the issuer . . . as the Commission determines . . . is necessary or useful for the protection of investors and in the public interest."[64] It was not until 2004 that the Commission adopted rules implementing this legislative directive.[65] The SEC did so by significantly expanding the Form 8-K to encompass specified events that previously were not called for under its prior regulations.[66] Nonetheless, the Commission left glaring gaps in the current disclosure regimen that are detrimental to sound corporate governance practices.

Two examples follow. First, no disclosure is required in the current Form 8-K of a company's loss, in the ordinary course of its business, of a significant contract with one of its major customers.[67] Undoubtedly, the subject company's management

---

[63] *Id.* ("In developed securities markets, it is axiomatic that, absent sufficient business justification, material nonpublic information must be promptly disclosed to the affected securities market(s).") (citations omitted). *See* Langevoort, *supra* note 52, at § 14:5 (observing that pursuant to the European Union's Market Abuse Directive passed by the European Parliament in 2013, "an issuer has a duty to disclose to the public, as soon as possible, inside information that directly concerns it," subject to specified exceptions).

[64] Section 409 of the Sarbanes-Oxley Act, *amending*, § 13(l) of the Securities Exchange Act, 15 U.S.C. § 78m(l) (2012).

[65] *See* Securities Exchange Act Release No. 49424 (2004).

[66] *See supra* notes 59–63 and accompanying text. As revised, SEC Form 8-K requires disclosure of specified events relating to the subject company's: business and operations, financial information, securities and trading markets, changes in its certifying accountant, corporate governance and management, amendments to its code of ethics, and Regulation FD disclosure. *See* 17 C.F.R. § 249.308 (2017).

[67] If material, the loss of such a contract would be required to be reported in the company's next periodic filing (e.g., Form 10-K or 10-Q), such as under Item 303 of Regulation S-K. Pursuant to Item 303, and more specifically the Management Discussion and Analysis (MD&A) contained therein, the SEC takes the position that disclosure must be made by the subject company "where a trend, demand, commitment, event or uncertainty is both presently known to management and reasonably likely to have material effects on the registrant's financial condition or results of operation." SEC Financial Reporting Release No. 36, 6 Fed. Sec. L. Rep. (CCH) ¶ 73,193, at 62,842 (1989). If a trend, demand, commitment, event or uncertainty is known, the registrant's management must consider the following:

1. Is the known trend, demand, commitment, event or uncertainty likely to come to fruition? If management determines that it is not reasonably likely to occur, no disclosure is required.
2. If management cannot make that determination, it must evaluate objectively the consequences of the known trend, demand, commitment, event or uncertainty, on the assumption that it will come to fruition.

   Disclosure is then required unless management determines that a material effect on the registrant's financial condition or results of operation is not reasonably likely to occur.

Id. See Panther Partners, Inc. v. Ikanos Commc'ns, Inc., 681 F.3d 114 (2d Cir. 2012); Securities Act Release No. 8350 (2003).

would prefer to delay disclosure of such adverse information as long as practicable. During the interim before the next periodic filing is due, perhaps new contracts can be obtained that would alleviate or replace the terminated contract(s). Immediate disclosure of such bad news could precipitate a "snowball" effect, whereby the company's financial condition would suffer further impairment.[68] This position, of course, conflicts with the prevailing approach taken by developed securities markets outside of the United States that, absent a sufficient business justification, shareholders and the securities markets are entitled to receive on a timely basis all material information.[69] Permitting subject corporations to delay disclosure of material information on the mere speculation or plan to replace irretrievably terminated contracts neglects investor interests and transparency in the securities marketplace. Investors are entitled to know such material information so that they can protect their financial interests. To act consistently with the disclosure objectives of the federal securities laws, the Commission should amend Form 8-K to require disclosure, *if material*, of such events as: the irretrievable termination of a customer contract, a known issue that raises liquidity concerns, and the occurrence of any other event that impacts the subject company's revenues, sales, or income.[70]

As another example, in its Form 8-K amendments, the SEC required that disclosure be made of an executive officer's resignation, retirement, or removal.[71] Unlike the situation with a director's resignation or removal where a description also must be provided of any disagreement between the company and such director,[72] the Commission declined to mandate that a subject company set forth the reasons for an executive officer's resignation or removal. The Commission reasoned that disclosure of the alleged reasons may embarrass such executive or precipitate a lawsuit by the executive against the company on defamation grounds.[73]

The SEC's position on this subject indeed is puzzling. An executive officer's resignation or removal strikes at the essence of corporate governance. Clearly, the fact of such resignation or removal often is material. Also, of great importance, are the

---

[68] *See* Marc I. Steinberg and Robin M. Goldman, *Issuer Affirmative Disclosure Obligations—An Analytical Framework for Merger Negotiations, Soft Information, and Bad News*, 46 Md. L. Rev. 923, 949–50 (1987).

[69] *See* discussion *supra* note 63 and accompanying text.

[70] *See* Steinberg and Goldman, *supra* note 68, at 950.

[71] *See* Form 8-K, Item 5.02.

[72] *Id.* (requiring in such circumstances "a brief description of the circumstances representing the disagreement that the registrant believes caused, in whole or in part, the director's resignation, refusal to stand for reelection or removal" and mandating that any written correspondence, including a letter, furnished by the subject director to the registrant concerning such circumstances be filed as an exhibit to such registrant's report on Form 8-K).

[73] *See* Securities Exchange Act Release No. 49424 (2004).

underlying reasons with respect to any disagreement that precipitated the subject officer's resignation or removal. In the current climate, institutional and other active shareholders are unlikely to be satisfied with the mere knowledge of such officer's resignation or removal.[74] Many of these shareholders will contact company personnel seeking to learn why this event occurred. Of course, if material, any such revelation selectively made to such shareholders would be in violation of SEC Regulation FD.[75] As a result, the subject company must maintain a closed-mouth posture with respect to such inquiries, thereby displeasing key shareholders, or disclose this material information to the investing public. The SEC's approach accordingly places subject companies in an awkward position that would have been avoided if the Commission had opted to treat key executive officers in this context on an equal footing as outside directors. As significant, the Commission's action permits a subject company to maintain secrecy with respect to an important disagreement between any of its executive officers and board of directors, thereby preventing investors from protecting themselves from financial loss that may ensue from any such disagreement. Hence, the SEC's position is an objectionable accommodation to corporate boards and management as well as antithetical to sound corporate governance practices.

B. FAILURE TO INVOKE STANDARDS OF PROFESSIONAL CONDUCT FOR ATTORNEYS

As discussed in Chapter 3 herein, attorneys practicing before the SEC are gatekeepers. Generally, gatekeepers are intermediaries who enhance market integrity and investor protection by exercising their diligence in certifying, assessing, or verifying facts surrounding the subject transaction or other event.[76] Depending on the circumstances, gatekeepers have the wherewithal to detect and deter fraud.[77] Gatekeeper accountability therefore comprises an integral component of transparency in the financial transactional context.[78]

---

[74] The role of active and institutional shareholders in the corporate governance framework is discussed in several chapters herein.

[75] Regulation FD is discussed in Chapter 3 herein. *See* Ben Dummett, *Akzo CEO Exits due to Health*, Wall St. J., July 20, 2017, at B3 (stating that the company's CEO resigned for health reasons).

[76] *See* John C. Coffee, Jr., *The Attorney as Gatekeeper: An Agenda for the SEC*, 103 Colum. L. Rev. 1293, 1296 (2003); sources cited in Chapter 3 herein.

[77] *Lawson v. FMR, LLC*, 134 S. Ct. 1158, 1170–71 (2014) ("Emphasizing the importance of outside professionals as 'gatekeepers who detect and deter fraud,' the Senate Report concludes: 'Congress must reconsider the incentive system that has been set up that encourages accountants and lawyers who come across fraud in their work to remain silent.'") (quoting S. Rep. No. 107-146, at 2 (2002)).

[78] *See* Marc I. Steinberg and James Ames, *From the Regulatory Abyss: The Weakened Gatekeeping Incentives Under the Uniform Securities Act*, 35 Yale L. & Pol. Rev. 1 (2016).

Hence, attorneys in the securities transactional setting are well-situated to deter fraud and other improper conduct. To effectuate this role, the lawyer may withhold essential services, such as declining to render a legal opinion essential to the consummation of the subject transaction.[79] Gatekeepers thus may have the leverage to prevent systemic frauds, such as those committed in Enron, WorldCom, Global Crossings, Tyco, and Adelphia.[80]

In the aftermath of these financial frauds, Congress perceived that attorneys did not proficiently perform their role as gatekeepers.[81] Enacting Section 307 of the Sarbanes-Oxley Act of 2002, Congress sought to incentivize legal counsel to act consistently with this objective. Pursuant to this statute, the SEC was directed to promulgate a rule:

> (1) requiring [a subject] attorney to report evidence of a material violation of securities law or breach of fiduciary duty or similar violation by the company or any agent thereof, to the chief legal counsel or the chief executive officer of the company (or the equivalent thereof); and (2) if the counsel or officer does not appropriately respond to the evidence (adopting, as necessary, appropriate remedial measures or sanctions with respect to the violation), requiring [such] attorney to report the evidence to the audit committee of the board of directors of the issuer or to another committee of the board of directors comprised solely of directors not employed directly or indirectly by the issuer, or to the board of directors.[82]

Implementing the directive, the Commission adopted its Standards of Professional Conduct for Attorneys.[83] Generally, these standards resemble existing ethical standards as prescribed by the American Bar Association and the vast majority of the states.[84] In this regard, the Commission declined to require that an attorney make

---

[79] *See United States v. Benjamin*, 328 F.2d 854, 863 (2d Cir. 1964) (Friendly, J.) ("In our complex society the accountant's certificate and the lawyer's opinion can be instruments for inflicting pecuniary loss more potent than the chisel or the crowbar."); sources cited notes 76–78 *supra*; Chapter 3 herein.

[80] *See* Steinberg and Ames, *supra* note 78, at 5 n.13 ("In each of these cases of large-scale fraud, attorneys and accountants allegedly failed to effectively perform their gatekeeping functions: they allegedly failed to minimize, let alone prevent, the violations by alerting the investing public or regulators.").

[81] *See* S. Rep. No. 107-146, at 2 (2002) (recognizing that attorneys, among others, serve as "gatekeepers who detect and deter fraud").

[82] 15 U.S.C. § 7245 (2012).

[83] Securities Exchange Act Release No. 47276 (2003) (codified at 17 C.F.R. pt. 205 (2017)).

[84] *See, e.g.*, American Bar Association, Model Rules of Professional Conduct, Rules 1.2(d), 1.6, 1.13, 1.16; Marc I. Steinberg, *Attorney Liability After Sarbanes-Oxley* § 3.02 at n.6 (2017) ("Today, over forty states permit or require an attorney to reveal a client's crime or fraud that threatens substantial financial loss."), *citing*, American

a "noisy withdrawal" in the client-fraud context;[85] instead, the Standards permit the subject attorney to make such a noisy withdrawal as such attorney "reasonably believes necessary: to prevent the issuer from committing [an illegal act] or a material violation likely to cause substantial financial injury to . . . the issuer or investors; . . . or to rectify the consequences of a material violation or illegal act in which the attorney's services have been used."[86]

Law Institute, *Restatement (Third) of the Law Governing Lawyers* § 67 comment b (2000). In part, the SEC Standards:

- require an attorney to report evidence of a material violation, determined according to an objective standard, "up-the-ladder" within the issuer to the chief legal counsel or the chief executive officer of the company or the equivalent;
- require an attorney, if the chief legal counsel or the chief executive officer of the company does not respond appropriately to the evidence, to report the evidence to the audit committee, another committee of independent directors, or the full board of directors;
- clarify that the rules cover attorneys providing legal services to an issuer who have an attorney-client relationship with the issuer, and who have notice that documents they are preparing or assisting in preparing will be filed with or submitted to the Commission;
- allow an issuer to establish a "qualified legal compliance committee" (QLCC) as an alternative procedure for reporting evidence of a material violation. . . . One way in which an attorney could satisfy the rule's reporting obligation is by reporting evidence of a material violation to a QLCC;
- allow an attorney, without the consent of an issuer client, to reveal confidential information related to his or her representation to the extent the attorney reasonably believes necessary (1) to prevent the issuer from committing a material violation likely to cause substantial financial injury to the financial interests or property of the issuer or investors; (2) to prevent the issuer from committing an illegal act; or (3) to rectify the consequences of a material violation or illegal act in which the attorney's services have been used; [and]
- state that the rules govern in the event the rules conflict with state law, but will not preempt the ability of a state to impose more rigorous obligations on attorneys that are not inconsistent with the rules. . . .

SEC Press Release No. 2003-13 (Jan. 23, 2003).

[85] Generally, a "noisy withdrawal" occurs when legal counsel resigns from representing the subject company and notifies the SEC, other regulator, or investors that he or she has withdrawn for professional reasons. The Commission proposed the inclusion of a "noisy withdrawal" mandate but subsequently declined to adopt such a provision. *See* Securities Exchange Act Release No. 46868 (2002) (proposing "noisy withdrawal" mandate); Securities Exchange Act Release No. 47276 (2003) (adoption of SEC Standards without a "noisy withdrawal" mandate). "The making of a noisy withdrawal, of course, sounds a siren that fraud or other grievous misconduct is afoot." Marc I. Steinberg, *Lawyer Liability After Sarbanes-Oxley—Has the Landscape Changed?*, 3 Wyo. L. Rev. 371, 374 (2003).

[86] *SEC Adopts Attorney Conduct Rule Under Sarbanes-Oxley Act*, Press Release No. 2003-13 (SEC Jan 23, 2003). The SEC's position is consistent with that of the vast majority of states. *See* note 84 *supra*. A small number of states require that an attorney make a "noisy withdrawal" under specified circumstances (*see, e.g.*, Tennessee Rules of Professional Conduct, Rule 4.1) whereas a few states prohibit an attorney's disclosure of client confidences and secrets in the financial harm setting (*see, e.g.*, California Business and Professional Code § 6068(e) (2004)).

Note that, pursuant to the American Bar Association's (ABA) Model Rules of Professional Conduct, in the event that the subject client continues to use the attorney's work product (such as a securities offering document) after the attorney learns that it is materially false, resignation alone may not be sufficient. Rather, in such circumstances, a "noisy withdrawal" may be required. *See* ABA Model Rule of Professional Conduct, Rule

Further analysis of the SEC Standards has been engaged in by this author[87] as well as several other commentators.[88] The focus of this discussion, however, is not whether the Commission's promulgation of these Standards constituted an appropriate implementation of Congress's mandate pursuant to the Sarbanes-Oxley Act.[89] Rather, attention is directed at the stark reality that the SEC has declined to initiate proceedings against attorneys who have violated these Standards. Although the Commission has brought enforcement actions and Rule 102(e) disciplinary proceedings against both in-house and outside counsel with some frequency,[90] it has not invoked its Standards of Professional Conduct for Attorneys. In spite of continual financial scandals, as evidenced by the passage of the Dodd-Frank Act of 2010[91] and subsequent debacles,[92] the SEC Standards have not been adequately utilized. In view of the legislative directive for the SEC to invoke these Standards as a means to address failures in attorney gatekeeper conduct and to deter like misconduct by members of the securities bar, the Commission's position may be viewed as an undue refusal to act consistently with its administrative authority.[93] Unfortunately, the

1.2 cmt. 10 (stating that "[i]n some circumstances, withdrawal alone might be insufficient" and that "[i]t may be necessary for the lawyer to give notice of the fact of withdrawal and to disaffirm any opinion, document, affirmation or the like"); ABA Model Rules of Professional Conduct, Rule 4.1 cmt. 3 (stating that "[s]ometimes it may be necessary for the lawyer to give notice of the fact of withdrawal and to disaffirm an opinion, document, affirmation or the like"); ABA Committee on Ethics and Professional Responsibility, Formal Opinion No. 92-366 (1992) (stating that "where the client avowedly intends to continue to use the lawyer's work product, this amounts to a de facto continuation of representation even if the lawyer has ceased to perform any additional work [hence signifying that] the representation is not completed, any more than the fraud itself is completed"). *See also*, Steinberg, *supra* note 84, at § 3.05; discussion Chapter 3 herein.

[87] *See, e.g.*, Marc I. Steinberg, *Lawyering and Ethics for the Business Attorney* 17–26 (4th ed. 2016); sources cited in notes 84, 85 *supra*.

[88] *See, e.g.*, Karl A. Groskaufmanis, *Climbing Up the Ladder: Corporate Counsel and the SEC's Reporting Requirement for Lawyers*, 89 Cornell L. Rev. 511 (2004); Thomas L. Hazen, *Administrative Law Controls on Attorney Practice—A Look at the Securities and Exchange Commission's Lawyer Conduct Rules*, 55 Admin. L. Rev. 323 (2003); Lisa H. Nicholson, *SarbOx 307's Impact on Subordinate In-House Counsel: Between a Rock and a Hard Place*, 2004 Mich. St. L. Rev. 559 (2004); Samuel J. Winer and Gregory S. Bruch, *The SEC Standards of Professional Conduct: Practicing Law Under the New Regime*, 35 Sec. Reg. & L. Rep. (BNA) 391 (2003).

[89] *See* discussion *supra* notes 81–82 and accompanying text.

[90] *See* discussion in Chapter 3 herein.

[91] The Dodd-Frank Act of 2010 is discussed in Chapters 5 and 6 herein.

[92] *See, e.g.*, Nate Raymond, *Law Firms to Pay $88 Million in Case Related to Mortgage Crisis*, Reuters (June 21, 2012).

[93] Pursuant to the Standards, the SEC clearly has authority to institute proceedings against subject attorneys and levy sanctions and discipline. As set forth in 17 C.F.R. § 205.6(a) (2017): "A violation of this part [namely, the Standards] by any attorney appearing and practicing before the Commission in the representation of an issuer shall subject such attorney to the civil penalties and remedies for a violation of the federal securities laws available to the Commission in an action brought by the Commission thereunder."

SEC's inaction has impaired the enhancement of the attorney's role as gatekeeper in the corporate governance framework.[94]

C. THE SEC'S NEGLECT WHEN INVOKING ITS STATUTORY RESOURCES

As stated by U. S. Senator Chuck Grassley, "[t]he SEC doesn't always use all of the penalties at its disposal, and it should."[95] The foregoing analysis provides one such example: the Commission's failure to institute proceedings against subject attorneys for alleged noncompliance with its Standards of Professional Conduct for Attorneys.[96] A more glaring failure is the subject of this discussion: the SEC's refusal to bring enforcement actions against corporate directors and executive officers based on alleged violation of Section 20(a) of the Securities Exchange Act, a statute that expressly provides for control person liability.[97]

Under Section 20(a), a person who controls another person who violates any provision of the Exchange Act or any SEC rule or regulation promulgated thereunder is jointly and severally liable unless such control person establishes that he or she "acted in good faith and did not directly or indirectly induce the act or acts constituting the violation...."[98] This statute is a far-reaching provision that encompasses key corporate insiders, including chief executive officers, chief financial officers, and outside directors who serve as lead directors or chair audit committees.[99] In the aftermath of the financial crisis, the SEC was severely criticized for its failure to pursue such insiders.[100] Instead, the Commission levied enormous money penalties

---

[94] The corporate and securities lawyer's role as gatekeeper is discussed *supra* notes 76–80 and accompanying text; discussion in Chapter 3 herein.

[95] Press Release, Office of Senator Chuck Grassley (Republican, Iowa), *Bill Seeks Tougher Penalties for Wall Street Fraud* (July 9, 2015), *available at* http://www.grassley.senate.gov/news/news-releases/bill-seeks-tougher-penalties-wall-street-fraud.

[96] *See supra* notes 76–94 and accompanying text.

[97] 15 U.S.C. § 78t(a) (2012).

[98] *Id.* Pursuant to SEC Rule 405, control is defined to encompass "the possession, direct or indirect, of the power to direct or cause the direction of the management and policies of a person." 17 C.F.R. § 230.405 (2017). Note that some courts require a showing of culpable participation by the control person—namely, that the control person was in a meaningful way a participant in the alleged securities violation. *See Sharp v. Coopers & Lybrand*, 649 F.2d 175, 185 (3d Cir. 1981).

[99] *See, e.g., Maverick Fund v. Converse Tech.*, 801 F. Supp. 2d 41 (E.D.N.Y. 2011); *In re Tronox, Inc. Sec. Litig.*, 769 F. Supp. 2d 202 (S.D.N.Y. 2011); *Salit v. Stanley Works*, 802 F. Supp. 728 (D. Conn. 1992).

[100] *See, e.g.*, Office of U.S. Senator Elizabeth Warren, *Rigged Justice 2016: How Weak Enforcement Lets Corporate Offenders Off Easy* (Jan. 2016), *available at* http://www.warren.senate.gov/files/documents/Rigged_Justice_2016.pdf.

against publicly-held companies,[101] which financially harmed shareholders of these companies.[102]

In many of these situations, the control person provision was available for the SEC to utilize against high level executives as well as certain outside directors of these companies. Yet, without explanation, the Commission declined to employ this provision. Indeed, although the discussion in Chapter 3 herein addresses a number of SEC enforcement actions against directors, the fact remains that the Commission has been reluctant to institute enforcement actions against these gatekeepers. As a former SEC Commissioner pointed out, "these matters are so infrequent that the agency does not currently maintain statistics on cases that are brought against directors."[103]

This hesitation is not based on the availability of the control person provision. By comparison, in private litigation under the federal securities laws, claims routinely are asserted alleging Section 20(a) control person liability against corporate officers and directors.[104] Undoubtedly, in many situations, it is difficult for the SEC to prove fraud against insiders of large publicly-held corporations. The control person provision significantly ameliorates this task by imposing liability against a subject control person unless such person shows that he or she acted in good faith and did not induce the violation(s).[105] For whatever reason, which the Commission has declined to articulate, it has not utilized this provision.

---

[101] *See, e.g.*, Press Release, U.S. Dept. of Justice, No. 14-884, *Bank of America to Pay $16.65 Billion in Historic Justice Department Settlement for Financial Fraud Leading up to and during the Financial Crisis* (Aug. 21, 2014); Press Release, U.S. Dept. of Justice, *Goldman Sachs Agrees to Pay More than $5 Billion in Connection with Its Sale of Residential Mortgage Backed Securities* (April 11, 2016); *JPMorgan Chase Bank, N.A.*, Securities Exchange Act Release No. 76694 (2015) (settlement involving payment of $307 million); *Citigroup Alternative Investments LLC & Citigroup Global Markets*, Securities Exchange Act Release No. 75710 (2015) (settlement involving payment of $180 million). For further discussion of these proceedings, *see* Marc I. Steinberg and Forrest C. Roberts, *Laxity at the Gates: The SEC's Neglect to Enforce Control Person Liability*, 11 U. Va. L. & Bus. Rev. 201, 217–29 (2017).

[102] *But see Statement of the Securities and Exchange Commission Concerning Financial Penalties*, Securities Release No. 2006-4 (2006) (stating that "a key question for the Commission is whether the issuer's violation has provided an improper benefit to the shareholders, or conversely whether the violation has resulted in harm to the shareholders"). This Statement, of course, assumes that the composition of shareholders in a publicly-held corporation remains static—which, of course, it does not in an actively-traded market of a company's stock. *See generally* Seth McNew, *Money Penalties Against Publicly-Held Companies: A Proposal for Restraint*, 37 Sec. Reg. L.J. 48 (2009).

[103] Luis A. Aguilar, SEC Commissioner, *Remarks at the 12th Annual Boardroom Summit and Peer Exchange: The Important Work of Boards of Directors* (Oct. 14, 2015), *available at* https://www.sec.gov/news/speech/important-work-of-boards-of-directors.html.

[104] *See, e.g.*, cases cited in Steinberg and Roberts, *supra* note 101, at 238 (also stating that "within the last three years, cases have been filed in every single U.S. circuit alleging Section 20(a) control person liability").

[105] *See* discussion *supra* notes 97–98 and accompanying text.

The financial scandals of the past two decades have shed light on the importance of sound corporate governance practices. As discussed in this book, the SEC frequently has emphasized the beneficial accountability impact of requiring adequate gatekeeper conduct. However, with respect to executive officers and directors of the large publicly-held companies, the Commission all too frequently has declined to pursue with sufficient vigor these gatekeepers. In its "tool chest," the Commission has the authority to initiate enforcement proceedings against these individuals by means of the control person provision. By invoking this provision in a reasoned and fair manner, the SEC has the leverage to effectuate enhanced corporate governance norms.[106]

VI. Conclusion

As discussed throughout this book, the federalization of corporate governance is a continual process, originating in earnest more than a century ago. As seen by such examples as the early efforts to require federal chartering, the SEC's promulgation of the shareholder proposal rule, and the proscription of insider trading in certain contexts, this process has been ongoing for several decades. Enacted in the first decade of this century, the Sarbanes-Oxley and Dodd-Frank Acts have accentuated the federalization of corporate governance. Yet, as this chapter has addressed, significant gaps remain that should be filled. Consistent therewith, the analysis set forth in this chapter identifies significant deficiencies that currently exist and recommends measures that should be implemented on the federal level to enhance corporate governance standards.

---

[106] *See* Steinberg and Roberts, *supra* note 101, at 247–48 (asserting that "[w]ithout explanation, the Commission has declined to meaningfully utilize [the control person] provision, and instead has tended to pursue gatekeepers only if they commit or aid in a primary violation [and that] with respect to the 'big players' on Wall Street, the SEC has declined to pursue any individual liability at all, except on rare occasions").

8

FUTURE FEDERALIZATION OF CORPORATE GOVERNANCE

I. Introduction

This book focuses on the federalization of corporate governance. Undoubtedly, such federalization has transpired. From proposals to require federal incorporation advanced early in the twentieth century through the enactment of the Dodd-Frank Act in 2010 and beyond, the presence of federal mandates as an essential component of the corporate governance landscape is manifestly clear. What the future will bring, of course, is uncertain. Nonetheless, to a significant extent, the federalization of corporate governance appears firmly entrenched.

II. Evolution of the Federalization of Corporate Governance

After providing an introductory chapter setting forth the book's framework, Chapter 2 addresses in depth the scores of proposals, commencing in the early 1900s, to require federal incorporation[1] or, alternatively, federal minimum standards.[2] The

[1] *See* Chapter 2, text at note 28 ("At no point in American history was the idea of federal incorporation more debated in Congress than the 1903–1914 period.").

[2] The most recent such proposal of significance was Senator Howard Metzenbaum's bill—"A Bill to establish Federal minimum standards relating to composition of corporate boards, duties of corporate directors, audit

The Federalization of Corporate Governance. Marc I. Steinberg.

bills analyzed therein (as well as the related development seeking the implementation of federal minimum standards through judicial recognition of Section 10(b) of the Securities Exchange Act to cover the "corporate universe"[3]) evidence the positions embraced by those proponents who advocated for the application of federal standards to normative corporate fiduciary conduct.

From these defeats, it may be posited that efforts to federalize corporate governance largely failed until the enactment of the Sarbanes-Oxley Act of 2002. Such a position is misplaced. As Chapters 3 and 4 of this book address, the realization of this federalization commenced with the enactment of the Securities Exchange Act of 1934. Although focused on the adequacy and sufficiency of disclosure, that Act also circumscribed the trading by corporate fiduciaries in their subject company's equity securities.[4] A few years thereafter, the SEC adopted the shareholder proposal rule.[5] Promulgated in 1942,[6] the rule plays an important role in providing shareholders with proxy access to bring matters of perceived significance to the attention of management, the board of directors, and fellow shareholders. For over 75 years, the shareholder proposal rule has demonstrated that vibrant federal corporate governance may serve to ameliorate state law shortcomings.[7]

From a historical perspective, several other corporate governance measures were instituted far before the passage of the Sarbanes-Oxley Act. As discussed in Chapter 3, one key example is the SEC's activism in regulating insider trading. Recognizing the lack of scrutiny given to this conduct by the states, the SEC seized the opportunity to federalize this aspect of corporate governance.[8] Another example is the Commission's focus on requiring disclosure of qualitative information with respect to the integrity and competency of directors and officers as well as their engaging in self-dealing transactions. These disclosure mandates, while seeking to provide a means to provide meaningful information to investors, also had the

---

and nomination committees, shareholders' rights, and for other purposes. . . ." S. 2567, 96th Cong. (1980). This bill is discussed in Chapter 2 herein.

[3] *See Santa Fe Indus., Inc. v. Green*, 430 U.S. 462 (1977) (requiring that manipulation or deception be shown, not solely breach of fiduciary duty or unfairness, in order for § 10(b) and Rule 10b-5 to apply), *discussed in* Chapters 2, 3 herein.

[4] *See* § 16(b) of the Securities Exchange Act, 15 U.S.C. § 78p(b) (2012), *discussed in* Chapter 3 herein.

[5] Rule 14a-8, 17 C.F.R. § 240.14a-8 (2017), *discussed in* Chapter 4 herein.

[6] Securities Exchange Act Release No. 3347 (1942).

[7] *See* discussion in Chapter 4 herein.

[8] *See* discussion in Chapter 3 herein; Stephen M. Bainbridge, *Insider Trading Regulation: The Path Dependent Choice Between Property Rights and Securities Fraud*, 52 SMU L. Rev. 1589, 1597 (1999) (stating that "insider trading was an ideal target for federalization [as] the states had shown little interest in insider trading for years [and that] federal regulation demonstrated the modernity, flexibility, and innovativeness of the securities laws").

implicit objective of improving standards of fiduciary conduct through the guise of disclosure.[9]

As discussed in Chapter 3, the SEC decades ago engaged in rule-making to ameliorate adverse court decisions, and, in so doing, impacted corporate governance standards. For example, the Commission's promulgation of Rule 13e-3, requiring the subject issuer to disclose whether it reasonably believes that the going-private transaction is fair or unfair to unaffiliated shareholders and the "material factors" upon which such belief is based,[10] was a response to the Supreme Court's *Santa Fe* decision[11] which precluded inquiry into the substantive fairness of the subject transaction under Section 10(b) and Rule 10b-5.[12] Hence, by invoking the authority to mandate disclosure, the SEC, in practical effect, enhanced the process and ultimate fairness of these transactions.[13] Likewise, the Commission's adoption of rules mandating that tender offers be open to all shareholders[14] was a reaction to the Delaware Supreme Court's decision in *Unocal*,[15] which upheld the use of discriminatory tender offers. In effect, with respect to tender offers made for publicly-held companies, the SEC's rules nullified the Delaware Supreme Court's decision in *Unocal*, thereby establishing a federal corporate governance norm that such offers must be open to all shareholders.[16]

As addressed in Chapter 3, the SEC's ordering of "undertakings" in its enforcement proceedings impacted corporate governance standards, at times dramatically. Commencing over four decades ago, far-reaching measures were ordered, including the appointment of independent directors, the retention of independent legal counsel to conduct a thorough investigation, and the appointment of independent consultants who were given extensive authority to make meaningful inquiries and recommendations.[17] That these types of expansive measures were ordered over

---

[9] *See* discussion in Chapter 3 herein in text after note 116 (stating that "disclosure of qualitative materiality, embraced by the SEC over fifty years ago, has a positive role with respect to improving standards of normative conduct").

[10] 17 C.F.R. § 240.13e-3 (2017), *discussed in* Chapter 3 herein.

[11] *Santa Fe Indus., Inc. v. Green*, 430 U.S. 462 (1977).

[12] *Id.* at 474 (holding that the going-private transaction "was neither deceptive nor manipulative and therefore did not violate either § 10(b) of the [Securities Exchange] Act or Rule 10b-5"). *See generally* Ralph C. Ferrara and Marc I. Steinberg, *A Reappraisal of* Santa Fe: *Rule 10b-5 and the New Federalism*, 129 U. Pa. L. Rev. 263 (1980).

[13] As pointed out in Chapter 3, state corporation law, particularly Delaware law, also has been instrumental with respect to improving the plight of minority shareholders in going-private transactions. *See, e.g., Kahn v. M&F Worldwide Corp.*, 88 A.3d 635 (Del. 2014); *Weinberger v. UOP, Inc.*, 457 A.2d 701 (Del. 1983).

[14] *See* Rules 13e-4(f)(8), 14d-10, 17 C.F.R. §§ 240.13e-4(f)(8), 14d-10 (2017), *discussed in* Chapter 3 herein.

[15] *Unocal v. Mesa Petroleum Co.*, 493 A.2d 946 (Del. 1985).

[16] Accordingly, the SEC's proactive promulgation of these rules signifies that such discriminatory tender offers no longer are available as a defense strategy to fend off a hostile takeover bid. *See* discussion in Chapter 3 herein.

[17] *See* discussion in Chapter 3 herein; Marc I. Steinberg and Ralph C. Ferrara, *Securities Practice: Federal and State Enforcement* (2d ed. 2001 & 2017–2018 supp.).

40 years ago should make it crystal clear that the SEC was an active participant in promoting the federalization of corporate governance.

With the federalization of corporate governance process set forth in its appropriate historical perspective, the more recent legislative, SEC, and stock exchange developments are the focus of Chapters 5 and 6. Undoubtedly, these measures have further entrenched the federalization of corporate governance. Such directives as a majority of the board of directors being comprised of independent directors, audit and compensation committees consisting solely of independent directors, the adoption and implementation of codes of ethics, prohibiting loans to executive officers and directors, and entitling shareholders to have an advisory vote on executive compensation provide ample illustrations of the increasing extent to which corporate governance has become federalized.[18] In conjunction with the Sarbanes-Oxley and Dodd-Frank Acts, stock exchange activism—although deemed self-regulation—largely has been generated from the directives set forth in these Acts as well as the SEC prodding the exchanges through the decades to adopt enhanced standards of corporate governance.[19] Accordingly, in its practical impact, stock exchange regulation serves as an important component of this federalization phenomena.[20]

Nonetheless, as explored in Chapter 7, there remain aspects of corporate governance that merit federalization. One clear example is the need for federal law application with respect to substantive tactics taken by insurgents and target boards of directors in connection with takeover bids of companies whose securities are traded on a national stock exchange. That national policy is determined in this context by state legislatures and courts (with great frequency, the Delaware legislature and courts) reflects an undue delegation by Congress. Hence, takeover bids that are of national as well as global magnitude should be subject to the parameters of federal law as statutorily determined by Congress, as administratively implemented by the SEC, and as construed by the federal courts.[21]

---

[18] *See* discussion in Chapters 5 and 6 herein.

[19] Indeed, the New York Stock Exchange's adoption in 1977 of a listing rule requiring that a subject company have an audit committee composed solely of independent directors provides one such example. *See, e.g., In the Matter of New York Stock Exchange, Inc.*, Securities Exchange Act Release No. 13346, 1977 WL 173602, at *1 (Mar. 9, 1977) (stating that "the Commission has urged strengthening the independence and vitality of corporate boards and has suggested that, at least initially, those principles could be implemented by amending the listing requirements of the NYSE and other self-regulatory organizations, rather than by direct Commission action"); discussion in Chapter 6 herein.

[20] *See* discussion in Chapter 6 herein (in that chapter's "Conclusion," observing: "Although technically not government regulation, the directives issued by federal legislation and the SEC (and thereafter implemented by the securities exchanges) make clear that SRO rules play a central role in the enhancement of sound corporate governance practices and policies.").

[21] Former SEC Chairman David S. Ruder, appointed by President George H.W. Bush, has advanced this position. *See* Remarks of SEC Chairman David S. Ruder, *Federal Preemption of State Anti-Takeover Legislation*,

Although already a component of federal corporate governance, the regulation of insider trading, as discussed in Chapter 7, merits codification. As interpreted by the U.S. Supreme Court and as regulated by the SEC, the law of insider trading in this country is erratic, ambiguous, and, all too frequently, treats similarly-situated persons in a disparate manner. Indeed, even though developed markets outside of the United States routinely consider U.S. disclosure and enforcement principles as sources for the adoption of their standards,[22] the U.S. regimen of insider trading has soundly been rejected.[23] To remedy this deficient framework, a straightforward insider trading statute should be enacted by Congress.[24]

III. Foretelling the Future of the Federalization of Corporate Governance

The federalization of corporate governance has been a process that commenced well over a century ago. A number of the instances where such federalization occurred as a result of SEC action may be perceived as subtle, such as the Commission's disclosure requirements focusing on the integrity and competency of directors and executive officers.[25] A number of others ostensibly were based solely on the SEC's enforcement authority to combat fraud, again based on a deficiency of disclosure rationale, such as with respect to utilizing Section 10(b) to pursue inside traders.[26] Yet, others may be viewed as seeking to more directly impact corporate governance, such as the SEC's shareholder proposal rule[27] and the Commission's use of undertakings and related measures, including the ordering that new directors be appointed and that independent legal counsel and consultants be retained to investigate and report.[28]

Before the 26th Annual Corporate Counsel Institute (Chicago Oct. 7, 1987) (asserting that "it is imprudent for states to use their authority over matters of internal governance as a means of regulating the interstate market for corporate control"); discussion in Chapter 7 herein.

[22] *See* Marc I. Steinberg, *International Securities Law—A Contemporary and Comparative Analysis* (1999).

[23] *See* discussion in Chapter 7 herein.

[24] Recently, U.S. District Judge Jed S. Rakoff suggested that Congress should enact an insider trading statute similar to the approach adopted by the European Union. *See* Alla Zayenchik, *Judge Rakoff Calls for Insider Trading Overhaul*, The Advocate for Institutional Investors at 14 (Summer 2017), *available at* www.blbglaw.com (quoting Judge Rakoff that: "Because the EU approach focuses not on fraud but on equality of access, it has virtually none of the difficulties that plague US law."); discussion in Chapters 3 and 7 herein.

[25] *See* discussion in Chapter 3 herein.

[26] *See* discussion in Chapters 3 and 7 herein.

[27] *See supra* notes 5–7 and accompanying text; discussion in Chapter 4 herein.

[28] *See supra* note 17 and accompanying text; discussion in Chapter 3 herein.

In a very visible manner, Congress entrenched the federalization of corporate governance by means of the Sarbanes-Oxley and Dodd-Frank Acts.[29] But far prior to that time, a number of legislative provisions signaled a federal presence. Indeed, as discussed in Chapter 3, the short-swing trading provisions contained in Section 16 of the Securities Exchange Act date back to 1934. A more recent example is Congress's codification in 1990 of the SEC's authority to procure officer and director bars.[30] Thus, to some extent, the federal codification of corporate governance has been a continual process, commencing from the enactment of the federal securities laws.

Undoubtedly, at times, this federalization process has stalled. This may have been due to legislative inaction, court decisions invalidating SEC rules or applying a more narrow interpretation to federal statutes than advocated, or a more restrained approach taken by the Commission itself.[31] Even during those periods, entrenched principles of federal corporate governance remained intact, being overseen by the Commission and the courts. In this respect, the shareholder proposal rule, the proscription against illegal insider trading, and disclosure of fiduciary self-dealing transactions serve as examples of the ongoing application of federal corporate governance.

This ebb and flow with respect to the intensity of federal corporate governance may not be explained by one political party rather than the other being in the majority. For example, the SEC's activist policies with respect to the foreign payments debacle largely occurred during the Ford Administration.[32] The Commission's adoption

---

[29] *See* discussion in Chapter 5 herein. Also, as discussed earlier in this chapter, *supra* notes 19–20 and accompanying text, and in Chapter 6 herein, stock exchange regulation has played a prominent role in the federalization of corporate governance.

[30] The Securities Enforcement Remedies and Penny Stock Reform Act of 1990, Pub. L. No. 101-429, 104 Stat. 931 (1990), *codified at*, § 20(e) of the Securities Act, 15 U.S.C. § 77t(e) (2012), § 21(d)(2) of the Securities Exchange Act, 15 U.S.C. § 78u(d)(2) (2012), *described in*, Marc I. Steinberg and Ralph C. Ferrara, *supra* note 17, at § 6:18 (stating that this provision "provides that any person who has violated Section 17(a)(1) of the Securities Act, or Section 10(b) of the Exchange Act, or the rules and regulations promulgated pursuant to Section 10(b), and who has also demonstrated 'substantial unfitness to serve as an officer or director' can be barred from serving as an officer or director of a corporation with a class of securities registered pursuant to Section 12 of the Exchange Act or a corporation that is required to file reports under Section 15(d) of that Act"). The Sarbanes-Oxley Act lowered this standard from that of "substantial unfitness" to that of "unfitness." *See* discussion in Chapter 5 herein. Note that, prior to the 1990 Act, the SEC procured officer and director bars as ancillary relief in its enforcement proceedings. *See* discussion in Chapter 3 herein.

[31] Examples include the U.S. Supreme Court's statutory analysis in the *Santa Fe* decision, 430 U.S. 462 (1977), and decisions by the U.S. Court of Appeals for the District of Columbia Circuit that invalidated SEC rules addressing disparate voting rights and shareholder access to a subject company's proxy statement to nominate directors. *See* discussion in Chapters 3, 4, 5, and 6 herein.

[32] *See, e.g.*, Report of the Securities and Exchange Commission on Questionable and Illegal Corporate Payments and Practices, Submitted to the Committee on Banking, Housing and Urban Affairs, U.S. Senate (May 1976) (discussing that the focus of SEC investigations with respect to such payments was on corporate accountability, disclosure, and governance); Statement of SEC Chairman Roderick M. Hills Before the Subcommittee on Consumer Protection and Finance, House Committee on Interstate and Foreign Commerce at 2 (Sept.

of rules that vitiated the Delaware Supreme Court's decision permitting exclusionary tender offers transpired during the presidency of Ronald Reagan.[33] And, as a last example, the Sarbanes-Oxley Act, the legislation that entrenched the federalization of corporate governance, was enacted when President George W. Bush was in office.[34] Although indications are that the Trump administration, Congress, and the SEC will not be active proponents of enhancing corporate governance principles,[35] the foundation for preserving these principles without undue impairment appears to be firmly established.[36]

In this regard, if the pendulum were to swing to a culture that encourages lax practices and weak enforcement, it may well be only a matter of a few years until financial scandals would ensue. Indeed, in 1995, Congress enacted legislation that many perceive as unduly favorable for defendants,[37] which was followed three years later by additional legislation that curtailed investors' interests.[38] Although one may

---

21, 1976) ("Disclosure of these matters reflects the deeply held belief that the managers of corporations are stewards acting on behalf of the shareholders, who are entitled to honest use of, and accounting for, the funds entrusted to the corporation and to procedures necessary to assure accountability and disclosure of the manner in which management performs its stewardship."); Thomas O. Gorman, *The Origins of the FCPA: Lessons for Effective Compliance and Enforcement*, 43 Sec. Reg. L.J. 43, 49–53 (2015) (discussing many of the SEC enforcement cases that named corporate officers as defendants in addition to the subject corporations, and also describing the SEC's volunteer program in which approximately "450 corporations stepped forward, conducted comprehensive internal investigations, and remediated the issues and provided their findings to the SEC staff and shareholders"); discussion in Chapter 3 herein.

[33] *See* SEC Rules 13e-4(f)(8), 14d-10, 17 C.F.R. §§ 240.13e-4(f)(8), 14d-10 (2017); *Unocal v. Mesa Petroleum Co.*, 493 A.2d 946 (Del. 1985); discussion *supra* notes 14–16 and accompanying text and in Chapter 3 herein.

[34] *See* discussion in Chapters 5, 6 herein.

[35] *See, e.g.*, *SEC Under Trump Slashes Rulemaking Agenda*, 49 Sec. Reg. & L. Rep. (BNA) 1162 (2017) (quoting Dennis Keller, president and chief executive officer of Better Markets, a watchdog group, that the SEC's agenda "falls far short of achieving the kinds of Main-Street-Investor oriented goals that the SEC exists for").

[36] *Id.* Thus far, the Trump administration and the SEC have not sought to rescind key provisions of the Sarbanes-Oxley and Dodd-Frank Acts or SEC rules and regulations promulgated pursuant to these Acts. In this regard, the role and influence of activist shareholders must be assessed as many of these provisions are now part of the corporate governance landscape that such investors view as not easily subject to abandonment. *See* discussion in Chapters 3, 4, and 6 herein.

[37] Pub. L. No. 104-67, 109 Stat. 737 (codified in various sections of 15 U.S.C. and 18 U.S.C.). In his veto message (which was overridden by Congress), President Clinton expressed concern with the bill's: (1) onerous pleading standards, (2) sanctions that treat plaintiffs more harshly than defendants, and (3) unduly broad "safe harbor" for companies that make forward-looking statements. Message from President William J. Clinton to the U.S. House of Representatives (Dec. 20, 1995). For discussion of this legislation, the Private Securities Litigation Reform Act of 1995, *see, e.g.*, Symposium, 51 Bus. Law. No. 4 (1996); Symposium, 106 Colum L. Rev. No. 7 (2006); Symposium, 24 Sec. Reg. L.J. No. 2 (1996).

[38] The Securities Litigation Uniform Standards Act of 1998, Pub. L. No. 105-353, 112 Stat. 3227 (codified in various sections of 15 U.S.C.). With certain exceptions, this Act preempts state law with respect to class actions involving nationally traded securities. Key exceptions include individual actions, derivative suits, and actions focusing on alleged misconduct in the merger and acquisition setting (such as mergers, tender offers, going private transactions, and the exercise of appraisal rights). For analysis of this legislation, *see, e.g.*, James Hamilton and

be hard-pressed to show that these Acts facilitated the perpetration of improper and illegal practices by instilling a culture of laxity and greed, the fact remains that four years thereafter, faced with financial debacles of exorbitant magnitude,[39] Congress enacted the Sarbanes-Oxley Act.[40]

Predicting the future of the federalization of corporate governance is challenging. What can be said is that, although the invocation of federal corporate governance will experience periods of vigor and stagnation (and perhaps retrenchment), its foundational principles now are acquiesced in, if not lauded, by many of the key constituencies implicated, including corporate fiduciaries, activist and institutional shareholders, and the SEC.[41] Moreover, if financial debacles of significant magnitude were to ensue, accompanied by perceptions of permissive federal or state law standards (thereby leaving a gap in norms that should be remedied), this country once again may witness congressional enactment of expansive corporate governance

---

Ted Trautmann, *Securities Litigation Uniform Standards Act of 1998: Law and Explanation* (1998); Lisa Casey, *Shutting the Doors to State Court: The Securities Litigation Uniform Standards Act of 1998*, 27 Sec. Reg. L.J. 141 (1999); Richard Painter, *Responding to a False Alarm: Federal Preemption of State Securities Fraud Causes of Action*, 84 Cornell L. Rev. 1 (1998).

Moreover, in 1996, Congress enacted the National Securities Markets Improvement Act of 1996, Pub. L. No. 104-290, 110 Stat. 3416. Among other provisions, this Act preempted state law with respect to certain exemptions from registration as well as the registration of securities listed on a national securities exchange. The state regulators retained their authority to pursue fraud. For an overview of this Act, *see* Robert Bagnell and Kimble Cannon, *The National Securities Markets Improvement Act of 1996: Summary and Discussion*, 25 Sec. Reg. L.J. 3 (1997).

[39] These financial debacles are referred to in several chapters herein. Federal legislation that ensued from major scandals include the Foreign Corrupt Practices Act of 1977, the Sarbanes-Oxley Act of 2002, and the Dodd-Frank Act of 2010.

[40] The Sarbanes-Oxley Act is examined in Chapters 5 and 6 herein. *See* Marc I. Steinberg, *Sarbanes-Oxley: A Note from the Editor-in-Chief*, 30 Sec. Reg. L.J. 358 (2002):

> After the enactment of three major acts of federal legislation in 1995, 1996, and 1998, seeking to foster capital formation and redress perceived abuses associated with class actions, the election of President George W. Bush and appointment of Harvey L. Pitt as SEC Chairman portended the continued deregulation of the securities markets and the affected players in the process. Instead, the very opposite has occurred: After the revelation of major financial debacles that have impaired the very foundation of the U.S. capital markets, Congress enacted the most pro-regulatory securities legislation since the passage of the Securities Exchange Act of 1934.

[41] Indeed, although not focused on federal regulation, acquiescence by corporate fiduciaries and their advisers of enhanced corporate governance principles is evidenced by such publications as the American Bar Association's (the ABA Committee on Corporate Laws) *Corporate Director's Guidebook*, the Business Roundtable's publication *Corporate Governance and American Competitiveness*, and the Conference Board's (Commission on Public Trust and Private Enterprise) Report on *Corporate Governance*. Another important publication in this respect is the American Law Institute's *Principles of Corporate Governance: Analysis and Recommendations*.

legislation.[42] Indeed, one may posit that, if state standards of corporate governance are perceived as unduly lax, it may well be only a matter of time before corporate governance will be predominantly within the purview of federal law and regulation.

IV. Conclusion

The existence of widespread perceptions that transparency is lacking in disclosures made by enterprises, fiduciary self-dealing is excessive, and private and government actions to redress misconduct are unduly stymied, would impede capital raising, reduce liquidity in the secondary markets, and induce the flow of investor funds to alternative types of investments. Such an eventuality would have serious adverse ramifications for the U.S. securities markets, its economy, and its global reputation. Congress and the SEC should be prepared, as they have shown in the past, to ensure that corrective measures are undertaken when lax state or federal standards facilitate the perpetration of miscreant behavior by those persons who are stewards. History has shown that, at times, state judicial and legislative determinations embrace practices that benefit corporate fiduciaries to the detriment of the subject enterprise, its shareholders, and other constituents. Congress, the SEC, and the federal courts should stand sentinel with their resources at hand to do what is necessary to maintain the preeminence of the U.S. securities markets, thereby continuing to attract needed capital and to provide sufficient comfort to those who part with their funds as active or passive investors. This endeavor is of monumental and continual importance.

The federalization of corporate governance, as in the past, thus is a process that will evolve and adapt to changing circumstances as they arise. The foreseeable future suggests that this federalization process will be a key determiner for the continuing stability of the U.S. capital markets and for enhancing investor protection. Hopefully, Congress, the SEC, the federal courts, and the national securities exchanges will admirably fulfill their respective responsibilities.

---

[42] Shortly prior to the passage of the Sarbanes-Oxley Act, this author remarked that "[h]opefully, Congress and the SEC, as the 'statutory guardians' of the investing public, will monitor this situation and seek to correct any undue imbalance that should arise." Marc I. Steinberg, *Curtailing Investor Protection Under the Securities Laws: Good for the Economy?*, 55 SMU L. Rev. 347, 355 (2002).

Index

The Federalization of Corporate Governance. Marc I. Steinberg.